TEACHING STRATEGIES

THAT FOSTER CONSTRUCTIVE BEHAVIOR

USING YOUR HEAD AND HEART

FIRST EDITION

SHARI HOLMES STOKES

cognella® ACADEMIC PUBLISHING

Bassim Hamadeh, CEO and Publisher

Susana Christie, Developmental Editor

Charlotte Andrew, Production Editor

Jess Estrella, Senior Graphic Designer

Alexa Lucido, Licensing Coordinator

Natalie Piccotti, Senior Marketing Manager

Kassie Graves, Director of Acquisitions

Jamie Giganti, Senior Managing Editor

Printed in the United States of America.

ISBN: 978-1-5165-1068-9 (pbk) / 978-1-5165-1069-6 (br)

cognella® | ACADEMIC PUBLISHING

Your heart will always make itself known
through your words.

—From a Chinese fortune cookie I received
while writing the book

TABLE OF CONTENTS

DEDICATION

This book is dedicated to

Lois Holmes Stokes

An artist with food, flowers, thread, and harp.
A gentle woman who beautified her home and her community and attended to its inhabitants.

And to

Charles Warbrook Stokes

A teacher and a preservationist who was as deft with garden hoe as he was with educators.
A gentle man who hummed along with any tune he heard but always did so in harmony.

Thank you both
for appreciating who I was and who I was becoming;
for providing so many good beginnings;
for being such remarkable models of living lightly on the earth and giving generously of
time, talents, and tender care to others.
I miss you, Mum and Dad. Time doesn't change that. I hope somehow you know about all this.
Jesse has played keyboard in a rock band; been a musical director for an *a capella* choir and high school and community
musicals; played for weddings and a "Haavad" alumni party ("Such a business!"); been in a musical himself; and has taught your
great-granddaughters to play piano.
Emma ["Hello, Beautiful!"] is a fine photographer and cinematographer. She has already worked on the taping of three TV shows
(with a walk-on in one) and several videos/movies. She has the eye for the beauty of the natural world and structures that you
did, and she bought herself a piano so she "shall have music wherever she goes."
Both are bright and creative, kind and gentle people in their own right, and each has a fine sense of humor.

And to

Stephanie, Greg, and Gavin Stokes

Wrenched from their lives and ours much, much too soon.
Your goodness remains among us. How we wish you were here, too.

This book is also dedicated to

Bear, The Divine Ms. Em, and Monsieur Le Bubbie Deau

better known to the rest of the world as

Jack, Emma, and Jesse Alling

For my one chance at existence, I cannot imagine having three better companions.
Here's to you—without, I promise, any of my "jazzy" singing or dancing during the celebration.
Each of you is simply the best
husband, friend, lover, life partner,
daughter,
son,
there could ever be for me!
Thanks for all the love and marvelous moments of lunacy, not to mention the learning you have afforded me.
How very fortunate I am to have had each of you in my life!
Bear, I carry you in my heart and will forever. Grief is my companion, but so are you, deeply and richly.
You live on in wonderful ways in so many people.
Each of us misses you terribly, but I think I do most of all.

PREFACE

All people are created equal. Then some become teachers.

—Anonymous

As a teacher, how fortunate I am to have been afforded the opportunity to hold up a mirror of possibility to another human being and to work with that person to see how far our work together could go, often to be pleased at how far it went—for the other person and for me.

My deep belief is that as teachers we all hold up that mirror of possibility for our students—a possibility of what they can learn, a possibility of who they can become. We can do this for any child, even under the most extreme circumstances. How often have we heard of someone who was in a horrible life situation and yet was able to be resilient and continue to learn and grow because of the efforts of one person, most often a teacher? We can not only help children cope; we can also enhance their capacity to do so. We can also go well beyond that, and within those relationships we can grow as well.

Teaching is challenging. Teaching for me is also the most giving of professions. What I give I am given back tenfold.

I wrote this book to support your efforts in being that mirror through good and difficult times. I also wrote it—and this is, perhaps, most important—because I believe you and I, we all, can do this in a constructive manner. As I come to the close of my writing, I realize that there is yet a third reason. I have written the book I wish I had had when I first started teaching. I needed solid grounding in what was possible and constructive. I also needed a book I could hold on to so I could refer to it when I wanted to refresh my mind about a particular concept or find yet another strategy that would support my efforts. My hope is that this will be a book that addresses your needs.

How have I set this book up to support your efforts in this important work of a teacher? I have done it though the content I share but also the structures I have chosen to use. The content will be described in the Beginning. For now, I would say it is an eclectic combination of all the best approaches I have pulled from what I have observed, the feedback I have received about my teaching, and the research in the fields of psychology, education, and special education. The focus is how to be proactive in preventing unconstructive behavior, how to respond on the spot should such behavior occur, and how to support more intensive or extensive behavior change. Included are any number of resource materials to allow you to go into more depth on particular topics.

The overarching structure is based on what we know from the field fosters the development of a learning community. First we connect—to the degree that we can—under the circumstances of author and reader. We get to know who we are as we begin this journey. Then, in the end, we close our work together. We look back, review what we have accomplished, celebrate our work, and say farewell.

In the chapters between the Beginning and the Closing, I use the structures that research tells us foster any learning experience. I get your brain ready, for example, by previewing the chapter's "agenda," inviting you to set a goal to help you frame your learning, accessing your prior knowledge or experience. I attempt to engage your emotions through a quote, a story, a thought-provoking question. I provide you ways to actively process what we are addressing with Active Learning Applications through the Cognella portal as well as opportunities to analyze and reflect. Woven within are anticipatory sets, story examples, and multiple ways to summarize what we have just addressed. As we begin each chapter, I also address two of the overarching questions of basic learning styles: "What will we address?" (i.e., what will you learn?) and "Why is this important?" Then, during the chapter, we address the other two questions: "How do you do this?" and "What are potential creative applications?"

I use these structures not only to facilitate your learning and memory but also to model for you what I state we as teachers need to do.

I offer many ideas and examples of strategies along the way. I do not do this to overwhelm but to provide ideas for all sorts of different teaching/learning styles. What I offer may not address all your needs nor be supportive of your work in all situations. I have not gone into depth about specific considerations for working with students who are gifted, who have disabilities, who are gifted and have disabilities, or who are learning English as a second (or third) language. But the principles and processes I offer should hold you in good stead for any child with whom you work.

I hope this book will support your efforts to hold up a mirror of possibility for any student you encounter and to have the empathy, perseverance, and grace to keep on in your work and to celebrate what you and your students are able to accomplish.

Let's begin.

ACKNOWLEDGMENTS

Sometimes our light goes out. But it is blown into flame by an encounter with another human being. Each of us owes the deepest thanks to those who have rekindled this inner light.

—Albert Schweitzer

Many people have helped. Some have encouraged me to continue to believe what I had to say was useful. Others have arranged opportunities for me to pursue my work or helped in the production of various drafts. During those times, when my light was so dim I barely knew it existed, I had the good fortune to be surrounded by people—young and old—who helped me rekindle my torch. They might have held up a mirror so I was able to see my value or said a word or two that showed deep understanding. Other times it was some well-timed cheerleading or feedback, or a note of thanks for the impact I have had that set my soul on fire yet again.

My deep appreciation to:

✦ Professor Frank Laycock at Oberlin College: for having faith in me and my work from the start.

✦ Administrators at Fitchburg State, including Drs. Patricia Spakes, Robert Antonucci, Michael Fiorentino, Paul Weizer, Annette Sullivan, Laurie DeRosa, and Ronald Colbert: for granting me sabbaticals to write.

✦ Dr. Elaine Frances, department chair, dean of education: for making my first sabbatical possible and giving me constructive support, feedback, and good fellowship (on and off campus), all these years.

✦ Dr. Anne Howard, my friend, coresearcher, copresenter, cowriter, coteacher, and brief office mate in a corner room painted peach: for every time she has told me my work is of value and for mentoring me (often unknowingly) since the first day we met.

✦ Dr. Nancy Murray, my friend, my colleague, and most recently, my department chair: for supporting me in countless ways, including her example of what working with a caring and competent person looks like and feels like.

✦ Lois Holmes Stokes, Betsy Holmes Summers, and Jan Ellis: for critiquing early chapters. Each has reached countless people through her hard work and role of mother as teacher. Mum, I miss you and Bets.

✦ Dr. Susan Stokes Ellis, Shelley Stokes Turnbow, and Celia Stokes, my sisters who have contributed greatly to the field of education: for supporting my life's efforts as mother, teacher, writer. Susan, your *extensive* editing, insights, and willingness to be a sounding board made all the difference in the book's content, and your unconditional support has made all the difference to me as an author and person. Shelley, your formatting made meeting my first deadline possible, and your ideas and feedback on wording, not to mention your support, have helped throughout.

✦ Dr. Mark Holmes Stokes, my brother, who supports adults in their learning: for encouraging my progress.

✦ Emma Stokes Alling and Jesse Stokes Alling, my bright, creative, empathic, wonderfully weird daughter and son: for cheering me on, for helping me grow in wisdom in countless ways, and for typing in the early days.

✦ Ashlee Alling, my talented daughter-in-law: for helping me with formatting, and with all devices technical, including my computer as I have interacted with the world of publishing.

- Lynn Sarda, former special education teacher and director of the Mid-Hudson Teacher Center at SUNY New Paltz, my mentor from my first days of teaching: for being my critic friend for my writing and my friend for life.

- Dr. Susan Swap, Dr. David Feldman, Dr. Michael Arcuri, Dr. William Meehan, Dr. Rosemarie Giovino, Judy Hersey, and Joseph Perez, my colleagues and friends: for seeing possibilities in me and my work at critical moments and cheering me on. Sue, when you died, we lost the quintessential model of competence and compassion in one human being.

- Veronica Kenney, Susan Cushing, Karen Kelleher, Laurie Collins, Becky Bennet Acheson, Karla Belliveau, Ita Murphy, Brenda Marcoux, Monica Winters, Kayleigh Pennell, Debbie Jeffries, Alyssa Serafini, Meryl Higgins, among many outstanding teachers: for offering me feedback, encouragement, and useful ideas as I watched them with students.

- The good people of Chelmsford (MA) Public Library: for providing a friendly environment for writing and light reading for escape when needed.

- All the students, teachers, and administrators I have had the pleasure of working with in this country and Canada: for making me think again and again about what I believe is right for children and young adults.

- Beth Lawrence, Tammy Soucie-Burke, Lindsey Duclos, Jill Pizza, Hannah Cote, Jessica Adams, Corie Hartenson, Josh Rosenthal, and Alexandra Creighton: for doing a fine job deciphering my handwriting as they typed material that ultimately became part of the book. Pat Jennings: for her consistently timely help at FSU Print Services. Jodie Lawton, FSU library: for her work obtaining all manner of support materials for my writing. Carolyn Hughes and Carla McGrath for their help in many ways, but most recently with helping the book-launch come to fruition.

- My team at Cognella: Annie Peterson, Claire Benson, Chelsey Rogers, Dani Skeen, Rose Tawy, Charlotte Andrew, Berenice Quirino, Beth Riley, Jamie Giganti, and Susana Christie, and the Cognella typesetters. I am a collaborator at heart. Each of these people played a different but important role working with me. Annie and Claire, thank you for helping me get this project off the ground. Jamie, thank you for your calm manner of showing me how to put my words into a format fit for publishing. Charlotte, you did a fine job of managing the project and all my questions and worries through the last steps. Susana, how talented you are as an editor. Your balance of support and structure contributed in no small measure to what the book has become. I could not have asked for a better person for a partner in this learning experience. Wow!

- The individuals whom I have referenced: for ideas that contributed to my thinking and writing.

- And last, but never least, former students at Fitchburg State, "I have learned a great deal from my friends. I have learned even more from my students" (the Talmud): for nurturing me in countless ways, including their gifts of powerful personal narratives, suggestions for books to read, quotations, text contributions, feedback, or suggestions about wording and kind words of support. Cassie Andrade, Brian Andy, Danaca Aho, Hilary Aho, Wendy Albert, Hannah Allen, Kristopher Ambrozewicz, Kerie Annichiarico, Stephanie Austin, Elisabeth Baer, Meghan Bahou, Tifany Bankowski, Gail Murray Barker, Amanda Barr, Aaron Barrett, Jen Barrett, Lauren Barry,

Melissa Bauer, Jeremy Bednarz, Jessica Beebe, Anne Bekeritis, Audrey Bekeritis, Amanda Bell, Karla Belliveau, Danielle Beaulieu, Hayley Bengtson, Becky Bennet (Acheson), Kayleigh Bennett, Katelyn Bernard, Brittany Berndt, Kristen Berquist, Elizabeth Beverage, Jill Bice, Dana Bickleman, Brittany Bilodeau, Megan Black, Vanessa Blake, Amy Bolduc, Sarah Brady, Shelby Bragel, Michael Bragg, Kristin Brekalis, Becky Briano, Mallory Brideau, Ruth Briggs, Laura Brouillette, Ali Brown, Chloe Brown, Gabrielle Brown, Betsy Brunell, Alison Bryant, Scarlett Budzinski, Kayla Bullock, Karen Burgess, Jamie Burns, Rebecca Bush, Vicki Bushey, Katelyn Caddigan, Meghan Callahan, Stephanie Canales, Emily Capone, Meghan Carroll, Katie Capuccio, Amber Cardwell, Megan Carlson, Sandra Charlestream, Heather Charest, Ainsley Carmon, Kelly Chase, Chris Cassavant, Chelsea Chaves, Stephanie Cercone, Melissa Chahowski, Julie Cicero, Kimberly Clapp, Sophie Cleghorn, Jeff Cole, Stasie Julie Cicero, Kimberly Clapp, Sophie Cleghorn, Jeff Cole, Stasie Coleman, Andrea Colleton, Nichole Comeau, Katie Conklin, Caitlin Conway, Cassandra Cook, Brandi Cooley, Caitlyn Corbett, Heather Corbett, Katie Cormier, Danielle Correia, Ryan Correia, Jen Corrigan, Dianne Cosgrave, Greg Costa, Sarah Costa, Meghan Coullahan, Kenzie Cournoyer, Sherry Courville Palazzi, Felicia Couture, Lauren Covey, Erica Coyne, Sam Cheek, Haleigh Crawford, Michelle Cree, Alexandra Creighton, Katie Cringan, Sydney Dalton, Lori Daniels, Angelica David, Jennifer Davis, Nicole Davis, Erica Debreceni, Lindsay Delorme, Heather DeLucia, Alex Desrosiers, Caitlyn Desrosiers, Carolynn DeWitt, Will DiFrancesco, Michelle DiLemme, Sarah Diminico, Christian DiRomualdo, Cheryl Dodge, Sarabeth Doe, Amanda Donadio, Lauren Donovan, Richard Drinkwater, Lindsey Duclos, Michelle Dunn, Amber Dutton, Briana Dyment, Katie Eccleston, Andrea Eddy, Ashley Eno, Amy Fahey, Keylla Falcon, Kristen Fearon, Christopher Feeley, Jaime Ferry, Joe Flanagan, Krystie Fleck, Meghan Fontaine, Vickie Forbes, Courtney Folsom, Ashley Forgues, Nicole Forrant, Allie Foss, Michelle Francouer, Katie Fratus, Annette Freeman, Carissa Fucillo, Michelle Gallagher, Kirstie Gallette, Patrick Galligan, Brooke Garnick, Katie Gelinas, Joseph George, Meghan Germain, Kristen Gilmore, Chelsea Giroux, Allyson Gnoza, Mary Goodsell, Heidi Gordon, Cheryl Gorman, Katie Gosselin, Kendra Gould, Dayna Green, Lisa Greenwood, Nate Gregory, Christina Gura, Jocelyn Haines, Kara Hand, Amanda Harris, Corinne Hartenstein, Christie Hawkes, Jessica Hebert, Sarah Henrie, Nancy Henry, Devin Hildick, Erin Hill, Kim Hilton, Ann Horgan, Lindsay Horowitz, Jillian Hughes, Dana Hurwitz, Natalia Illarraza, Lindsay Irons, Meg Jacobs, Kayelane James, Kristin Jarmusik, Amy Jette, Jenny Jo, Samantha Johnson, Betsy Johnston, Sarah Jolicoeur, Alex Joseph, Lauren Kahn, Tanya Kalantari, Heidi Kalinowski, Becca Landers, Kate Kane, Cortney Kelly, Tammie Kettle (Smith), Amelia Kilborn, Meagan Killion, Haley King, Danielle Kirdulis, Destiny Kirker, Lois Kolofsky, Tracy Kolofsky, Sarah Kowalsky, Katie Kotowski, Kara Kovac, Camille Kurzanski, Amanda Lacouture, Lea Lafond, Matt Lamey, Michaela Lally, Brittany Lanza, Allyssa Lariviere, Colleen Leary, Emily Leary, Kristen Leary, Julie LeBlanc, Jessica LeClerc, Tricia Leduc, Kim Leesha, Heather Leger, Kathryn LeSage, Jenn Lewin, Annika Leydon, Aline Lima, Joe Lindberg, Jenn Lizotte, Jenna Lomano, Christy Lonardo, Stephanie Lord, Victoria Lorden, Jessica Loscalzo, Amanda Lovell, Allie Lynch, Kassi Mainville, Kate Malone, Kate Manning, Amy Mansell, Carrie Marion, Jamy Marquez, Samantha Martin, Sheila Martin, Camilla Marques, Nick Mazzaglia, Rebecca McClure, Patty McCormack, Brendan McWilliams, Jess Martel, Joshua Mello, Kendra Mielcarz, Carol Miller, Maureen Mitchell, Ryan Monaghan, Caitlyn Mondello, Kretsy Mondesir, Anthony Montesion, Shawn Morandi, David Morgan, Kathy Morin, Ali Morse, Heather Morse, Katie Mullen, Sarah Mullin, Arlyn Murphy, Danielle Mutrie, Jo-Ann Nalette, Ashley Newton, Lauren Nichols, Lisa Nobrega, Corey Odell, Jillian Oliviera, Amy Orlando, Alison Orecchio, Jennifer Orne, Shatara Otero-Hurte, Alissa Palange, Janel Pelletier, Michelle Peters, Maggie Peterson, Alicia Rocco, Saralyn O'Rourke, Katherine Paquette, Danielle

Pardee, Stephanie Parent, Kaylyn Parker, Amanda Patrick, Nicole Pelzer, Melanie Pinto, Jill Pizza, Kacie Powers, Marie Powers, Kimberly Priestley, Jill Quastello, Louis Ray, Isa Rebholtz, Erin Reddick, Craig Reid, Rosemary Reidy, Ashley Reilly, Brittany Respass, Michael Reyes, Tara-Lee Reynolds, Chelsey Richardson, Samantha Riley, Lisa Rivera, Jackie Robar, Barbara Renzi, Jordan Roberge, Rachel Robidoux, David Robinson, Ashley Robison, Nick Roger, David Romanowski, Kate Rouleau, Carlie Roy, Rebecca Ruston, Mel Saari, Vanessa Sackett, Gia Santaniello, Kristen Sauvageau, Leigh Sawyer, Stefanie Scaglione, Erika Scarpignato, Jessica Schoorens, Brett Sczylvian, Kim Seguin, Michael Seitz, Kendra Sheppard, Barbara Sheridan, Alyssa Serafini, Melissa Shikles, Jessi Shimkus, Dana Shoults, Amanda Siciliano, Kaitlyn Silva, Katie Silveira, Mary Kate Simmons, Erin Simon, Mandy Simpson, Michael Siplas, Katelyn Sletterink, Carly Smith, Sam Smith, Brittany Spencer, Corrin Snay, Kasondra Sporbert, Michelle Soini, Becca Stankowski, Juliana Steadman, Michelle Steele, Genevieve Steere, Lauren Steeves, Angie Stetson, Becky St. Jean, Jess St. Pierre (Vezina), Emily Swan, Robin Szymakowski, Nicole Taft, Lindsey Tait, Jayce Tamulevich, Ellen Tansey, Hannah Tasso, Alex Teixeira, Sherry Tetreault, Chris Thibodeau, Joslyn Thiem, Courtney Thompson, Lynn Tokola, Lisa Torgersen, Meagan Trainor, Thea Triehy, Nina Trobaugh, Sarah Turgeon, Lauren Twomey, Jessica Tyler, Christina Valenti, Janelle Vautour, Becca Walsh, Leanna Walsh, Melissa Ward, Jacob Watkins, Felicia Weaver, Jason Weeks, Kim Wheeler, Rachel Weiland, Courtney Westcott, Brittany Whiting, Sara Whitney, Sam Wilkinson, Nick Wilson, Ari Winters, Macy Woodard, Marie Zacek, and Amanda Zorzenella, Despena Zouzas. The world is a better place for their work.

If I have omitted a name, it is my memory, not my gratitude, that is lacking. Forgive me, and tell me who you are.

—Shari Stokes

May 1, 2017

UNDERSTANDING THE DYNAMICS BEHIND BEHAVIOR

The complexity of our behavior requires a complex set of explanatory ideas.

—Susan Krauss Whitbourne

Before we can begin to address how we as teachers can support constructive behavior in students, we need to consider the dynamics behind behavior: How does our brain function? What basic needs drive our behavior? What seems to trigger a specific behavior in any given moment—whether that behavior is constructive or unconstructive in our eyes? If a behavior is triggered, what makes it likely that it will occur again under similar circumstances?

Section I provides the conceptual underpinnings that will help us begin to answer these questions. The first chapter in this section offers an overview of the book's perspective. The remaining three chapters provide more details about how we can better understand what drives behavior and, based on this understanding, how we can use this perspective to work with students to support their constructive behavior.

BEGINNING

Introductions and Reflections

*The best of a book is not the thought
it suggests, just as the charm of music
dwells not in the tones but in the echoes
of our hearts.*

—Oliver Wendell Holmes, Jr.[1]

---

[1] If you are someone who enjoys personal connections, then it might be fun for you to know that Holmes was my great grandfather's cousin. Of course, I take no credit for the work he did on the Supreme Court championing free speech with Justice Louis Brandeis, but I am pleased to know that a relative worked hard for people's rights.

Introduction to the Author

I teach who I am. I write who I am. Therefore, this introduction is here to give you a context in which you can place all the concepts and strategies you'll find in this book.

I frequently begin my work with others with a quote. This quote from George Bernard Shaw seems the right choice for my introduction because it so clearly describes how I feel:

> Life is no brief candle to me. It is a sort of splendid torch which I have got hold of for the moment, and I want to make it burn as brightly as possible before handing it on to future generations.

My great passion in life is ensuring the well-being of children and young adults. Teaching chose me. I have taught people of many different ages. My work began in a demonstration site with 18-month- to 3-year-old children who were challenged by multiple disabilities. Then, in three different elementary schools, I taught a self-contained class for students who were labeled as having learning and behavior difficulties. I hated the labels but loved the children. My teaching experiences have also included working for several years with students in elementary and middle school resource rooms, along with coteaching in general education classrooms. I have tutored adults with disabilities. I have taught in undergraduate and graduate teacher preparation programs at private and public universities. For the last 25 years, I have had the pleasure of working at Fitchburg State College which, in 2010, became Fitchburg State University in Massachusetts in both the Special Education Department and, more recently, the Education Department. I am fortunate to work with a number of extraordinary professionals there at the university and in nearby public schools.

I am not a perfect teacher by any means, but I am definitely a passionate one. Once, when I asked students in an undergraduate course to pick a word to describe themselves, someone chose "almost." He explained that he felt he was almost many things—almost through school, almost a teacher, etc. I would say I, too, feel "almost." I am "almost" the teacher I would like to be. Then again, I will probably "almost" be the teacher I want to be when I am 96. Always, I will be committed to working with others to make a difference in the lives of children and young adults through effective teaching.

My best to you as you make a difference on behalf of the students with whom you work.

Introduction to the Book

Many years ago, an important finding in the research on learning (Caine & Caine, 1994) explained that people understand and remember more when they are actively engaged in the learning process. I have written this book in a way that enables you to interact with the material. The following are some aspects I hope will make the materials engaging and that will draw you in.

Quotes

Quotes can crystallize an idea or feeling in a way that gives it an added punch while at the same time validating an idea. Quotes usually evoke emotions. We know from the research on brain functioning (Gregory & Kaufelt, 2015; Immordino-Yang, 2015; Jensen, 2015a; Jensen, 2015b;) that positive emotions facilitate learning and memory. I want to support your emotional engagement. I hope the quotes facilitate this.

Another reason I use quotes is that I want to connect with you. Often after a class or workshop, someone talks with me about a quote I used or shares one of his favorites. If you also like quotes, I encourage you to add yours in the margin. If you have more information about a quote whose source is unknown to me, or if you have one you want to share, I invite you to send it to me.

Readying the Brain for Learning

At the beginning of a chapter, there is an overview of the content and an opportunity for you to consider your goals. Within a chapter, there are possibilities to access prior knowledge and experiences and to react to the content. Each time we come to the end of a chapter, there will be an opportunity to review important points and to preview the next chapter. These anticipatory sets and reviews provide an enticement to read and a map to foster your thinking and your retention of the material. The research on learning (R. Hunter, 2014; M. Hunter, 2004; Jensen, 2015a; Jensen, 2015b; Wolfe, 2001) clearly indicates these opportunities are essential to foster understanding and remembering.

Reflection Opportunities

While I have strong beliefs about the kind of teaching that fosters constructive behavior, I do not have all the answers. What I do have is the deep conviction that each of us has a capacity to change, to grow. Our hope for doing that rests in our ongoing consideration of practice. Throughout each chapter, Reflection Opportunities give you room to consider what you think or your teaching practices.

Each time there is an opportunity for you to access prior knowledge or experience, to reflect, to react to the content, or to summarize what you have read, I have provided space for you to write, if you have chosen a notebook or paper bound version. I understand that writing in a book may not be a match for your learning style/needs or the form of book you have. You might choose to use a large sticky note or a piece of regular paper, if you have an ebook or one that is paper bound. If you have the text in notebook form, you could use paper that has three holes, so you can insert your ideas into the book wherever they belong. I encourage you to do whatever works best for you.

Introduction to the Perspective

I believe that as teachers we do not teach life skills, functional academics, mathematics, English/language arts, art, music, etc. We teach children and young adults. Our subject matter is a medium—a vehicle through which we empower future adults with the skills, information, values, and attitudes to lead rich, productive, meaningful lives that add to, rather than deplete, the world around them. This job is not ours alone; however, while many other people may contribute, our role as teachers is crucial.

Children and young adults are not born knowing how to interact constructively with others, nor how to form a community, nor how to reflect on the effect of their behavior. They need to learn these skills just the way they learn how to do anything else. School is an essential place to learn them; yet in many schools, these skills are not taught. Then, when students make mistakes in their behavior, what will often occur? As Colvin (in Jones & Jones, 2016, p. 287) explains, the usual approach to students' behavior is quite different from the strategies we use when we teach academics. The chart below shows Colvin's (2004) comparison of the two kinds of problems we as teachers encounter in schools and what we often do as a result. As you look at Table B-1, consider the degree to which you believe this is an accurate representation of what occurs in many classrooms.

Table B-1. Procedures for Academic Problems Compared to Social Problems[i]		
Kind of Error	Procedures for Academic Problem	Procedures for Social Problem
Infrequent	Assume student is trying to make correct response	Assume student is not trying to make correct response
	Assume error was accidental	Assume error was deliberate
	Provide assistance (model-lead-test)	Provide negative consequence
	Provide more practice	Practice not required
	Assume student has learned skills and will perform correctly in future	Assume student will make right choice and behave in the future
Frequent (chronic)	Assume student has learned the wrong way	Assume student refuses to cooperate
	Assume student has been taught (inadvertently) the wrong way	Assume student knows what is right and has been told often
	Diagnose the problem	Provide more negative consequences
	Identify misrule or determine more effective manner in which to present the material	Withdraw student from normal context
	Adjust presentation. Focus on rule. Provide feedback. Provide practice and review	Maintain student removal from normal context
	Assume student has been taught skill and will perform correctly in the future	Assume student has "learned" lesson and will behave in future

i G. Colvin, from Comprehensive Classroom Management, ed. V. Jones and L. Jones, p. 287. Copyright © 2004 by Pearson Education, Inc.

When students make academic mistakes, we help them learn the appropriate way to do whatever they are learning. We need to take the same approach when children behave inappropriately.

We decry the current level of violence in our world, yet people continue to treat children, emotionally and physically, in violent ways—both small and great. There are still classrooms where children are not allowed to move out of their seats for long periods of time, lunchrooms where children are not allowed to talk, and even schools that use corporal punishment. Children are shamed, humiliated, and embarrassed by adults. To make matters worse, this often happens in front of others.

My sense is that when we as adults do this, we do not intend to be mean or hurtful. We simply do not have an alternative strategy to employ. In addition, some of the packaged strategies that teachers might use ask adults to be even more assertive about their rights when dealing with children. Over and over, I see the words *behavior management* when people describe what they believe to be effective teaching strategies. When all this happens, I shout (to myself), "We do not manage behavior. We manage classrooms. Who is nurturing our children? Who is providing structure to help them develop constructive behavior? Who is enabling them to learn from their mistakes, all the while keeping their positive senses of themselves intact?"

My experiences teaching and working with teachers, not to mention my adventures as a mother, have convinced me that children want to be the best they can be. No child wants to behave unconstructively; no young adult wants to act like a so-called jerk. Children are born with the innate capacity and desire to be happy, constructive human beings.

Our responsibility as adults is to foster that process. It is not only that shame, embarrassment, punishment, and humiliation are not helpful—they are harmful, not only to those who are on the receiving end but also to those who employ such practices. These practices are unnecessary. We do not need to manage children. We do not need more power. We need strategies that provide structure and nurture students.

Introduction to the Approach

The approach I share with you is *proactive and constructive*. Rather than suggesting the use of strategies to suppress inappropriate behavior, this approach supports strategies that help students learn positive behavior patterns in the first place or alternatives to replace unconstructive behavior.

The approach I share is *eclectic*. While many people working with students use strategies from one theoretical perspective, I draw on principles and approaches from many different ones, including those that may at first seem to contradict one another. Some of what I draw on may be considered an example of a *behaviorist* approach, while other ideas are considered *psychodynamic*.

The approach I share is *ecological*. To be effective teachers, we need to consider *more* than just what an individual student brings to the learning situation. We need to consider the student *within* a particular environment and *among* the myriad interactions that occur between that student and others. Any learner is part of an ecosystem—a set of components that are related to each other for that student at that time. Change one component in the system, and the others are affected. Using this lens, the behavior of any student is seen as the result of the *interaction* between what is inherent in that individual and whatever is in the surrounding environment as well as the nature of that student's social interactions with other human beings.

The approach I share is *comprehensive*. An aspect of the book that may surprise you is the inclusion of so many instructional strategies. I want to be supportive of your competence in all areas because I know that the better we are at facilitating learning, the better our strategies to support constructive behavior will be. These go hand in hand.

The approach I share is *complex*. It is not simple or mechanistic. This approach pervades all aspects of our work. Implementing it takes time, patience, and an ability to reflect on practice, refine, and then try again. I do not say this to scare you. Rather, I warn you because when we try something new, we often get worse before we get better. One moment we may do fine and the next take two giant steps backwards. If you try a strategy that is new for you, you may find yourself getting discouraged or frustrated. The implementation of these strategies is a lifelong process of learning. Like you, I am always trying to get better at doing what I believe is right for students.

While the approach is complex, the book offers a lot of *practical* "how-to's" that describe steps for the processes and give examples of how to apply the steps.

This book is meant to be a *broad but thorough overview* of what I believe is possible in our work with students. I have provided references and resources I find helpful. These can support you if you wish to pursue a particular topic in greater depth.

This is *an approach you can feel good about using*: It is positive and respectful; it is *theoretically sound and fully grounded in research and evidence-based practices; it is effective*.

Note: After attempts at different solutions to fostering gender equality, I found the least cumbersome to be the random assignment of male and female pronouns throughout the book. I hope you find it unobtrusive.

Consideration of You as the Reader

You are unique in all the world. While I may not know you, I support you in your efforts to be the best teacher possible. As you read, consider *your* values and the strategies *you* use while also asking yourself: How can the strategies in this book support my work? How can I use these ideas to help me continually realize my values?

· ·

REFLECTION OPPORTUNITIES

The reflection in Activity A to this Beginning section of the text gives you an opportunity to consider what you value. Write your answers as directed. There are **no** right or wrong answers. This is *not* a time to analyze or criticize. Just write as quickly as possible, because speed kills the critic in your brain. I placed the reflection in Activity A following this section so that when we revisit your values later in the book, you can easily find it.

Our philosophy and the values inherent in it are the underpinnings of our decision-making and therefore determine the strategies we use with students. Before we go any further, answer questions to reflect on some philosophical assumptions you bring to your work. I also placed this reflection in an activity following this Beginning section (Reflection B) so that when we revisit these beliefs later in the book, you can find the reflection readily.

· ·

Final Thoughts

The Beginning portion of this book addresses important aspects of our work together. I wanted to introduce myself so that you might understand the basis for what I share with you. The second aspect of this introduction is the nature of the book's contents. My hope is that providing you an overview will foster your connection to the material. The third focus of the introduction is you. I wanted you to reflect on who you are as you read the book. Much of what we gain from any learning situation rests on what we bring. Offering you the opportunity to consider who you are as the basis for your responses to the book's contents brings this to a more conscious level for you.

Looking Forward: Preview of the Rest of the Book

In Section I, you will read four chapters that provide a conceptual underpinning of basic human needs, how we provide structure and nurture students to meet those needs, and the ecological perspective to working constructively with students. With these concepts as our basis, in the first two chapters of Section II, our focus shifts to the teaching strategies we utilize to prepare the learning environment and establish the community of learners. In in final two chapters of Section II, we consider strategies for sustaining a learning community. Section III addresses the question: What if the strategies we use to establish and sustain a learning community are not enough? Four chapters in this section give us an opportunity to look at how we can support positive behavior change over the long term. The Closing facilitates our drawing our work to an end. In our Introductions and Reflections, we took time to join together. In our Closing we take time, as we need to do in the final portion of any learning experience, to look back and to bring our work together to a close.

References

Caine, R. & Caine, G. (1994). *Making connections: Teaching and the human brain*. Reading, MA: Addison Wesley.

Hunter, M. (1982). *Mastery teaching*. El Segundo, CA: TIP Publications.

Hunter, M. (2004). *Mastery teaching* (2nd ed.). Thousand Oaks, CA: Corwin Press.

Hunter, R. (2014). *Madeline Hunter's Mastery Teaching: Increasing instructional effectiveness in elementary and secondary schools*. Thousand Oaks, CA: Corwin Press.

Immordino-Yang, M. (2015). *Emotions, learning and the brain*. New York, NY: W.W. Norton & Co.

Jensen, E. (2005) *Teaching with the brain in mind* (2nd ed.). Alexandria, VA: Association for Supervision and Curriculum Development.

Jensen, E. (2015a). Guiding principles for brain-based education. Retrieved from www.brainbasedlearning. net/guiding-principles-for-brain-based-education/

Jensen, E. (2015b). What is brain-based learning? Retrieved from www.jensenlearning.com/what-is-brain-based-research.php

Jones, V. & Jones, L. (2016). *Comprehensive classroom management* (11th ed.). Boston, MA: Pearson,

Wolfe, P. (2010). *Brain matters: Translating research into classroom practice* (2nd ed.). Alexandria, VA: Association for Supervision and Curriculum Development.

ACTIVITY A

BEGINNING REFLECTION A: *WHO ARE YOU?* QUESTIONS

On a separate piece of paper that you can keep in a readily available place, write the title "Beginning Reflection A" at the top. Below that write "Who Am I?" Below that write your answers to each of these questions. **Tip:** I encourage you to use key words from the question in each answer, so when you return, what you have written will be readily understood.

1. What positive words describe you as a person?

2. Why did you want to become a teacher?

3. At this point, what are your dreams for your work as a teacher?

4. As a teacher, what would be a nightmare for you?

5. What are your strengths, special skills, talents, and abilities as a teacher?

6. When you look back, which teacher do you remember as being a support to you as a person? What did s/he do or say that you found nurturing?

7. Think of people who have taught you how to do something in a way that you found positive. What did that person do that was constructive?

8. When you finish working with students, what do you hope the students will remember about learning with you?

9. Long after students leave you, what do you hope they will remember about what you taught them?

10. Long after students leave you, what do you hope they remember about you?

WHO ARE YOU? ANALYSIS

Your hopes and dreams (questions 2, 3, 7, 8, 9, and 10) are those aspects of teaching that are particularly important to you—values to maintain or to work towards. Your nightmare (#4), on the other hand, includes those aspects of teaching you hope will not happen. Nightmares are aspects of your life you want to work against—to prevent, if at all possible. The nature of the nurturing (#6) and structure (#7) that you found helpful also speaks to what you value.

WHAT YOU VALUE AS A TEACHER

Extract what you value from your analysis. Below your answers to "Beginning Reflection A: Who am I?" write "What I value as a teacher" and summarize your values—what is important to you, including what you want to avoid as a teacher. As you write, if other values come to mind, include those, too. Remember: there are no right or wrong items.

YOUR TOOLS TO HELP YOU REALIZE YOUR VALUES

Some of the tools you have to help you make your dreams a reality and prevent your nightmare can be found in the positive words you used to describe yourself (#1) and the skills, talents, and abilities you identified (#4). Below your writing on what you value, write the title "Tools to Help Me Integrate What I Value Into My Teaching." Then list your tools.

ACTIVITY B

MY PHILOSOPHY REGARDING THE NATURE OF BEHAVIOR AND BEHAVIOR CHANGE: QUESTIONS FOR REFLECTION

What I Believe about the Nature of Human Behavior

Write what you believe about the nature of human behavior on a piece of paper that you label "Beginning Reflection B: What I Believe about the Nature of Human Behavior." As with your responses to Beginning Reflection A keep this in a readily available place until we use it later in the text. Again, I encourage you to use key words from each question in your answer, so when you return, what you have written will be readily understood.

1. Do I believe that all teachers would pretty much agree with me what constitutes appropriate behavior, or do I think it varies from teacher to teacher?

2. Is there such a thing as "good" behavior? If so, what would I consider to be "good" behavior?

3. Is there such a thing as "bad" behavior? If so, what would I consider to be "bad" behavior?

4. Is there such a thing as a "good" student? If so, what characteristics would a "good" student have?

5. Is there such a thing as a "bad" student? If so, what characteristics would a "bad" student have?

6. Is it always possible to change behavior, or are there some children who are just "bad" or who are "all bad"?

7. In what ways, if any, do a student's cultural background and values affect her/his behavior?

8. In what ways, if any, might my cultural background and values affect my perspective about a student's behavior?

What I Believe about Behavior Change Support

Now write the title "What I Believe about Behavior Change Support", and below that your twelve answers.

1. Who do I think has the primary responsibility for controlling student behavior in the classroom?

2. Who do I think should develop the rules in a classroom?

3. In what ways, if any, might my culture affect my response to a student's behavior?

4. As a teacher, do I think I always have a right to change the behavior of one of my students? Why or why not?

5. As a teacher, do I think I always have a responsibility to change the behavior of one of my students? Why or why not?

6. How important do I think individual differences are when I address unconstructive behavior?

7. As a teacher, do I think behavior change support is solely my responsibility? If it is not, then who else should be involved?

8. As a teacher, do I need a student's permission or agreement to proceed with a behavior change support strategy? If so, under what conditions? Do I need a caregiver's permission? If so, under what conditions?

9. What do I believe about the use of rewards to support behavior change? Would I ever use them? If so, under what conditions?

10. What do I believe about the use of punishment to support behavior change? Would I ever use it? If so, under what conditions?

11. Is any strategy appropriate to use when changing a behavior; that is, do the ends justify the means one uses as a teacher? What would I be willing to do to support behavior change? Is there anything I would not be willing to do to address behavior or support behavior change?

12. What, if any, ethical considerations should I have when supporting change in a student's behavior?

CHAPTER 1

An Ecological Approach To Supporting
Constructive Behavior

The way we look at a situation will in large measure determine how effectively we can address it.

—Shari Stokes

What Will This Chapter Discuss?

We will consider how an ecological approach can help us determine ways to meet the emotional needs of any students. This chapter describes the basic emotional needs and how we can meet these needs by providing structure and nurturing. It also addresses the importance of balancing these two.

Why Is This Important?

For most people, what is going on in the surrounding environment has an influence on their behavior and their learning. How they act and how much they learn vary widely from learning situation to learning situation. To be effective teachers, we need to consider students as individuals who bring talents and needs to any learning situation. We must also consider more than just the student: we must consider the student within a particular environment and among the myriad of interactions occurring between that student and others. To support us in maintaining accurate perceptions of student's needs and in utilizing effective intervention strategies, we will use this ecological perspective. We will view any student as having an ecosystem: a set of components that are related to each other in space and time. Change one variable in that system, and the others are affected. Using this lens, the behavior of any individual is seen *as the result of the interaction* between the variables within that person and whatever variables are external to that person, including the nature and location of physical objects, instructional strategies, and the behavior of other human beings. When we say "as the result of," we do not mean that the individual is passive—that experiences just happen *to* her. The person has an active role; she affects the components of the system.

What Will You Learn?

By the end of this chapter, you will be able to

- describe the ecological approach and its components:

  - how what is going on in the environment inside the student's body (neurologically, chemically, emotionally, etc.) affects the student's behavior (physiological environment variables);

  - how what is in the environment outside the student (the nature of instructional strategies being used, the nature of the student's chair, the room temperature, the sights and sounds in the room) affects the student's behavior (physical environment);

  - how the student is relating (verbally and nonverbally) to others, how others are relating to the student, and how those factors affect his behavior (psychosocial environment); and

  - how what this student brings to the learning experience (talents, temperament, disabilities, emotions, mood states, etc.) interacts with the nature of his external environment variables (temperature, lighting level, instructional strategies) and with the nature of his interactions (verbal and nonverbal) with others, and how all of this affects the student's behavior;

+ compare and contrast the ecological approach to other approaches; and
+ explain the advantages of the ecological approach.

What Do You Want To Accomplish?

What goals do you have as you study the basic needs of students and consider an ecological approach to addressing those needs and creating a learning environment? Write your responses here or on a piece of paper.

_____

_____

_____

ACCESSING PRIOR KNOWLEDGE AND EXPERIENCE

To prepare for this chapter, think about a time and place when you were not comfortable engaging with the people around you or in the task itself. Take a few minutes to jot down here or elsewhere why you were not comfortable. What did you need that was not available in that situation?

_____

_____

_____

Now, think about a different time and place when you felt good about yourself, what you were doing, and the people you were doing it with. Take a few minutes to jot down here or elsewhere what you were getting from that situation that helped you feel that way.

_____

_____

_____

Given my reading, personal experiences, analysis, and reflection for all these years, I have come to believe that as human beings we not only have certain physiological needs for rest, nourishment, and so on. We also have certain basic emotional needs. I believe if we are going to feel open to growing, learning, and furthering our relationships with other people, these emotional needs must be met. In my opinion, the most important are those listed below.

+ A need for **safety** (for both our bodies and the feelings within them): If we don't feel safe in a classroom—if we are worried that the teacher or someone else will hurt us (perhaps grab or hit us) or that someone will hurt our feelings (perhaps berate, expose, or embarrass us)—then we will not be open to learning.

+ A need for **caring and love:** The need to feel cared for includes the need for appropriate affection in words, manner, and touch. Feeling cared for includes the need to be paid attention to and understood. If someone cares for us, she will want to focus on what we say. She will do so because it will be of value for her to understand what we are thinking and feeling. On the other hand, if our teacher or coach does not pay attention to us, value us, try to understand who we are—how we learn, what we think and feel—then how can *we* feel we have something to bring to the learning situation and the development of positive relationships with others?

+ A need to **belong:** Each of us needs to feel a part of a group, a class, a team, a partnership. We do not have to be *with* the group all the time, but when we are, we do need to feel a part of it, not just *in* it. Moreover, we need to feel that the part we play in the group is important—that we have something to contribute and will gain something from the group. Connection gives meaning to our lives.

+ A need to feel **competent:** This is a need for power in the most positive sense of the word. We need to feel that we not only have something to contribute but also that we are capable of doing what we want to do or what is being asked of us. We can develop our abilities. We can be useful members of society. We are competent human beings.

+ A need for **joy, play, recreation, merriment:** This need goes beyond the physiological need for cognitive and sensory stimulation. It is a need to take pleasure in experience—intellectual or physical—regardless of the nature of the task. We need opportunities to be curious and use our imagination. We need experiences that allow fluidity, dynamism, and spontaneity. These experiences may include whimsy, humor, frivolity. They may include reciprocity with another person. They may include a sense of "I've got it!" They always include being nourished and replenished.

REFLECTION OPPORTUNITY

What do you think about this list of basic needs? If you were to make a list, how would it be similar to or different from the list I developed? Write your responses to these questions on a separate piece of paper or in the space provided.

_____

_____

_____

_____

As we look at these basic needs more closely, we see they share two important characteristics. The first characteristic is that these needs are not hierarchical in their nature: they are all equally important. However, while they are equally important, every individual will prioritize them differently based on his or her own life experience. For example, if many important people in one's life have died, one may feel more alone than one would choose. In many situations, one may have a stronger desire to belong—to be part of a partnership, team, or group—than someone else might. Certainly, one will still need to have the other four needs met, but the desire to feel that sense of belonging will be more intense than what others might feel.

The second characteristic of basic needs is that all five needs are interdependent. If one of the needs is not met, that affects the degree to which the others are met. Indeed, interdependency may be the litmus test for any need being a basic one. Let me offer an example to illustrate this last characteristic: If I do not feel emotionally safe in a class for an extended period of time, then I will likely feel that my teacher does not care enough about me to grasp my discomfort and help me feel safer. I feel a bit lost, isolated. This is not a learning community within which I feel that I belong. Because I feel unsafe, any sense of efficaciousness is much lower than what I might typically feel. Clearly, under such conditions there is no joy. If one need is to be met, then all other needs must be reasonably met.

How Do We Meet Basic Emotional Needs?

If basic emotional needs are to be met _and_ students are going to learn subject matter and skills while also learning positive, useful behavior patterns, what must we the adults do in these situations? How do we foster learning?

We foster learning by nurturing children and providing them with structure. Children and young adults need both nurturing and structure if they are to develop into emotionally healthy, happy, and productive adults.

When we nurture, we send an important, powerful message to the other person: "I care about you. I willingly care for and support you in the ways you need." This is a message of _un_conditional positive feelings towards another—unconditional because the message is based on how we feel about the person, *not* what the person does or says. We nurture someone when she makes mistakes because nurturing is not based on perfection. (Besides, making mistakes is a normal, necessary part of growth. Mistakes are useful lessons.) We nurture someone when he behaves in a way that we feel is inappropriate. People express this sentiment by saying "I like you, but I don't like what you are doing", or "I care deeply for you; that hasn't changed—I just feel very angry about what you did." On the other hand, nurturing someone does not mean never setting limits. As we will discuss, limit setting provides structure.

Children are not born loving themselves or others. If we nurture them—if they see our unconditional care and support for them—they can come to care for themselves unconditionally. Sadly, the opposite is also true: if what is mirrored in our eyes is disgust or shame, or if we refuse to nurture a child, then she will likely find it difficult to love herself or others. There are many individuals who do harm to themselves or other people because they never learned to care. No one nurtured them.

Again, the *un*conditional nature of this caring is important. When we love ourselves, there should be no strings attached. This is not a love based on being better than someone else. Nor should these good feelings exist only when we are doing everything right. *Really* loving ourselves means being able to make mistakes. (Of course, there are extremes in behavior that are not the kinds of mistakes we are describing here.)

Another part of this message is the importance of patience and tolerance. We may not be able to do something the way we would like to right away. It's all right to take time to learn. A third part of this self-love is the message that we can learn from our experiences. We can be open to and make healthy, productive decisions based on both the positive *and* the constructive negative feedback we gain from the experiences that come our way.

When children are very young, we principally nurture through care. The younger the child, the more we respond as soon as we determine what she needs. As a child matures, our care becomes more of an offer—she can accept or reject this care freely. Also, as children mature and are more able to take care of themselves, our care turns to what might more appropriately be called support.

Is nurturing enough? No, it isn't. Structure is also needed. Without structure, there would be chaos. If being nurtured gives us positive power, then being given structure helps us learn the appropriate boundaries for our power. Structure also sets expectations and standards for our behavior. Structure helps us learn the positive consequences of what we do. Appropriate structure also helps us learn from the negative consequences. We learn how to avoid making the same mistakes over and over again. With appropriate external structure, a person develops internal structure and self-discipline.

Structure includes not only rules for how to get along in life. It also includes the skills needed to be successful at what we do, to function independently. Being successful requires many skills. We need to be able to size up a situation to determine what is required to negotiate it successfully; to establish one or more goals; to determine options; to make choices; to start, carry through, and complete one or more tasks; to evaluate what we have accomplished; and to fine-tune our actions if changes are necessary.

How Do We Balance Nurturing and Structure?

These days, we hear a lot about the need for more discipline. Is structure more important than nurturing? No. With too much nurturing and too little structure, a child may be smothered by care and become unable to fend positively for himself. Another consequence could be that the child or young adult will not have the right boundaries. She might be too thin-skinned or overstep other people's personal boundaries much too often. In contrast, too little nurturing and too much structure could create a child who is joyless and lacking in spontaneity. She might be anxious because there are so many rules but not enough support for all that needs to be accomplished. Another result might be that a student becomes extremely uncomfortable without explicit rules and procedures. He might be a perfectionist who only feels good about himself when everything is done "perfectly" according to "all the rules." Nurturance and structure contribute in different but equally important ways to addressing basic emotional needs, and so they must be appropriately balanced.

Nurturing and Providing Structure to Create a Sense of Safety

Being nurtured sends the message "You are safe with me. I will not hurt your body or your feelings. You will feel the ease of both mental and physical well-being. I will teach you with material that is appropriate for your developmental level and your learning style." Providing structure teaches students how to care for themselves, how to keep themselves safe. It also teaches them how to show that they care about the well-being of others and respect their safety. "Today's learning target is 'I can deal with teasing.' We will talk about what we say when someone teases us."

Nurturing and Providing Structure to Create a Sense of Love

Being nurtured communicates "I care about you. I'm here to support you." Nurturing encourages students to feel worthy. It provides a model for how to care for themselves and others. Being nurtured also sends the message "I like you and respect you for who you are as an individual, not for what you do. I will take the time to get to know you as an individual." Being given structure tells students that someone cares enough to teach them the concepts, skills, habits, rules, and boundaries that will enable them to be successful in life.

Nurturing and Providing Structure to Create a Sense of Belonging

Being nurtured tells students "You are one of us; you are an important member of this partnership, group, team, class." Being given structure teaches them how to effectively collaborate and function interdependently with others. "In our morning meeting today, we will practice listening respectfully. Let's make a list of how we show others that we are listening to what they are saying."

Nurturing and Providing Structure to Create a Sense of Efficacy

Being nurtured says "You can; you are capable." Being provided structure says "This is how to do it." Being given structure teaches students the skills to be capable, as an individual *and* in their work and play with others.

Nurturing and Providing Structure to Create a Sense of Joy, of Well-Being

Being **nurtured** says "We have an innate desire to be happy. Look for delight in what you do. Find things that give you joy. All labor and no enjoyment is not a good balance in everyday life." Being given **structure** teaches students how to nourish themselves alone and in a reciprocal fashion with another person.

If your learning style is helped by material presented in chart form, Table 1-1 below provides this.

Table 1-1. **How Nurturance and Structure Address Basic Needs**		
Basic Need	**How Nurturance Addresses the Basic Need**	**How Structure Addresses the Basic Need**
Safety (emotional, physical, cognitive)	Being **nurtured** sends the message, "You can be assured that you are safe with me. I will not hurt your body or your feelings nor will I ask you to take actions that will harm you. I will present material to you that is high challenge, but not too hard nor more than you can learn at one time."	Receiving **structure** tells us how important it is to respect our own safety and that of others. Being given structure teaches us how to keep ourselves safe and how to respect the safety of others.
Love	Being **nurtured** communicates, "I care for you. I respect you. I'm here to support you." Nurturing encourages us to feel worthy. It provides a model for us to care for ourselves and for others.	Receiving **structure** says that someone cares enough to teach us the skills, habits, rules, boundaries that will enable us to be successful in life. Being given structure provides us examples/models for how one cares for oneself and others.
Belonging	Being **nurtured** tells us, "You are one of us; you are an important member of this partnership, group, team, class. We need you."	Receiving **structure** tells us that being a part of a group takes skill. Being given structure teaches us how to function interdependently with those around us.
Efficacy	Being **nurtured** says, "You can, you are capable."	Receiving **structure** says, "This is how to do it." Being provided structure teaches us the skills to be capable both as an individual and with others.
Joy	Being **nurtured** says, "Look for delight in what you do. Find things that give you joy. Labor without enjoyment is not emotionally helpful in everyday life. We all need fun. We all need to have times in which we enjoy what we are doing."	Receiving **structure** communicates to us that joy can go hand in hand with learning and living. Being provided structure teaches us how to nourish ourselves and how to nourish others in a reciprocal fashion.
In Summary:	**Nurturance** supports who we *are* as an individual. **Nurturance** helps us to *feel* good about being us, about being alive.	**Structure** supports what we do. Structure gives us the skills with which we can lead fulfilling lives.

If children and young adults are to learn, we as teachers must create classroom environments that are conducive to learning. People are most open to learning when their emotional needs are being met. To meet basic emotional needs, we must nurture and provide structure in an appropriate balance. A summary of these ideas in mathematical formula would look this:

EFFECTIVE TEACHING =

providing nurturance (care and support) + structure (reasonable, slightly challenging expectations, opportunities to learn ideas/skills, and constructive feedback)

To teach effectively—to nurture *and* provide structure—is a complex process. We can certainly do it, but do not let anyone ever tell you that teaching is either simple or easy. It takes time to build up the strategies. Why? **No two of us are alike.** While all people have certain emotional needs, how these are realized varies widely from person to person. Think of the children in any family you know. Are they all alike? Even identical twins are not really identical. So it is when we think about teaching children and young adults: no two students are alike. There are certainly some strategies that will be helpful for most children, but even then, the degree of helpfulness can vary from one student to another.

An Ecological Approach to Nurturing and Providing Structure

How do we both nurture and provide structure? Our ecological perspective will help. Before we begin, I want to set the stage.

REFLECTION OPPORTUNITY

Does your behavior change when you are in different learning environments? On a separate piece of paper or in the following space briefly describe an example. Explain why you think this change happened.

_____

_____

_____

_____

There are many approaches to teaching and learning. Before exploring the ecological approach, we will briefly consider a few others to analyze how they are like the ecological approach and how they are different from it.

Many approaches to working with the behavior of children and young adults focus principally on one environment of a student's existence, while others focus on two. For example, the medical approach to intervention focuses principally on the physiological (internal) environment of the student. Mood states, extreme aggression, and attention deficit disorders are viewed as the result of a chemical imbalance that affects thinking and behavior. Diagnosis is done through discussion, written assessments such as personality or other inventories, checklists and reports of behavior, and possibly the completion of medical tests such as Magnetic Resonance Imaging (MRI). Internal states are inferred from information about behavior and thinking patterns gleaned from the student and, perhaps, information from others. Intervention is then done medically. For example, a pharmaceutical drug might be prescribed to help a student address depression or attention deficit disorder.

A group of approaches that have as their foci variables in the physiological *and* psychosocial (interaction) environments are derived from humanistic psychology and the work of Maslow (1968), Rogers (1969, 1983), Purkey (1970), and Gordon (1991), to name a few. Sometimes these approaches are called psychodynamic. Information is gathered by a teacher or a counselor through interview, observation, and perhaps survey instruments to determine what the child is thinking and feeling, the sources of conflict or tension, the student's internal needs, and the nature of the student's interactions with significant other people. This information is used to develop an intervention in both the student's physiological environment (where variables such as emotions lie) and the psychosocial environment (in which human interaction variables exist). The intervention might consist of counseling or therapy. Humanistic interventions might also be implemented in the classroom's psychosocial environment and include, for example, strategies that address the nature of the teacher–student interaction or activities such as class or small-group discussions on certain topics and role play.

The third example, the behaviorist approach, looks at a student's verbal and nonverbal behavior (variables in the psychosocial environment) and intervenes in the external (physical) environment by using variables in the teacher's instructional strategies. These might include cues to encourage a certain student behavior to occur, followed by reinforcement after the behavior occurs to encourage it to occur again under similar circumstances. What cannot be observed is not considered. B. F. Skinner (1968, 1983), who espoused this approach, believed that behavior was a response to external events or stimuli: if one looked at student behavior and determined what events triggered it and what the consequences were for that behavior *from the perspective of the individual,* one could determine the variable(s) in the environment that needed to be manipulated to change the behavior. He did not use the term "physical environment," but that is where interventions occur for behaviorists.

None of these approaches takes an ecological perspective. None look at variables in *all three* environments. None consider *the interaction of variables in all three* in the provision of nurturance and structure to support constructive behavior in children and young adults. None look at variables in all three environments when collecting information, when analyzing the data, and when designing an intervention to support change.

Why Should We Use the Ecological Approach?

What is going on in the surrounding environment influences students' behavior. How they act and how much they learn varies widely from learning situation to learning situation. To be effective teachers, we need to consider students as individuals who bring talents and needs to any learning situation. We must also consider *more* than just the student—we must consider the student *within* a particular environment and *among* the myriad of interactions occurring between that student and others.

There are three aspects of the student's ecosystem that are important to consider in any learning situation. We will call these aspects environments. They are the physiological, the physical, and the psychosocial environments. Let us examine what is included in each.

The physiological environment includes those variables that exist within the individual:

+ brain functioning, including all that is stored in the brain's memory;
+ health factors such as nutrition, stamina, temporary illnesses, and chronic conditions;
+ natural abilities and learning needs such as temperament, learning style, intelligences, and disabilities;
+ neurobiological conditions such as attention deficit disorders;
+ mood disorders such as depression and bipolar disorder;
+ toxic substances such as lead and certain drugs; and
+ affective variables, including the feelings and internal mood states of the child.

The physical environment includes variables in a classroom or in the **physical world** *outside* the student *that do not include personal interaction*:

+ the nature, location, and arrangement of the furniture, equipment, and objects;
+ the nature of the lighting, the level of the temperature, the noise level, and the displays around the room; and
+ the nature of instructional strategies and materials.

The psychosocial environment includes variables that exist within the verbal and nonverbal interaction of the student and other people (words used, tone of voice, facial expressions, hand movements and other body language) and the student's internal interactions (e.g., talking to himself).

To be able to teach and support the development of constructive behavior—to be able to provide structure and to nurture—we need to look at the student *not only* as an individual but *as an individual who has an ecosystem.* How the variables in our ecosystem affect each of us varies from individual to individual. Any student has his own ecosystem, but he is simultaneously a part of a much larger ecosystem that includes everyone else (with his or her own ecosystem) in the learning situation at any one time.

Using the ecological perspective requires us to ask four key questions as we develop our perception of a student, her needs, what is affecting her—what might be contributing to the level of her learning and to the nature of her behavior.

The first three questions relate to variables in each of the environments.

1. Physiological environment variables: What is going on in the environment inside the student's body (neurologically, chemically, emotionally, etc.), and how are these internal variables affecting him and, thereby, affecting the student's behavior?

2. Physical environment variables: What is the environment outside the student like (the nature of instructional strategies being used, the nature of the student's chair, the room temperature,

the sights and sounds in the room), and how are these external variables affecting the student and, thereby, affecting his behavior?

3. Psychosocial environment variables: How is the student relating (verbally and nonverbally) to others? How are others relating to the student? How are these interactions affecting him and, thereby, affecting his behavior?

The fourth question addresses the interconnectedness of the three environments:

4. How does what this student brings to the learning experience (variables in his internal environment such as talents, temperament, disabilities, emotions, mood states, etc.) interact with the nature of his external environment variables (temperature, lighting level, instructional strategies) and the nature of his interactions (verbal and nonverbal) with others? How do all these interactions among variables have an impact on the student's behavior?

We will look at behavior in a context. Therefore, *all four questions need to be asked* if an ecological approach to assessing need, to responding, and to evaluating the results is to be effectively carried out.

What Are the Advantages of the Ecological Approach?

Viewing behavior within a context provides three advantages. The first occurs during the data collection and assessment phases of the behavior change support process. If we gather and analyze information about variables in *all three environments*, we are more likely to discover useful information about patterns of variables that may contribute to the occurrence of the behavior. Also, we are more likely to gain information that will allow us to conceptualize the whole picture of how these variables might interact.

The second advantage occurs when we design our intervention—our instructional strategy. If we consider what changes are needed in variables in *all three environments*, we are more likely to be successful in addressing the student's needs.

The third advantage occurs during the implementation of our strategy. If we address variables in *all three environments*, we are much more likely to effect the changes necessary to support the student's development of constructive behavior.

Application Activity: Addressing Basic Needs within an Ecological Approach

PART I: THINKING ABOUT THE ECOLOGICAL PERSPECTIVE FOR CONSIDERING BASIC NEEDS

Take a few minutes to review the ideas in the chapter. Then, write your answers below or on elsewhere to the following questions in the space provided or elsewhere.

1. Can you remember one way in which the ecological approach is different from the others?

   _____

   _____

2. In what ways, if any, is this approach different from what you have been using so far?

   _____

   _____

3. In what ways, if any, is this approach similar to what you have been using so far?

   _____

   _____

PART II: THINKING ABOUT BASIC NEEDS

Directions   Research indicates that drawing a picture of something helps us remember a concept. In the following space or on a separate page, if needed, draw a picture that represents each of the five basic needs. Don't worry about artistry; just enjoy coming up with an image that speaks to you and helps you understand and remember something you've learned.

Final Thoughts

We began by looking at basic needs of students. We talked about how teachers nurture and provide structure to meet those basic needs. We also considered the ecological perspective, one way to conceptualize what might be affecting a student's behavior at any given moment. We said that with the knowledge of basic needs and the ecological perspective, we can effectively nurture and provide structure and thus support constructive behavior. We also discussed how the ecological approach includes elements of other approaches as well as how it is different. We concluded that the differences of the ecological approach offer advantages over others.

Looking Forward

In the next three chapters, we will consider the three environments that exist for any individual: the physiological, the physical, and the psychosocial environment. We will examine specific variables contained within each environment to determine how they might affect variables in the other environments and affect learning and behavior.

References

Armstrong, T. (1998). *Awakening genius in the classroom*. Alexandria, VA: Association for Supervision and Curriculum Development.

Armstrong, T. (2009). *Multiple intelligences in the classroom* (3rd ed.). Alexandria, VA: Association for Supervision and Curriculum Development.

Bocchino, R. (1999). *Emotional literacy: To be a different kind of smart*. Thousand Oaks, CA: Corwin Press.

Brophy, J. (1998). *Motivating students to learn*. Boston, MA: McGraw-Hill.

Caine, R. & Caine, G. (1994). *Making connections: Teaching and the human brain* (2nd ed.). Reading, MA: Addison-Wesley.

Clarke, J. & Dawson, C. (1989). *Growing up again*. New York, NY: Harper and Row.

Cohen, J. (1999). *Educating minds and hearts*. New York, NY: Teachers College Press.

Dean, C., Hubbell, E., Pitler, H., & Stone, B. J. (2012). *Classroom instruction that works: Research-based strategies for increasing student achievement* (2nd ed.). Alexandria, VA: Association for Supervision and Curriculum Development.

Evans, W., Evans, S., & Schmid, R. (1993). *Behavior and instructional management: An ecological approach*. Boston: Allyn & Bacon.

Gardner, H. (1993). *Multiple intelligences: The theory in practice*. New York, NY: Basic Books.

Glasser, W. (1986). *Control theory in the classroom*. New York, NY: Harper & Row.

Glasser, W. (1992). *The quality school: Managing students without coercion* (2nd ed.). New York, NY: HarperCollins.

Glasser, W. (1998). *The quality school teacher* (3rd ed.). New York, NY: Harper Perennial.

Goleman, D. (1996). *Emotional intelligence*. New York, NY: Bantam.

Goleman, D. (2006). *Social intelligence: The new science of human relationships*. New York, NY: Random House.

Gordon, T. (1991). *Discipline that works*. New York, NY: Plume/Penguin Books.

Hyman, I. (1997). *School discipline and school violence*. Boston: Allyn & Bacon.

Jensen, E. (2015). Guiding principles for brain-based education. Retrieved from www.brainbasedlearning. net/guiding-principles-for-brain-based-education/

Kessler, R. (2000). *The soul of education*. Alexandria, VA: Association for Supervision and Curriculum Development.

Kohl, H. (1998). *The discipline of hope: Learning from a lifetime of teaching*. New York, NY: Simon and Shuster.

Kohn, A. (1996). *Beyond discipline: From compliance to community*. Alexandria, VA: Association for Supervision and Curriculum Development.

Marzano, R. (2007). *The art and science of teaching: A comprehensive framework for effective instruction*. Alexandria, VA: Association for Supervision and Curriculum Development.

Marzano, R., Gaddy, B., Foseid, M, C., Foseid, M. P., and Marzano, J. (2005). *A handbook for classroom management that works*. Alexandria, VA: Association for Supervision and Curriculum Development.

Maslow, A. (1954*). Motivation and personality*. New York, NY: Harper and Bros.

Maslow, A. (1968). *Toward a psychology of being* (2nd ed.). New York, NY: Van Nostrand.

Maslow, A. (1972). *The farther reaches of human nature*. New York, NY: Viking Press.

Purkey, W. (1970). *Self-concept and school achievement*. Englewood Cliffs, NJ: Prentice-Hall.

Rogers, C. (1961). *On becoming a person*. Boston: Houghton Mifflin.

Rogers. C. (1969). *Freedom to learn*. Columbus, OH: Merrill.

Skinner, B. F. (1968). *The technology of teaching*. New York, NY: Appleton-Century-Crofts.

Skinner, B. F. (1983*). A matter of consequences*. New York, NY: Knopf.

Sylwester, R. (1995). A *celebration of neurons: An educator's guide to the human brain*. Alexandria, VA: Association for Supervision and Curriculum Development.

United Nations General Assembly. (1959). *Declaration of the rights of children*. New York, NY: United Nations.

Wolfe, P. (2010). *Brain matters: Translating research into classroom practice* (2nd ed.). Alexandria, VA: Association for Supervision and Curriculum Development.

CHAPTER 2

The Effects of Physiological Environment Variables on Behavior

What lies behind us and what lies before us are tiny matters compared to what lies within us.

—Ralph Waldo Emerson

What Will This Chapter Discuss?

We will consider a broad range of categories of physiological environment variables: typical brain functioning, temperament, mindset, learning style, intelligences, disabilities, health issues, drugs, mood disorders, neurobiological conditions, toxic substances. Some we will analyze briefly; others we will examine in greater detail.

Why Is This Important?

As we said in Chapter 1, many current approaches to supporting behavior change look at the effects of some of the variables we will consider, but none look at all. Doctors look at medical issues; behaviorists look at observable behavior and setting events; developmentalists and those in the psychodynamic schools of thought look at internal variables in what is often called the psyche. None addresses the full range of variables in what we are calling the physiological environment. Yet as we consider each of these variables, we will see how any one could affect a student's learning and behavior. If we are to be thorough in our assessment of what might be contributing to a student's behavior, I believe we cannot ignore all the elements that comprise the physiological environment.

What Will You Learn?

In this chapter, you will learn about:

* the internal variables that can affect behavior; and
* the internal variables that can affect the ability to learn and, therefore, a student's behavior.

What Do You Want To Accomplish?

What would you like to learn about internal variables that can affect learning and behavior? Write your responses here or on a piece of paper.

_____

_____

_____

_____

What Are Key Variables in the Physiological Environment of Every Student?

We address the physiological environment first because it allows us to begin with you, the reader, since you are an example of one learner. As you read, consider how the variables we analyze affect your learning. What ways can you bring that understanding to the effects these variables might have on the learning and behavior of each student with whom you work?

I do not expect that you will remember the details of each category. What is important is your understanding that there are any number of internal variables that can affect a person's ability to learn and can affect behavior in a variety of ways. You can use the references at the end of the chapter for greater details and a deeper understanding of any of the topics whenever the need arises.

Brain Functioning

Understanding how typical human beings respond to, take in, and process what they are experiencing is basic to all other topics. In the last 25 years, there have been major breakthroughs in our understanding of brain functioning and its implications for teaching.

Our capacity to learn is inexhaustible. Each healthy human brain, irrespective of a person's age, sex, nationality, or cultural background, comes equipped with a set of exceptional features. As Caine and Caine (1994) describe them, they are:

- the ability to detect patterns and to make approximations;
- a phenomenal capacity for various types of memory;
- the ability to self-correct and learn from experience by way of analysis of external data and self-reflection; and
- an inexhaustible capacity to create (p. 3).

The human brain seeks novelty. There is another aspect of brain functioning that is important to consider. Each brain is wired for novelty. It is always seeking new stimuli with which to work. If teachers do not provide novelty in learning experiences, (students are passively involved for long stretches, or the lesson structure is the same day after day), students' brains will seek novelty elsewhere. They may be attracted by watching something outside the window, imagining a scene in their mind, or drawing on nearby paper (or the back of their hand). Teachers often say, "She is not paying attention." But she is. The question is: To what is she paying attention? As Saphier, Haley-Spec, and Gowen (2008) remind us, students' brains are always paying attention to something. If what we as teachers offer is not interesting, meaningful, or novel enough, students will pay attention to something that draws their focus elsewhere.

The human brain seeks to connect with others. "Neuroscience has discovered that our brain's very design makes it sociable, inexorably drawn into an intimate brain-to-brain linkup whenever we engage with another person" (Goleman, 2017). Every encounter we have with another human being affects both her brain and ours. The longer, the more frequent the interactions and the more important the person is to us, the greater the impact.

We learn from our entire experience. Our learning includes what we are absorbing through all our senses and the connections we are making within that experience and from that experience to any we have had in the past. Simultaneously, our brain is holding those connections ready to link to any experiences in the future. It follows then that the richer our experiences, the greater the connections in our brain. Environment quite literally affects the brain physiologically.

There are Three Layers of the Brain that Interact with Each Other

Looking at the specific physiology of the brain provides useful information to aid our understanding of some important aspects of learning. The Triune Brain Theory of how our brain functions is one of the many ways to conceptualize brain functioning. This model comes from the work of Paul MacLean (1978, as cited in Caine & Caine, 1994). He proposes that there are three layers to our brain: the brain stem, the limbic system, and the neocortex; thus, the name *TRI*une. The brain stem is the oldest portion of the brain from an evolutionary perspective. Most of its functioning is automatic. It controls all the functions of the body that enable us to survive, such as circulation, digestion, and elimination. This is also the portion of the brain that controls all our emotional reactions to potentially dangerous situations, such as our "flight or fight" response when we feel threatened. The limbic system, MacLean theorizes, was the next area of our brain to evolve. This portion mediates memory and houses our major centers of emotion. Here is where the two amygdalae lie—one on either side of the brain. The amygdalae are the parts of the brain that control emotions (Goleman, 1995). All feelings, including fear, affection and passion, are tied to them. All emotional memory is stored there. The most recent area of our brain to evolve, according to the Triune Brain Theory, is the neocortex. This is the largest portion (about 5/6) of the brain. Whereas the brain stem controls automatic responses, the neocortex is the center of "thinking." This is where sensory information is processed, where our language occurs, where we recall the past and plan for the future.

Emotions

Happiness, frustration, anger, sadness, disappointment, and envy are but some of the emotions we experience. Each is a variable in the physiological environment of every student.

Some emotions can invite us to think about certain things. Other emotions can affect how we perceive a situation and on what we choose to focus in any situation. As we have said, all emotions prepare us for response. When we experience emotion, how we respond and how quickly we do so are other important pieces of the emotion → action picture. Understanding the mechanism of any emotion can help us to respond constructively when we feel an emotion and can also help us to support constructive behavior in students when they experience feelings.

From a biological, neurological perspective, any emotion is an impulse to act (Goleman, 1995). We feel; we are urged by that feeling to act. Over time, evolution has instilled instant neurological plans in us for addressing our emotions. Each emotion plays a distinct role in preparing our bodies to respond. Two contrasting examples demonstrate this point. The first is anger and the second is happiness.

> With *anger,* blood flows to the hands making it easier to grasp a weapon or strike at a foe. Heart rate increases, and a rush of hormones, such as adrenaline, generates a pulse of energy strong enough for vigorous action (Goleman, 1995, p. 6).

By contrast, consider happiness. When we are happy, there is an activity increase in the part of our brain that simultaneously enhances our energy and quiets our negative thoughts and worries (Goleman, 1995, pp. 6–7). There is a shift in our physiology that helps our body recover from the arousal of upsetting emotions. Happiness offers the body, in Goleman's (1995) words, "a general rest, as well as readiness and enthusiasm for whatever task is at hand and for striving towards a variety of goals" (p. 7).

Emotion Plays a Key Role in Thinking, Memory, and Learning

The three areas, or layers, of the brain interact. Note the word *interact*. Each layer is interconnected with the other two. I stress this point because in education we are likely to view learning (and, therefore, how we should teach) as involving cognition—thinking. We rarely include emotion in the picture. Yet emotion plays a key role in learning. Memory has no personal meaning without emotion. Deprive learning of its emotional content and we limit a student's capacity to remember.

When we teach, of course we want that emotion to be constructive. Notice I did not say positive. Do you remember an event or experience that had a powerful effect on you that was not positive? I still remember, as if it were just moments ago, seeing TV footage of police dogs attacking peaceful demonstrators during the civil rights movement. What I felt then, and feel today just as vividly every time that picture comes to mind, does not involve any *positive* emotion. However, the learning was *constructive*. In fact, it led to my taking several steps then and continuing to take steps to ensure that human beings are not treated that way anywhere. By anyone. I learned more about the violation of basic human rights in that one emotional moment than I had in many hours spent reading and talking about civil rights. Emotion certainly plays a key role in facilitating memory and, therefore, in learning (Caine, Caine, McClintick, & Klimack, 2005).

Emotion can also have a muting effect on learning. When we perceive ourselves at risk, parts of our neocortex shut down. Consider Claude: Students in his class are talking about a story character, Chuck, whose family is struggling to make ends meet. Chuck hides the fact. Because he can't afford sports equipment or the rental of an instrument, he doesn't join any activities. No one understands why he isn't going out for sports or the band. He's good at both. They try to persuade him he should. As the class discussion about the character's choice progresses, some students do not seem to understand how the character Chuck couldn't afford the items he needs. One or two understand that but wonder why Chuck won't tell anyone. Claude is having increasing difficulty being a part of the discussion. His mom just lost her job. No one knows, and he wants it that way. He is upset that some of his friends don't understand that good people can get into a situation like that. He becomes very uncomfortable with the discussion. He is embarrassed and also angry about what some other children are saying. He is also worried that somehow his situation will be exposed if he tries to explain how he thinks Chuck might be feeling or reacting. Claude withdraws and doesn't say a word.

We shut down even more of our neocortex when we feel helpless, when we feel we have no control over the outcome of the situation. Hart (1982, as cited in Caine & Caine, 1994, p. 69) calls this "downshifting." The name is apt because the control of functioning is *shift*ed from the higher-reasoning neocortex *down* to the lower, automatic layers of the brain: the limbic system and the brain stem. In threat situations, the body needs to respond quickly, so such downshifting promotes survival. In a classroom, however, students should never experience a threatening situation. Students should have no reason to need to react immediately, to flee or to stand and defend. The need to "downshift" in a classroom is detrimental to learning; in fact, it prevents learning, if by learning we mean reasoning. The kind of learning that might occur under fear has no place in our classrooms. The research on brain functioning clearly supports students' need to feel emotionally safe if they are to learn constructive behavior patterns.

Downshifting also occurs when we feel angry. This is true whether the anger is felt directly as a primary emotion, experienced as a mask for other feelings we are too frightened or defended to feel (feelings such as fear, anxiety, or a sense of abandonment), or felt as a secondary emotion, following on the heels of other feelings. Do we always have to be victims of our anger's call to quick response? No. We can develop personal responses for the moment that will buy us enough time to let our "thinking mind" take over, to let reason precede our response to the situation or another person. Knowing how strong emotions like anger can trigger instant behavior is an important basis for our later consideration of how we can support constructive responses when the "emotional mind" is triggered by emotions.

The Research on Brain Functioning Clearly Supports Students' Need to Feel Emotionally Safe

Later in the book, we will address the implications of brain functioning for nurturing and providing structure to foster constructive behavior in students. For now, we need to remember that what goes on in the brain, including memory (in the student's physiological environment), affects and is affected by what is going on in that student's physical environment (variables such as classroom arrangement and instruction, to name but two) and psychosocial environment variables (interactions with other students and teacher).

Social Intelligence

The pathways in our brains are highly sensitive to what is going on around us. Our experiences with others change the nature of our circuitry. As Goleman states (2006), "Our social interactions operate as modulators … that continually reset key aspects of our brain function as they orchestrate our emotions (p. 5)." How others behave towards us affects not only how we behave in the moment but also how we develop the social skills to behave constructively in the future.

Social intelligence includes the skills that allow any person to use emotions thoughtfully, to maintain a balance between emotions and reasoning, and to interact constructively with others of any age. Goleman (1995, 1996, 2006, 2017) delineates these competencies or domains as those that contribute to social intelligence. As you read these, you may notice that the first four are internal processes, whereas social skills put those processes into action.

- **Self-awareness:** ability to name feelings and talk about them clearly
- **Self-management of emotions:** ability to ease emotions or change moods; skill in resolving a conflict constructively, even if it entails strong emotions
- **Self-motivation:** a mindset of "I can," a sense of resilience, and an ability to maintain inner drive and persistence
- **Empathy:** ability to grasp what another person is feeling and to "feel" for that person
- **Social skills:** ability to interact constructively with others of all ages. Include:
  - **Synchrony:** getting mannerisms and movements in synch with those of the person with whom one is interacting

- ♦ **Self-presentation:** ability to present oneself in a way that makes the desired impression

- ♦ **Influence:** ability to use tact and self-control to constructively shape the outcome of an interaction

- ♦ **Concern:** tendency to turn empathy into action

Clearly, the variable of social intelligence and the skills therein can profoundly affect a student's behavior in any interaction in the classroom—whether it is with the teacher or other students.

Mindset

Our mindset is not something with which we are born. We don't inherit it. We develop it. From an early age, as we go through life, we form perceptions about our capacities. We base these on our experiences, but perhaps even more, we base them on what people who are important to us *say* about our ability and how important people *react* to us as we work at everyday challenges. A growth mindset (Dweck, 2006) is the belief that abilities can be developed through hard work and persistence, or "grit," as Duckworth (2016) describes it. A fixed mindset is framed by the belief that what we can do, we can do. No more. Effort will not make a difference.

Our mindset affects how we approach learning, how we solve problems, and the habits we develop. In other words, how we think about our abilities affects our behavior in any number of ways. Ultimately, our mindset profoundly affects the degree to which we fulfill our potential. As Henry Ford once said, "If you think you can, you can. If you think you can't, you can't."

The effect of our talents is vastly overrated. Yes, we do need some ability, but what really counts is what we do with what we have. That is based on our belief that what we do makes a difference. If we feel our efforts will enable us to master whatever is in front of us, we will persist even when things get difficult. We will think about learning. We will focus on effort. We won't worry about how competent or smart we are. We will think, instead, about the strategies we are using and whether or not they are the best for the problem at hand. We will persist. We will practice because we know (if we are practicing the skill correctly) we will improve. Those with a growth mindset believe, as Winston Churchill is quoted as saying, "Success is not final, failure is not fatal: it is the courage to continue that counts."

IMPORTANT POINT ABOUT BRAIN FUNCTIONING, EMOTIONS, SOCIAL INTELLIGENCE, AND MINDSET

The research on brain functioning, emotions, social intelligence, and mindset clearly supports students' need to feel emotionally safe if they are to learn.

Values

As human beings, we are likely to perceive, to interpret what we see, based on our own beliefs and values of the moment. If we have particular values, then we are likely to behave a certain way that reflects those beliefs and values.

Teacher Values

Examples

1. If we are female and became particularly interested in science in the sixth grade, when we are teaching middle school students, we might expect middle school-age girls to be similarly inclined. Our expectations would likely lead us to invite their active participation in scientific activities, to encourage them to ask questions about whatever they are exploring in class, and to give them time to think before having to answer a question because we know their processing of information is an important part of learning.

2. If we value quietness in our room, our beliefs about the importance of quietness will affect how we behave with students—both those who are quiet and those who are not.

3. If we value the kind of respect shown by the direct gaze of students from Western cultures, then students from Asian, Hispanic, and Native American cultures who show respect by averting their eyes will likely *not* get the same kind of response from us.

Student Values

Examples

1. If a student believes "real girls" should not be athletic, he might tease any girls who want to spend time participating in any kind of sports activity.

2. If a student values the experiences of others, she might be apt to listen to teachers or peers when they share in a team or large-group discussion.

IMPORTANT POINT ABOUT VALUES

Our values, which often include our feelings and memories of previous experiences regarding these values, affect our behavior choices. These choices will, in turn, affect others.

Temperament

Another way to describe temperament is to say behavioral style. We are born with our temperament. Research on temperament was first published over 45 years ago by three investigators, Thomas, Chess, and Birch (1968), who did a 10-year study of the development of 136 individuals (including several sets of twins). The investigators observed the children's behavior from infancy frequently and interviewed their parents and teachers about that behavior. The researchers concluded that there are nine distinct categories of behavior, which they called temperament.

- ✦ Activity level: How active are we throughout a typical day?
- ✦ Rhythmicity: What is the degree to which our eating, sleeping, and other daily habits occur at the same time, last for the same duration, or are of the same amount on most days?
- ✦ Approach/withdrawal: Given a new situation (that is safe), what is the likelihood that we will get involved or withdraw?
- ✦ Adaptability: How quickly can we adapt and become comfortable with new situations when change occurs?
- ✦ Threshold responsiveness: How much stimulation is needed and how intense must it be for us to respond?
- ✦ Attention span/persistence: Once we begin a task, how long does our usual attention span last? How easily are we distracted?
- ✦ Intensity of reaction: When we respond, how much energy and intensity is in our typical reaction?
- ✦ Quality of mood: What is our typical mood? Is it happy, friendly, and pleasant or sad, unfriendly, or "grumpy"?

These behavior styles are readily apparent from birth and persist consistently over the course of an individual's lifetime (Thomas, Chess, & Birch, 1970b).

As Thomas and Chess continued their study (Thomas & Chess, 1977; Chess & Thomas, 1984), they found that constitutional differences in behavior styles or temperament are vulnerable to temporary as well as long-term environmental influences. Goleman agrees (1995). From his chapter aptly given the title "Temperament is Not Destiny," he writes:

> The emotional lessons of childhood have a profound impact on temperament, either amplifying or muting an innate predisposition. The great plasticity of the brain in childhood means that experience during those years can have a lasting impact on the sculpting of neural pathways for the rest of the life. (p. 221).

Perhaps we could best summarize the role of temperament by saying temperament is tendency, not totality.

From the nine categories, the researchers delineated three major temperament styles, each with its own characteristic approach to situations. Keep in mind there is no right or wrong temperament style; rather, the degree to which a style matches those of the key people around the individual is the critical issue. We will discuss the implications of that in a moment. The three major styles as *labeled by the researchers* are listed below.

The difficult child temperament: Of the nine categories, the characteristics that fit into this style include irregular biological rhythms, difficulty in adapting to change, withdrawal rather than approaching new experiences, moodiness, or typically unhappy mood state.

The slow-to-warm-up temperament: Characterized by some irregular biological rhythms, some adaptability to change, initial negative responses to new situations; however, given time and support, will shift to positive responses.

The easy child temperament: Characteristics include regular biological functions, positive response to new situations and people, readily adaptable, moderate to positive moods.

· ·

REFLECTION OPPORTUNITY

For each part of the reflection write your responses in the space provided or on a separate piece of paper.

What is your reaction to the particular words researchers gave the temperament styles? From whose perspective do the titles describe the child's temperament—the adult's or the child's?

_____

_____

_____

_____

_____

_____

I find it interesting that the words chosen to name the styles use terms that describe how the child affects others. I find these labels laden with judgments. Two even seem to carry an implicit warning: "This is going to be a child who is hard to teach!" I would ask: Is it not more useful to label the behavior styles *functionally*? For example:

The child who needs significant time and support to adapt to change

The child who needs some time and support to adapt to change

The child who finds change easy and adapts readily

If we used these revised labels, we would know what the world is like from the *student's* perspective and what we need to do to meet that individual's needs. Typically, I do not like labels, but if they are to be used, I would prefer ones that give me insight about the student rather than foreshadow difficulty. From our ecological perspective, the important questions are: How does this student's temperament affect the rest of the variables in her ecosystem? How is the student's temperament affected by the variables in the rest of her ecosystem? Consider the following scenarios and then write your responses to the questions for each in the space provided or on a separate piece of paper:

Scenario #1: You are a student who warms up and adapts slowly. Change is not easy for you. What do you think it would be like to be in a class in which the teacher frequently uses new strategies and alters activities?

_____

_____

_____

_____

While those around you are switching activities readily, you would need to know what is coming next and require some support for the change, such as warnings about upcoming transitions.

Scenario #2: You are a student who is shy and who does not find being friendly easy. What would it be like for you to be placed in a situation where you were designated the leader of a group? How would you feel about having group members have to count on your ability to lead a team, when for you such work is difficult?

_____

_____

_____

_____

What might a teacher do to help you adjust to such a situation?

_____

_____

_____

A significant discrepancy between a student's temperament and the learning environment is likely to create stress for the teacher and the student. The teacher might lack the knowledge about styles to address the situation objectively. He could think the student is *being* difficult rather than *having* difficulty because of the student's natural temperament style. As a result, the teacher might respond defensively rather than intervening effectively to ameliorate the situation. A second possible reason for the strain is that the child's emotional needs are not being met. If so, the student may resist what is occurring because she feels uncomfortable or unsafe or doesn't know what to do to approach the situation successfully.

Teacher temperament as a variable may also play a role in the interactions between a student's temperament and the variables in her three environments. For example, a positive effect would occur if a teacher has difficulty adapting to change. She might have developed strategies to help *herself* cope, and she also applies these to support students. Her empathy, which comes from knowing that adapting is not second nature for some people, might make her more likely to help students who need similar support. In a different example, a difficult effect could arise if a teacher readily adapts to change *but* does *not* realize that adaptation is not as easy for others. Then, the student might be left to struggle with transitions and other changes in routine, activities, subjects, classes, and teachers.

IMPORTANT POINTS ABOUT TEMPERAMENT

✦ Temperament is a student's *behavioral* style.

✦ While Temperament is a variable in the physiological environment that affects student learning and behavior, temperament is tendency, but not totality, nor is it destiny.

Intelligences

More than 20 years ago, Howard Gardner (1983) became a champion of the idea that intelligence is multifaceted and includes many more capacities than have been traditionally evaluated on intelligence tests. The categories Gardner has delineated thus far are described below (Armstrong, 2009). Note that there are many ways to be intelligent in each category. As you read the descriptions, do not be misled by the fact that each intelligence has been described separately. Intelligences do not work in isolation. They are described that way solely to help you to understand the unique features of each.

✦ Verbal/linguistic intelligence: People who have this intelligence are facile, comfortable, and adept with language in at least one of its many forms (humor, poetry, storytelling, writing, abstract reasoning, symbolic thinking, similes, metaphors, public speaking, explaining, teaching, and persuading). People who have developed this intelligence may be fluent in more than one language. Their memory and recall are excellent.

✦ Logical/mathematical intelligence: People with this intelligence are skilled at reasoning, both inductively and deductively. They have developed the capacity to work with abstract symbols, see relationships between parts of something including bits of information, recognize patterns, and perform complex calculations.

✦ Visual/spatial intelligence: People with these skills are particularly effective in forming mental pictures. They can visualize objects and the space around them from different perspectives. They have active imaginations. They are the artists, architects, mapmakers and navigators, chess players, and industrial designers in our world.

✦ Bodily/kinesthetic intelligence: People who have developed this among their intelligences are good at using their bodies to communicate, to express emotion, to create or invent something, to build something, to handle objects skillfully, to play a sport, or to participate in a field that relies on the body such as dance or mime.

- ✦ **Musical, rhythmic intelligence:** People who have developed this intelligence are sensitive to sounds. They recognize and use patterns of rhythm and tone. They can use music to communicate ideas and feelings.
- ✦ **Interpersonal intelligence:** People with this intelligence work well with others. They are good at picking up subtle cues from people, empathic about people's feelings, and effective at communicating verbally and nonverbally.
- ✦ **Intrapersonal intelligence:** People with this intelligence are able to step back and think about themselves. They are skilled in matters that are within people: intuition and self-reflection. They think about and try to understand thinking and feeling and have a range of emotional responses available. They know their strengths and weaknesses.
- ✦ **Naturalist intelligence:** People with skills in this arena feel particularly happy when they are in the midst of nature. They often enjoy collecting natural objects: rocks, seashells, or flowers to press. They are good at identifying, distinguishing among (and thereby categorizing), and using features of the natural world. They try to understand the connections between groups of natural things, both those that once lived and those alive today.

REFLECTION OPPORTUNITY

Write your responses in the space provided or on a separate piece of paper.

Which intelligences would seem to be your current strengths? _____

_____

Are there times you can recall when you were taught in ways that matched any of your intelligences? Were there times when you were not? _____

_____

When you compare the two experiences, what effect do you believe addressing a student's intelligences might have on student's sense of efficacy? On a feeling of ease and well-being while learning? _____

_____

_____

We know that skills are the tools with which students come to know the world. When teachers provide lessons that invite students to use intelligences in which they are strong, their understanding of the "what," the "how," the "why," the "what if," and the chance for a connected emotion—and, therefore, the memory of what was learned—would more likely be there.

IMPORTANT POINTS ABOUT INTELLIGENCES

✦ Each of us has *multiple* intelligences. Some of us are strong in some; others are strong in different ones. Although most people have developed only a few, Gardner (1983) believes each of us can develop all intelligences to an adequate level—given opportunities to learn.

✦ There are many skills within an intelligence. Having strength in one intelligence does not mean that we excel in all skills within that intelligence.

✦ Not being strong in the intelligence most commonly tapped in school—linguistic intelligence—does not mean that an individual is not intelligent.

✦ Given appropriate learning experiences, nearly all of us can develop an intelligence to an adequate level.

Learning Styles

For more than 30 years, many people have investigated personal styles in learning, thinking, and reading. David Kolb was one of the earlier researchers (Boyatzis & Kolb, 1991; Kolb, Boyatzis, & Mainemelis, 2001; Kolb & Kolb, 2005). He differentiated four predominant styles of learning. Anthony Gregorc found four clusters of characteristics that he calls minds styles. He named them according to the dominant "transaction abilities" (concrete or abstract) and the manner of reasoning (sequential or random) (Gregorc, 1982, 1985a, 1985b; Gregorc Asssociates, Inc., 2015). If we synthesize the work of these two investigators, the following four groupings of learner styles emerge.

✦ Analytic learners: those whom Kolb characterizes as excelling in watching and thinking. Gregorc describes these people as abstract sequential thinkers who reason in a linear fashion. These are the conceptual thinkers who would rather deal with theories and ideas in the abstract than the concrete world. They perceive the world through ideas and do so reflectively. These are the so-called "thinkers." The art historian or English professor might be characteristic of this style.

✦ Common sense learners: those whom Kolb characterizes as excelling in thinking and doing. Gregorc describes these people as concrete sequential thinkers who are structured, practical, thorough, and predictable. They perceive the world through ideas and do so actively—the kind of thinking that pilots, engineers, and applied scientists do well.

✦ Dynamic learners: those whom Kolb characterizes as excelling at doing, sensing, and feeling. They learn by experience, through social interaction. Gregorc describes these people as abstract random thinkers who work most comfortably with ideas but are divergent thinkers. Their ideas go in all directions. They are the "dreamers." They process reflectively and seek personal meaning in what they do. They tend to be expressive, sensitive, sociable people who love sharing whatever they enjoy. They often excel in creative endeavors as artists, actors, and writers.

✦ Imaginative learners: those whom Kolb characterizes as excelling in watching, feeling, and sensing. Gregorc describes these people as concrete random thinkers who deal readily with the here and now but do so in a creative fashion. They seek hidden possibilities. They learn through experience and do so by processing actively (rather than reflectively). They are comfortable exploring relationships, people, ideas, places, and things. These people are experimenters and problem solvers because they readily see many possibilities for solutions. They are original, intuitive, and investigative in their thinking. These folks are dreamers, inventors, agents of change, and sometimes revolutionaries.

McCarthy (2000a; McCarthy 2000b; McCarthy 2000c; McCarthy & McCarthy, 2006), one of the foremost investigators in learning preferences, suggests that an effective way to conceptualize the needs of these four groups of learners is to think of each as having a favorite question:

- **Analytic learners** need to know <u>what</u>. "What is it?" "What are the facts?" "What is the concept?" "What is the theory?" "How does this fit into what I already know?" "What do the experts think about this?" Analytic learners need details to analyze and critique in order to form concepts.
- **Common sense learners** want to know <u>how</u>. **"**How does this work?" "How do I do this?" "How can I use this?" They need clear, concrete, linear, step-by-step, hands-on learning experiences. They want to know the practical application of what they are learning. They need a chance to apply the concept or skill.
- **Dynamic learners** want to know <u>why</u>. "Why are we learning this?" "What difference will this make to my life if I learn this?" They want to know the personal meaning of what they are learning. They need to examine and connect with what they are learning.
- **Imaginative learners** want to know <u>if</u>. "What if I did it this way instead—would it still work?" "What can it become?" "What can I make of this?" They are "big picture." holistic learners who bring action to their learning. They see things in many different ways and are interested in the creative application of what they are learning. They want to refine, share, and celebrate their learning.

Whether you favor Kolb's, Gregorc's, or McCarthy's taxonomy of styles, there is evidence to conclude that while nearly all of us can learn particular content or skills, *how* we come to master the material is affected by our style. In many classes, the focus is on concepts and skills without regard to the other questions: why ("Why is this important for me to learn?); how ("How will I use this in my life?"); and what if ("What are the creative possibilities for what I have just learned?"). How might the narrower focus on "what?" affect the learning of those who best grasp what is being taught when they are able to understand the other three questions?

Lately, some theorists, including Butler (2014), encourage educators *not* to label someone this or that kind of learner. Instead, they encourage us to see that a student might favor one approach to learning in one context. In another, that same student might use a different approach to learning. Given what I believe about the interaction of variables in the student's environments and the effects on a student's learning and behavior, it does not surprise me to hear this shift away from boxing a student into one style. In other words, if one or more variables were to change in the physical environment (for example, the setting or learning agenda) or in the psychosocial environment (say, the grouping of students for a particular task), then the learning style variables in the student's physiological environment might be affected to such a degree that the student's approach to learning would change in response.

REFLECTION OPPORTUNITY

Many people have ideas about the conditions under which students learn best. What have you read or heard people say? Put a check next to each or create a list on a separate piece of paper.

Students learn best:

  + early in the morning;
  + in brightly lit rooms;
  + in rooms in which the temperature falls in a range between 68-70 degrees;
  + when seated in chairs that are "formal" in nature; and
  + in a quiet environment.

All these ideas were long held by many (and still are by some today). However, towards the end of the last century, researchers began to dispel these "notions" (Dunn, Griggs, Olson, Gorman, & Beasley, 1995). As a result, we now know that physiological variables that affect individual learning style and preferences go beyond temperament and how a student thinks. Other characteristics appear to be preferences in any of the three environments. These learning styles or preferences might include the nature of variables:

In the physiological environment:

  + time of day best for learning;
  + visual, auditory, or hands-on kinesthetic learning;
  + frequency with which there are opportunities to take breaks, to move around;

In the physical environment:

  + light (soft, dim to bright, incandescent, fluorescent, natural);
  + temperature of the room (cool to warm);
  + noise level (silence or background noise or music);
  + degree of formality in seating; and

In the psychosocial environment:

  + social arrangements (working on a learning task independently, with a partner, or in a team); and
  + interaction with an adult (degree of availability of teacher/coach during a task)

Perhaps the best way to summarize the findings (Barrett, Zhang, Moffat, & Kobbacy, 2012; Dunn, Thies, & Honigsfeld, 2001; Dunn & Griggs, 2003; Dunn, Honigsfeld, Doolan, Bostrom, Russo, Schiering, Suh, & Tenedero, 2009; Sousa & Tomlinson, 2011) is to say that we cannot make any generalizations about the physical environment variables in the design, contents, and ambience of a room that support all students' learning. The research shows that different students have different needs. These preferences—for example, the time of day when they learn best—may change over time as their bodies grow and their sleep and wakefulness cycles change.

IMPORTANT POINTS ABOUT LEARNING STYLES

✦ Most students *can* learn the same skill or concept, but *how* students best learn varies from individual to individual, depending on the learning style/needs of the student and the nature of the material to be mastered.

✦ In some situations, a mismatch between what the student is asked to do and what the student is able to do does not derive from how the student learns but how the curriculum is presented.

Disabilities

Some aspects of a student's physiological environment *can* interfere with learning and behavior. I have carefully chosen the word "can" because far too many people in our culture assume that "disability" is synonymous with "inability." Certainly, there are some conditions in the body that—without correction, adjustment, or modification—can profoundly affect growth and development. Legal blindness that cannot be corrected *could* affect whether or not that student is able to take in information *if* learning experiences that utilize other sensory channels are not provided. A student with minimal hearing who counts on concrete references to comprehend language could have difficulty with language that is full of idiomatic expressions, plays on words, and similes. Cognitive disabilities, learning disabilities, and certain kinds of brain damage certainly affect learning. In all instances, the important question to ask is: Does this physiological variable affect functioning? If so, how? What Universal Design for Learning elements would help (e.g., multiple means of representation, engagement, action and expression)? What other adaptations and accommodations would facilitate learning and social interaction?

Competent people have disabilities, and people with disabilities are competent. Edison had a profound learning disability that affected his ability to read, yet his persistence in trying sources for filaments made the light bulb possible. Einstein had a disability too, yet think of the contribution he made to our understanding of how the universe functions. Therefore, while disability needs to be included in a discussion of conditions in the physiological environment that *can* affect learning, the point must be emphasized that disability in and of itself is not synonymous with inability.

Sometimes the so-called disability does not exist within the child, although people describe the situation as if it did. Educators will say that a student has a learning disability when sometimes the condition is a mismatch between the learning style of the student and the teaching strategies being employed: if other strategies were utilized, the "disability" would vanish. Sometimes it is not the physiological condition that is the disability but rather the attitudes of other people. Instead of looking at what the student can do, some people only see what the student can*not* do. They see problems, not strengths—they assume that if a typical avenue to learning is closed, then all avenues must be closed. They see locked doors rather than invitations to be creative in their approaches.

Cognitive-Social Disabilities

Autism spectrum disorder (ASD) is the name for a group of disabilities that includes a wide range (thus the term "spectrum") of skills and levels of functioning. Included in this category is Asperger syndrome. Students on the spectrum may have any of the following *to varying degrees*:

- difficulty communicating across a variety of contexts and relationships;
- difficulty interacting with others socially;
- repetitive behaviors;
- limited interests or activities; and/or
- the need to have the same schedule and the same routines within that schedule day after day.

On the other hand, students on the autism spectrum can have the following strengths and abilities:

- above-average intelligence (the Centers for Disease Control reports that 46% of ASD children have above-average intelligence);
- being able to learn things in detail and remember information for long periods of time;
- being strong visual and auditory learners; and
- excelling in math, science, music, or art.

Note: Some students are mildly impacted, while others have severe difficulties as a result of autism spectrum disorder (Autism Speaks. Retrieved 2017 from https://www.autismspeaks.org/; National Institute of Mental Health. Retrieved 2017 from https://www.nimh.nih.gov/health/topics/AutismSpectrumDisorders).

Attention Deficit Disorders

ADHD includes developmentally inappropriate or underdeveloped attention skills that can play out in hyperactivity or inattentiveness and/or internal preoccupation or impulsivity (Hopkins Medicine, 2017). Some students have attentional problems and/or impulsivity but not learning difficulties, while others have both. Still others may also have emotional or behavioral difficulties with their disorder (CHADD, 2016). Evidence to date suggests that there is a genetic predisposition to ADHD disorders.

Psychostimulant medications can help because they balance the chemicals in the brain that prevent the student from controlling impulses and maintaining attention. These medicines, however, can have side effects, including insomnia, decreased appetite, headaches, and jitteriness. Also, some children and young adults can have a rebound effect; when the medication wears off, there may be an increase in hyperactivity or impulsiveness for a period of time (Hopkins Medicine, 2017). Antidepressants and anti-anxiety medications to decrease either the symptoms of ADHD or concurrent difficulties may also be helpful.

IMPORTANT POINTS ABOUT DISABILITIES

✦ Disability does not have to be synonymous with inability.

✦ Sometimes it is the attitude of other people that creates the disability.

✦ Given creative teaching, many "disabilities" have diminished impact to some degree, if not entirely.

Health Factors

There are a number of health factors that can affect a student's functioning. Among these are nutrition, rest, stamina, allergies, temporary illnesses, chronic health conditions, mood disorders, neurobiological conditions, toxic substances, prescription and over the counter medications, and emotions.

ACCESSING PRIOR KNOWLEDGE AND EXPERIENCE

When you have not had much sleep, how does this affect your focus, tolerance for frustration, stamina, and ability to learn? In the space provided or elsewhere describe how lack of sleep affects you. _____

_____

_____

_____

_____

Nutrition, Rest, and Stamina

All the energy for thinking and behavior is fueled by food and replenished by rest. Lack of essential elements in our diet can also affect our ability to participate fully in the learning experience. For example, lack of carbohydrates and protein affects our muscles, stamina, thinking, and memory. The lack of sufficient rest can both subtly and profoundly affect the ability to learn, and interact with peers. Carbohydrates are fuel for action and brain metabolism. Proteins keep tissues, hormones, enzymes, and antibodies working as they should. An inappropriate diet may have more than just a temporary effect: if key substances are not available during critical periods in a child's development—either before or after birth—the actual structure of the brain, not to mention how it functions, can be seriously impaired. In the extreme, if vitamins such as B6 are consistently missing, seizures that damage brain cells may result (Batshaw, Roizen, & Lotrecchiano, 2013).

Allergies

Not only might a student with allergies have difficulty breathing adequately, but medications to help with the primary effects of allergies may also make a student sluggish, sleepy, or irritable. Some allergies create skin reactions such as hives that can distract from the learning at hand. Other allergies cause stomach and intestinal pain.

Chronic Conditions

Asthma is an example of a health issue that can affect functioning in a classroom—from a mild to an extreme degree (Taras & Potts-Datema, 2005; Heller, Alberto, Best, & Schwartzman, 2009). When airway linings are swollen and become narrowed, breathing is difficult. The airways in a person with asthma are also much more sensitive than most people's and react to "triggers" in the environment such as changes in temperature, pollen or dust mites, strenuous exercise, extreme emotions, infections such as colds and sore throats, paint, perfume, cleaning products, and other vapors. Wheezing, coughing, and/or serious difficulty breathing—in other words, an asthma attack—can occur. Symptoms and severity vary widely from student to student. Stamina, not to mention the ability to move even short distances, may be compromised. Playing a musical instrument or full participation in informal or organized sports—two important group experiences for children and young adults—can be limited by the effect that chronic conditions like asthma have on stamina. A student with severe reactions may miss school and lose out not only on learning experiences but also on opportunities to develop and sustain friendships.

Temporary Illness

Although an illness may be temporary, it can affect students of any age in the classroom. You probably know from your own experience the last time you went to class with a bad cold that your ability to be a part of whatever is going on, and to feel that you are competent, are compromised by your illness.

Mood Disorders

A mood disorder being diagnosed more frequently in younger children is depression (Rudolph & Lambert, 2007). This is not the temporary sadness or sense of discouragement anyone can feel from day to day (or even weeks and months) if we experience a significant loss such as moving away from a familiar community or losing someone we love. Chronic depression exists in a student when her feelings of sadness, despair, and passivity; her loss of appetite, stamina, and sleep; and her feelings of personal worthlessness—even if they are tied to a specific event—are extreme, last for a year or more, and disable her from functioning. If you have ever been sad, discouraged, or even temporarily depressed, then you know how this could affect a student. For those suffering from serious depression, even getting out of bed in the morning to go to school may be an insurmountable task.

Other students (usually those who are older) suffer from extreme deviations in mood in both directions—a bipolar depressive disorder (Youngstrom, 2007). For a while, they may be depressed. Then they may become full of energy, sometimes to the degree that they have difficulty sleeping. In this manic phase, they may make rash decisions that they do not remember once they swing back away from the mania.

For many children, medication can help, but it may take several trials of different kinds of medication until the right match is made. Antidepressant medications can help but can also have side effects, including *increased* depression. Students taking a medication need to be alert to these symptoms, as do the adults who are around them.

Neurobiological Conditions: Obsessive-Compulsive Disorder

Obsessive-compulsive disorder, commonly called OCD, appears in different ways in different people, which means not every student has the same symptoms. Many have combinations of symptoms. In general, those who have OCD suffer from unwanted, intrusive thoughts that they cannot seem to get rid of (obsessions), which often compel them to repeatedly perform ritualistic behaviors and routines (compulsions) to try and ease their anxiety (Mayo Clinic, 2016). It's not uncommon that OCD symptoms may accompany depressed mood, elevated mood, or both.

Those who have OCD, particularly the older they are, may be aware that their thoughts and actions are irrational, but they are not able to stop them. Moreover, they may spend several hours every day focusing on these thoughts and performing rituals involving hand-washing, counting, or checking to try to ward off persistent, unwelcome thoughts, feelings, or images. These rituals can interfere with a student's normal routine, schoolwork, and social activities. Trying to concentrate on schoolwork may be difficult when obsessive thoughts intrude. If OCD symptoms are already present, stress can worsen them. Anxiety, fatigue and illness—even the stress associated with holidays, vacations, and other positive events—can affect OCD.

There is evidence that hereditary factors may contribute to a predisposition to having OCD. Stress doesn't *cause* OCD. However, stress or trauma can trigger symptoms. Childhood illnesses do not cause OCD, "although there is growing evidence that strep throat, the flu, or other severe bacterial or viral infections may trigger the sudden onset of symptoms in children who are genetically predisposed to OCD" (Anxiety and Depression Association of America, 2017).

As with bipolar depressive disorder, relief from obsessive and compulsive thoughts and rituals can occur with the proper medication.

Note: While some children do seem to have a series of related "symptoms" that legitimately appear to be ADHD, many behaviors associated with attention deficit disorders are also associated with bright, energetic students who do not fit the demands of the particular teacher or of certain environments. Many factors could lead a student to behave as if she had ADHD, including a creative nature that has difficulty fitting into conforming requirements, lack of consistent love and care, a mismatch between teacher strategy and individual student's needs, student anxiety due to abuse or neglect, and inappropriate educational and behavioral expectations.

Ingested Toxic Substances

Many toxic substances can have a transitory or even a profound effect on a student. Lead is one. It can be ingested in many ways. We can breathe it in from polluted air or tiny leaded paint chips from renovated homes or drink it in water that has sat in leaded pipes. Lead in the bloodstream blocks the ability of the blood to carry oxygen. Nausea, dizziness, and headaches can result in the short term. If a child ingests lead—particularly while the brain is going through rapid growth in the first six years—damage to the brain cells can result. Learning issues and irritability in behavior are two of the possible results.

Ingested Medications, Recreational Drugs, and Related Substances

Recreational Drugs and Related Substances Can Have a Toxic Effect

These variables can have a deleterious effect on a child long before he begins school. There is some evidence that hallucinogens consumed by the parents prior to pregnancy may alter genetic material. Alcohol consumed during pregnancy can have an effect so profound that there is a specific condition named for it—Fetal Alcohol Syndrome (FAS). Children born to mothers who consumed alcohol in excess may be highly irritable and may have mild to significant learning, health, and behavioral difficulties and an attention deficit disorder with hyperactivity. They are more likely to have congenital heart defects, developmental delays—particularly in the area of language—and may, on the extreme end, be profoundly brain damaged. After birth, there is a possible second layer of damage to the child. Many children with FAS may need to be removed from their homes because of abuse or neglect by the alcoholic parent. Abuse, neglect, and removal from one's family—a secondary issue that may result from alcohol addiction—can also profoundly affect the physiological environment of children (Batshaw, Roizen, & Lotrecchiano, 2013).

The overuse or careless use of addictive substances from nicotine and caffeine to narcotics falls under the category of toxic variables in the physiological environment. The disruption of sleep and/or irritability that results from levels of caffeine that are too high for any student may have subtle effects on learning and interaction with others. Arriving at a class under the influence of stimulants such as cocaine, depressants such as alcohol, or hallucinogenic drugs such as marijuana or mescaline will clearly have an effect. Table 2-1 presents the effects of some drugs.

Table 2-1. **The Effects of Some Drugs**		
Type of Drug	**Drug**	**Observable Effects**
Stimulant	• amphetamine • cocaine	Increased level of activity, hallucinations, dilated pupils, appetite loss
Depressant	• alcohol • heroin • Quaalude	Decreased level of activity, slowing of reaction time, drowsiness, loss of coordination, irritability
Hallucinogen	• marijuana • mescaline	Hallucinations, inability to concentrate, mood swings, dilated pupils

Note: What may be overlooked—but is nonetheless an important variable in the physiological environment—is student use of drugs and related substances for the purposes of self-medication. Whether knowingly or not, many young adults use drugs such as alcohol under the guise of making themselves "more sociable" when what they are actually trying to do is counteract or address personal problems. What people often do not understand is that this use of drugs can mask serious problems such as depression. (Alcohol is itself a depressant, so its use to cope with depression—or any problem, for that matter—is particularly counterproductive.) Diagnosis of the situation may focus solely on the symptom (i.e., excessive drinking) as a factor to address but miss the underlying problem that also needs thoughtful intervention.

Medications Can Have a Positive Effect

As we have stated, mood disorders may be eased by drug therapy. Medication(s) can address neurobiological conditions such as attention deficit disorders. One 10-year-old student I worked with described the change when he was on one such drug by saying, "I can finally think. My brain is no longer just black." Easing some of the effects of health conditions such as the breathing difficulties associated with asthma or the pain and inflammation from juvenile arthritis is another positive effect of prescription drugs. Therefore, when we think about the effects of the variable of drugs/medications in a student's physiological environment (and, as a result, the effect of this variable on the student's behavior), we need to consider both positive and negative effects. At times, we need to consider both simultaneously because each effect will, in turn, affect the student's needs and behavior.

Medications Can Be Toxic Substances

Even when thoughtfully monitored by a physician or psychiatrist, the effect of any medicine is potentially damaging for a child. We could have included them in the toxic substances analysis above, but since these drugs also have the potential to be helpful, we will analyze them under this category. The potential negative effects of prescription drugs have to be weighed against the positive results. For example, medications may stop seizures (an obvious positive result), but their toxicity to the liver or other organs is a risk over time (a potential negative—even a life-threatening—result).

IMPORTANT POINT ABOUT HEALTH FACTORS

In addition to the effects of the health issue/disorder on learning and social interaction, there are other variables to consider. Key would be the effects of medication being used to treat the condition as well as absences from school and the resulting loss of learning and social experiences.

Application Activity: Shaping Up a Summary of Variables in the Physiological Environment

Complete each sentence stem from what you have read about variables in the physiological environment and their possible effects on students:

 Something that SQUARES with my beliefs is:

 A question going AROUND in my mind is:

 Three POINTS I want to remember are:

1.

2.

3.

Final Thoughts

Some of the variables in the physiological environment are those with which the student is born, although these may not express themselves until later in the student's development. On the other hand, a variable such as mindset is not something with which a student is born but rather a learned habit of mind, a way of approaching learning, social experiences, and indeed life. While not genetic, mindsets can be engrained enough that they might appear to be a part of a student's makeup, along with green eyes and curly brown hair. Though internal, mindset, like behavior, is learned, and a new mindset can be developed.

Most physiological variables are not destiny. They are only tendencies. Examples: Students can develop more depth in an intelligence, or more intelligences, if given the opportunity to learn how. Mindset can be changed. Yet any of the physiological environment variables we have discussed can influence behavior.

We cannot say for sure in advance in what ways a variable will impact a particular student and how that student will respond. This will depend on the nature of the variable and its pervasiveness within the individual. Yet even nature and pervasiveness will be realized differently in each individual. Various therapies, including medications, can certainly help to ameliorate negative effects of some physiological variables. The strategies we as teachers use in our learning communities can have a profound effect, too. The question remains: What effect will our teaching have? We will address this question in later chapters.

Looking Forward

Now that we have had an opportunity to consider variables in the internal physiological environment and their possible effects on students, we are ready to address variables in the second of the three environments in the ecological approach. In Chapter 3, we will look at variables in the physical environment. We will discuss how the arrangement and contents of a classroom, as well as the instructional strategies employed by the teacher, have an effect on behavior.

References

Anxiety and Depression Association of America. (2017). Obsessive/compulsive disorder. Retrieved from https://www.adaa.org/understanding-anxiety/obsessive-compulsive-disorder-ocd

Appleton, P. (2008). *Children's anxiety: A contextual approach*. New York: Routledge.

Armstrong, T. (2009). *Multiple intelligences in the classroom* (3rd ed.). Alexandria, VA: Association for Supervision and Curriculum Development.

Autism Speaks. (2017). Retrieved from https://www.autismspeaks.org/.

Barrett, P., Zhang, Y., Moffat, J., & Kobbacy, K. (2012). A holistic, multilevel analysis identifying the impact of class design on pupils' learning. *Building and Environment, 59*, 678–679.

Batshaw, M., Roizen, N., & Lotrecchiano, G. (Eds.). (2013). *Children with disabilities.* (7th ed.). Baltimore, MD: Brookes.

Boyatzis, R. & Kolb, D. (1991). Assessing individuality in learning: The learning skills profile. *Educational Psychology: An International Journal of Experimental Educational Psychology, 11*(34), 279–295.

Brock, S., Jimerson, S., & Hansen, R. (2009). *Developmental psychopathology at school: Identifying, assessing and treating ADHD at school.* New York, NY: Springer.

Butler, K. (1988). *It's all in your mind.* Columbia, Ct: Learner's Dimension.

Butler, K. (1987). *Learning and teaching style: In theory and practice.* Columbia, Ct: Learner's Dimension.

Caine, R., & Caine, G. (1994). *Making connections: Teaching and the human brain.* Reading, MA: Addison Wesley.

Caine, R., Caine, G., McClintick, C., & Klimack, K. (2005). *12 brain/mind learning principles in action.* Thousand Oaks, CA: Corwin Press.

CHADD.org. *Children and Adolescents with ADD.* Retrieved 2016 from http://.www.CHADD.org

Chess, S., & Thomas, A. (1984). *Origins and evolution of behavior disorders in children: From infancy to early adult life.* New York, NY: Brunner/Mazel.

Davis-Berman, J. & Pestello, F. (2010). Medicating for ADD/ADHD. *International Journal of Mental Health and Addiction, 8*(3), 482–492.

Dean, C., Hubbell, E., Pitler, H., & Stone, Bj. (2012). *Classroom instruction that works: Research-based strategies for increasing student achievement* (2nd ed.). Alexandria, VA: Association for Supervision and Curriculum Development.

Dopheide, J. & Pliszka, S. (2009). Attention-deficit/hyperactivity disorder: An update. *Pharmacotherapy, 29*(6), 656–679.

Duckworth, A. (2016). *Grit: The power of passion and perseverance.* New York, NY: Scribner.

Dunn, R., & Griggs, S. (Eds.). (2003). *Synthesis of the Dunn and Dunn Learning-Style Model Research: Who, What, When, Where, and So What?* New York, NY: St. John's University.

Dunn, R., Honigsfeld, A., Doolan, L., Bostrom, L., Russo, K., Schiering, M., Suh, B., & Tenedero, H. (2009). Impact of learning-style instructional strategies on students' achievement and attitudes: Perceptions of educators in diverse institutions. *The Clearing House: A Journal of Educational Strategies, Issues and Ideas, 82*(3), 135–140.

Dunn, R., Thies, A., & Honigsfeld, A. (2001). *Synthesis of the Dunn and Dunn learning-style model research: Analysis from a neuropsychological perspective.* Jamaica, NY: St John's University School of Education and Human Services.

Dweck, C. (2006). *Mindset: The new psychology of success.* New York, NY: Ballantine Books.

Evans, W., Evans, S., & Schmid, R. (1989). *Behavior and Instructional management: An ecological approach.* Boston, MA: Allyn and Bacon.

Gardner, H. (1983). *Frames of mind: The theory of multiple intelligences.* New York, NY: Basic Books.

Glanzman, M., & Blum, N. (2013). Attention deficit and hyperactivity. In Batshaw, M. (Ed.), *Children with disabilities* (7th ed., pp. 345–365). Baltimore, MD: Brookes.

Goleman, D. (1995). *Emotional intelligence.* New York, NY: Bantam.

Goleman, D. (1996). On emotional intelligence: A conversation with Daniel Goleman. *Education Leadership,* *53*(1), 6–11.

Goleman, D. (2006). *Social intelligence: The new science of human relationships.* New York, NY: Random House.

Goleman, D. (2017). The most fundamental discovery of this new science: We are wired to connect. Retrieved from http:\\www.danielgoleman.info/topics/social-intelligence/Gregorc Associates, Inc. (2015). Retrieved from http:\\www.gregorc.com

Gregorc, A. (1982). *An adult's guide to style.* Columbia, CT: Gregorc Assoc., Inc.

Gregorc, A. (1985a). *Inside styles: Beyond the basics.* Maynard, MA: Gabriel Systems, Inc.

Gregorc, A. (1985b). *Gregorc style delineator.* Columbia, CT: Gregorc Assoc., Inc.

Heller, K., Alberto, P., Best, S., & Schwartzman, M. (2009). *Understanding physical, health and multiple disabilities.* Upper Saddle River, NJ: Pearson.

Hopkins Medicine. (2017). Attention-Deficit/Hyperactivity Disorder (ADHD) in children. Retrieved from http://www.hopkinsmedicine.org/healthlibrary/conditions/mental_health_disorders/attention-deficit_hyperactivity_disorder_adhd_in_children_90,P02552/

Kline, L. (2008). A baker's dozen: Effective instructional strategies. In Cole, R. (Ed.), *Educating everybody's children: Diverse teaching strategies for diverse learners* (2nd ed., pp. 21–45). Alexandria, VA: Association for Supervision and Curriculum Development.

Kolb, A., & Kolb, D. (2005). *The Kolb learning style inventory—version 3.1: Technical specifications.* Boston, MA: Hay Resources Direct.

Kolb, D., Boyatzis, R., & Mainemelis, C. (2001). Experiential learning theory: Previous research and new directions. In R. Sternberg and L. Zhang (Eds.), *Perspectives on thinking, learning, and cognitive styles,* 228–247. Mahwah, NJ: Lawrence Erlbaum Associates.

Lazear, D. (1999). *Eight ways of knowing: Teaching for Multiple Intelligences.* Arlington Heights, IL: Skylight.

Lazear, D. (2004). *Higher order thinking the multiple intelligences way.* Chicago: Zephyr Press.

MacLean, P. (1978). A mind of three brains: Educating the triune brain. In J. Chall & A. Mirsky (Eds.), *Education and the brain* (pp. 308–342). Chicago, IL: University of Chicago Press.

Maslow, A. (1954). *Motivation and personality*. New York, NY: Harper and Bros.

Maslow, A. (1962). *Toward a psychology of being*. New York, NY: Van Nostrand.

Maslow, A. (1972). *The farther reaches of human nature*. New York, NY: Viking Press.

Mayo Clinic. (2016). Obsessive compulsive disorder. Retrieved from http://www.mayoclinic.org/diseases-conditions/ocd/basics/symptoms/con-20027827

McCarthy, B. (1981). *4MAT System: Teaching to learning styles with right-left mode techniques*. Barrington, IL: Excel.

McCarthy, B. (2000a). *About learning* (2nd ed.). Wauconda, IL: About Learning, Inc.

McCarthy, B. (2000b). *About teaching: 4MAT in the classroom*. Wauconda, IL: About Learning, Inc.

McCarthy, B. (2000c). *4MAT in the classroom*. Wauconda, IL: About Learning, Inc.

McCarthy, B., & McCarthy, D. (2006). *Teaching around the 4MAT cycle*. Thousand Oaks, CA: Corwin Press.

National Institute of Mental Health (2017). Autism spectrum disorder. Retrieved from https://www.nimh.nih.gov/health/topics/autism-spectrum-disorders-asd/index.shtml

Rogers, C. (1961). *On becoming a person*. Boston: Houghton Mifflin.

Rudolph, K., and Lambert, S. (2007). Child and adolescent depression. In E. Mash & R. Barkley (Eds.), *Assessment of childhood disorders* (4th ed., pp. 213–252). New York, NY: Guilford.

Saphier J., Haley-Spec, M., & Gower, R. (2008). *The skillful teacher: Building your teaching skills* (5th ed.). Acton, MA: Research for Better Teaching.

Sousa, D. & Tomlinson, C. (2011). *Differentiation and the brain: How neuroscience supports the learner-friendly classroom*. Bloomington, IN: Solution tree Press.

Sternberg, R., and Zhang, L. (Eds.). (2001). *Perspectives on thinking, learning, and cognitive styles*. Mahwah, NJ: Lawrence Erlbaum Associates.

Taras, H., & Potts-Datema, W. (2005). Childhood asthma and student performance at school. *Journal of School Health, 78*(7), 389–396.

Thomas, A., Chess, S., & Birch, H. (1970a). *Temperamental and behavior disorders in children*. New York, NY: New York University Press.

Thomas, A., Chess, S. & Birch, H. (1970b). The origin of personality. *Scientific American*, 102–109. Retrieved from http://www.acamedia.info/sciences/sciliterature/origin_of_personality.htm

Thomas, A., & Chess, S. (1977). *Temperament and development*. New York, NY: Brunner/Mazel.

Turnbull, A., Turnbull, R., Wehmeyer, M., & Shogren, K. (2016). *Exceptional lives: Special education in today's schools* (8th ed.). Columbus, Ohio: Merrill.

Wolf, P. (2010). *Brain matters: Translating research into classroom practice* (2nd ed.). Alexandria, VA: Association for Supervision and Curriculum Development.

Youngstrom, E. (2007). Pediatric bipolar disorder. In E. Mash & R. Barkley (Eds.), *Assessment of childhood disorders* (4th ed.), 253–304. New York, NY: Guilford.

Website Resources

Children and Adolescents with **ADD**. Retrieved 2016 from http://www.CHADD.org

National Resource Center on **ADHD.** Retrieved 2016 from http://www.help4adhd.org

Anxiety and Depression Association of America. Retrieved 2017 from https://www.adaa.org/understanding-anxiety/obsessive-compulsive-disorder-ocd

Thomas **Armstrong**'s *American Institute for Learning and Development*. Retreived 2015 from http://www.institute4learning.com

Autism Speaks. Retrieved 2017 from https://www.autismspeaks.org/

Autism Spectrum Disorder. National Institute of Mental Health/National Institute of Health. Retrieved 2017 from https://www.nimh.nih.gov/health/topics/Autism Spectrum Disorder

Kathleen **Butler**'s *The Learner's Dimension*. Retrieved 2015 from http://www.learnersdimension.com

Rita **Dunn**'s & Kenneth **Dunn**'s *International Learning Styles.* Retrieved 2014 from http://www.learningstyles.net

Daniel **Goleman**'s website on emotional and social intelligence. Retrieved 2017 from http://www.danielgoleman.info

Anthony **Gregorc Associates.** Retrieved 2015 from http://www.gregorc.com

Hopkins Medicine. Retrieved 2017 from http://www.hopkinsmedicine.org/healthlibrary/

David **Kolb**'s *Learning from Experience*. Retrieved 2015 from http://www.learningfromexperience.com

David **Lazear**'s *David Lazear Group/Multiple Intelligences.* Retrieved 2015 from http://www.davidlazeargroup.com

Mayo Clinic. Retrieved 2017 from http://www.mayoclinic.org

Bernice **McCarthy's** *About Learning.* Retrieved 2017 from http://www.aboutlearning.com

Universal Design for Learning. Retrieved 2017 from http://www.cast.org or http://uldcenter.org

CHAPTER 3

The Effects of Physical Environment Variables on Behavior

We shape our buildings and they shape us.

—Winston Churchill

What Will This Chapter Discuss?

The physical environment comprises all those aspects of the classroom that are seen, heard, felt, and experienced—with the exception of interpersonal interactions. (The latter belongs in the third environment we will discuss in the next chapter.) There are three categories of physical environment variables: 1) instruction—both the class curriculum and the teacher's strategies; 2) the nature of the room contents, including instructional materials; and 3) the room arrangement—the furniture, equipment, and materials; the location of the windows and doors and, therefore, what can be seen and heard through them; the extent and nature of the lighting and heat; the location of signs and other materials posted throughout the room; the high-traffic areas. We begin with the arrangement of the space and the physical objects in the room because doing so gives us the "big picture" within which we can place the contents and instruction.

Why Is This Important?

Analyzing the physical environment enables us to understand how variables in the room external to the students affect learning and behavior. Our intent as teachers is to meet the basic needs of each student for many reasons, not the least of which is to minimize the likelihood that unconstructive behavior will occur. We will analyze these variables to determine how we can use them in ways that *do* address basic needs and thereby affect a student's learning and behavior.

What Will You Learn?

By the end of the chapter, you will be able to:

- ✦ state the three kinds of variables in the physical environment and give at least two examples of each kind;
- ✦ state the four considerations we need to keep in mind to consider student's physiological variables, address their basic needs, provide structure, and nurture when arranging the furniture, equipment, and objects in the room in order to be proactive in our support of constructive behavior; and
- ✦ critique a room to determine the degree to which the four considerations have been addressed.

What Do You Want To Accomplish?

Do you have goals beyond that? If so, write them down here or elsewhere so you can refer back to determine if you are addressing them as you read: _____

_____

_____

ACCESSING PRIOR KNOWLEDGE/EXPERIENCE

Think back to the various classrooms in which you learned. In the space below or on a separate piece of paper, list the aspects about the arrangement of furniture, equipment, and contents that addressed your basic needs (safety, belonging, a sense of value, competence, joy/play) and those that did not.

Aspects that addressed your basic emotional needs: _____

_____

_____

_____

Aspects that did not: _____

_____

_____

How Can Room Variables Nurture Students by Meeting their Basic Needs?

We have said nurturing gives people the sense that they are safe, they are important in their own right, they are cared for as individuals, they can do, they belong. How might room arrangement and contents nurture students and provide structure? They do this by addressing each of the basic needs. As we consider these variables, ask yourself: Does anything we discuss resonate with your experiences?

How Do We Meet Students' Need to Feel Safe?

To meet the need of physical safety, equipment and furniture would be solidly built, not easily able to be tipped over, and lacking in parts that splinter easily or have jagged edges. There would be no broken windows, no chipping paint, or any other aspect of the classroom in need of physical repair that would be a safety risk.

Any display that values each and all students would address the need for emotional safety. Displays would offer a variety of choices to allow students to make something that they feel competent creating. A bulletin board with different kinds of items posted, a celebration display that was multimedia in nature, or a science show that contained all kinds of experiments would allow students to feel safe as they shared what they had learned. On the other hand, any posted statement, list, summary of accomplishments for which the awards are limited in number, or that advertise (even unwittingly) that some cannot do the skill as well or as fast as others risks loss of student's emotional safety. Specific examples would be: class lists of students who have mastered particular math facts or prepositional phrases, or a chart that shows how many books every class member has read. Do you remember being on such a list, or if not, can you imagine what it might feel like? For those not included, these kinds of lists can leave some students feeling embarrassed, ashamed, angry, or defeated. Even students on the "top" can feel emotionally "unsafe"—either because they are not sure they can stay there or because of the feelings apparent in other students. Such lists are factors in the physical environment that diminish emotional safety.

How Do We Meet Students' Need to Feel Cared About, Valued?

One way that the physical environment of a classroom can send students a message that each is cared about as an *individual* learner is by offering a learning environment and learning experiences that meet his or her needs. We can do this in many ways.

We Provide Brain-Compatible Instruction

Does the room appear to be arranged so that brain-compatible instruction can occur? For example, is there a lesson agenda to provide a road map for students' brains and, thereby, foster their learning? Is there evidence of activities that ready students' brains for learning by accessing prior knowledge, such as displays that contain student predictions? Are there materials and equipment that would support active engagement in learning? Can the students readily process what they are learning by talking about it with others nearby because the room is arranged in a manner that facilitates collaborative learning? If the current arrangement does not foster dialogue among students, could the students readily reconfigure the seats and desks/tables to allow collaboration to happen? Are there "mind maps" or evidence of other learning experiences that offer opportunities to summarize what has been learned to facilitate retention? Is there any evidence to suggest that the curriculum content is integrated across subjects? Is there any evidence to suggest that differentiated instruction occurs, so that all can study a topic, but with materials written at different levels of difficulty or address a topic at different levels of complexity?

We Address Individual Learner Needs

In Chapter 2, we discussed how different learners have individual preferences for how they learn. If we are to create a learning environment that is optimal for students, we need to think not only of the entire group in any class but also of individuals. One important way variables in the physical environment can nurture students is by offering variety and choices to make it possible for students to meet their individual learner needs. Such a physical environment could include different kinds of learning areas and/or different content that would address variables in the ways listed below.

+ Lighting: well-lit areas; some more dimly lit areas; areas with fluorescent lights; areas with incandescent lights; areas that receive natural light through windows.
+ Noise: an area with headphones for those who are supported in focusing by having continual background stimulation or for those who need "white noise" to help them tune out ambient

sound; an area away from random noise distractions (such as the doorway and open windows) for those who need quiet to concentrate.

- **Seating:** straight-backed as well as more informal chairs or cushions are available.
- **Instructional groupings:** students could have choices available for working alone or with others—there might be carrels for working as individuals and a table or movable desks to arrange for collaborating with others.
- **Timing in the day:** students could have choices about whether they study a subject in the morning or afternoon—not all advanced algebra classes would be taught during second and third periods.
- **Materials for learning:** the materials about the room could offer students choices about whether they learn with music, art, props for role play, journals, manipulatives, items from the natural environment, books on tape, graphs, and maps.

We Recognize the Value of Each Student as an Individual

Another way the contents of the physical environment can send a message to students that they are cared about is by telling them that they are not measured in comparison to anyone else; moreover, their worth is not derived from what they *do* but who they *are*. Displays that offer all students an opportunity to share what each feels good about and eliminates comparisons would be one example. Other evidence might be subtle, such as any materials that suggest everyone's ideas are respected, everyone's effort is honored, and that it is fine to arrive at a solution in many different ways. Evidence to the contrary would include any acknowledgment of "The one best _____ " or displays that honor only some learners, such as Student of the Month (unless there are 10 or fewer students in the class).

The curriculum, as evidenced by displays in the room and the content of books, is another portion of the physical environment where messages about student value occur. Who is valued in the displays? Are both genders validated: are there displays about boys *and* girls, men *and* women participating in positively regarded activities? Are many ethnic groups represented, including those of whom the students are members? Are there people shown who happen to have disabilities as well as those who do not? What is valued: unusual feats or everyday contributions? Effort or just accomplishment? Beauty on the outside, or beauty within?

How Do We Meet the Students' Need to Feel a Sense of Belonging?

The arrangement of space and objects in the physical environment can send a message to students that they belong, that this is their class; they are citizens, not tourists; they are members of the learning community, not visitors. Desks arranged so students can work together signals potential for belonging. By contrast, one desk segregated from the others—particularly one facing the wall or placed next to the teacher's desk—suggests isolation.

Displays made by the students or students and the teacher signal shared ownership. (On the other hand, displays created only by the teacher signal that the teacher owns the room.) Shared ownership in the running of the learning community would be signaled by a posted list—developed by the students and teacher—of jobs needed to carry out the class, from shoelace helper to computer sign-up manager, attendance taker, or room arranger for particular activities. Shared ownership of personal rights and responsibilities would be in evidence if there were a posted list of behavior expectations for students *and* teacher (as well as any other adult who works in the room) developed by *all* the people in the class—teacher, students, aides, student teachers—all members of that learning community and would be signed by all.

How Do We Meet Students' Need to Feel Efficacious?

One item to notice is the location of the teacher's desk. Is it the "tollgate" near the door to the room; that is, do people have to pass by it to gain access? Such a location suggests greater than necessary power on the part of the teacher. A teacher's desk in front of rows of students signals "I am the one who can. You will listen to me; you will learn from me." The teacher's desk off to the side, with the students' desks/ tables arranged in an arrangement (such as a U) that facilitates collaborative learning says, "We all have something to contribute. We will learn from each other. You can, and I can, and we all can, together." Of course, when we look at classroom arrangements, we need to be careful about making assumptions. For example, a room can be arranged in a U, but within that room a teacher can spend all the time lecturing to the students and not actively engaging them. On the other hand, a room of desks in rows can be rearranged into a U or into groups of four or five students positioned for group work any time the need arises in a lesson. So, arrangement alone cannot tell us all we need to know, but it gives us a start.

Another aspect of room arrangement that can empower students comes from the strategic location of learning materials. When materials are kept away or only distributed by the teacher, that sends a message that the teacher has the power; students can*not* proceed with their learning without "goods" granted by the teacher. On the other hand, closets and shelves that are positioned so that students can get their own supplies when needed (and through appropriate procedures, which we will discuss later) encourage students to take charge of their learning. The same is true for a room that has objects and furniture arranged to support the nature of activities that require them (for example, sinks next to the tables where science experiments are being performed or art projects are being created, but *not* next to computers). This arrangement sends the message "You can!" to learners.

The contents of a classroom can meet the need to be efficacious by providing students with goals for their behavior and work and processes that support the meeting of those goals. As mentioned before, process posters and a list of five to seven rules created by the community and posted in a prominent place would support understanding of what is expected in their work and how students can be successful in their interactions. An agenda for the day or the lesson posted where all can see would help students feel a sense of competence by providing them with a path through the day or through the activities of a lesson.

For students who learn in different classrooms and whose schedule rotates on an other-than-5-days-a-week basis in a middle school, providing information beyond the confines of a room can be helpful. Posters—placed in the school office, the hallways, just outside classroom doors, and near the doors inside rooms—indicating which "day" (A through F, for example) is today's schedule supports students' feeling of competence (and helps create a feeling of competence in teachers and staff, too!). This posting throughout the school supports students' ability to get to the right room at the right time. Posters reminding them what materials they need for work in that particular room support their having what they need once they get to where they need to be.

When students are settled in the room and able to begin a learning experience, the nature of the contents in the room (and their ready availability) can support feelings of efficacy by providing tools for learning experiences that utilize many different abilities and talents. Materials that enable students to access skills and ideas, process these, and be evaluated through a variety of intelligences (in addition to the normally heavy emphasis on linguistic and logical/mathematical intelligences) foster feelings of efficacy. Contents that support the use of music, cooperative learning structures, art activities, role play, multimedia, field trips, and inner reflection, for example, will help many more students feel competent and experience success as they learn.

For English-language learners, providing labels that in their primary language as well as the English equivalent and books in their native language for content (even as they learn their second language) can support their feelings of efficacy. Offering recorded books for students whose comprehension of ideas is above their ability to decode words can help them feel competent during English/language arts, book, and history/social studies discussions.

How Do We Meet Students' Need to Experience Joy, a Sense of Well-Being?

The room and the objects and materials in it can be arranged in such a way that they invite curiosity and support students' desire to discover, to find out about many different things. Such a room would be fun to walk into—a festival for the senses. It would be festooned with students' work through many different intelligences. Those bulletin boards that did not celebrate students' discoveries would be interactional in nature. There might be evidence of a sense of humor, but none that is sarcastic.

How Can Room Content Variables Provide Structure?

Variables in the contents of a classroom can provide structure for student behavior by sending messages about behavior expectations. We all need guidelines for our behavior. Without structure, students cannot be sure how they should behave in a given situation. If there are no clear expectations, students will try to discover them ourselves by testing and testing until the teacher's responses provide the much-needed guidelines. Under such conditions, the students' (if not the teacher's) anxiety will be raised because they are unsure of what to do—what is okay and what is not. Messages in the contents of a classroom about expected behavior come in various forms.

Posted Classroom Rules, Contract, Pledge, Charter, Constitution, or Class Promise Provide a Reminder of Class Agreed Upon Expectations

Each is a statement of what class community members want to gain from participating in the class and what they feel they need to give to the learning community to have it function well. With the exception of rules, the statements are means of collaboratively establishing and reminding students of expectations and are usually quite detailed. They contain a list of the rights and responsibilities of class members and are usually created with older students—grades four and up.

Table 3-1. Example of a Class Contract Created with Older Students	
Contract for Our Learning Community	
Students' Rights (To be safeguarded by the teacher and/or student)	**Students' Responsibilities** (To be fulfilled by the student)
To have a teacher who does her best.	To be responsible: To do my homework, to come to school, to be on time, and to do my best.
To have choices about the way I learn and how I show what I have learned.	To tell people my learning needs.
To be trusted.	To be trustworthy. To trust others.
To feel I can share what I am thinking. To "pass" when I don't want to contribute during class. To to make mistakes.	To share "air time". To be open to others' ideas; to disagree with ideas, not people. To contribute to a class that is safe.
To get clear directions on assignments. To get clear due dates for assignments. To get helpful feedback about what I do well and about how to improve.	To listen to helpful feedback—both about what I do well and about what I need to change. To use feedback to improve.
To be understood. To understand. To get answers to my questions.	To ask until I understand. To help others understand.
To have a class that helps me learn.	To tell people my needs. To think about others' needs.
To have a class that is kind.	To be responsible for my own learning and helpful to others'. To help make learning fun for all, and to not allow myself to "clam up."
I am willing to assert my rights and uphold my responsibilities in this contract. Student: _____ Date: _____ Teacher: _____ Date: _____	

On the other hand, a set of rules is a list of three to five (or more) specific, concrete guidelines that address how community members will behave in class, including how they will treat each other, the materials, and the environment. A sample set of rules would be as follows in Table 3-2:

Table 3-2. **Example of a Set of Rules**
Rules We Want for Our Work Together

1. Be kind to ourselves and others.
 	
2. Help each person feel a part of our community:
 	
    Help make this a place in which everyone feels safe.
 	
    Encourage others to speak in a discussion.
 	
3. Come ready to learn and to help others learn:
 	
    Do our work the best we can; ask if we don't understand.
 	
    Help others when they ask for it.
 	
4. Celebrate happy occasions.
 	
5. Treat others the way we want to be treated:
 	
    When we listen to and when we talk about what other people say;
 	
    In our humor—no teasing or sarcasm.

How rules are formulated and their nature can provide structure (and nurture) students. They need to be created with the students, and they need to be taught: "What do we mean by 'We respect others'?" Review and reminders are also needed. All the while, we keep the rules posted to provide guidelines and reminders—visual reinforcement of what has been learned.

Posted Procedures Remind Students How to Carry Out Expected Behavior

Probably the most important procedures that need to be at eye level—and in letters (and icons) large enough and at the appropriate reading level for students to read—would be the steps to take when there is a fire drill or a lockdown drill. Other procedures for any given class might be, for example, how to use the bathroom, how to turn in finished work or homework, what to do about work missed when absent, etc. Note: We will address the process of creating rules and procedures in Chapter 6.

Posted Signs Cue Students About What Behavior is Expected Where

Another form of communication about behavior expectations comes from signs that direct behavior for particular sections of a room. They name the nature or kind of activities that are acceptable in a particular section, or they delineate how many students can be in the section at one time. Sometimes these signs are just that—written signs such as those in Table 3-3.

Table 3-3. Examples of Signs that Provide Expectations for Behavior in Sections of the Room		
MATH RESOURCES	*FOR QUIET THINKING ONLY*	2 per lab station at a time

Other signs might appear on a whiteboard or bulletin board, usually with a box to frame the contents and help separate them from day-to-day information. Such reminders could include the next day's homework or, like the one below, long-term project due dates. Often teachers use a particular color to highlight the importance of these signs.

Table 3-4. Example of a Sign that Provides Expectations Regarding Assignments	
Project Steps	Due
Scaled floor plans for dream house	4/23
Cardboard model	5/2

Posted Schedules and Agendas Cue and Remind Students of Expectations

Daily, weekly, or course rotation schedules can help students anticipate what will occur (and when) in their school lives. In a similar vein, if a schedule—the agenda for a class or learning experience, in particular—is reviewed at the beginning of and throughout a lesson, it helps to set expectations for what will come next and what, therefore, students might be expected to do. An agenda also helps the students' brains to establish an "anticipatory set" to create a context within which the students can frame their learning.

Stating Curriculum Standards/Learning Targets Provides a Focus for Constructive Behavior

While curriculum standards/learning targets do not directly provide structure for students' behavior, such standards do tell students what the focus of their work should be: what is it that they should be working on during this week—a broader agenda than the day's lesson. In addition, the standards provide statements of what behavior is the "standard" for students in a grade level (i.e., what is expected of students while they are in that particular grade). For example, there are speaking and listening standards that state what students are expected to do when participating in a conversation with others. Having the expectation *posted in student-friendly words* would help provide a source of structure for student work and behavior.

Posted Process and Product Expectations Remind Students of What is Expected and How to Meet Specific Expectations

Other messages about behavior come in the form of posters or charts (published or handwritten). These might include, for example, the steps (process) students could or are expected to use to solve a math problem. Below is an example I saw posted in a classroom.

Table 3-5. Example of a Sign that Provides Process Suggestions: Ten Solution Strategies[i]		
1) Act out the problem or use objects.	4) Make an organized list.	8) Use logical reasoning.
2) Make a picture or diagram.	5) Guess and check.	9) Make it simpler.
3) Use or make a table.	6) Use or look for a pattern.	10) Brainstorm
	7) Work backwards.	

i   Creative Publications. (1989). *Ten solution strategies*. Mountain View, CA, Publisher.

Other posters might cue students to the expectations for products. In elementary and middle school classrooms, I have observed many variations of the following expectations for the end result of any written piece:

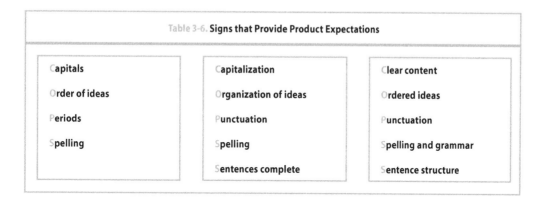

Table 3-6. Signs that Provide Product Expectations		
Capitals	**C**apitalization	**C**lear content
Order of ideas	**O**rganization of ideas	**O**rdered ideas
Periods	**P**unctuation	**P**unctuation
Spelling	**S**pelling	**S**pelling and grammar
	Sentences complete	**S**entence structure

Often these signs include acronyms (such as COPS[i] in the previous examples) that are mnemonic devices to help students remember the steps or contents—to remind students of ways to "police" their writing. Indeed, this form of providing signals is intended to do just that—remind students of expectations. Teachers would have taught the content, and periodically they would also provide a review, but all the while the poster is there to help students maintain the expected behavior.

Signals in a Room Cue Students About What Behavior is Expected Where

Signals provide messages by virtue of the arrangement of contents in a section of the room: Art supplies and extra paper near an easel say "Artists Invited." Various measurement tools and objects of different shapes with written problems to solve that require measurement invite a particular kind of math behavior. A series of earphones, scripts of two or three Shakespeare plays, and a CD player with CDs that contain marvelous renditions of the plays call out "Come, listen to Shakespeare here!" While signals are not written, adding a sign encourages students to interact with the materials.

How Can Room Arrangement Variables Provide Structure for Students' Behavior?

We have said that structure teaches students how to do things and provides expectations for the quality of performance. How might the variables of room arrangement provide structure? Before we address this question, take a minute to consider what you already know regarding the relationship between these categories of variables in the physical environment and behavior.

· ·

REFLECTION OPPORTUNITY

Write your responses to in the spaces provided or on a separate piece of paper.

Picture a class in which there are lots of barriers between most students and areas of the room that are frequently used—the pencil sharpener, water fountain, shelves for essential resources, lockers/cubbies. How do you think that would affect behavior—of the students who were trying to get to these places and of the students who were seated near the pathways to these frequently used locations? _____

_____

_____

Consider a room in which the teacher could not see some students because bookshelves or equipment walled off sections of the room. Suppose these same objects made it hard for the teacher to get quickly to students who needed help or for a student to get to a teacher or classmate to ask a question or check in for an "okay" to go on to the next step. How might that affect student behavior? _____

_____

_____

Imagine a room in which the space just behind where the teacher was teaching was filled with mobiles of shiny paper or a display that included many photos of students. Picture a room in which light from the window made a glare on the board every afternoon after lunch. How might such arrangements of objects or materials distract or interfere with students' ability to focus? _____

_____

_____

· ·

Visibility of Teacher(s), Students, and Lesson Foci Fosters Constructive Behavior

In order to facilitate learning—to monitor students' behavior for feedback, to anticipate needs, and to be proactive about implementing strategies—teachers need to be able to readily see all the students. At the same time, to participate effectively in the lesson, students need to see the teacher, other students, and materials that are an integral part of the learning experience. Included in these materials would be the lesson agenda, student-friendly objectives, process and product posters that are key to the lesson—all at eye level—and all safety procedures (such as fire drill instructions) that all students can read.

Proximity of Students and Teacher Supports Constructive Behavior

Teachers need to be able to get to each student in the shortest amount of time possible to facilitate and manage the learning experience and to troubleshoot problems that might arise. Students, in turn, need to be able to get to teachers as quickly as possible for support or clarification in order to be able to move constructively through the learning experience. Therefore, the room should be arranged so that there is the least distance and the fewest barriers between the teacher(s) and students and between students and teacher(s).

Accessibility of High-Traffic Areas Facilitates Constructive Behavior

In order to learn, students need ready access to places such as the drinking fountain (if there is one in the room), the pencil sharpener, and other important resources in the room without bothering other students or upsetting materials nearby. These high-traffic areas need to be free of congestion to diminish potential "downtime" and the possibilities for problems as students are retrieving and putting away supplies or other resources.

Elimination of Distractibility Enhances Constructive Behavior

In order to learn, students must also be able to focus on either people (e.g., a teacher or classmate who is speaking) or materials (e.g., computer screens, recordings, books, papers, objects, words, numbers, or formulas being written on a board). If attention is taken away by attractive but irrelevant objects (such as those hanging from the skylights or ceiling), by glares or reflections, by the movement from other students squeezing their way past to get to frequently used resources, or by noise coming from any source, then students' behavior cannot be constructively focused on the learning task at hand.

Further Exploration: There are many useful references on the effects of classroom variables. One from which I drew the ideas about visibility, proximity, accessibility, and distractibility that you can explore further is "Managing Classrooms: A Framework for Teachers" by Carolyn Evertson (1987). While this was written many years ago, it is based on classroom research carried out over an extended period of time. The ideas are relevant to any classroom today or in the future. Three current references are: Emmer and Evertson (2017); Evertson and Emmer (2017); and Marzano (2007). Complete references appear at the end of the chapter.

· ·

Application Opportunity: Four Considerations for Room Design

What are the four considerations you want to keep in mind when arranging the furniture, equipment, and objects in a room to address students' physiological variables and basic needs, provide structure, and nurture students?

1. _____

2. _____

3. _____

4. _____

Answers can be found in the book's Appendix A: Answer Key under "Chapter 3: C3AK: Four Considerations for Room Design—Answers."

· ·

How Can Instruction Provide Structure and Nurture Students?

For our analysis of the effects of variables in the physical environment on student behavior, I chose to present the classroom arrangement and contents first because I wanted to heighten your sensitivity to variables that are often overlooked. When people observe in classrooms, more often than not they are drawn to the action. They watch the teacher and students interact or students interacting with other students. Important aspects of the physical environment may be missed.

Now we are ready to address instructional strategies within that room. Instruction is made up of both curriculum and teaching strategies—what students are taught and how they are taught.

Curriculum Content Provides Structure

Instruction provides structure for constructive behavior when it effectively enables students to learn functional, empowering academic *and social skills*. Probably the most obvious example of curriculum content that can support constructive social behavior would be the Johnson and Johnson approach to cooperative learning called Learning Together (Johnson, Johnson, & Holubec, 2008). Attention is drawn to this particular approach because Learning Together includes the teaching of social skills as a major component. None of the other approaches does. For example, students are taught how to listen empathically, disagree constructively, and include everyone on a team in the work of the team. We will consider this approach in detail in Chapter 7.

Another example of curriculum content that would provide structure for constructive behavior is a conflict resolution or peer mediation programs such as the ones developed by the Johnsons (Johnson & Johnson, 2006; 1995a; 1995b; 1995c). In all of these programs students in a class are taught the skills.

A third kind of curriculum comes from a variety of sources; each offers a means to teach specific social skills. Massachusetts General Hospital (2015) has designed a Think: Kids program[ii] that teaches, among other skills, collaborative problem solving for work with students whose behavior is particularly challenging. These examples illustrate how instructional content can directly provide structure because the choice of *what* to teach supports the learning of constructive behavior.

Our Instructional Strategies Foster Constructive Behavior

How we teach can provide structure for students' thinking and learning. We have known for a long while now what teaching steps are compatible with brain functioning (Hunter, 2004; Rosenshine & Stevens, 1986; Berliner & Rosenshine, 1987).

> Introduction: helping the students to get ready for the lesson itself by providing an anticipatory set in the form of an agenda and a source of motivation to grab their attention and help their brains anticipate what is about to occur. The introduction also needs to help the

students develop a mental set for understanding the skill or concept. This includes providing and accessing prior knowledge to ready their brains for the learning that is about to take place. (The agenda and objectives are then reviewed at natural points in the lesson.)

Explanation: teaching the students what they need to know to grasp the concept or carry out the procedure.

Demonstration or model: demonstrating the procedure or providing a model of the concept. (In some schools, this is called the "I Do" portion of the lesson; this is when the teacher does whatever is being taught.)

Checking for understanding: being sure students fully comprehend the concept or what it is they are to do in the procedure before they begin to put what they have learned into action.

Coached practice: providing supportive supervision to nurture the unfolding of the learning process in each student as he works with and applies the concept or carries out the procedure. (In some schools, this is called the "We Do" portion of the lesson; this is when the teacher and the students together do whatever is being taught.)

Closing—summarization: engaging the students actively in summarizing the key ideas or steps in the procedure.

Solitary practice: providing meaningful opportunities to practice the skill (procedure) or apply the concept that are designed in such a way that the success rate is about 75% or better. (In some schools, this is called the "You Do" portion of the lesson; in other words, this is when the students on their own do whatever is being taught.)

Periodic reviews with the students.

Instruction can nurture students if it is provided in a way that matches their learning needs, whether the instruction responds to the elements in the room mentioned above (heat, light, kinds of seating, etc.), uses many different intelligences over time to support learning, or responds to any of the other variables we addressed in Chapter 2.

Application Opportunity: Instruction That Meets Basic Needs

The chart below briefly describes examples of instructional content (curriculum) and processes (strategies) that would *not* meet each basic emotional need. By contrast, for each emotional need there is room in the first column for you to fill in examples of instruction that *would* nurture students. You could also write the Need on a separate piece of paper and next to it examples of instruction that *would* meet that emotional need,

	Table 3-7. The Role Instruction Can Play in Addressing Basic Emotional Needs	
Need	Instruction that *would* meet the emotional need	Instruction that would NOT meet the emotional needs of students
Emotional safety		• Use "one size fits all" instruction; • Use the same processes most of the time; • Use competitive structures; • Use ranking for evaluation; • Speak critically about students publicly; e.g., to another teacher or student. • Make evaluation of student work public; • Display student work without permission; • Use sarcasm or ridicule; • Use materials that omit the contributions of cultural groups or represent them disrespectfully.
Belonging		• Pit students against others; • Single out student(s) publicly for judgment of any negative nature; • Speak negatively about one student to others; • Minimize opportunities for students to learn about each other; • Use only individualistic structures for learning.
Personal value		• Tell the students the class rules; • Make all the decisions and do all the management tasks yourself; • Boss rather than lead or foster; • Use large group instruction most of the time; • Discount or ridicule a student's ideas; • Single out a student who needs help; • Make one student's success be dependent on another's failure, e.g., "Well, Leah doesn't know the answer; do you, Amy?"

Table 3-7. **The Role Instruction Can Play in Addressing Basic Emotional Needs (Continued)**		
Efficacy		• Instruct beyond students' stretch; • Lecture at students; • Address private issues publicly; • Criticize publicly; • Criticize instead of providing constructive feedback; • Expect perfection; • Expect accuracy before fluency is achieved; • Use comparative evaluation; • Use evaluation criteria or processes that are not known to students in advance.
Fun, joy, recreation, a sense of well-being		• Provide no variety in nature, pacing, social configuration, setting, timing, momentum, materials; • Use rigid, authoritarian strategies; • For in-school and homework assignments rely on text and paper and pencil learning; • Control all decision-making and everything that goes on in the room.

In the book's Appendix A: Answer Key, under C3AK Table 3-7, "Chapter 3: The Role Instruction Can Play in Addressing Emotional Needs—Possible Answers," I have provided examples of strategies gathered from working with teacher candidates and teachers in the field and from my work with children and young adults. See if you agree. Did you have some to add?

• •

Final Thoughts

When we think about teaching, we tend to focus on instruction. Certainly, how we teach children and young adults is an essential consideration for supporting the development of constructive behavior. While we have spent some time in this chapter talking about considerations for effective instructional strategies, these alone will not enable us to provide the needed structure and nurturance for students, nor will specific curriculum. We also need to think about the design of the space within which we teach—how we arrange the furniture, equipment, and materials. These elements either support our instruction or undermine it. How we design our room either fosters our ability to nurture students and provide structure or prevents us from effectively fostering students' learning.

Looking Forward

In the next chapter, we will turn to the final of the three environments—the psychosocial environment. We will discuss how the variables in the informal interactions (both between a teacher and students and among students) can affect behavior.

References

Armstrong, T. (2009). *Multiple intelligences in the classroom* (3rd ed.). Alexandria, VA: Association for Supervisi on and Curriculum Development.

Berliner, D., & Rosenshine, B. (1987). *Talks to teachers*. New York, NY: Random House.

Cole, R. (Ed.). (2008). *Educating everybody's children: Diverse teaching strategies for diverse learners* (2nd ed.). Alexandria, VA: Association for Supervision and Curriculum Development.

Creative Publications. (1989). *Ten solution strategies.* Mountain View, CA: Publisher.

Deshler, D., & Shumaker, J. (1986). Learning strategies: An instructional alternative for low achieving adolescents. *Exceptional children, 52*(6), 583–590.

Emmer, E., & Evertson, C. (2017). *Classroom management for middle and high school teachers* [loose-leaf version] (10th ed.). Boston, MA: Pearson.

Evertson, C. (1987). Managing classrooms: A framework for teachers. In D. Berliner & B. Rosenshine (Eds.), *Talks to teachers*, 54–74 New York, NY: Random House.

Evertson, C., Emmer, W., Clements, B., & Worsham, M. (1997). *Classroom management for elementary teachers* (4th ed.). Boston, MA: Allyn & Bacon.

Evertson, C., & Emmer, W. (2017). *Classroom management for elementary teachers* [loose-leaf version] (11th ed.). Boston, MA: Pearson.

Evertson, C., & Neal, K. (2006). Looking into learning-centered classrooms: Implications for classroom management. *NEA Research Best Practices Working Paper.* Washington, DC: National Education Association. Retrieved from http://files.eric.ed.gov/fulltext/ED495820.pdf

Evertson, C., & Weinstein, C. (Eds.). (2006). *The handbook of classroom management: Research, practice, and contemporary issues.* Mahwah, NJ: Lawrence Erlbaum.

Freiberg, J. (1996, September). From tourists to citizens in the classroom. *Educational Leadership 54*(1), 32–36.

Hunter, M. (1982). *Mastery teaching.* El Segundo, CA: TIP Publications.

Johnson, D., & Johnson, F. (2016). *Joining together: Group theory and group skills* (12th ed.). Boston, MA: Allyn & Bacon.

Johnson, D., & Johnson, R. (1989). *Cooperation and competition*. Edina, MN: Interaction Book Company.

Johnson, D., & Johnson, R. (1994). *Learning together and alone: Cooperative competitive and individualistic learning* (4th ed.). Boston: Allyn & Bacon.

Johnson, D., & Johnson, R. (1995a). *My mediation notebook* (3rd ed.). Edina, MN: Interaction Book Co.

Johnson, D., & Johnson, R. (1995b). *Reducing school violence through conflict resolution*. Alexandria, VA: Association for Supervision and Curriculum Development.

Johnson, D., & Johnson, R. (1995c). *Teaching students to be peacemakers.* Edina, MN: Interaction Book Co.

Johnson, D., & Johnson, R. (2006). Conflict resolution, peer mediation and peacemaking. In C. Evertson & C. Weinstein (Eds.), *Handbook of classroom management* (pp. 803–832). Mahwah, NJ: Lawrence Erlbaum Associates.

Johnson, D., & Johnson, R. (2009). An educational psychology success story: Social interdependence theory and cooperative learning. *Educational Researcher, 38*(5), 365–379.

Johnson, D., Johnson, R., & Holubec, E. (2008). *Cooperation in the classroom* (8th ed.). Alexandria, VA: Association for Supervision and Curriculum Development.

Jones, V. (2015). *Practical classroom management* [loose-leaf version] (2nd ed.). Boston, MA: Pearson.

Jones, V., & Jones, L. (2016). *Comprehensive classroom management: Creating communities of support and solving problems* [loose-leaf version] (11th ed.). Boston. MA: Pearson.

Levin, J., & Nolan, J. (2013). *Principles of classroom management: A professional decision-making model* (7th ed.). Boston, MA: Pearson.

Marzano, R. (2007). *The art and science of teaching: A comprehensive framework for effective instruction.* Alexandria, VA: Association for Supervision and Curriculum Development.

Massachusetts General Hospital. (2015). *Collaborative problem solving: Think Kids introductory training.* Boston, MA: Massachusetts General Hospital.

Rosenshine, B., & Stevens, R. (1986). Teaching functions. In M. Wittrock (Ed.), *Handbook of research on teaching* (3rd ed.). New York, NY: MacMillan.

Schussler, D., Poole, I., Whitlock, T., & Evertson, C. (2007, July). Layers and links: Learning to juggle one more thing in the classroom. *Teaching and Teacher Education, 23*(5)**,** 572–585.

Tomlinson, C. (2001). *How to differentiate instruction in mixed-ability classrooms* (2nd ed.). Alexandria, VA: Association for Supervision and Curriculum Development.

Tomlinson, C. (2014). *The differentiated classroom: Responding to the needs of all learners* (2nd ed.) Alexandria, VA: Association for Supervision and Curriculum Development.

Resources

American Institute for Learning and Development. (2014). Retrieved from http://institute4learning.com

Evertson, C. (1987). Managing classrooms. In D. Berliner & B. Rosenshine (Eds.), *Talks to teachers,* 54–74. New York, NY: Random House.

Evertson, C., & Emmer, W. (2017). *Classroom management for elementary teachers* (11th ed.). Boston, MA: Pearson.

Evertson, C., Emmer, W., Clements, B., & Worsham, M. (1997). *Classroom management for elementary teachers* (4th ed.). Boston, MA: Allyn & Bacon.

Evertson, C., & Neal, K. (2006). Looking into learning-centered classrooms: Implications for classroom management. In B. Demarest (Ed.), *Benchmarks for excellence.* Washington, DC: National Education Association.

Freiberg, J. (1996, September). From tourists to citizens in the classroom. *Educational Leadership 54*(1), 32–36.

Jones, V., & Jones, L. (2016). *Comprehensive classroom management: Creating communities of support and solving problems* (11th ed.). Boston. MA: Pearson.

Marzano, R. (2007). *The art and science of teaching: A comprehensive framework for effective instruction.* Alexandria, VA: Association for Supervision and Curriculum Development.

Massachusetts General Hospital. (2015). *Collaborative problem solving: Think Kids introductory training.* Boston, MA: Massachusetts General Hospital.

Endnotes

i   Note: To my knowledge, COPS appeared originally in Deshler, D., & Shumaker, J. (1986). Learning strategies: An instructional alternative for low achieving adolescents. *Exceptional Children 52*(6), 583–590.

ii Thank you, Katie Silva, for sharing this material with me (personal communication, 2016).

CHAPTER 4

The Effects of Psychosocial Environment Variables on Behavior

The person['s] ... heart withers if it does not answer to another heart. His mind shrinks away if he hears only the echoes of his own thoughts and finds no other inspiration.

—Pearl S. Buck

What Will This Chapter Discuss?

The variables in this third and final environment focus on verbal and nonverbal human interaction. We will address the effects of both student–student and student–teacher social interactions on student behavior.

Why Is This Important?

As discussed in Chapter 2, as human beings we are hardwired to connect with others. "Neuroscience has discovered that our brain's very design makes it sociable, inexorably drawn into an intimate brain-to-brain linkup whenever we engage with another person" (Goleman, 2017). Every encounter we have with another human being affects both their brain and ours. The longer and the more frequent the interactions are and the more important the person is to us, the greater the impact of our experiences with others is on the nature of our circuitry. As Goleman (2006) states, "Our social interactions operate as modulators ... that continually reset key aspects of our brain function as they orchestrate our emotions (p. 5)."

How others behave not only affects how students behave in the moment but also how they develop the social skills needed to behave constructively in the future. To review, these social skills include, according to Goleman (1995; 1996; 2006; 2017),

- **synchrony:** getting mannerisms and movements "in synch" with those of the person with whom one is interacting;
- **self-presentation:** ability to present oneself in a way that makes the desired impression;
- **influence:** ability to use tact and self-control to constructively shape the outcome of an interaction; and
- **concern:** tendency to turn empathy into action.

As a result of this latest research on the effects of social interaction on the brain, when we think of variables in the psychosocial environment affecting behavior, we can look at the moment of interaction and analyze which variables seem to be contributing to the behavior of the individuals involved. We can also look at the nature of that interaction as one more learning experience that has the potential to affect the brain's circuitry and, thereby, affect student's increasing capacity to be socially intelligent.

As teachers, we can not only understand a student's behavior more thoroughly by analyzing the variables in an interaction and their possible effects on that behavior; we can also use our knowledge about the plasticity of the brain to construct (to the extent possible) the interactions students have, so each interaction fosters that student's social intelligence. As we facilitate students' learning of mathematics, English/language arts, art, and music, science and social studies so we can help them develop self-awareness, an ability to manage emotions, the capacity to be empathic and to act on it, self-motivation, and social skills. Each interaction can be considered to be a "teacher," an experience from which a student's social intelligence can be enhanced.

What Will You Learn?

In this chapter, you will learn about:

- ✦ the effects of student–student social interactions on student behavior; and
- ✦ the effects of student–teacher social interactions on student behavior.

What Do You Want To Accomplish?

Before we discuss the psychosocial environment, let us give you an opportunity to set a goal for yourself. You have now learned about variables in two of the three environments in the ecological approach. Below or on a separate piece of paper write what would you like to learn about the variables in this environment.

_____

_____

_____

_____

· ·

REFLECTION OPPORTUNITY

Write your responses to this reflection in the spaces provided or on a piece of paper.

List three very different people or groups of people with whom you interact informally on a peer or collegial basis—not people who are your superiors. For sources, you might consider friends, coworkers, family, relatives, or others in a class.

Person or Group A: _____

Person or Group B: _____

Person or Group C: _____

Picture yourself interacting in your usual manner with each of these different people or groups of people. Describe the nature of your typical behavior with each. Include how you feel as you interact with them. Some suggestions are shown below, but you do not need to limit yourself to these.

1. To what degree you are formal in how you communicate
2. How much you listen, talk
3. What you talk about
4. How much you joke, fool around, laugh, tease
5. The nature of your body language

6. How you sit, stand, move
7. To what degree you are active and assertive or shy and reserved
8. To what degree you are sensitive to others, thoughtful
9. How you feel as you interact with this person or these people

My behavior and feelings with person or group A: _____

_____

_____

My behavior and feelings with person or group B: _____

_____

_____

My behavior and feelings with person or group C: _____

_____

_____

How my behavior and feelings were different with each of these people or groups: _____

_____

_____

What variables do you think contributed to which behavior? _____

_____

_____

How Do Student–Student Social Interactions Affect Student Behavior?

One variable that affects student behavior in any interaction is other people's behavior. Did you find this was true for you as you reflected on your experiences above? The effect of other people's behavior can be made more complicated by a number of factors.

Who is Behaving a Certain Way Has an Effect

If a person has high status in a student's eyes, then that person's behavior is likely to encourage the student to behave in a way that is similar to them. The effect of one student's behavior on one or more other students can be quite impulsive. Redl and Wineman (1951) called this "group contagion." One student reacts and, as a result, others are set off by that reaction. Then quickly, still others follow suit. Even students who typically exhibit constructive behavior can get caught up by the excitement of the moment. A low-status group member's behavior would not have the same ripple effect.

A student may also act a certain way to get the attention or approval of a high-status group member. This is particularly true with adolescents. In middle and high school, students are more concerned with peer acceptance than they are with academic success. The degree to which they view their interactions with others as positive affects nearly every aspect of their school experience. The more important the other person, the greater the effect is on attitudes, interests, productivity, and, ultimately, academic achievement (Henley, 2006).

When a student wants to be noticed, particularly by someone to whose gender that student is attracted, all sorts of behavior can occur. (I call it "peacock behavior" because, like the male peacock who flutters his beautiful tail plumage, this behavior is intended to get the eye of another.) Sometimes students go to what seems a bit of an extreme of poking or knocking into another person in the hopes of getting noticed. On the other hand, think of the behavior you have seen when someone is trying not to be seen. Perhaps he is shy or is trying to avoid another student who is giving him more attention than is wanted. If the person someone wanted to attract or avoid were not in the group, then the "peacock behavior" or the slinking away behavior would not likely be triggered.

Who is In the Group Has an Effect

Our consideration of who is in the group leads us to consider the familiarity of each member to every other member and the level of comfort with each one. Students who don't know others in a group may be more reticent to take a risk and speak. Some students may not want to work with another student based on their familiarity with that person's behavior in past group work. Both familiarity and comfort level can have a positive or negative effect on a person's social interaction.

The Size of the Group Has an Effect

The nature of a student's social interaction behavior may vary in different sized groups. Size and all the variables it can bring can affect a person's social interaction stimulation level—in a positive or negative way. Large groups can encourage some students to be particularly active and even louder than usual. For other students, large groups are overwhelming. Think of a student with difficulty hearing, auditory processing problems, or who is learning English as a second (or third) language. For these students and others, screening out extraneous noises as they try to follow the conversation of many people can be difficult.

How Others in the Group Treat the Student Has an Effect

How the student acts in a group or team will depend, in some measure, on how the members treat her. If others seem happy to have the student on their team and invite her to share ideas, the student is likely to feel safe enough, with a sense of belonging and of value enough to contribute. When the student completes a task, if others give him helpful, constructive feedback and recognize his contribution, the student is likely to feel efficacious and to therefore continue contributing. On the other hand, if the student feels unwelcomed and like an outsider because of how others react to her being a team member—if others ignore the student's contribution, put down the work of the student, or tease her—those behaviors will also affect how the student feels and behaves in response. Research (Bellmore, 2011) reports that elementary students who were rejected by peers not only had more negative attitudes towards school; they were absent more often than their peers and showed evidence of lower academic growth (as indicated by measures such as standardized test scores and grades). Other research shows that when students do not feel that they belong, they are much more likely to behave in ways that are oppositional to adults and aggressive to peers (Sturato, van Lier, Cuijpers & Koot, 2011). In fact, how students respect, value, and, therefore, treat others in their class (and school) is a significant factor in the extent to which bullying will exist (Carrera, DePalma, & Lameiras, 2011).

How Do Student–Teacher Social Interactions Affect Student Behavior?

. . . .

REFLECTION OPPORTUNITY

What happens to your behavior when you interact with teachers who have different social interaction styles? Give yourself time to think about your experiences by completing this reflection in the space provided or on a separate piece of paper.

Think of two teachers (A and B) you have had whose social interaction with you is quite different.

Picture yourself interacting with teacher A. How would you describe that teacher's style? _____

_____

_____

How did you behave? How did you feel? _____

_____

_____

Picture yourself interacting with teacher B. How would you describe that teacher's style? _____

_____

_____

How did you behave? How did you feel? _____

_____

_____

Did you behave differently with teachers who had distinctly different social interaction styles? In what ways, if any, were your behavior and feelings with teacher A different from those with teacher B?

_____

_____

_____

Because of the nature of our social interactions with them, students may not only interact differently in informal interactions; they may also behave differently in class when interactions are more formal.

* *

What Might Be the Effect of a Teacher's Social Interactions on a Student's Behavior in a Class?

Example: The effect of teacher behavior on student behavior was continuously brought home when I taught in a middle school. Often, during our grade-level meetings, one or more teachers would express concern about how a student was behaving in class. For example, they would describe the student as one who never talked to them, never spoke in class, never contributed to a discussion. Nearly always, one or two other teachers would express surprise. Their sense of the student was quite different. They saw a student who chatted with them about a number of topics before class or after school, who took on a leadership role in teamwork during class, who contributed during discussions. While some of the variables that contributed to the student's behavior were *not* psychosocial (for example, the way the class sessions were designed and how the teachers taught), some variables *were* psychosocial. These included whether or not the teacher approached the student informally to talk about topics of interest to the student and whether or not the teacher expressed interest in what was going on in the student's life in school and outside of class. Those teachers who had similar social interaction styles with students were the ones who had a similar perception of the student's behavior—either concern or no concern. Had we, as a team, assumed that the student's behavior was what either group of teachers observed—a "nontalker/noncontributor" or a "talker/contributor"—we would have lost sight of the whole child—someone who contributed in some classes but did not in others. We would also have lost sight of the effect of particular psychosocial environment variables on any student's behavior. Some students flourish with particular kinds of teacher interactions. Other students do not.

What Might Be the Effects of the Social Skills Learned Outside School on Student Behavior?

There is another reason why social behavior may not be consistent. As with all other skills, students come to school with different levels of emotional intelligence and different social skill development. As we have said before, children are not born socially adept. They need to learn certain social skills in the same way they need to learn the concepts and skills of mathematics, language arts, and many other disciplines.

What Children Learn Outside School May Not Be the Full Range and Depth of Skills Needed to Function Effectively in the Classroom and in the World

Some models that children may observe in video games, television shows, and their personal lives may not offer the constructive approach required in school (Groves, 2003; Jensen, 2013). Therefore, when students come to school, they may not be able to respond constructively to variables in their psychosocial environment. They may not be as capable of interacting as "mindfully," as Goleman (1995) describes it, as they need to be.

Skills Learned at Home and in the Neighborhood May Not Be Generalized to the Classroom

First of all, we know from research on brain functioning and learning that generalization does not occur automatically. Secondly, characteristics of families are different from class communities. The school setting, the demographics for age, and the number of people are different enough to hamper generalization; in other words, what you can do effectively one-on-one with an older or younger sibling may not be effective in a group of 23 to 27. Third, behavior that may be appropriate in the neighborhood may not be what is expected in school (Jensen, 2010, 2013, 2016; Jensen & Snider, 2013; Lelli, 2014; Payne, 2008).

Opportunities to Teach Social Skills within a Family are Often Spontaneous Moments that Occur in Public Situations Fraught with their Own Issues

Something is about to "run amuck" socially (or already has), and suddenly parents need to intervene in public. The difficulty in these situations is that parents feel on display, as though not only what their children are doing but how they are responding are a clear indication of their effectiveness as parents—there for all to see. For some parents, this public exposure may not be a problem. For most, it creates a climate in which they definitely are not at their best. They don't feel safe. They become embarrassed, self-conscious. Their brains shut down; their choices seem to evaporate. They respond with what seems to be the most efficient way to immediately put a stop to the situation or extricate their family from it rather than seeing the moment as an opportunity to teach social skills.

While opportunities for parents to teach through modeling do occur on a daily basis, the drawback to counting on these for teaching *social* skills is that children rarely see their parents in situations that are similar to a class community. Moreover, as children get older, they are likely to turn away from their parents and instead look to peers for their examples of "appropriate," "cool," "okay" behavior.

For many reasons, counting on constructive skills being taught at home is not practical. As teachers, we are in a good position to integrate the teaching of social skills side by side with skills needed in specific disciplines. We can support students in addressing the variables in their psychosocial environment more often and more effectively (Brackett & Rivers, 2014; Gibbs, 2001; Henderson, 2007; Lelli, 2014; Noddings, 2005; Payne, 2008; Souers & Hall, 2016; Yeager & Walton, 2011). We will discuss how we do this in future chapters.

How Do Variables in the Student's Physiological and Physical Environments Affect Social Interaction?

In Chapter 2, we said that a person responded to everyday life, including social interactions, according to that person's temperament. Yet we see inconsistencies. How could that be? First of all, we need to keep in mind that (as we said before) variables in our physiological environment are only *tendencies*, not our destiny. We *tend* to act a certain way—we have a propensity to be shy or not, we tend to have a certain level of energy, we tend to have a certain mood level, we tend to have a degree of rhythmicity in our daily behavior. We also know from our ecological perspective that variables in any of the individual's environments interact with others. So it is with temperament. Interaction with other variables plays a role in how temperament is realized in any social situation. A person may be shy, but the reticence may be increased or decreased based on the effect of other variables in the physiological and physical environments: for example, the level of tiredness or current medication being taken; the location of the social interaction; or the team task at hand. Another factor that contributes to the effects of temperament is the relative degree of the power of each variable at any given moment; that is, one variable may have a more profound effect than another variable in the mix. Therefore, one or more of the student's variables in any environment may have a stronger effect than the temperament variable involved. Example: A particular medication may cause a student to feel drowsy and fuzzy headed, so he withdraws, even though his tendency to adapt is usually high.

Whenever I think of the effects of physical variables on a student's social interactions with others, I am reminded of a student with whom I worked for a period of time each day in a resource room. We worked together on reading and writing, but reading decoding gave him the most difficulty. As you might imagine, in the learning experiences in which reading and writing on the spot were frequently required, he struggled. He was quiet and rarely participated. At times, he completely withdrew. I would guess he was overwhelmed. The teacher in whose class this occurred had a sense of the student as someone who was not interested in the subject because he never spoke. As that teacher described it, the student was "not particularly bright" and did not "pull his weight" in class by interacting with others.

For English/language arts, we addressed one of the difficulties by asking adults in the community to record the books being used in class. For this student, the recorded books were a gift. He could go to class and participate fully in the comprehension and application discussions. He did so enthusiastically in small groups and whole-class discussions. He had insights to share, reasons to support his ideas.

Science class was an even better match. He was an eighth grader, so of great importance to him was his relationships with his peers. He was a highly valued member of his cooperative team. Most of the work in class was done through carrying out science experiments and then reporting the results and the possible reasons behind them. Reading material was limited to short spurts. This could be done by the team member who had that job. Some writing was needed. However, since specific jobs were determined by team members, he offered to do the jobs he was good at. What was required every day in class was a number of social interactions—cooperative skills. These he excelled at, without a doubt. He worked well with others. He listened. He was calm. He was an effective problem solver. He had a wealth of knowledge about the topics and enthusiasm for the work assigned. He had a high social intelligence. In that class, the teacher told me, all the students wanted the student on their team. He did particularly well in science class. This teacher had a very different sense of the student's ability to work with others and within the class.

The student's behavior in science class and, to a lesser degree, in English/language arts was quite different from that in social studies. The tasks required of the students in that class led to different psychosocial variables. The results had a profound effect on the student's social interaction and his success in class.

ACCESSING PRIOR KNOWLEDGE/EXPERIENCE

In the space below or elsewhere list some social skills you think would be important for students to develop over time.

_____   _____

_____   _____

_____   _____

_____   _____

I believe the following list would characterize constructive social skills, an appropriate level of emotional and social intelligence, and effective means of addressing psychosocial environment variables as they affect behavior. I have developed this list for myself from my years of reading, teaching, and life experiences. (Note of clarification: while aspects of these social skills—namely, empathy and emotions—reside in the physiological environment of the student, the student's skill in being aware of them and using them constructively are variables that reside in the psychosocial environment.) I feel my list is always open to revision. As you read it, do you think any important skill has been omitted?

My overarching goal for all students is for them to continually enhance their capacity to develop constructive behavior patterns and habits. Specific skills would include:

- To identify their feelings, talk about them, and use them to make constructive decisions
- To manage emotions, control impulses, resolve problems and conflicts constructively
- To anticipate the likely consequences of their decisions, and with this understanding to make reasonable decisions based on their values, safety, and their respect for themselves and for others
- To interact successfully with people:
  - To listen in ways that foster their understanding of what people are saying
  - To act with thoughtfulness towards others
  - To be assertive about their needs and advocate effectively for their ideas
- To develop interdependent relationship with others
- To engage effectively in social activities
- To take and fulfill responsibilities, be motivated to complete work or meet a goal
- To remain optimistic when there are setbacks and frustrations
- To lead a life that is physically and emotionally safe, healthy, self-affirming, productive, and happy

As you compare my list against the one you wrote, are there any skills you would add or delete?

_____   _____

_____   _____

_____   _____

_____   _____

Final Thoughts

The behavior of others as they interact with us socially (psychosocial environment variables) affects our behavior, which in turn affects our chemistry (physiological environment variables), which in turn affects our behavior. Simultaneously, how we are interacting socially affects the emotions and behavior of those with whom we are interacting, and their emotions affect their thinking and their behavior. The physical context in which we interact with others affects our social skills (psychosocial environment variables) and our thinking and internal feelings, not to mention our sense of self and our perception of our capabilities (physiological environment variables). And so, it goes.

Understanding why students behave as they do (and why we as teachers behave the way we do) is a complex process. I hope you are beginning to realize that the reason I use an *ecological* approach to understanding behavior is because it is the only approach that fosters the kind of insight into the complexity of behavior functioning we as teachers need in order to be effective in our assessment and intervention with students.

We have a list of important social skills to keep in mind. In later chapters, we will address how we can foster these skills in students to enable them to effectively address variables in their psychosocial environment so that they can interact constructively with others.

Looking Forward

In these first chapters, we have considered the ecological perspective—its nature and the advantages of using it as an approach to fostering constructive behavior in students. We have looked at the variables in each of three environments and briefly considered how each set of variables could contribute to the nature of behavior at any given moment. With these ideas as our context, we are ready to consider how we can be proactive in supporting constructive behavior through the ways in which we set up a classroom and, within it, how we establish a community of learners. All the while, we will take into consideration students' physiological environment variables as we use variables in the physical and psychosocial environments to nurture and provide structure.

References

Bellmore, A. (2011). Peer rejection and unpopularity: Association with GPAs across the transition to middle school. *Journal of Educational Psychology, 103*, 282–295.

Bocchino. R. (1999). *Emotional literacy: To be a different kind of smart.* Thousand Oaks, CA: Corwin Press.

Brackett, M., & Rivers, S. (Eds.) (2014). *International handbook of emotions in education.* New York, NY: Routledge, Taylor and Francis Group.

Carrera, M., DePalma, R., & Lameiras, M. (2011). Toward a more comprehensive understanding of bullying in school settings. *Educational Psychology Review, 23*(4), 479–499.

Charney, R. (2002). *Teaching children to care* (2nd ed.). Greenfield, MA: Northeast Foundation for Children.

Dweck, C. (2006) *Mindset: The new psychology of success.* New York, NY: Ballantine.

Elias, M., Zins, J., Weissberg, R., Frey, K., Greenberg, M., Haynes, N., Kessler, R., Schwab-Stone, M., & Shriver, T. (1997). *Promoting social and emotional learning: Guidelines for educators.* Alexandria, VA: Association for Supervision and Curriculum Development.

Evans, W., Evans, S., & Schmid, R. (1993). *Behavior and instructional management: An ecological approach.* Boston, MA: Allyn & Bacon.

Gibbs, J. (2001). *Tribes: A new way of learning and being together.* Windsor, CA: Center Source.

Ginot, H. (1972). *Teacher and child.* New York, NY: Avon.

Goleman, D. (1995). *Emotional intelligence.* New York, NY: Bantam Books.

Goleman, D. (1996). On emotional intelligence: A conversation with Daniel Goleman. *Education leadership*, *53*(1), 6–11.

Goleman, D. (1998). *Working with emotional intelligence*. New York, NY: Bantam Books.

Goleman, D. (2006). *Social intelligence: The new science of human relationships*. New York, NY: Random House.

Goleman, D. (2017). The most fundamental discovery of this new science: We are wired to connect. Retrieved from http://www.danielgoleman.info/topics/social-intelligence/2017/

Grove, B. (2003). *Children who see too much*. Boston, MA: Beacon Press.

Henley, M. (2006). *Classroom management: A proactive approach*. Boston, MA: Pearson.

Henderson, N. (2007). *Resiliency in action: Practical ideas for overcoming risks and building strengths in youth, families and communities*. Solvang, CA: Resiliency in Action.

Jensen, E. (2010). Different brains, different learners. San Diego, CA: Corwin.

Jensen, E. (2013). *Engaging students with poverty in mind*. Alexandria, VA: Association for Supervision and Curriculum Development.

Jensen, E. (2016). Poor students, rich teaching; mindsets for change—raising achievement for youth at risk. Bloomington, IN: Solution Tree Press.

Jensen, E., & Snider, C. (2013). *Turnaround tools for the teenage brain: Helping underperforming students become lifelong learners*. New York, NY: John Wiley & Sons.

Lelli, C. (2014, July–September). Strategies to help the traumatized student in school. *Kappa Delta Pi Record 50*(3), 114–118.

Noddings, N. (2005). *The challenge to care in schools* (2nd ed.). New York, NY: Teachers College Press.

Payne, R. (2008, April). Poverty and learning: Nine powerful practices. *Educational Leadership, 65*(7), 48–52.

Redl, C., & Wineman, D. (1951). *Children who hate: The disorganization and breakdown of behavior controls*. New York, NY: Free Press.

Souers, K., & Hall, P. (2016). *Fostering resilient learners: Strategies for creating a trauma-sensitive classroom*. Alexandria, VA: Association for Supervision and Curriculum Development.

Sturato, C., van Lier, P., Cuijpers, P., & Koot, H. (2011, May/June). The role of peer relationships in the development of early school-age externalizing problems. *Child Development, 82*(3), 758–765.

Yeager, D., & Walton, G. (2011). Social-psychological interventions in education: They're not magic. *Review of Educational Research, 81*(2), 267–301.

ESTABLISHING AND SUSTAINING A COMMUNITY OF LEARNERS

We do not believe in ourselves until someone reveals that deep inside us is valuable, worth listening to, worthy of our trust. ...Once we believe in ourselves, we can risk curiosity, wonder, spontaneous delight, or any experience that reveals the human spirit.

—e. e. cummings

If any student is to develop constructive behavior—behavior that supports the student's growth and learning and that contributes to the community of which the student is a member—then as teachers we need to meet the student's basic emotional needs and provide the student a balance of structure and nurturance. A powerful overarching strategy to nurturing and providing structure for appropriate behavior is the establishment of a learning community. In the next chapters, we will address how we establish and maintain this community using our ecological approach. We will consider how we address variables in all three of students' environments. Note: While as teachers we *do* have access to the variables in students' physical and psychosocial environment variables, we *do not* have direct access to their physiological variables. Therefore, even when we address these internal variables (such as supporting students' discovering their learning styles and needs), we will utilize strategies that exist in the students' psychosocial and physical environments.

CHAPTER 5

Designing a Classroom and Our Instruction Within

Design is not just what it looks like and feels like. Design is how it works.

—Steve Jobs

What Will This Chapter Discuss?

We focus on the ways competent, caring teachers can create a productive learning environment. As teachers, we need to create a physical environment that provides structure and nurturing through the arrangement of our rooms and our choices about their contents. We also need to create an interpersonal (psychosocial) environment that provides structure and nurtures students. We do this through the connections we create as we establish a sense of community. We begin *our* work *before* school begins. Our focus is on the arrangement of elements in the room, our choices about the nature of the contents, and our design of learning experiences for our students

Why Is This Important?

The research is clear. Being proactive distinguishes effective teachers from less effective ones (Emmer & Evertson, 2017; Evertson & Emmer, 2017; Evertson & Weinstein, 2006; Jones, 2015; Jones & Jones, 2016). A few weeks of investing in establishing a constructive learning environment is worth months of reacting to unconstructive behavior. Success is the most effective, efficient teacher. From the start of our work with students, we want to empower them to be successful with constructive behavior.

Being proactive means we begin even before students arrive. We arrange the physical environment variables—the furniture, equipment, materials, displays—in such a way that they guide constructive behavior. Being proactive means we start, on the very first day, to create a community of learners. To do this effectively, we use variables in both the physical and psychosocial environments to meet all five basic emotional needs. We nurture students and their connections (to us and to each other) to create a learning community that is safe and caring and that fosters a feeling of belonging and well-being. We provide structure by setting expectations for student behavior with the students and then teaching or reviewing the skills and procedures needed to meet those expectations. All of these elements empower students to contribute constructively to the work of the community and to feel that they can expand their capacities well beyond where they are at the moment.

> Feeling valued, cared for, and supported by others in a community is a positive motivating force that promotes attachment to the group and commitment to school, motivation to engage in learning tasks, and value for learning. The support, encouragement identification, and commitment engendered by a caring school benefits all students, but especially to [sic] those who do not get much support outside of school. Community benefits all students, but especially to [sic] those who do not get much support outside of school.
>
> —Good & Brophy (2008)

What Will You Learn?

By the end of the chapter, you will be able to:

- ✦ design a room and its contents to foster constructive behavior;
- ✦ design a room to create a nurturing learning community;
- ✦ design structured learning experiences that nurture students;
- ✦ design interactions with students that provide structure and nurture constructive behavior; and
- ✦ cultivate awareness of a teacher mindset that continually fosters a classroom community.

What Do You Want To Accomplish?

What would you like to learn about designing rooms and designing instruction? Write your responses here or on a piece of paper. _____

_____

_____

_____

How Do We Design a Room to Foster Constructive Behavior?

We Ask Essential Questions

When planning room design, we ask: What are the goals of the curriculum? What kinds of learning activities will support students' reaching these goals? How often will there be individual, small group, and whole class work? Where will these take place in the room? Where and how will print and other visual information such as PowerPoints, videos, displays, and posters be provided? What technology will be used to support learning? Given the answers to these questions, how do the furniture, equipment, and displays need to be arranged to support the nature of the teaching and learning that will occur?

There are Five Considerations for Successful Room Arrangement

In Chapter 3, we addressed four considerations for a room arrangement that can provide structure through establishing expectations and nurture students by addressing their learning needs. These considerations are accessibility, visibility, minimization of distractibility, and proximity. We will examine these in greater detail and add a fifth—placement of adjacent areas (Barrett, Zhang, Moffat, & Kobbacy, 2013; Emmer & Evertson, 2017; Evertson & Emmer, 2017; Evertson, Poole, & the IRIS Center, 2002; Marzano, 2017; Saphier, Haley-Spec, & Gowen, 2008; Scott, 2017).

Accessibility of High-Traffic Areas Is One Consideration

Classrooms have more people per square foot than most other learning and working places. The potential for congestion is huge. Tight spaces increase physical contact and the possibility of tension between students. The degree to which we can minimize this potential right from the start will support constructive behavior.

If their behavior is to be constructive and their learning and basic needs are to be met, students need easy access to their materials, a water fountain, the pencil sharpener, the waste basket(s), books, etc. Accessibility has two elements: ease in getting to high-traffic areas and, once there, ease in securing what is needed. As we set up our rooms, we need to think about the route to supplies, cubbies/lockers—all the high-traffic areas. Is there a clear path for any student to get where she needs to go from wherever she is sitting *without* disrupting other students or their learning? Is there sufficient space in each of these areas, meaning is there enough room for more than one student at a time to easily get what is needed without the conflict that can invite unconstructive behavior? When accessibility is thwarted because certain supplies are limited, we need to develop a fair system for providing materials in a timely manner to all who need them so that students do not compete to get what they need for the projects on which they are working.

> Tip: To enhance accessibility, remove unnecessary equipment or furniture.

At the same time that we are planning access, we need to consider areas of the room or materials and equipment to which there should *not* be access. We can be proactive about preventing some problems simply by considering how the room design will appropriately limit accessibility. Are there places we don't want students to get to? Are there paths we do not want them to take? Are there pieces of equipment or materials that are fragile, confidential, or used only for a particular activity? Are there limited amounts of certain supplies or equipment that we need to distribute rather than having them available on a "first come, first served" basis? Where can we keep things safe and avoid tempting the students to try to use them?

One way to enhance success when considering accessibility is to draw a simple floor plan—an outline of all the furniture in the room, as close to scale as possible. The goal is to be able to see the relationship among objects without spending inordinate amounts of time on measurements. I find graph paper helps me to do this. Once all the pieces in the floor plan are in place, we can look at where open space occurs. Does the design foster the movements of the students in and out of the room and to high-traffic areas like resource books, the "homework bin," etc.? Does the arrangement keep traffic from flowing to areas where students should *not* be—such as near your personal supply drawers or cabinets?

Visibility of Lesson Foci is a Second Consideration

Teachers need to be able to see all students. Students need to see the teacher as well as all other people and materials that are important in the learning experience. Given the room arrangement, can the teacher see all of the students at any time, no matter where each is located in the room? We often joke about teachers having eyes in the backs of their heads. However, being able to see everyone maximizes our ability to be proactive about addressing needs wherever they arise (and sometimes even to anticipate them before they arise) anywhere in the classroom. For students, being able to see the teacher and to know the teacher can see every student provides an important source of structure. The students realize whatever they are doing can be noticed by the teacher.

There are many objects—sources of print material, fixtures, etc.—that people need to be able to look at in any classroom to meet students' learning needs. The key questions for visibility are: Who can see what, when? If we want to direct students' attention to a particular focus—a display, the steps in a procedure, or a person's face—can this be readily accomplished? Are the key ongoing displays easy to see, and can students, thereby, readily refer to the class rules, the goals for the lesson, calendars of homework assignments, reviews of procedures, or key curriculum elements such as mathematical algorithms or grammar rules? Can all students see the steps for emergency procedures?

> **Tip:** To increase space for postings to provide important visual information in locations where students can readily view it, we can close a portion of the blinds and use those as backdrops for what we want to post.

I find it helpful to create a plan of the walls in any room I teach to figure out the best choices for posting material. I consider not only where in the room I will place the materials but also the distance from the floor and the size of words. This is essential for those displays that students need to see all the time (e.g., emergency procedures, assignment deadlines).

While bookshelves, file cabinets, and other large pieces of furniture or equipment are needed in most classrooms, we have to give careful thought to the placement of tall items. While cordoning off one or more portions of the room for specific activities can be a helpful use of physical environment variables, where we place these is important to consider. Their location cannot obstruct the various foci of learning—a projection site, the teacher's face, the faces of students. Imagine an amphitheater setup (whether the floor is flat or graduated) with all tall items placed against the walls. Students can see the whiteboard/projection site and anyone speaking in the front of the room, but can students readily see each other when they are contributing to a discussion or asking questions? If they cannot, how will this affect their focus on others during the lesson, and how will the possible lack of focus affect those speaking? If students cannot see each other's faces, how will this meet the learning needs of those whose hearing is enhanced by lip-reading (e.g., English-language learners and students with either hearing disabilities or auditory processing difficulties)?

> **Tip:** Because students sitting in their chairs are much shorter than we are as teachers when we stand, it is easy to lose track of what can be seen in the room and what cannot. Our sitting in various chairs and looking full circle around the room provides us a student's-eye view of what is visible and what is not.

Proximity of Students and Teacher is the Third Consideration

When we consider proximity, the goal is for us to be readily able to reach students and for them to be able to reach us easily. We do not need to be close to each student; we need to be able to get to each, and each student needs to be able to get to us. As we noted in Chapter 3, what makes this possible is the fewest barriers and the least distance between the teacher and each student and between each student and the teacher—no matter where students and we are in the room. This allows us to monitor learning and step in to support or redirect and thus nurture students and provide structure for their behavior, if need be. At the same time, if we can be readily reached when needed by a student, our ability to clarify, to cheer on a student's efforts, to provide any kind of support and, thereby, nurture students, is possible.

On the other hand, if we cluster desks in groups of more than four or if desks are placed in rows with limited space in between those that are side by side, this can diminish the capacity for proximity. Such arrangements make it harder for students to circumnavigate the desks to reach us and also for us to reach them to provide support and feedback and to respond on the spot to what might be moving towards inappropriate unconstructive behavior. (We will address many ways we can respond on the spot in a later chapter.)

Eliminating Distractions is the Fourth Consideration

The information pathways in the room—both sight and sound—need to be clear between student and instructional foci (including key people). We have already addressed the need for students to see the foci of learning. Anything that distracts them from that impedes learning and can contribute to unconstructive behavior. Different students find different people, noises, sights, and sounds distracting. We may not be able to eliminate all distractions for all students; however, we can diminish many. We need to be sure, for example, that displays (such as those hanging from the ceiling or lights) are not in students' line of sight; that the door can be readily closed when others are passing by; that shades can be drawn when cars in a nearby parking lot reflect glare from the sun; and that the windows can be closed when the class is adjacent to a parking lot or playground from which noise can be a source of distraction. We can also locate individual and group work areas away from computer screens to diminish having those colorful images and sounds (if there are no headphones) divert students' attention when they are not using the computers.

Variables such as public address announcements and other interruptions by adults need to be controlled so their intrusion on learning is minimal. In a middle school where I worked, the teachers asked to have intercom announcements limited to the few minutes before the first class began and the last few minutes after the last class. These teachers worked with administrators to rearrange their class schedule to ensure that those who needed to make announcements would have the time to do so, but that instruction would be minimally affected.

Variables such as heating, lighting, and ventilation need to be manipulated (to the extent possible) *to provide choices* for students. We can supplement the often-present fluorescent lights with floor and desk lamps to offer incandescent lighting alternatives. Huge pillows and director's chairs (or other kinds of chairs) added to rooms can provide different *choices* for seating during various learning experiences. We can offer carrels for students to

> **Tip:** As teachers, if we do a lot of standing up and walking around, the heat—as it naturally rises in the room—warms the upper portion of our bodies, whereas students, particularly younger ones whose bodies are closer to the floor of the room, will have the cooler air around them. We may feel warmer than the students and need to remember this as we consider adjusting the temperature.

put on their tables/desks to provide a sense of greater solitude and possibly diminish visual distractions when working on individual tasks. Students can be encouraged to wear clothing in layers so that they can adjust their warmth to respond to various heat levels in different sections of the room or to weather changes. If permitted by school rules, students can have water bottles at their desks and be given time for snacks that don't disrupt learning. We can set up stations where white noise or quiet, calm classical music can be available for those who need it to diminish the distracting ambient noise in a room.

Sights and sounds are not the only distractions. We need to think about smells that could distract. Is the room close to the cafeteria or grass that gives off its own "perfume" when being cut? Close to the bus loading area where the diesel fumes can drift into the room? Do some of the adults who work with the students wear cologne that may irritate nostrils? What do we need to do to minimize students' attention being drawn away by these smells? Can we find a place or two where we can safely place a fan or two to cool the room's air while windows are closed? Can we be sure nothing is in the way so we can easily close the door when we can anticipate noise in the hallway? We can ask other adults to limit their use of perfume and aftershave/cologne to support the students' learning need to not be distracted.

I find all these considerations important enough that before each class I teach in a room shared with other teachers, I take a few minutes to arrange the furniture in a U so all students can see all foci of learning, and so I consistently send them a message that we are all learning together—each has something to offer. I close the windows and blinds so distractions, including glare on the board, are minimized. (If I forget, a student will raise a hand to ask that I do. While I am grateful the request is made, it creates a pause in the lesson that I prefer to avoid.) I place materials we will need in class on the students' desks. I write the agenda on the board, along with the title under which I will write assignments throughout the class session. I set up the projection devices so they are ready on the spot. I find these steps so important to the success of the class that I often make myself a written list (which I attach to my lesson notes) of what I need to do that might be unique to a given lesson beyond the everyday steps for getting ready.

Appropriate Placement of Adjacent Areas is the Final Consideration

A final aspect of room arrangement to be considered is which areas are placed adjacent to others. Are safety rules posted near where they need to be applied and at a level that matches the sight line of the students? Is electrical equipment housed and used in areas as far away from water as possible to ensure student (and equipment) safety? Are activity areas near where the supplies of needed materials are located, and are areas where students need to talk of sufficient distance from where other students will need relative quiet to proceed successfully? Some of these questions may seem obvious, but teaching is complex. We may be so busy focusing on one aspect of the room that we forget another variable that needs to be considered.

REFLECTION OPPORTUNITY

Consider students with whom you have worked or are currently working. In the space provided below or on a separate piece of paper describe one way you can use room arrangement variables to nurture those students. Then describe one way you can use room contents to nurture those students by addressing their learning needs. _____

_____

_____

_____

_____

How Can We Design a Room to Nurture Students?

We nurture students by creating a learning community. In Chapter 7, we will address how a sense of community of learners can be built through our instructional strategies. However, before the students arrive, there are aspects of room arrangement that we can address (Emmer & Evertson, 2017; Evertson & Emmer, 2017; Evertson, Poole, & the IRIS Center, 2002). How we arrange desks or tables where the students do much of their work sends strong messages to students as soon as they walk in the room. Many classrooms use rows or an amphitheater design. Either communicates that the teacher is the expert and that students' knowledge is of lesser value, as is their contribution. To nurture students—to establish a community in which all feel that each contributes—we need a different design.

In contrast to rows of desks, consider what message a U design sends to students: "We are all in this together. Each of us can contribute. We are all valued. When one of us speaks, others can see that person (addressed under 'Visibility' above) and will be more readily able to hear that person." The learning experience is shared.

We Use Flexible Seating Arrangements that Support Students' Needs

With chairs that can be lifted and desk/tables that move students can shift the furniture into a U shape (or any other configuration) when appropriate. Flexibility allows the U design needed for whole class work while enabling the shift in seating students need when working in groups teams so that each can see all other students with whom she is working. The Johnsons call this KKEE, or knee-to-knee, eye-to-eye (Johnson, Johnson, & Johnson Holubec, 1994). KKEE enables students' need to be close enough to others in their group to share ideas and materials while being far enough from other groups to minimize distractions. Sufficient distance between groups also encourages each group to do its own thinking rather than being swayed by the ideas heard from an adjacent group. The ideal arrangement of desks/tables must be such that teachers or students can change grouping configuration quickly and quietly. Because there are times when collaboration will mean shifting from working in pairs to working in a team of four or five to working alone (all in the space of 30 minutes), flexible arrangements that maximize possibilities for seating configurations are essential.

Platform: Application Opportunity

In this active-learning platform, you'll have an opportunity to apply all the ideas we have addressed to design the ideal classroom for you and the children you will teach.

How Can We Use Room Content Variables to Provide Structure?

Keep in mind that feeling safe and valued, feeling that you belong, and understanding and enjoying activities and learning are the basic student needs to think about when planning room content variables. Below are guidelines that help ensure a classroom meets these needs.

We Post Rules

In Chapter 3, we said that competent, caring, and empowering teachers establish expectations for constructive behavior *with* community members. Room contents also ought to reflect this joint effort; therefore, as soon as we create rules with students, we need to post rules in a location that everyone can readily see to provide structure in the form of reminders about behavior expectations. If students are not able to read, we need to use symbols, icons, or pictures that illustrate the ideas. Note: We will talk more about how we develop rules with students in Chapter 6.

We Use Signage

Signs and/or pictures that label key room sections, such as "Library," "Math Lab," or "Writer's Workshop Publication Site," provide cues for expected activities/behavior. Note: If students are emergent readers or learning English as a second language, our signs include illustrations in the form of icons, photos, or pictures cut from a magazine or obtained from the Internet.

We Post Assignments and Due Dates

Usually a particular corner of the whiteboard, bulletin board, or website for the class is a useful location for posting assignment details in a consistent fashion within view of any student.

We Post Process and Product Expectations

We create (or invite students to create) posters and signs that signal process or product expectations, such as the COPS or Ten Solution Strategies illustrated previously. As with posted assignments, a consistent location for these expectations is needed.

We Thoughtfully Arrange Equipment and Materials

The contents of a classroom need to be configured to signal the behavior that would be appropriate. If we want students to carry out a particular activity in any section of the room, we arrange the equipment and materials in a way that invites students to carry out that learning experience and facilitates their being efficacious as they do it. Examples: If we want them to research information, then by arranging a number of resource books alongside a computer, tablet, Chromebook, or iPad with a stack of note-size cards, pencils and pens in containers, and a series of engaging questions posted in plain sight, we are "stating" our expectation: "Research is done here." If we place a container with a variety of pens, pencils, markers, and packets of various kinds of paper on a table with a few examples of what might be done with the materials, then we are making it clear that in this part of the room we expect that students will design and make an illustration and/or a cover for a writing piece.

How Can We Make Content Arrangement Choices in a Shared Room?

There are alternatives for addressing the use of space: integration, parallel use, or division by some manner. If we use the same room for a number of different learning communities, we have a conversation with *each* class and build a fair degree of consensus on the general design of the room, including how to parcel out various aspects of the room. If we share the room with another teacher, then the conversation includes the needs of the students in her classes. Whosever needs we are addressing, we decide where rules, process and product expectations, and assignments with due dates will go and provide a heading for each with the class or teacher's name. To address the arrangement of displays, we can have a space allotted for each class—a bulletin board, a poster display space on the wall, an exhibit space or shelf—or we can rotate access to portions of the room: one month, Classes 1 and 3 divide the allotted space; next month, Classes 2 and 4; and so on.

If we design a room and arrange its contents in ways that match students' needs and readily facilitates their learning, they have every reason to behave constructively.

How Can We Design Learning Experiences to Provide Structure and Nurturing?

As we get ready for the new class to arrive, we need to plan the learning experiences we will share with the students during the first week or a bit later. Planning ahead for the early days with a new community of students takes careful consideration. We want to keep in mind how the brain functions so we can match our design elements to the latest research. We also want to be sure we provide structure for the students' learning—a path for their brains through the learning experience. We want to nurture their well-being—give them a sense that they are safe, we care about them and their learning, they belong in this class with others, they are a welcomed part of this community, they are competent individuals, and there is enjoyment to be had in the learning that is going on. In any lesson, safety and efficacy must be felt, and no other needs can be thwarted by the content or processes. We may not be able to touch on all the basic needs in each lesson, but over a series of lessons, all five needs must be addressed.

ACCESS PRIOR KNOWLEDGE/EXPERIENCE

Think back on a teacher you had that you found boring. When he was, what did he do, or what did he not do that you found boring? _____

_____

_____

Clearly, none of us wants to be boring. What can we do to avoid this? In the last fifteen years, we have learned a great deal about brain functioning and how to foster learning (Ambrose, Bridges, DiPietro, Lovett, Norman, & Meyers, 2010; American Psychological Association, n.d.; Armstrong, 2016; Center for Educational Research and Innovation, 2008; Hinton, Miyamoto, & Della-Chiesa, 2008; Jensen, 2013, 2015a, 2015b; Johnson, 2011; Semrud-Clikeman, n.d.; Sousa & Tomlinson, 2011; Willis, 2006). Given this information and our desire to nurture and to provide structure, we consider three parts of a lesson. The beginning is designed to engage and prepare students emotionally and cognitively to learn the material, to achieve the cognitive and social objectives. The middle fosters processing and understanding of the material. The final portion facilitates summarization and retention of what was learned. Note: As you read about the lesson structure, you will find that the ideas of Madeline Hunter (M. Hunter, 2004; R. Hunter, 2014) and Charlotte Danielson (2007; n.d.) are integrated within. Actual written lesson plan structures in use will vary from one teacher preparation program to another and from one school district to another.

We Ready Students for Learning

Given what we know about how brains function as well as what we have learned (in the first weeks, our learning curve about our students is sharp, indeed) about the variables in our students' physiological environments—their learning needs, their talents and interests—we choose processes that will "prime" their brains and activate their desire to learn. We set the focus—where we are headed in this lesson; we use an anticipatory set to give the students an enticing preview of what is to come in the lesson (R. Hunter, 2014; M. Hunter, 2004); we provide an advance organizer—the path we will take to get there; we provide a motivator to grab the students' attention and stimulate their desire to go on the learning adventure with us (e.g., show materials that whet their curiosity; pose a dilemma); we set the purpose/meaning—why this destination (e.g., suggest usefulness of concept/skill; connect the focus to students' lives). We also access prior knowledge to gather and refine students' previous information about this concept or skill and to get the dendrites in their brains receptive to new information.

Note: The particular order of these components is not crucial. What is essential is that all are included in the launch of the lesson.

We Foster the Processing of Material

Hopefully, we have engaged the students in the learning journey, the route is established, and their dendrites are "ready to roll." Now we state goals for comprehension or expectations for the lesson outcomes, including social skills or other behavior (i.e., tell students what they can hope to accomplish by the time they reach the destination goal[s]) and thereby give their brains another bit of structure to organize what is about to be learned; we tell them how they will demonstrate the concept or skill—what the end product will look like or sound like. Then we provide a means of achieving the goals according to the nature of what is to be learned. Whether we are teaching a concept or a skill, we provide clear explanations at a level the students can grasp.

If we are teaching a concept, after we have prepared students in the first portion of the lesson by fostering their recall, we associate new information with what they already know. We organize the conceptual information to create a meaningful pattern. To do this, we actively engage students in constructing knowledge of the concept (e.g., invite students to refine predictions; intersperse a variety of questions; provide opportunities for dialogue between us and students and among students about ideas or consideration of skills/processes; facilitate the students' revision of predictions and confirm/disconfirm in a nonjudgmental manner). We represent or invite students to represent the concept(s) in a way to be remembered, and we provide opportunities for students to experiment with/analyze the concept.

On the other hand, if we are teaching a skill, after we foster recall in the preparation stage and build this skill on what students already know, we develop a model for the process, demonstrate, and provide guided practice with constructive feedback. If appropriate, we also review or teach vocabulary within the context in which it is used. We ask questions that invite more than rote recall.

We check for understanding beyond asking "Do you understand?" or "Do you have any questions?"

We Facilitate Student Retention and Transfer

We provide the students an opportunity to summarize orally, in writing, or by drawing a visual illustration. We may offer an opportunity to generalize to new examples or apply in different contexts; if not, we do that within the next lesson(s). We also offer a means to reflect on and evaluate work.

We Include Other Elements Throughout the Lesson

We also give clear directions—orally and visually—in appropriate chunks because we know directions are an essential form of structure. Our clarity extends to the directions we provide to foster students' behavior though transitions from one portion of the lesson to the next, to a new activity, to the next lesson.

We Assess What Was Learned

We also offer ourselves a means of evaluation and reflection. If we have designed an effective lesson, the objective(s) could be assessed within or by the end of the lesson. As we assess our work to determine to what degree we provided an effective lesson, we ask, "To what degree could the objective(s) be assessed within or by the end of the lesson, and to what degree did each student meet those learning objectives?" A checklist for supporting our including all the essential pieces in a lesson is provided at the end of the chapter in Appendix A, Table 5-2.

If we include these elements of an effective learning experience in each of our lessons, not only do we foster students' learning; we also prevent nearly all unconstructive behavior from occurring. Engaged students whose learning is facilitated have little to no reason to behave in other than constructive ways.

REFLECTION OPPORTUNITY

Think of a lesson you have taught or might teach. On a separate piece of paper or in the space provided describe how the design of the learning experience might provide structure (a path through the learning process and clear cues about appropriate behavior) and nurturance for students through meeting their basic needs with the strategies you choose to ready students for the learning experience, to foster their active engagement in processing the content, and to support their summarizing of the lesson. _____

_____

_____

_____

_____

How Can We Use Instructional Content to Provide Structure and Nurturing?

The content of the learning experiences we create is as important as the design of the lesson pieces. We can nurture students during the first days of school by including key topics that address their emotional needs and their concerns, that build community, and that establish expectations for their behavior and for procedures—in both academics and the running of the class (Armstrong, 2016; Brooks, email newsletter, September 1, 2004; Charney, 2002; Jensen, 2013; Noddings, 2005; Souers & Hall, 2016).

REFLECTION OPPORTUNITY

Think back to the most recent time that you first entered a classroom. What questions did you have? Write your answer in the space provided or on a separate piece of paper. _____

_____

_____

_____

Below are a few examples of the key things students often want to know:

+ Am I in the right place?
+ Where should I sit?
+ What will the teacher be like?
+ Will I like my teacher?
+ What am I supposed to do in this class?

We Integrate Lesson Topics that Help Establish Expectations and Build Community

Appropriate lesson topics will often depend on the students' development levels. In addition, while some topics can easily be covered in a couple of lessons with guided practice, other topics will need more time. As you look at the list of potential topics below, consider their appropriateness for different developmental levels and the length of time you think each topic would require.

+ Procedures for daily running of the class (e.g., attendance, use of bathrooms, lunch count, jobs assignment and how each is carried out)

- Getting-acquainted processes
- Materials procedures: how and when pencils get sharpened; what other materials are available to be gotten when needed; what materials are for teacher use only
- Safety procedures (e.g., fire, lockdown, severe weather alerts)
- Procedures for moving in the room: how to enter and leave; how to move about room while minimizing disruptions
- Procedures for moving about the school: how to move through the hallway (elementary); how to go to the nurse, library (passes or notes needed, if any; nature of walking, etc.) and what to do once you get there
- How to gain teacher attention during whole class work, small-group work, or when the teacher is working with an individual student
- Academic procedures (e.g., who can get what materials where and when; where work goes when completed)
- Assessment activities to identify how students learn and what students know/remember
- Review of concepts and skills from previous class/year on which to build
- Preview of the key topics and skills that will be addressed—at least initially—during the class

If we are to create a climate in which constructive behavior and learning can flourish, in the early days the major focus needs to be on building all aspects of the community, assessing current skills and concepts, and reviewing essential previous learning. After that, the students are ready for us to preview the learning ahead.

We nurture students through the lesson content. We take advantage of the opportunity the first days (and the weeks beyond) offer us to provide learning experiences that connect the community members to each other and to us. This will help students be more involved in their own education, more motivated to learn, and more capable of coping with their frustrations (Armstrong, 2016; Brooks, email newsletter, September 1, 2004; Charney, 2002; Jensen, 2013; Noddings, 2005; Souers & Hall, 2016).

We provide structure for students through our lesson content. They need to know the standards for behavior—procedures and rules. If they do not know how to carry out procedures, or if they have been told the rules but not participated in the development of them, they may not be clear about what is expected, or they may not be as likely to "buy into" the standards. Unconstructive behavior is more likely to occur (Armstrong, 2016; Emmer & Evertson, 2017; Evertson & Emmer, 2017; Jones, 2015; Jones & Jones, 2016).

We Use Those First Days to Gather Assessment Information

This information enables us to choose the content level of learning experiences to match students' development of concepts and skills, as well as their strengths and talents, thereby facilitating their success. Note: Specific ideas for how to build connections, how to establish rules and procedures with the students, and how to gather assessment information on students' learning needs and talents are provided in Chapter 6's content and appendices.

REFLECTION OPPORTUNITY

On a separate piece of paper or in the space provided describe how the content of a lesson can provide structure and how the content can nurture students. _____

_____

_____

_____

How Can We Design Our Interactions to Provide Structure and Nurturance?

We Understand the Role of Cues or Triggers

Behavior—unconstructive or constructive—does not occur randomly. It is always triggered or cued by something internal or external. Behaviorists call these antecedent conditions, antecedent events, or setting events (Alberto & Troutman, 2013; Shea & Bauer, 2011; Wolfgang, 2009). If we want to foster *constructive* behavior, we need to create antecedent conditions *that cue the specific behavior we hope to facilitate.* We can do this within a lesson. We also do this when we interact informally with students. Note: We have more control over some cues than others. As we consider kinds of cues, over which do you think we have more control?

Students continually receive external and internal cues. *External* conditions cue students through the five senses in the physical and psychological environments: a) verbal cues ("For this part of the activity, raise your hands and wait to be addressed before responding."); b) physical cues (a gentle tap under the upper arm to suggest that the arm needs to be raised); c) visual cues (written directions, invitations, or signs, such as "Science Area" and "3 People Only"; symbols, such as icons on a communication board or poster that inform students about what is expected); d) smells (coming from food being prepared in the cafeteria or car/truck fumes from the road below); e) sounds (music, class change buzzers, PA announcements); f) sensations (warmth from a radiator). *Internal* conditions cue students through what they experience in their physiological environment, such as hunger pangs, tiredness, an itch, and feelings, such as remorse, frustration, delight, or curiosity. Over which of these cues do you think we as teachers have more control?

Note: What triggers one student's behavior may not work for another.

Of the two types of antecedent conditions, internal cues are the ones that we as teachers have the least power to manipulate. Therefore, we will focus on external cues we can control. There are many. We can specifically cue a constructive behavior through what we say in conversation and when we give verbal and written directions in a lesson. We can arrange variables in the student's physical environment beyond our instructional strategies (e.g., equipment, furniture, posters, signs). We can also arrange variables in the student's psychosocial environment. For example, we can choose with whom the student works to provide peer cues that can foster constructive behavior. Should these cues not be effective, we can provide additional prompts for the student to support success in exhibiting the constructive behavior.

We Maximize the Power of Effective Cues

✦ If we want a behavior to happen (e.g., moving quietly and safely to the next station in the lesson), then, much like any other skill, we provide the direction (cue) each time the behavior is needed until the behavior becomes a learned habit. Then we need to provide the cue periodically to maintain the behavior in the student's repertoire.

✦ We provide the cue close in time to when the student behavior is needed. If our cue isn't in close proximity to the needed behavior, then all sorts of other cues in the students' internal and external environment will trigger other behavior instead.

✦ We provide a cue that works *for the student(s)*. We avoid stating a direction when students are chatting because they may not differentiate our voice from others'. We avoid using just a spoken cue because many students will not retain it if their learning styles/needs are attuned to focusing on and remembering visual directions instead.

We Understand the Role of Consequences

There is another set of conditions we can facilitate from Day 1. These occur after a behavior we want to foster. Behaviorists (Alberto & Troutman, 2017; Shea & Bauer, 2011; Wolfgang, 2009) call these consequent events or consequent conditions because, as the word 'consequent' suggests, these occur as a result of the behavior. When we want to foster a student behavior to happen more than once, not only do we need to cue it in advance (as we said above); the student must see some value in the behavior—must derive some pleasure, satisfaction, or sense of well-being from doing the behavior—or the likelihood of it happening again is minimal and there is no chance of its becoming a habit. Therefore, we orchestrate what occurs afterwards *close in time* so the student perceives that her action brings about a pleasant change—a "reinforcer," as the behaviorists call it—in at least one of her environments. If the consequence does not occur quite soon after her behavior, she won't connect the two into a cause–effect memory pattern. No pattern perceived; no habit learned. Then, we need to be sure some reinforcement is available thereafter to maintain the behavior in the student's repertoire.

We Maximize the Power of Constructive Consequences

We have two ways to ensure that something positive occurs following a constructive behavior. We can: 1) be sure something occurs that is pleasant *from the student's perspective* and seems connected to the constructive behavior she has just exhibited (what behaviorists call positive reinforcement because something pleasant is added); or 2) remove something unpleasant *for the student close in time to* and as *a result of* the constructive action (called negative reinforcement because something is taken away, yet the result is pleasant). I say "for the student" or "from the student's perspective" because a reinforcer does not work unless the student perceives it as pleasant and an effect of her action. This close timing enhances the "cause–effect" relationship in the student's mind. Two warnings: We can make the mistake of assuming that what we *think* would be positive is actually not positive for the student, and we can arrange to have the possible pleasant consequence occur too long after the behavior. We need to be observant about the effects of what we think might be reinforcing and its timing to determine if it is actually working.

As we consider facilitating constructive behavior through the effects of consequences, we need to be wary of misusing particular words that can to trip up people. Positive reinforcement is called positive not because the result is pleasant for the person who exhibited the action (that is the reinforcement part of the term) but because something has been added. I am helped by thinking of the plus sign we use to indicate we are adding something. The plus sign (+) is a "positive" sign. On the other hand, if something unpleasant is removed (as a consequent event), behaviorists use the term "negative (for something taken away) reinforcement" because its result is pleasant, so the behavior is likely to happen again under similar circumstances. This consequent condition is *not* punishment, because the effect is pleasant. I am helped to remember that "negative" isn't the effect on the student; it is the direction of what happened as a result of the behavior—something was removed—*just like the minus sign (–)*, the *negative* sign in mathematics, can mean something is taken away or removed. Example: Berenise sat next to two other girls in her class to watch a video she wanted to see. One girl constantly whispered loudly enough that Berenise couldn't hear the dialogue. Berenise quietly got up and moved to a seat where her surroundings were sufficiently quiet that she could hear what was going on. The cue was the whispering and, with it, not being able to hear the video. The action was moving her location. The negative reinforcement was the *removing of the unpleasant* whispering so Berenise could accomplish what she wanted—hearing the video, which was something pleasurable for her. Under similar circumstances, Berenise is likely to shift seats because she has been negatively reinforced, so she feels good (efficacious) about what she did. She was not punished, because her behavior allowed her to experience hearing the video—something she wanted.

Another important cause—effect relationship we keep in mind is that cues and consequence can also decrease the likelihood that a behavior will occur in the future. If we do *not* want a behavior to occur, we eliminate (or at least greatly diminish) the cue/antecedent and the pleasant consequence the student experiences (reinforcement). One of the most effective ways to begin to eliminate unconstructive behavior is to avoid having it triggered in the first place. As teachers, we cannot control all triggers—some because we don't expect them to occur and others because they are internal triggers that are beyond our control. However, there are many moments in a class when we can control the triggers to an unconstructive behavior. If we try in advance to eliminate these and we make sure there are cues for constructive behavior that are even stronger than the cues for possible unconstructive behavior, we start moving towards decreasing unconstructive behavior while simultaneously fostering constructive behavior.

A particularly effective way to begin to eliminate unconstructive behavior is to avoid having it reinforced in the first place. Punishing events that occur right after a behavior decrease the likelihood that the behavior will occur in the future. There are two subcategories of punishment, just as there were two subcategories of reinforcement. In one subcategory of punishment, something "yucky" or unpleasant to the student occurs quite soon after an unconstructive behavior. This is called positive (for something being added) punishment (because it was unpleasant for the student and, thereby, discourages the behavior's happening again under similar circumstances). Note: I am unequivocally against the use of positive punishment. I even find it upsetting to provide an example, but I will for purposes of our discussion: yelling at someone who has just done something.

In the other subcategory of punishment, something pleasant or desirable to the student is removed quite soon after the unconstructive behavior; this is called negative (for something being taken away) punishment (because it was unpleasant for the student and thus discourages the behavior's happening again). Logical and natural consequences fall under this subcategory. Examples: 1) The student does not treat equipment with care/respect as outlined in the class rules. Logical consequence = she is not allowed to use the equipment (something pleasant was removed) until she is ready to follow the rules. 2) The student does not study new material. Natural consequence = he earns a low grade on a quiz. These examples are both unpleasant experiences that will likely decrease the use of the unconstructive behavior under similar circumstances; however, the students are not shamed or embarrassed by someone else's treatment of them. The consequences are rational. Fair. Students are taught that what they do has an effect. We want them to learn the cause–effect relationship of their behavior and its consequences, just as we want them to learn how to write with accurate punctuation, to speak with expression, and to use their creative ideas to solve problems.

Another way we discourage an unconstructive action in a particular context is to make sure *in advance* that we eliminate external reinforcing consequences for the unconstructive behavior. This is called extinction, *not* punishment, because we do not do something *after* the behavior has occurred. Instead, we arrange the variables *in advance* so if the behavior occurs, the student does not experience a positive external result. Example: A student who acts in a way that seeks attention from us, but we do not give that attention after the action occurs. Over time, the student is less likely to exhibit what, for her, was not successful behavior.

Often unconstructive behavior occurs because the cue and reinforcement for constructive actions were not clear. So, to be effective in our proactive fostering of constructive behavior during our first days with students, we utilize the power of antecedent conditions. We fill our room with helpful cues provided by the arrangement and materials. We review our plans to be sure our visual and verbal directions clearly and consistently trigger the needed student behavior. Such clear cues are essential when we are establishing processes and procedures in a lesson, but they are equally important when we are shifting our expectations from one segment to another, from one activity to a different one, or from one location to another spot in the room or building. We also remember the power of reinforcement. We design the room and the learning experiences so there are sources of pleasure and feelings of well-being and accomplishment to reinforce constructive learner behavior. We also establish logical consequences for students—consequences to implement that teach students the effect of their behavior should unconstructive actions occur.

We Remember Essential Ideas about Antecedents/Cues and Consequences

Clear antecedent conditions and consequences that are reinforcing, or, if need be, are natural or logical in their punishing consequences provide structure. They tell students "This is what is expected" and "This is what can be gained/lost from doing an action." The cue and reinforcement also provide nurturance. Both give students an opportunity to feel efficacious because they know what to do and, having done it, to feel good about what they just did.

We will further discuss natural and logical consequences later in the text. We will also address in greater detail how we can work with antecedent and consequent conditions or events.

If we connect with students and help them connect with others in ways that foster a sense of belonging and community, and if we interact with students through our instruction using strategies that address their needs and facilitate their learning the curriculum and social skills, they have every reason to behave constructively.

How Can We as Teachers Be Aware of Our Ongoing Mindset?

The overarching element that makes the creation of a class community possible is our mindset as teachers. The assumptions we make about ourselves and others form the basis for the choices we make regarding our informal communication with students (variables in their psychosocial environment) and our instructional strategies (variables in their physical environment). While most of us have a growth mindset—we believe capacities, including intelligence, can be developed (Dweck, 2006)—we need to keep examining our work to be sure it continues to be congruent with this growth mindset as we plan our learning experiences and as we interact with students through the thousands of actions we take and responses we make every day. We also need to nurture our constructive growth mindset. Teaching is complex, difficult, and, at times, particularly frustrating. If we are to be successful in our contribution to creating a community, we need to continually check our perspective so that we consistently believe in the value of each student and that we believe in that student's capacity to learn and grow, and we demonstrate these beliefs (Dweck, as interviewed by Gross-Loh, 2017). Our choice of strategies, our words, and equally important, our nonverbal language will communicate this belief to every student. We may not agree with what students say, or we may not think that their behavior in any given moment is constructive, but we do need to value them and care about their well-being. We believe in their capacity to learn and grow (and in ours, too), even when they have taken what may seem like two steps backwards. We try to find their "islands of competence" (Brooks, 1991). We treat them with kindness and respect throughout our relationship with them.

If we do not treat each student with kindness and respect, how can we expect each of them to treat others with kindness and respect? If we do not show that we care, how can we expect them to care about themselves and others? If we do not believe that each can contribute something to the learning community, how will each feel he has something to contribute and be willing to take the risk to do so?

We also need to believe that investing time and energy in creating a learning community is of value to the students and to us. The research tells us it is. But we have to be believers, or the incongruence between our beliefs and our actions will be loud and clear to students.

. . . .

REFLECTION OPPORTUNITY

In the space provided or on a separate piece of paper describe how your own growth mindset could help foster a constructive class community. _____

_____

_____

_____

. . . .

Application Activity: Three Rooms to Analyze

Table 5-1. **Application Activity: Three Classroom to Analyze**

The activity below is designed to provide you an opportunity to analyze three classroom designs and, in so doing, apply what you have learned in this chapter. The room designs appear below the questions.

Read each question separately. Then, analyze the three room designs to determine your answers to each part of the question. Write your analysis in the space provided or on separate pieces of paper.

1) In what ways, if any, are students nurtured by each room arrangement (A, B, and C):

a) What nurturing messages are being sent to the students by the room arrangement that suggest the basic emotional needs of safety, love/care/value, belonging, efficacy, and play/joy are being met?

Classroom __A____

_____

_____

_____

Classroom __B____

_____

_____

_____

Classroom __C____

_____

_____

_____

2) To what degree, if any, is structure being provided by the room arrangement:

a) **Accessibility:** What evidence suggests that high traffic areas accessible in each room?

Classroom __A____

_____

_____

_____

Classroom __B____

_____

_____

_____

Classroom __C____

_____

_____

_____

b) **Visibility:** What evidence suggests that important points of focus (the teacher, the faces of others students if they are speaking, the display areas) visible to the students in each room? What evidence suggests that the teacher can see any of the students to be proactive about facilitating learning and troubleshooting issues?

Classroom __A____

_____

_____

_____

Classroom __B____

_____

_____

_____

Classroom __C____

_____

_____

_____

c) **Distractibility:** What evidence suggests that important points of focus in each classroom are distraction free?

Classroom __A____

_____

_____

_____

Classroom __B____

_____

_____

_____

Classroom __C____

_____

_____

_____

d) **Proximity:** To what degree does it appear that all students could be in close proximity to the teacher wherever he stood or sat? To what degree could the teacher be in close proximity to each student no matter where the student was working? What is the evidence?

Classroom __A____

_____

_____

_____

Classroom __B____

_____

_____

_____

Classroom __C____

_____

_____

_____

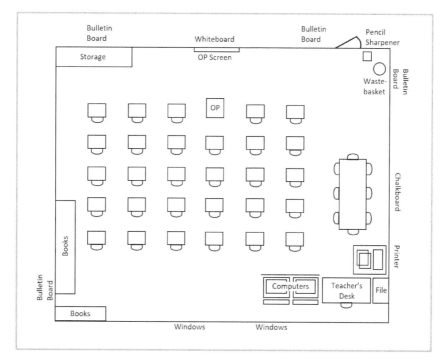

Classroom A

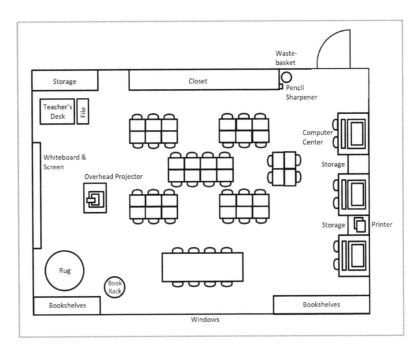

Classroom B

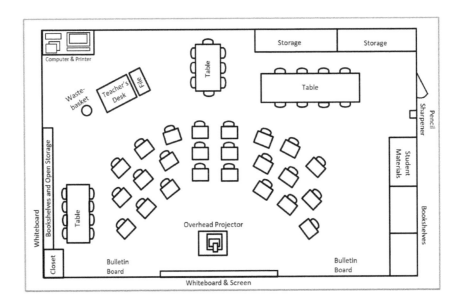

Classroom C

REFLECTION OPPORTUNITY

What can you 'harvest' from your analysis that you can apply to your work in the field? Write your answer either here or on a separate piece of paper. _____

_____

_____

_____

Final Thoughts

We have considered the contribution of a teacher's use of physical environment variables to establish a constructive learning community. You have summarized key points throughout the chapter. What two points do you want to focus on in your work with students? Write your answers either here or on a separate piece of paper, if need be._____

_____

_____

Looking Forward

Chapter 6 focuses on fostering a nurturing classroom community. In the physical environment, this includes clear strategies for maximizing constructive behaviors while minimizing the triggers and cues that spark unconstructive ones. We will also look at variables in the psychosocial environment that contribute to establishing a learning community. As we do, we will consider a number of strategies that we, as caring, competent, and empowering teachers, can use.

References

Alberto, P. & Troutman, A. (2017). *Applied behavior analysis for teachers* (9th ed.). Boston, MA: Pearson.

Ambrose, S., Bridges, M., DiPietro, M., Lovett, M., Norman, M., & Mayer, R. (2010). *How learning works: 7 research-based principles for smart teaching*. San Francisco, CA: Jossey-Bass.

American Psychological Association. (n.d.). *Research in brain function and learning. The importance of matching instruction to a child's maturity level*. Retrieved 2017 from http://www.apa.org/education/k12/brain-function.aspx

Barrett, P., Zhang, Y., Moffat, J., & Kobbacy, K. (2013, January). A holistic, multi-level analysis identifying the impact of class design on pupils' learning. *Building and Environment*, (59), 678–689. Retrieved from http://dx.doi.org/10.1016/j.buildenv.2012.09.016

Brooks, R. (1991). *The self-esteem teacher*. Loveland, OH: Treehaus Communications.

Brophy, J. (2010). *Motivating students to learn (3rd ed.)*. Boston, MA: McGraw Hill.

Burden, P. (2012). *Classroom management: Creating a successful learning community*. New York, NY: Wiley.

Cangelosi, J. (2013). *Classroom management strategies: Gaining and maintaining students' cooperation (7th ed.)*. New York, NY: Wiley.

Center for Educational Research and Innovation. (2008). *Understanding the brain: The birth of a learning science*. Paris, France: Organization for Economic Cooperation and Development. Retrieved from www.oecd.org/site/educeri21st/40554190.pdf

Charney, R. (2002). *Teaching children to care* (2nd ed.). Greenfield, MA: Northeast Foundation for Children.

Danielson, C. (n.d.). *Model lesson plan template*. Retrieved from http://www.montana.edu/fieldplacement/documents/PDFs/DanielsonFrameworkLessonPlan.pdf

Danielson, C. (2007). *Enhancing professional practice: A framework for teaching.* Alexandria, VA: Association for Supervision and Curriculum Development.

Dean, C., Hubbell, E., Pitler, H., & Stone, Bj. (2012). *Classroom instruction that works: Research-based strategies for increasing student achievement*. Denver, CO: McREL.

Dweck, C. (2006). *Mindset: The new psychology of success*. New York, NY: Ballantine Books.

Emmer, E. & Evertson, C. (2017). *Classroom management for middle and high school teachers* [loose-leaf version] (11th ed.). Boston, MA: Pearson.

Evertson, C. & Emmer, E. (2017). *Classroom management for elementary teachers* [loose-leaf version] (11th ed.). Boston, MA: Pearson.

Evertson, C., & Neal, K. (2006). Looking into learning-centered classrooms: Implications for classroom management. Washington, DC: National Education Association.

Evertson, C., Poole, I., & the IRIS Center. (2002, 2017). Effective room arrangement. Retrieved from http://iris.peabody.vanderbhttps://iris.peabody.vanderbilt.edu/wp-content/uploads/pdf_case_studies/ics_effrmarr.pdf

Evertson, C. & Weinstein, C. (Eds.). (2006). *The handbook of classroom management: Research, practice, and contemporary issues*. Mahwah, NJ: Lawrence Erlbaum.

Goleman, D. (2006). *Social intelligence: The new science of human relationships*. New York, NY: Random House.

Good, T. & Brophy, J. (2008). *Looking in classrooms* (10th ed.). Boston, MA: Pearson.

Gross-Loh, C. (2016, December 16). How praise became a consolation prize. *The Atlantic*. Retrieved from https://www.theatlantic.com/education/archive/2016/12/how-praise-became-a-consolation-prize/510845/

Harmin, M. (1994). *Inspiring active learning*. Alexandria, VA: Association for Supervision and Curriculum Development.

Henderson, N. (2013). Havens of resilience. *Educational Leadership: Resilience and Learning, 71*(1), 22–28.

Hinton, C., Miyamoto, K., & Della-Chiesa, B. (2008). Brain research, learning and emotions: Implications for education research, policy and practice. *European Journal of Education, 43*(1), 87–103.

Hunter, M. (1982). *Mastery teaching: Increasing instructional effectiveness in elementary and secondary schools*. El Segundo, CA: TIP Publications.

Hunter, M. (2004). *Mastery teaching: Increasing instructional effectiveness in elementary and secondary schools* (2nd ed.). Thousand Oaks, CA: Corwin Press.

Hunter, R. (2014). *Madeline Hunter's mastery teaching: Increasing instructional effectiveness in elementary and secondary schools*. Thousand Oaks, CA: Corwin Press.

Jensen, E. (2013). *Engaging students with poverty in mind*. Alexandria, VA: Association for Supervision and Curriculum Development.

Jensen, E. (2015a). *Guiding principles for brain-based education*. Retrieved from http://www.brainbased-learning.net/guiding-principles-for-brain-based-education/

Jensen, E. (2015b). *What is brain-based learning?* Retrieved from http://www.jensenlearning.com/what-is-brain-based-research.php

Jensen, E. (2005). *Teaching with the brain in mind* (2nd ed.). Alexandria, VA: Association for Supervision and Curriculum Development.

Johnson, L. (2011). *Teaching outside the box: How to grab your students by their brains* (2nd ed.). San Francisco, CA: Jossey-Bass, John Wiley & Sons, Inc.

Johnson. D., Johnson, R. & Johnson Hollubec, E. (1994). *The new circles of learning: Cooperation in the classroom and the school*. Edina, MN: Interaction Book Company.

Jones, V. (2015). *Practical classroom management* [loose-leaf version] (2nd ed.). Boston. MA: Pearson.

Jones, V. & Jones, L. (2016). *Comprehensive classroom management: Creating communities of support and solving problems* [loose-leaf version] (11th ed.). Boston, MA: Pearson.

Kohl, H. (1998). *The discipline of hope*. New York, NY: Simon & Shuster.

Marzano, R. (2017). *The new art and science of teaching*. Alexandria, VA: Association for Supervision and Curriculum Development.

Marzano, R., Marzano, J., & Pickering, D. (2003). *Classroom management that works: Research-based strategies for every teacher*. Alexandria, VA: Association for Supervision and Curriculum Development.

Marzano, R., Gaddy, B., Foseid, M., Foseid, M., & Marzano, J. (2005). *A handbook for classroom management that works*. Alexandria, VA: Association for Supervision and Curriculum Development.

McCabe, M. & Rhoades, J. (1990). *The nurturing classroom*. Sacramento, CA: ITA Publications.

Nelson, J., Lott, L., & Glenn, S. (2013). *Positive discipline in the classroom* (4th ed.). New York, NY: Three Rivers Press.

Nelson, J., Escobar, L., & Portolan, K. (2001). *Positive discipline: A teacher's A–Z guide: Hundreds of solutions for almost every classroom behavior problem!* (2nd. ed.). New York, NY: Three Rivers Press.

Noddings, N. (2005). *The challenge to care in schools* (2nd ed.). New York, NY: Teachers College Press.

Piaget, J. & Inhelder, B. (1969). *Psychology of the child*. New York, NY: Basic Books.

Ridnouver, K. (2006). *Managing your classroom with heart: A guide to nurturing adolescent learners*. Alexandria, VA: Association for Supervision and Curriculum Development.

Saphier, J. & Haley, M. (1993). *Activators*. Carlisle, MA: Research for Better Teaching.

Saphier, J., Haley–Speca, M., & Gower, R. (2008). *The skillful teacher: Building your teaching skills* (6th ed.). Acton, MA: Research for Better Teaching.

Scott, T. (2017). *Teaching behavior: Managing classrooms through effective instruction*. Thousand Oaks, CA: Corwin Press.

Semrud-Clikeman, M. (n.d.). *Research in brain function and learning: The importance of matching instruction to a child's maturity level*. Retrieved from http://www.apa.org/education/k12/brain-function.aspx

Shea, T. & Bauer, A. (2012). *Behavior management: A practical approach for educators* (10th ed.). Boston, MA: Pearson.

Souers, K. & Hall, P. (2016) *Fostering resilient learners*. Alexandria, VA: Association for Supervision and Curriculum Development.

Sousa, D. & Tomlinson, C. (2001). *Differentiation and the brain: How neuroscience supports the learner-friendly classroom*. Bloomington, IN: Solution Tree Press.

Sternberg, R. (1994, November). Allowing for thinking styles. *Educational Leadership, 51*, 36–40.

Thelan, H. (1981). *The classroom society*. London: Croom Helm.

Thousand, J., Villa, R., & Nevin, A. (2002*). Creativity and collaborative learning: A practical guide to empowering students, teachers, and families* (2nd ed.). Baltimore, MD: Brookes.

Villa, R. & Thousand, J. (2017). *Leading an inclusive school: Access and success for ALL students*. Alexandria, VA: Association for Supervision and Curriculum Development.

Willis, J. (2007). *Brain-friendly strategies for the inclusion classroom*. Alexandria, VA: Association for Supervision and Curriculum Development.

Wong, H. & Wong, R. (1991). *The first days of school*. Mountain View, CA: Harry Wong Publications.

Wong, H., Wong, R., Johndal, S., & Ferguson, D. (2016). *The classroom management book*. Mountain View, CA: Harry Wong Publications.

Wolfgang, C. (2009). *Solving discipline and classroom management problems* (7th ed.). New York, NY: John Wiley & Sons.

Wormeli, R. (2016, September). What to do in week one? *Educational Leadership: Relationships First, 74*(1), 10–15.

Yeager, D. & Dweck, C. (2012). Mindsets that promote resilience: When student believe that personal characteristics can be developed. *Educational Psychologist, 47*(4), 302–314.

Website Resources for Room Arrangement

Evertson, C., Poole, I., & the IRIS Center. (2002). *Effective room arrangement study unit*. Retrieved from http://iris.peabody.vanderbhttps://iris.peabody.vanderbilt.edu/wp-content/uploads/pdf_case_studies/ics_effrmarr.pdf

Project Ideal is a project of the Texas Council for Developmental Disabilities that includes activities, video, and other resources. Retrieved 2017 from http://www.projectidealonline.org/v/arranging-classroom

Appendix A

Table 5-2. **Elements of an Effective Lesson Plan Check Sheet**[i]	√
Beginning—To prepare the students for the lesson:	
Introduction: Sets focus; **provide advance organizer**, e.g., previews agenda; suggests questions that lesson could answer.	
Primes students' brains: Sets **purpose; provides an anticipatory set;** provides **motivation/meaning;** e.g., asks engaging question; connects focus to students' lives.	
Reviews or teaches **vocabulary** to be used [if appropriate].	
Accesses **prior knowledge** to refine old information & attach new concept/skill: Associates new information to old; helped create meaningful pattern to foster understanding and retention. If this is a reading/literature lesson, supported students in making predictions.	
Middle—To support active processing:	
Sets a **goal for comprehension** or **expectations** for the lesson outcome, including social skills or other behavior.	
Matches **teaching strategy** to nature of learning:	
If a **concept**: Fosters recall and associates new information with what students already know; organizes information to create a meaningful pattern; represents/invites students to represent information in a way to be remembered; provides opportunities for students to experiment with/analyze concept.	
If a **skill**: Fosters recall and builds on what students already know; develops a model for the process; demonstrates; provides guided practice with constructive feedback; fosters student reflection on skill application.	
Actively **engages** students in constructing knowledge of concept or skill; e.g., invites students to refine predictions; intersperses a variety of questions; provides opportunities for dialogue about ideas or consideration of skills/processes. If reading/literature lesson, facilitates revising of predictions or confirming/disconfirming in a non-judgmental manner.	
End—To support retention (memory) and transfer:	
Closure: Provides opportunity to: **summarize** orally/in writing, **generalize** to new examples, **apply** concept or skill in different context [generalize], and/or **reflect** on work.	
Throughout lesson:	
Provides **transition** from previous portion or lesson to next portion or lesson.	
Gives clear **directions—orally and visually—**in appropriate chunks.	
Provides clear **explanations**.	
Asks questions that invite more than rote recall.	
Checks for **understanding** beyond asking, "Do you understand?" or "Do you have any questions?"	
As a result of the lesson:	
Lesson objective(s) could be **assessed** within lesson.	

i Note: You will find the ideas of Madeline Hunter (2004, 1982) and Charlotte Danielson (2007; 2017) are integrated within.

CHAPTER 6

Establishing Community Connections and Expectations

> A beginning is the time for taking the most delicate care that the balances are correct.
>
> —Frank Herbert[i]

What Will This Chapter Address?

The students have arrived! There is much to be done to get the new school year or class off to a good start. We have already spent time getting ready as we considered variables in the previous chapter. Now we can put those strategies into place with the students. During the opening weeks of school, we have two essential tasks: 1) to establish a community that fosters connections among members and—with that community—establish expectations for the work to be done; and 2) to assess the ways these students learn and where they are in their skill development and content understanding so that we can effectively review and ready them to learn the new curriculum. Both tasks take thought and time.

Why Is This Important?

While in our excitement we may want to surge ahead into teaching the curriculum and we may feel at times that focusing on anything else seems to take away valuable time from the students' learning, the research is clear: if we do not take time to foster connections and establish expectations during the first weeks, we will be thwarted throughout the remainder of our work to foster content and skill development (Emmer & Evertson, 2017; Evertson & Emmer, 2017; Jones, 2015; Jones & Jones, 2016; Marzano, 2017). The more we invest proactively in providing structure and nurturance to address students' basic emotional needs, the more likely students will exhibit constructive behavior. Eight powerful strategies build a learning community. Two utilize variables in the psychosocial environment. Six utilize variables in the physical environment. We will address each.

What Will You Learn?

By the end of the chapter, you will be able to describe how to establish a community of learners, including how to:

+ foster connections between you and students;
+ foster connections among learning community members;
+ establish expectations for constructive behaviors; and
+ integrate collaborative structures and social skills into the learning experience.

What Do You Want To Accomplish?

What would you like to learn about establishing a community of learners? Write your responses here or on a piece of paper. _____

_____

_____

REFLECTION OPPORTUNITY

Form a picture of a community of learners in your mind. Think about what characteristics you would want in such a community. Early in Chapter 1 after you set your chapter goals, you had an opportunity to access prior knowledge/experience about a time when you did not feel comfortable learning and what contributed to your lack of comfort. Then you thought about a situation in which you felt good about yourself and about what you were doing—when you felt open to the experience, to learning, to getting to know or becoming closer to the people you were with. I asked you to list some of the characteristics of that situation and the person/people facilitating it that helped you feel open. You also wrote what emotional needs you thought were being met in that situation. To add to your current thoughts about important learning community characteristics read your responses in that reflection. Write a summary of what characteristics you would want in a community of learners here or on a piece of paper: _____

_____

_____

_____

As you continue to read the chapter, keep in mind what you want in a learning community. Take note of how the ideas we address will support your achieving what you believe a community should be. I would encourage you to make notes of the ideas you want to implement as soon as you are able.

What are the Characteristics of a Community of Learners?

A community of learners is characterized as one in which each individual is respected as a person, as is that individual's right to learn. People listen to each other. No one teases or is teased. No sarcasm is used. No one slights or is slighted. This is a group in which everyone belongs, no matter what gender, age, race, religion, background, sexual orientation, learning style or rate, disabilities, strengths, intelligences, or needs rather than selective categories of children or adults. No one is isolated. Everyone is accepted and accepting of others (Wormeli, 2016).

> Such a classroom community seeks to meet each student's need to feel competent, connected to others, autonomous. … Students are not only exposed to basic human values, they also have many opportunities to think about, discuss and act upon those values, while gaining experiences that promote empathy and understanding of others (Child Development Project, 1991).

Everyone feels safe in this kind of community. Research (Feinstein, 2013) tells us that feeling safe and supported in class increases dopamine in the brain, which in turn increases a student's sense of optimism and self-satisfaction. These feelings are essential if students are to be open to the vulnerability of learning and the change it brings.

In a community of learners, students have comfortable relationships with their teacher. They know that the teacher cares for them and that she sees, hears, or feels what they are trying to convey (Charney, 2002; Noddings, 2005; Scott, 2017). Teachers work *with* students rather than doing things *for* them or *to* them (Jensen, 2013; Rimm-Kaufman & Sandilos, 2016). The underlying assumptions are that each person has something to offer; each is an active, contributing member; and everyone has something to gain. Students play an active role in making decisions. Problems are solved in ways that ensure everyone wins. The community is learner centered, and everyone—adult and child alike—is considered a learner.

The environment is alive with the pleasure of learning. Curiosity, creativity, imagination, humor, inventiveness, sensitivity to the world around and the people within the community, and a sense of wonder abound. Many moments are filled with the sheer joy of discovery, and only rarely do members encounter the agony of utter frustration. The talents of each flourish. Establishing a community of learners is about creating a high-quality, equitable, excitement-filled environment for all the students and all the adults in the room.

Caring learning communities are intentionally built. How can we go about creating such an environment in our first days with students? We will focus on those strategies that are powerful in providing structure and nurturing constructive behavior. These strategies apply during any "first days," whether we are beginning our student teaching, facing a new school year, starting to teach a subject class, or substituting with a new group of students.

Whatever we do, we need to keep in mind, "Nothing without love!" This use of the word love is *not* meant to denote, in Noddings's (2005) words, "… infatuation, enchantment, or obsession, but a full receptivity" (p. 16). The form of love of which I speak denotes positive regard for every student. If we do not approach each interaction with genuine caring solely because this person is a human being, then nothing we teach will be of value. Do students push our buttons sometimes? Yes! Is the work frustrating beyond belief some days? Of course! Teaching is complex, multifaceted, and difficult. It asks us to be the best we can be, moment after moment, day after day after day.

As we have said, We do not have to agree with what students say or be pleased with how they act, but we do need to care about them in a way that fosters their learning and their personhood.

"Nothing without love" also speaks more broadly. It includes deep positive feelings for the work we do. If we are to effectively create an environment that provides structure and nurtures students—one that meets their basic emotional needs and fosters their full development—we need to feel that we have something to offer, something we give readily, and also that we are open to learning something new.

How Can We Foster the Kind of Interactions that Nurture Students?

We Foster Connections Between Us as People and Students

· ·

REFLECTION OPPORTUNITY

Think of a teacher who made a difference in your life. What about your being with that teacher inspired you, made you want to learn, and do your best? In the space provided or elsewhere write what comes to mind. _____

_____

_____

_____

· ·

In most instances, human beings do their best when they feel what they are doing is important and they like or respect the person who is leading them. They also feel competent and know that if they run into difficulty, they will be supported in figuring out what to do next. There is an added bonus if they like the leader, too. So it is for students in a learning situation (Rimm-Kaufman & Sandilos, 2016). The *person* in each teacher is as important as the *teacher* in each teacher. In fact, the two are inextricably interwoven. The relationship between teacher and students is key to constructing a learning community (Jensen, 2013; Ridnouer, 2006; Rimm-Kaufman & Sandilos, 2016; Scott, 2017; Souers & Hall, 2016; Wormeli, 2016). Glasser (1998a) tells us students "should know you well enough and like [respect] what they know enough to see you as the best person they have ever met outside their family. You should not settle for less."

For older students who are struggling with identity and autonomy, knowing us as people shows our humanness. We are not some unfeeling autocrat telling them what to do. Each teacher is a person who was their age once, who struggled with and had fun with being that age, just as those students are doing now. It is harder for them to brush us off with, "Oh, she's saying that because she is a teacher." When students know us and our choices, then our decisions and actions appear to be based on our whole personhood, not just our "teacherhood." Moreover, the more students know about us, the more opportunities they have to connect with us. Within these connections lies the possibility for adding quality to their lives in any number of ways. We can, for example, be a person who suggests potential to students: "Wow, she did that! Well, then, maybe I can, too." We can suggest interesting opportunities: "I never thought of hiking to see the leaves in the fall. She sounds like she had a good time," or "I've never tried reading Jack Vance. If he digs Vance, maybe I would, too." We can provide insight into human nature: "He felt that way when his dog died. I am not the only one who feels that way."

The importance of this connection cannot be overemphasized (Jensen, 2013; Jones, 2015; Jones & Jones, 2016; Noddings, 2005; Ridnouer, 2016; Souers & Hall, 2016). Not only does it help the students; it invigorates us as teachers. "We are more willing to invest in students when we feel connected to them" (Wormeli, 2016, p. 11). What can help to make this connection?

✦ We have a welcome sign on our door and a welcome mat at the entrance to our room.

✦ We create a welcoming display about the class members and, if possible, about the class content (if there is a particular focus). **Examples:** 1) On the inside of a math class door is a drawing of a large pie with a student's or adult's name on each piece. The sign below reads "Here we are, all a piece of the PY." 2) A ruler with a sign saying "We all measure up in this room" could also be used. 3) Working *with* the students to choose a content-related, themed sign to give the message of being a community would provide an added bonus.

✦ We learn students' names as soon as possible (Payne, 2008), and we learn how to pronounce them correctly. "All of us feel honored when others whom we respect think our names are worth remembering. In that simple act, we make a connection" (Wormeli, 2016, p. 10).

> *"The sweetest sound in the world is the person's own name."*
>
> **—Dale Carnegie**

✦ Whenever possible, we stand at the door or sit at a table just inside (if we need a spot to collect materials) to greet and welcome each student by name. Being there not only provides a teacher an eye for whatever is going on, but for many students, having a welcoming figure can help ease the anxiety they feel crossing the threshold to any class. Moreover, welcoming a student by name reestablishes that important connection.

Tip to Help Learn Names: Tent cards with names on both sides can help everyone (who reads) learn others' names because they can be easily seen in their raised position. Students can decorate around the edge of the cards with colors, items, and words that say something about them—their interests, talents, or aspects of their personality. Cards are taped to desks if students stay in the room. Those who move to other rooms are responsible for keeping the cards in a safe place (a pocket in a notebook or assignment book would be a possibility) until used again.

✦ We grab moments to chat briefly with students about their lives—what they enjoy, how events in their lives—such as a game, club outing, volunteer work, concert, or debate—went, what they did to amuse a younger child when babysitting recently, etc. I am reminded of Joseph Tarrant's quote: "Attention is the most basic form of love. Through it we bless and are blessed." Glasser (1998a) suggests that we also look for occasions to talk with students about the following:

♦ **Who they and we are:** interests; what food, music, sports, and books we like; how families are shaped

- What we stand for: our opinions and beliefs—not as the only ones, but as ours

- Their hopes, their beliefs

Neither person is to be judged, just understood. We can connect with students about their lives, their hopes, and their beliefs in person and online. We can develop a series of questions offline or online: If you could have a superpower, what would you choose and why? What is your favorite color? What makes you smile? If you could go anywhere, where would you go and why? What would be a perfect day for you (that was one my sixth-grade teacher asked us)? If the questions were online, we could ask students to select three or four to answer, either by responding below the question or creating an audio recording sent directly to us through email via Google Drive or Google Voice (Tucker, 2016).

We Foster Personal Connections Among Learning Community Members

We provide opportunities for class members, both students and adults, to not only learn each other's names but to know each other as people, so students have comfortable relationships with one another. As students work together with our support and lesson design, they also make the kinds of connections with each other that help weave a community network. We invest time in establishing "we-ness."

> Sing me your song, and I will teach you my dance!

We Integrate Community Connection Activities into our Curriculum

We can use many different kinds of activities, but whatever we choose needs to be enjoyable for both students and teachers *and low risk*. Members should be able to carry out the activity without feeling personally threatened or overly challenged. There can be *no* judgment or criticism of what is done. The focus is on sharing oneself with others in a reciprocal, supportive, inviting environment. Below are several activities that help to build a classroom community.

All members of the community, including adult(s), can create a class quilt by having each person design a same-sized square that represents what is important to that individual. A similar activity invites individuals to decorate a pre-cut, interlocking puzzle piece in a manner that describes or represents them. An adult or class members then assemble the pieces to form the whole. Quotes, such as "Each of us is an important piece of our class," can be added to the display. In Appendix A of this chapter, you will find directions for creating a class quilt.

Note: Be sure to tell the students in advance if their quilt, puzzle piece, banner, shield or coat of arms will be posted publicly and who will be able to see it, so students can choose what information they feel safe about sharing.

An alternative would be for members of the community to create coats of arms, shields or banners that represent what is important to them in their lives, that depict interests, talents, and important beliefs. This project could include one or more sentences that describe how the elements in the coat of arms, shield, banner relate to the individual. When the students briefly share their shields, or quilt squares, we can facilitate connections by paraphrasing or extending what we hear and see (e.g., "Cecilia, work with older people sounds important to you," or "Max, you like the trumpet. Do you play in a band?"). We can also facilitate students' appreciation of diversity by supporting their understanding of how they are *different in positive ways*: "We have variety: three people like jazz; others like classical; others like rap."

We can also use verbal activities:

✦ Students can **introduce themselves** and share what they like: favorite food, color, game, sport, music. For an introduction activity based on the eight intelligences, see Appendix B of this chapter.

✦ An **interview process** can help make connections. Students take turns interviewing each other using questions we give them or questions the class develops as a whole from individual, pair, or small-group work. In the one-step interview design, two students are randomly paired and carry out the interview. In the two-step design, after two students have interviewed each other and written notes in the spaces provided, they find a second group of two. Each interviewer summarizes the information from her partner for the new pair. A sample form with questions designed in advance appears below.

Table 6-1. **Interest Interview**	
Partner's Name: _____	
A favorite color: _____ A favorite past-time: _____ A hero/heroine: _____ A favorite place: _____	A favorite food: _____ A favorite animal: _____ A favorite indulgence: _____ A favorite part of school: _____

✦ **Online connections:** We can post a series of icebreaker questions online. Any student can respond and have conversations with other students about their responses in a chat room format—after we have addressed or reviewed safety rules for responding and interacting respectfully online.

We can use visual activities:

✦ Individuals, pairs, and teams can **create displays** that acquaint others with them. "Community Member/Table/Team of the Week" is one concept for such a display. It can be done on a bulletin board alone or include items displayed on a shelf or table below the board. In order for this to be a connecting rather than an exclusionary activity, every member of the learning community must at some point have an equivalent amount of time and space to provide a display. This includes adults in the community.

✦ Each community member can create an **acrostic poem** with the letters in his name. First (or first and last) names are written down the left side of the paper. Then each letter is used to begin a word or two or a phrase that describes that person. If I were to write an acrostic with my name, it might look like this:

The acrostic poem for each student people could be is glued to a cutout in the shape of a person. Each student could color in details on his "person" that match his own hair and eye color, etc. The "people" are posted side by side to make a chain of people connected to all the others. For younger students a face or a whole person could be colored in without the use of a poem.

As we share the results of any of these connection activities we can use a "Quick Whip", so all are heard, but the process moves quickly. As with all processes the students need to be taught how to do this, so the sharing does not drag.

How to do a "Quick Whip"

We ask a number of students to take turns sharing whatever amount of information we feel would be helpful and to do it quickly about what they will say. They will need a moment to plan their quick response. As soon as one person is done, the turn "whips" to the next one. Give them a moment to plan their brief and quick response. Portions of two or more sessions can be used to limit the time for the process at any one sharing as well as the amount of information being absorbed.

We Choose Activities that Foster Our Goal

If acquaintance alone is the goal, any of the above activities would be useful. If connections *and* an increased sense of the nature of community are the goals, then the process is greatly enhanced if there are activities that create a final product to serve as a visual reminder of the important contribution each member makes to creating the whole. That is what communities are all about.

The possibilities for each connection activity are furthered by providing opportunities for the community members to talk in small groups about what is important about or to individual members. We need to design the discussion questions so the members uncover similarities in ways that facilitate connections and frame differences in a positive way.

We Choose Activities to Address Multiple Goals

There is no need to limit the process of making connections to just one activity. Nor is there any reason not to have instructional objectives integrated simultaneously. We can choose a means of getting acquainted that can be woven into our curriculum. The quilt square and the coat of arms, banner, shield activities can be part of a larger study of how these two pieces of artwork were made and their place in cultures of old and those of today. Students could learn about the mathematics behind the symmetry and geometric design of squares or the historical importance of the directions provided by "crazy quilts" (those without geometric designs) for people escaping slavery through the Underground Railroad. There are many fine pieces of literature—short and long—in which quilting and quilt squares play an important part in the theme and/or the plot. The role of coats of arm banners, shields in history—their symbolism, the mathematical proportions used to create them, the use of a particular medium, material, tool, or all of the above—could be a part of an integrated unit in which the students' creating their own is just one (perhaps, culminating) piece of history/social studies lessons.

How Can We Use Instructional Variables to Nurture Students and Provide Structure?

Supporting constructive behavior cannot be separated from the teaching of curricular content. The better we become at facilitating learning, the better we will be at choosing strategies that support constructive behavior in students (Weisen, 2013).

We Create a Class Tone That Communicates Possibility

The most effective way to foster students' social, emotional, and cognitive development is through establishing an instructional class tone. When we communicate possibility, we create an environment most conducive to the learning of *everything*—academic content and skills, social skills, problem-solving across all areas of life—everything. The literature supporting this kind of learning environment has been clear for years and years (Hunter, 1982; McCabe & Rhoades, 1990; Smith, 1998; Jensen, 2005; Dweck, 2006; Marzano, 2017; Cole, 2008; Dean, Hubbell, Pitler & Stone, 2012; Gregory & Kaufeldt, 2015; Jensen, 2013; Jensen, 2015a; Jones & Jones, 2016; Ridnouver, 2016; Souers & Hall, 2016; Hoerr, 2017; Duckworth, 2017).

In the last 15 years, research in neuroscience, psychology, and education has provided additional rationale for such a climate. When we facilitate students' understanding of their possibilities, of the malleability of their capacities, and of their ability to develop and maintain what many are calling a *growth mindset* (Dweck, 2006) as they address everyday situations in and out of school, we offer students the power of persistence and, with it, resilience (Anderson & Forkner, 2013; Duckworth, 2017; Henderson 2013; Hoerr, 2017; Jensen, 2013; Saphier, 2017; Souers & Hill, 2016). The mental capacity to see possibility and to persist in working through whatever situations arise in life—both within school and without, both now and in the future when school is far behind them—provides students with the ability to take what they have learned at any grade level and use it to be successful in life, no matter their path.

There are no exacting steps to creating such a climate. Rather, there is an attitude we cultivate that comes from a belief system and with it an approach that is possible, if we are willing to adopt what Kohl (2000) calls "the discipline of hope." In his book by this title Kohl describes this discipline as the refusal to accept any limits on what students can learn or on what we as teachers can do to foster that learning. Establishing a climate of possibility means adopting the discipline of hope and throwing our talents and energy behind implementing the strategies described in these chapters.

We establish our climate with the norms we create with our students. In this case it would be particularly helpful if the green title below were closer to this introductory statement.

The First Norm We Establish Is: Everyone in Our Community Has Potential

Included in that potential is the possibility for change, for enhancement of what already exists within (Dweck, 2006; Duckworth, 2016; Saphier, 2017). Each of us needs a mirror to show us our value. Each of us has potential. Many possibilities exist for each of us. We do not have to be limited to what we are today. Teachers are that mirror. When students look into our eyes, they need to see their possibilities. They need to see hope. They need to see respect. We have the skills, the wisdom, the experience in life, and the tools to nurture the unfolding of whatever is in each student.

The Second Norm Is: We Are All in This Process of Becoming Together

As teachers, we say: *"**We** help each other out." "How can **we** solve this?"* We post signs such as those below.

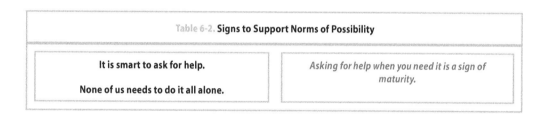

Table 6-2. **Signs to Support Norms of Possibility**	
It is smart to ask for help. **None of us needs to do it all alone.**	*Asking for help when you need it is a sign of maturity.*

The Third Norm We Establish Is: We Expect Progress and Perseverance, Not Perfection

We can communicate this with the signs we post: "Practice makes better and better" (this suggests possibility) instead of "Practice makes perfect." No one is perfect. Encouraging students to strive for perfection sets them up for disappointment. On the other hand, "Triumph = try + umph!" is a message that encourages possibility and perseverance. Perseverance is what matters if progress is to be made (Duckworth, 2017; Dweck, 2006; Hoerr, 2017; Saphier, 2017).

Our Fourth Norm Is: Mistakes Are Not Only a Natural Part of Learning; They Are Also Sources of Useful Feedback

Howard Gardner (1997) tells us that highly creative people—those whom others unquestionably regard as being capable individuals—have three things in common: They have the ability to leverage their strengths. They take time each day to reflect. They reframe "failures" so they are seen as a natural part of the creative process—food for thought, "stuff" to be added to the soup of experience that will nurture further creative ideas and actions. I would say that these highly talented people have created for themselves a climate of hope and possibility and, with it, the capacity to persist.

Admittedly, some students do not exert appropriate or sufficient effort. And while there can be no success without effort, I would contend that most mistakes—most of what is considered "failure" in schools, most of what is circled in red by teachers—is simply *not yet success*. We need to support students' understanding that mistakes are not only a natural part of the learning process—mistakes are an *important* part of the learning process. Mistakes teach. They tell us where to focus in order to improve, to make lasting progress: Do we need to gain a better understanding of a concept or skill or to practice applying either more accurately? As teachers, we help students befriend their mistakes any time we help them build their growth mindset or their capacity for grit when we support their understanding that their capacities can grow and their brains are malleable. Therefore, when we give written feedback, we shift from red (for "wrong!") to other colors (for "Let's figure out how to fix this"). When we respond to oral reports and written pieces of any kind, we honor students' effort and foster the development of their skills and ideas by providing both encouragement and constructive feedback that helps them become better and better at what they are learning to do (Saphier, 2017). We post signs such as those below.

Table 6-3. **Examples of Signs**	
Mistakes are natural. **We learn from them.**	Take **chances, get messy, make mistakes.**[i]

i Catchphrase from "Miss Fribble and the Amazing School Bus" book series.

When something does not work out or when something is not accurate, the perspective in a constructive learning community is: *"Yes, this may be disappointing. At the same time, now you have information that is an important part of learning. You can better understand the choices and the results. If not, you may be closer to asking a question or asking for the kind of help that will support your efforts. You have the power to change the situation."* Personal effort in using information at hand to parlay into improved responses in the future and the perseverance to do so is what counts (Duckworth, 2016; Dweck, 2006).

This perspective on using feedback to enhance what we do is essential for teachers, too. How often our students teach us. We share this as we model the usefulness of feedback from experience: *"Your questions made me think more about what I was saying in yesterday's class. I want to go back and revisit our discussion on _____ and see if I can be clearer about the perspective I was sharing." "This morning when I gave you materials for your projects, I could tell from some of the elbow bumping that there could be a better way to arrange things. What suggestions do you have?"*

When a student is stuck on a process, we can ask, *"What were you trying to do?"* When a student answers a factual oral question incorrectly, we can respond by saying in a neutral voice, *"Can you tell me how you came up with that answer?"* or *"Can you tell me more?"* or *"Help me see the connection between what we were talking about and that thought."* Our response can uncover some fascinating thought processes that were going on or a slight slip in reasoning that led the student down an inaccurate path. We can help with either. Sometimes asking for more information gives the student a chance to consider her own thoughts and, in the process, clarify her own thinking to come up with a more accurate response. Sometimes that "aha!" moment comes solo. Sometimes other students can help—always in an effort to support. We are all in this learning together.

Another way we can respond to an incorrect answer to a question regarding factual information is: *"That would be the correct answer for _____. Now, what would be the answer for _____?"*

Mistakes are also useful information for us as teachers. *What can I learn from a student's mistake?* We can use what the student has done to assess what the student was thinking, what choices the student made, and what tensions might have been operating that were blocking him from being successful. With that information, we figure out how we can respond. We can help him to become clearer in his thinking—always in the service of learning. When a student has made a mistake, if we say, *"Does someone else have a different answer?"* we have lost the opportunity to help that student, and probably others in the class, come to a better understanding of the material.[ii] On the other hand, it can be very helpful to set up the expectation that there are many ways of looking at a problem or question and that various answers can help us clarify our thinking. In that case, asking if anyone has a different answer can enable the whole class to compare and think about two ways of responding to the question.

Jean Piaget, in the early years of his study of intelligence, became fascinated with the so-called *wrong* answers that children gave on their intelligence tests. He saw in those answers the possibility of understanding how children think. And it was this work that led him, after many years, to his important theories on children's cognitive development (Piaget & Inhelder, 1969). Like Piaget, we can learn much about our students by looking at *how* they get the answers they do and *what* those answers are. Then we have the opportunity to help them to the next step in the process, whatever it might be.

The Fifth Norm for Our Work with Students Is: Learning Requires Active Engagement

We respect students as the ones who need to be the doers if their potential is to be reached. We do not do *to* them or *for* them but *with* them. We facilitate *their* thinking so they come to realize that their brains can do the reasoning needed and can discover the solutions desired, whether the focus is learning content or changing behavior.

The Sixth Norm Is: Behavior Can Change and Progress, Like Any Other Kind of Learning

As we have said, we act with respect towards the person, even when we may not respect the person's behavior. Moreover, we do not *react*; we *respond* (knowing that sometimes we may need a moment to ease away from a strong emotional reaction). We use an observational, neutral tone of voice. If the intrusion is minimal, we replace versions of "no" or "stop" with a redirection, or we empower students to think about their choices by asking, "What's the rule you need to be following?" "What's the task to be done?" or "What's your job?" If more than redirection is needed, we work *with* students to address the situation as a problem to be solved. We use the opportunity to teach. After all, discipline means to teach. (How to address unconstructive behavior will be addressed further in Chapter 9 and beyond.)

A Seventh Norm Is: The Climate of Possibility Includes the Value of Celebrating Growth—Everyone's Growth

"Look how far we've come since we first started _____!" "Do you remember what it was like when you were _____? How much you've learned!" "I have gained so much from working with you. You have helped me to look at this issue from a different perspective."

IN SUMMARY: A learning community needs to be a place where students want to be. The feeling and tone are positive (students know what they can do instead of what they cannot) and nonthreatening but appropriately challenging, with a clear focus on learning (Jensen, 2013). Inherent in a climate of possibility is the perspective that each has the ability and ongoing potential for change. None need stay as she is. For years we have known that this emotional atmosphere is the one most conducive to learning (Hunter, 1982).

How Can We Foster Connections Between Us as Facilitators of Learning and Students?

To create a safe and supportive learning community and to choose effective teaching strategies, teachers need to know the intelligences, learning styles, and needs of their students (Wormeli, 2016). Observation checklists and questionnaires can be used to gather such information. Thomas Armstrong (2009), Bernice McCarthy (2005), Marie Carbo (2014), and others have created multiple intelligences, learning styles, and reading styles questionnaires. Teacher-created questionnaires can also be used (Sousa & Tomlinson, 2015). At the beginning of our work with students, we can ask them (online or offline) to give us advice on how to be the best teacher for them. For example, we could have them think about times when they felt most successful learning and then ask what the teacher or coach did that helped make this possible. For younger children, careful thought needs to be given to both wording and length of questions or statements. If a student is not yet a fluent reader, an adult or older student can read the questions or statements to the student. Instead of writing in answers, students can indicate their preferences by circling a face with an appropriate expression (smile, straight-lined mouth, or frown).

Reading students' IEPs and 504 Plans and finding out which students are learning English as a second language as well as how long their minds have been balancing the use of two (if not more) languages can also provide essential information about strategies to support and facilitate student learning.

In the absence of other information, we tend to assume that people learn as we do. We then teach as we learn. As we gather information on how students learn, we are reminded that people learn in a variety of ways, many of which are different from our own. We are also given information with which to enhance our instruction for *particular* students. Often, we find these approaches help other students as well. Many can benefit, including those who are teaching.

Discovering what kinds of learners the students are also allows us to share that information with them. Students need to learn about themselves as learners—about the significant variables in their physiological environment. Armstrong (2002) has written a book to support students in understanding multiple intelligences. If we support students in becoming *constructive* advocates for their learning needs, they are much more likely to ask appropriately for what they need.

Analyzing different learning styles and needs can also benefit the collaborative efforts of the class community. When the class has respectful discussions about different styles and needs, students come to appreciate that not everyone sees the world and learns the same way they do. Moreover, they come to understand why peers behave as they do in class. "Oh, so that's why you _____. Now I understand." "You do need to know why we are learning something before you can get it." "So, if I look directly at you, you can read my lips and listen to what I am saying, and that helps. I can do that. Understanding how community members learn, as well as how each can support the learning of others, has benefits for everyone.

REFLECTION OPPORTUNITY

On a separate piece of paper or in the space provided write your responses to the questions.

Which of the strategies to foster connections have you used already? _____

_____

_____

Which of the strategies you have not yet used would you consider adding to your "teacher toolbelt"?

_____

_____

_____

How Can We Establish Expectations for Constructive Behavior?

Students of any age do not walk into a class knowing what will be expected in that particular learning situation. Establishing expectations gives students predictable boundaries, sets the conditions for accountability, and thereby empowers them. With the knowledge of what is expected and how it is expected, students are able to make choices and decisions about their behavior (Emmer & Evertson, 2017; Evertson & Emmer, 2017; Jones, 2015; Jones & Jones, 2016). However, if *we* as teachers state the expectations, *our* brains are doing the thinking, not the students'. When we establish expectations *with* the students, the process invites *them* to think about and learn how to create useful structure for their behavior. Developing expectations *with* students ensures that they better understand how their behavior affects others and how a good experience in a class is not dependent solely on the actions of the teacher. Establishing expectations *with* the students also helps to gain their cooperation. They are much more likely to feel ownership of, and be willing to live within, a structure that they have helped create.

We Establish Expectations Through the Creation of a Class Community Contract

Some classes call their contract a class pledge, charter, or promise. A sample of one kind of contract was included in Chapter 4. Such a contract is developed through teacher facilitation of discussions.

> We, the seventh-grade English/Language Arts class, will work together to create a calm, safe, learning environment in which we can all work together. To create this environment, we will come to class ready to learn. We will listen to each other's ideas and feelings with respect, whether we agree or not. When we disagree, it will be with ideas, not people. We will work together to solve problems. We will support each other, not hurt each other. We will not accept bullying in any form by anyone. We pledge to make this a good year for everyone in our class.

The results are the foundation for everyone understanding that all members have rights and responsibilities in any community. The next portion/stage of the small, then large, group discussions addresses other important questions: What do students think their rights are in this community? What are their responsibilities? What are the teacher(s) responsibilities? What kind of behavior contributes to a community in which everyone feels safe, cared about, and respected and has a sense of belonging, competence, and joy. These discussions then lead to the creation of a contract.

Often teachers add two lines at the bottom of the contract—one where they sign and one where the student signs. With both having signed, each student is given back a copy to keep in a safe place and revisit later. (Reviewing the contract will be addressed in Chapter 7.) To the left is an example of a pledge, class charter contract.

An important focus for a contract—whether it is for a class, grade-level team, or school-wide—is anti-bullying. Leominster Public Schools in Massachusetts (2016) uses a contract from the Owleus Anti-Bullying Program.[iii] The contract includes the agreement you see below which all students signed.

> + We will not bully.
> + We will try to help students who are bullied.
> + We will try to include students who are left out.
> + If we know someone who is being bullied, we will tell an adult at school or an adult at home.

Of course, simply signing a contract is not enough, but it is an important step in helping students develop constructive behavior and diminish every aspect of bullying. (We will discuss more strategies to address bullying later in the book.)

We Establish Expectations Through the Creation of Community Rules

Unlike a contract, the focus of a set of rules is principally the *actions* of the students. Rules are also much more specific than contracts. For many learning communities, the list of class rules is a distilled version of some aspects of the contract. While contracts may involve a long list, a list of rules should be short—indeed, the fewest possible in number—to address crucial behaviors for the well-being and operation of the community. Creating a contract *first* helps because those discussions can form the basis for developing more specific rules. The choice of which behavior to address in rules will vary from class to class and may need to be revised as the community develops. Often the consequences for not following the rules are explained in the contract and/or with students. However, those consequences do not appear on the rules statement.

Differences Between Rules and Procedures

Rules state expectations or standards for behavior. Rules tell students how to act.

> Example of a rule: Listen while others are talking.

Procedures address specific activities and provide steps for completing tasks.

> Example of a procedure: When you are done with your work, put your finished product in the basket labeled "Done." Return materials to their appropriate place.

Important Characteristics of Effective Class Rules

* The list is short—preferably 3–5 rules. The average human brain remembers material in chunks of five, plus or minus two items. If we want rules to be remembered, limiting them is necessary.

* Rules are stated positively. Stating what *not* to do does not establish an expectation for what a student *is* to do. If the sign says "No food in the auditorium," a question might be "Okay, I can't eat food, but how about drinking water?" Positive statements teach. "Enjoy your food and drink outside the auditorium" establishes a clear expectation. Telling students what to do increases the likelihood that they will make correct choices. Moreover, a positive statement is less likely to be challenged because it does not invite the power struggle that might be encouraged by what sounds like a demanding tone.

* Rules are stated clearly.

* Rules conform to the school rules. When creating rules, if a student suggests one contrary to school rules, we have the responsibility to intervene with an explanation. An important part of the discussion would be the teacher's role: to carry out school rules and be responsible for the safety for all.

* Rules are age and context appropriate. While this may seem an obvious characteristic, I saw a rule that stated: "Children will sit with their hands folded on their desks facing front at all times." This degree of quiet is not developmentally appropriate for any students, nor is it sound educational practice.

Below are examples of rules for different grade levels. For the primary level pictures or icons accompany the words.

Table 6-4. Examples of Rules for Different Grade Levels		
Primary Level	**Upper Elementary Level**	**Middle School Level**
• Be kind.	• Be kind to others.	• Listen when others speak.
• Listen to others.	• Ask for help, when you need it. Help others when you can.	• Respect the feelings and ideas of others; resolve differences with respect.
• Raise your hand to speak.	• Try your hardest to do your best.	• Keep yourself and others safe.
• Take care of the classroom.	• Listen when someone else is speaking; raise your hand to speak.	• Respect your property, that of others, and the school's.
• Walk in the room and the halls.	• When you disagree, do it peacefully.	• Come to class and be in your seat on time and prepared with materials and homework.
		• Turn assignments in by due date.
		• Follow all school rules.

✦ **Finally, effective rules are those created with the students.** As we have said, Inviting the students to be part of building the rules increases their sense of efficacy because they feel they have an influence on, and are more in control of, what happens in the class. As a result, they are more likely to follow them (Armstrong, 2016; Emmer & Evertson, 2017; Evertson & Emmer, 2017; Jensen, 2013; Jones & Jones, 2016).

Platform: Application Opportunity

On the Active Learning Platform under Chapter 6, you have an opportunity to apply the ideas we have addressed regarding rule development.

How Can We Establish Rules with Students?

Step 1: Discuss the value of rules. Students are more likely to buy into rules if they understand their purposes and benefits. Students need to understand that they value certain behavior in others. Given the developmental level of your students, questions to ask might be: What is important to you about how everyone behaves in this class, or how do you want others to behave towards you/treat you? What rules do you think would be helpful for us, or what rules would remind us how to treat each other well?

Step 2: Create a list of the rules students (and we) think would **be helpful.** If possible, we start by working in small groups that allow more active student engagement. (However, this depends on the developmental level of students and their experience working in small-group brainstorming.)

- Teach/remind students of the purpose of brainstorming: to get as many ideas as possible in a limited period of time.
- Teach/review the rules for brainstorming: 1) get as many ideas down as quickly as you can; 2) no judgments; 3) piggybacking on other's ideas is all right.
- Direct the students to use positive terms (What to do). This may require a few examples.
- Remind students class rules must conform to school rules. Do a quick review of school rules with a copy all students can see as you review them and as they work in groups. Icons to illustrate the rules would help students whose reading skills would be helped by such support.
- Direct the groups to choose a secretary to write *just* what was said. *No* editing. (Be sure they know this person can contribute, also.)
- Tell students how much time they have.
- Release the students with directions to do the group work.
- Combine lists in the large group. Remove duplications. Delete rules that do not conform to school rules. As we discuss the rules, we talk about whether the students feel each rule helps the group do its work effectively and helps students feel good. Also, if we have rules that are nonnegotiable, as the teacher we need to integrate these into the mix.
- Discuss the usefulness of having 3–5 rules. Talk about how rules can be combined or how one can be subsumed under another (perhaps if a rule is stated more broadly). Direct students to return to their small groups to pare down the combined list to what groups feel is essential.
- Work as a whole class to create a final list of 3–5 that everyone feels are *essential.* Foster the group's work to edit, combine similar ideas, and omit ones subsumed under others.

Step 3: Be sure that the rules are understood. The strategy I have found most helpful is to ask, "What would this look like and/or what would this sound like?" Such a question helps make abstract words like "respect" and "polite" more concrete.

Step 4: Gain commitment for the final list. Work with the class to be sure everyone can live with the rules. Some minor tweaking may be needed. If some students feel a particular rule is not appropriate, there are options. The first is to have the students present their reasoning to the whole class and work with everyone to reach a solution, either through changing the rule's wording or by deleting that rule because not everyone agrees that it is vital. A second option would occur if the first does not produce consensus. We ask those who do not agree to try out the rule for a week and come back together to discuss the results, including whether the rule needs editing.

Step 5: Teach the rules. For details, see below under "Steps for Teaching Rules and Procedures."

Step 6: Determine with the students what will occur if each rule is followed or not. Before you choose to take this step with students, I encourage you to reflect on your own philosophy regarding discipline. We will address possibilities below.

Tip: If you choose to send a copy of the rules home, I encourage you to provide the caregiver with a context. This might include your philosophy statement about classroom management, how the rules were formulated collaboratively, and what you and the students have decided will occur if the rules are followed and what should occur if they are not. This process presents the rules and their formulation in a positive manner that describes their relationship to effective instruction and student learning.

Step 7: Have the students sign the rules to indicate their agreement and willingness to uphold them. Usually one copy of the rules is turned into a poster large enough for all in the class to read. Students then sign at the bottom or around the edge as a frame. In some classes, I have seen posters on which students have traced their hands and then signed within.

Step 8: Post the rules in a way that makes them clear for students and in a location that is easy for everyone to see. If the students are emergent readers or learning English as a second language, icons or pictures cut from magazines, found on the web, or drawn—by students or us will be needed to illustrate each rule. When creating the poster, provide specific examples under the more general rules, soliciting these from the students. **Example:** In a second-grade classroom, under "Keep our classroom clean," were: Push in chairs when you leave a spot. Keep tables clear.

Step 9: Provide copies for students. Many teachers not only make copies for the students but also request/require that the students have a parent or guardian sign to indicate that she or he has also read the list. The rules are then returned to school by a certain date, and students keep a copy in a particular location, such as the front of their binder in their classroom desk or mailbox, or in their cubby, so that the list can be referred to readily.

Step 10: Test the students on the rules orally or in writing in a way that enables them, and you, to determine that everyone understands each rule and knows how it applies. The ultimate goal is for everyone to understand completely. If clarification is needed, work with students until it is reached.

Step 11: Periodically review the rules. The need to review a rule may become apparent. Students' behavior can provide helpful cues. However, even if there is no evidence that rules are being forgotten, being proactive about reviewing them can contribute to preventing unconstructive behavior.

As you read these steps, do you find yourself saying, "This would take too much time away from the curriculum content!"? If you do, remind yourself of the research on proactive management (Emmer & Evertson, 2017; Evertson & Emmer, 2017; Jones & Jones, 2016; Marzano, 2017). Either we spend the time when the community is forming, or *even more time* will be needed later to address the problems that arise because we did not. Establishing rules does not have to be separated from the class curriculum. A class I visited was studying the Constitution of the United States. They wrote their rules in the form used in the Constitution and included some of the wording. A mathematics class expressed each rule in the form of an equation as well as words.

How We Establish Consequences with Students

We consider our choices and carefully choose consequences that match our climate of possibility.

Below is a chart that compares the traditional approach to discipline with the restorative one. The restorative approach has been around for a long time[iv] but is regaining in popularity (Smith, Fisher, & Frey, 2015). As you read the columns, consider which approach would best teach constructive behavior.

Table 6-5. Comparison of Traditional Approach to Discipline to Restorative Approach[i]	
Traditional Approach	**Restorative Approach**
School and rules violated.	*People and relationships* violated.
Justice focuses on *establishing guilt.*	Justice identifies *needs and obligations.*
Accountability = punishment.	Accountability = understanding impact, repairing harm.
Justice is directed at the offender, victim ignored.	Offender, the victim, and school all have direct roles in justice process.
Rules and intent outweigh whether outcome is positive/negative the outcome for offender and victim(s).	Offenders is responsible for harmful behavior, repairing harm, and working toward a positive outcome.
No opportunity for remorse or amends.	Opportunities given for amends and expression of remorse.

i   D. Smith, D. Fisher, and N. Frey, from *Better Than Carrots or Sticks*, p. 2. Copyright © 2015 by Association for Supervision and Curriculum Development (ACSD). Adapted from: San Francisco Unified School District. (n.d.). Restorative Practices Whole-school Implementation Guide, p. 19.

The Traditional Approach Uses Punishment

A major drawback of this is that punishment (with the exception of natural and logical consequences, which we will address below) is not effective because it does not teach what *to do*. Moreover, whatever caused the student to act unconstructively is not addressed. Because the underlying need is unresolved and an alternative constructive means of addressing that student's need was not learned, the student is likely to act in the same way in the future.

The Traditional Approach Uses the Power of Rules and School Authority to Suppress Behavior

The focus is blame, and the result, more often than not, is shame. Punishment, with its inherent blame and shame, does not teach understanding and empathy. Blame and shame do not restore the community. Rather, schisms are created—between teacher and student and among students. In addition, the "offender" may want to strike out in revenge or retaliation against authority because his needs were also violated and he was left with no way to address this.

The Restorative Approach includes Natural, Social, and Imposed but Logical Consequences to Teach Constructive Behavior

A natural consequence occurs without teacher intervention; for example, if Bernie does not do homework, a *natural* consequence might be that he lacks practice, so he will not have learned the material and will do poorly when the learning is evaluated. An *imposed* but *logical* consequence would be that he does not receive credit for that assignment. A combination natural and social consequence might occur the next day if Bernie were asked to do small-group work that depended on having done the homework and he could not uphold his portion of the group work (natural); his group work would suffer, and members might be frustrated or angry with him (social consequence). He would then make amends by explaining to the teacher that it was his work, not the rest of the group's, that hadn't been done. He would discuss with the teacher and group members what he might do to make things right. Of these consequences, team members could determine the logical ones with the teacher, if all agree that the imposed consequences are needed "to teach."

The Restorative Approach Supports Change

It offers the opportunity (and space) for the student whose behavior was unconstructive to feel vulnerability of remorse. This approach is more likely to foster the understanding that there are consequences for choices made, to lessen shame and, equally important, to enhance empathy. The result is a useful life learning experience.

The Restorative Approach Maintains the Community

In fact, if done well, the restorative approach enhances the positive feelings in the community.

I encourage us to work with students to implement this approach as rules and consequences are being established.

We Establish the Use of the Restorative Approach

As a community, we discuss (as is appropriate for the developmental level of the students) the natural consequences that occur if students follow each rule and if they do not. Then, if appropriate, we have the students develop with us an agreement of what, if any, contrived or imposed logical consequences would occur. The discussion should include both the positive and *constructive* negative consequences. As facilitators, we need to ensure that imposed consequences are fair and will be experienced by anyone. We also need to ensure that imposed consequences are logical and, thereby, directly connected to the behavior in question. Imposed consequences must also be respectful and safe and thereby address students' emotional needs so that constructive learning can occur. They need to *maintain the connection between the students and the learning community because* they do not cut off the student through embarrassment, humiliation, or any form of harm. Examples of imposed, logical consequences:

- If you are disrespectful with materials, you must put them down and leave the activity until you are ready to follow the class rule.
- If you have broken the materials, you must clean up your mess and contribute to replacing them to the degree that you can.
- If you are disrespectful to a person, you must "clean up your mess" by talking with the person to resolve the conflict constructively and make amends.

We Establish Expectations by Creating Procedures

In addition to working with students to establish general class rules, teachers need to provide two kinds of procedures that outline their expectation (Jones & Jones, 2016). The first explains how to behave during certain activities; for example, how students will behave in a cooperative learning experience, during an exam, when transitions occur, at the close of class for the day, or when walking in line. An example appears on the right. The second discusses how to be accountable and responsible; for example, by knowing when work is due, what to do to make up work if absent, or how clean the room should be at certain times or after certain activities.

The following areas are addressed in procedures (Emmer & Evertson, 2017; Evertson & Emmer, 2017):

4 Behaviors for Walking in Line[v]

1. **Behind the person in front of you (not next to) and leaving a space in between** (with an illustration of two stick figures facing forward and an arrow indicating space between the two).

2. **Resting mouth** (with an illustration of a profile with lips closed and hand with the first finger near the mouth indicating no noise coming out).

3. **Walking feet** (with an illustration of a stick figure walking).

4. **Hands and feet to self** (with an illustration of figure with both hands at her side and feet underneath her body).

- Students' use of classroom space and facilities, along with room maintenance.
- Students' behavior during specific times, such as when they arrive, at the close of the class or day, at snack time, when a visitor enters the room, or when there is a fire or lockdown drill.
- Students' behavior outside the classroom. (This is typically addressed with elementary students in more depth than those in middle school.)
- Students' academic accountability. (Not surprisingly, this area is addressed more often by middle school teachers, than elementary ones where greater independent accountability is expected.)
- Administrative procedures that must be handled during class time: for example, taking attendance or doing the lunch count.
- How to respond when signals are used by the teacher.

We Use Signals as Procedures to Support Constructive Behavior

As procedures signals can cue students to start an activity, stop one, or gain their attention in the midst of one. Signals can be auditory or visual. Examples include playing music associated with a particular activity, such as cleaning up or turning off lights (but not flickering them, since that can be unsettling to students and, in the worst case, cause seizures). Some signals infuse fun into the experience; e.g., the word "freeze" tells students to freeze their movements, no matter what. This signal usually results in a bit of laughter because of the "poses." If students are talking in small groups, a visual signal may be more effective, since a spoken one may be difficult to distinguish over their conversations. An effective sound other than the human voice, like a train whistle, chime, bell, or musical alarm on a cell phone, could also capture their attention. Other useful auditory signals include:

+ Clapping in a particular rhythm. Students respond in kind. The teacher changes the rhythm. Students must listen to be able to respond. (Variety in the rhythms makes it fun.)
+ Teacher: *"1, 2, 3, all eyes on me."* Students: *"1, 2, all eyes on you."*
+ Teacher: *"Uno, dos, tres, please look at my face"* or *"5, 4, 3, 2 … eyes should be on me … and 1."*
+ Teacher: *"Finish what you are writing/saying [pause until the level of noise quiets a bit]. May I have your attention, please."*
+ Teacher: *"Give me five"* while raising hand with fingers outspread. The five fingers are reminders to: 1) put materials down; 2) still bodies; 3) be silent; 4) look at teacher; and 5) listen to next direction.

We Teach the Procedures We Use, Review, and Implement Consistently

Students may not fully understand what certain procedures mean. Moreover, for each class the procedure may be slightly different. How a student has learned to turn in work with one teacher does not mean she will be prepared for the unique expectations of another. Students also need to be aware of the consequences for following procedures and those for not following them. For example, if learning logs are turned in on Fridays, what happens? If they are not turned in, then what is the result?

The steps for teaching procedures are the same ones we addressed earlier that are effective for teaching any new skill that.

Teaching rules and procedures when they are first addressed is not enough. As Levin and Nolan (2014) remind us, some students do not learn rules or procedures right away. Other students learn the procedures and rules but forget to utilize them. Over time, any rule or procedure might be forgotten. When this occurs, we quickly review. We can ask students to look for (anonymous) examples of incidents when people are correctly following a rule or by asking students to write a letter to a parent explaining the meaning of one or more procedures. Initially, these reviews should happen frequently. As students become more successful, the time in between reviewing rules can lengthen. The younger the students and the more complex the procedure, the greater the need for review.

We need to implement the system consistently. We monitor compliance. Ensure positive results for students who follow the rules and procedures. We evaluate the effectiveness of the system with the students by, for example, asking the question: "Does some aspect of this rule need to be changed?"

We Provide Expectations for Student Responsibilities in Running the Classroom

Establishing a system of classroom jobs helps build community and provides opportunities for students to carry out responsibilities that contribute to a supportive learning environment. As students carry out the responsibilities, they can feel that they are giving something back to the learning community.[vi] This feeling can be fostered by giving those who carried out the jobs some appreciation at the end of the week, especially when expressed by the whole community. A silent cheer, "applause" in American Sign Language, or a "thumbs up" are examples.

An effective way to build social skills and community responsibility is to ask the students (in trios and then with the whole class) to come up with a list of jobs that would make the room a good place to be. As with rules, determining responsibilities *with* the students gives them a greater sense of importance and competence in the community. We can add delight to the process by inviting students to come up with names for the roles (including having them consider using alliteration for the titles). In some rooms, someone is given the job of answering the door, while someone else runs errands (UPS/USPS Delivery Person). In elementary grades, Line Leader is often a favorite. Noise Navigator and Officer in Charge of Time can be helpful, particularly whenever teamwork activities occur during the class. Materials Handler (often called Handout Helper in primary grades) is a helpful job at any grade level. Chair Chief, Table Tidier, and Floor Fancier[vii] are delightful names for three jobs any room could benefit from having. These could be combined and given the title of "Room Manager" in middle school grades. Possibilities for this role include making sure the room is clean, desks and tables are clear of unnecessary materials, and chairs are where they need to be, along with checking that all is ready for the next activity or when the next group enters. This role could also include, if appropriate, turning out the lights when everyone has gone and no one will be there for a while. The person in this role is a facilitator for getting these tasks done by collaborating with classmates and contributing himself. As you might imagine, mentoring for this role by the teacher is needed. This would include having a class conversation about how to go about asking others to help with what needs to be done (That is an important life skill.).

The jobs chart, with dates, needs to be posted where everyone can see it. In some classes, a sign adjacent to the jobs list reads, "If I am absent, _____ will help by doing this job until I return," or, to make the choice of a substitute easy, the next name on the list of students waiting for a turn is used. I have seen elementary classes that have weekly job lists with responsibilities for *everyone* in the class. This is accomplished by having many jobs and many people assigned to any given job, such as Breakfast Delivery People, Lunch Box Delivery People (two wagons for lunch bags or boxes taken to the cafeteria), Room Manager, Book Distributor, and Materials Gatherer. The final job (with two spaces) was "Job Substitute."

We Provide Expectations at the Beginning of Each Lesson

As we have said, each lesson needs a launch that includes a statement of expectations for learning/learning targets and for the behavior that is the focus of the student's work. These provide clarity about where the lesson is headed and what students need to do to be successful in reaching that destination.

We Teach Constructive Community Behavior by Example

Modeling is a powerful teaching tool. We can be an ongoing example that contributes to creating a learning community.

> ✦ We are fair, unbiased, and without prejudice.

"Students have more need of models than critics."

— Joseph Joubert

- ✦ We use respectful language, even if we disagree.
- ✦ When a problem arises, we describe the situation objectively as a problem to be solved, not as students to be criticized for their feelings or behavior.
- ✦ We avoid using racist, sexist, or ageist language or telling jokes that ridicule any group of people.
- ✦ We learn about and use our knowledge of the cultural behavior patterns of the students we teach.
- ✦ We honor what a student is feeling whether we agree or not.
- ✦ We use individual performance or criterion references for evaluation.
- ✦ We deal with private matters privately.
- ✦ We model a passion for learning, for the content we teach, and for our work with the students.
- ✦ We express caring and compassion.
- ✦ We never use sarcasm.
  - ♦ **Sarcasm is a mixed message** that at once draws someone into the content of the communication and pushes him away with the tone. Pushing students away thwarts their basic emotional needs to feel cared for, to be connected to us, and, thereby, to belong.
  - ♦ **Sarcasm is confusing.** Does a student pay attention to the words or the tone of voice we are using? The often-subtle disparity between the tone and content would be particularly confusing to a student who has a hearing disability, a student with language processing problems, or some students on the autism spectrum. For those who can sense the mixed nature of the message, the question becomes "What do I do?"
  - ♦ **Sarcasm implies criticism.** *But what is the nature of the criticism?* Sarcasm does not meet the need to enable a student to feel efficacious.
  - ♦ **Sarcasm misses the purpose of communication**—to send a clear message to someone. If the sarcastic tone is a reflection of frustration, then we need to say, "I am frustrated." If our reaction is to something just said, then that reaction needs to be stated: "I don't agree. Here's why …"
  - ♦ **Sarcasm is not authentic.** If we want students to be authentic as speakers, we need to provide models of authentic communication when we are speaking. We need to be examples of how to communicate effectively.

Teaching is *not* doing; teaching is being. We cannot effectively teach what we are not already ourselves.

How Can We Integrate Collaborative Structures into the Learning Experiences and Constructive Social Skills into the Curriculum?

We Use Many Structures to Facilitate Students Supporting Other Students in a Learning Community

Ask Three Before Me ("three" refers to other students, and "me" refers to the teacher). This process is one that can be established for portions of a class, when appropriate.

Help Wanted. For various activities, students fill out and post signs that look like the old-time sheriff's "wanted" posters or those found in our post offices today. Other students print their name below to indicate their willingness to help with particular content or a skill. An example would be:

Table 6-6. **Example of How to Foster Collaborative Structures**

~WANTED~	I can help:
Someone who can help with:	_____
_____	_____

Resource People for Particular Skills. Provide students (and adults) in the learning community an opportunity to make a list (perhaps with the help of classmates, friends, family, other teachers) of the talents they have, from whistling to creating web sites to creating illustrations for books, poetry, maps, or three-dimensional geometric objects. Then, as a class, determine (according to the developmental level of the children) how best to display such information. Some examples that I have seen include having each student sign up under topics on a chart and listing names by topic in a resource directory that was typed on a word processor so additions could be made later. Imagine the opportunities for students to learn other skills (depending upon their grade level) while compiling resources: brainstorming, categorizing, indexing, alphabetizing, etc.

Homework Buddies. A middle school science teacher with whom I worked used this strategy in all his classes. Students were invited (if, after reading an explanation of the process from the teacher, the students had been given written adult permission) to give their phone numbers to members of their cooperative team. A student could call another for clarification for support. (The teacher had worked with all the students on how to help without giving answers). A buddy could also call to cheer a teammate on towards homework completion by the due date so all on the team would earn points for completing assignments on time.

Potential Peer Coaches. We can provide some means for students who have indicated that they are comfortable enough to support others to coach another student on a skill being learned in class. I have seen kindergarten children sign up as helpers for anything from secretary (writing another student's ideas down) for the narrative of a book to reading a story aloud. In a middle school class, the skill focus would be different. Since learners are unique, the process needs to be driven by those who want help—it is they who need to define what is needed and when it would be helpful. No one is forced to be a coach or to use a coach, but the expectation is that folks will take advantage of the opportunity if they are stuck. Needs change with time and content focus: today, a student may be able to help with math; tomorrow, that same student may be stumped on how to apply a particular algorithm; therefore, whatever mechanism is developed needs to allow fluidity.

Peer Tutors. We can make it possible for students to become academic or activity (sports, music, the arts) tutors for others. Peer tutors have ongoing relationships with their tutees for any focus and with a variety of age combinations. The focus may be on supporting the tutee in learning, or the tutor, or both. The opportunity for the tutor to revisit material or skills in the process of explaining it or demonstrating it to someone else and to organize it, yet again, aids retention. Tutors can also gain feelings of self-worth and competence as they see the success of their work. **Note:** Students who catch on the fastest to a new skill may not be the best tutors; rather, those who have about average speed in learning are often the most effective at explaining and demonstrating to others and incorporating the necessary patience and timing into their tutorial. Being a good tutor is not easy, nor does one "just do it naturally" (Johnson & Johnson, 1995a). To be successful, tutors need content focus that they have already mastered; a structured, prescribed format for the lessons; and opportunities to learn how to tutor under the support of a teacher-coach.

Peer Teaching: We can have two or more students form a team to explore a focused topic of interest, given whatever we are studying at the time. With a class discussion of what makes learning interesting and likely to be grasped, students can create a brief presentation including visuals/music and activities to support peer learning.

Peer Mediators. We can teach students how to mediate to help peers negotiate conflicts—training, practice, and effort are needed. All community members need to be taught how to mediate. Then having a fair means of choosing each day who will be the mediators is needed, as well as a means of evaluating the program. One characteristic of successful programs is that they are grade level or school-wide. Each step is facilitated by the trained peer mediator (Wolfgang, 2009). The steps include:

Step 1: Agreement to mediate by all parties involved—a neutral location is chosen;

Step 2: Gathering of everyone's points of view—done respectfully without blaming or criticizing others;

Step 3: Gathering of information about what it is that each wants;

Step 4: Creation of win-win options for resolving the conflict without any judgements or evaluation;

Step 5: Evaluation of the options from Step 4 so each person feels the potential solution meets his needs;

Step 6: Creation of an agreement that is formalized, written down, and signed by all parties involved;

Formal peer mediation programs are not necessary; however, a designed curriculum is often a helpful starting place. Most programs begin at the fourth grade.

Resources

References can be found at the end of the chapter under "Resources for Students Supporting Students" and "Resources for Peer Mediation."

Cooperative Learning Experiences: Cooperative learning structures are reciprocal. Each student is invested in his own learning *as well as* that of other members in the group. The goal is to work together cooperatively in such a way that all are teachers and all are learners—each gives and each gains. Cooperative learning is done in pairs or small groups. There is a common task that is appropriate for all group members, although what each gives to and gains from the learning experience may be different. Interdependence is fostered by our design of the activity. All are responsible. Each is held accountable for the work done by the group and the material that was to be learned.

One source for cooperative structures comes in the form of curriculum-specific packages. These focus on the design of cooperative learning experiences that are uniquely tailored to specific content, such as math, science, integrated reading, and composition. These are lockstep approaches with prescribed procedures. Examples of curriculum packages include Team Accelerated Instruction for Math and Cooperative Integrated Reading and Composition—both by Richard Slavin (Slavin, Madden, Chambers, & Haxby, 2009; Slavin and Madden, 2001). While not specific to one content, the Group Investigation Method by Sharan & Sharan (1992) from the ideas of Thelan (1981) would be used for those subject areas in which investigation of ideas is appropriate.

Another source of collaborative, cooperative structures includes those developed to be used with any curriculum content. One example was developed by Aronson and Patnoe (1997). It is called Jigsaw. A second example falls under the Structural Approach of Kagan (1990; 1994; 2009). This latter approach offers structures rather than procedures for addressing specific curriculum. Structures are broken down into elements (e.g., "brainstorm," "write," "check,"" interview") so that a teacher can create a lesson manipulating the smaller elements within a structure. I believe that the drawbacks of the Structural Approach include that it does not require that both a social and an academic task goal be made explicit for each lesson nor that team monitoring occur.

A third form of cooperative learning called Learning Together was designed by members of the Johnson family (Johnson, Johnson, & Holubec, 2008). Learning Together is *content independent*. It can be used with any curriculum. What makes Learning Together distinct is that it specifically builds social skills. While the Kagan approach does offer structures for team skills, I find the Johnsons' approach holds me in better stead when I teach social skills. In Chapter 7, we will address how to implement this approach. For now, references under the Johnsons' names appear at the chapter's end.

Marzano (2017) believes that of all the group strategies possible, cooperative learning is likely to be the most powerful. If you want to use a form of cooperative learning in any content area, Appendix C to this chapter contains an extensive list of a variety of quick starters for all ages. These are good to use any time, but they would be helpful for easing into cooperative learning structures and processes as you are getting to know the students, their learning strengths, and their needs.

We Minimize the Use of Unhealthy Competitive Structures

....

ACCESSING PRIOR KNOWLEDGE/EXPERIENCE

Recall your own experience in a team-against-team competition. What was the behavior of the participants when they were winning and when they were losing? Did everyone on the winning team seem to enjoy the experience? If not, why not? Did everyone on the losing team enjoy losing? If not, why not? When the competition was done, how did the winners treat the losers? How did the losers treat the winners? How did each respond to the treatment of the others'? From what was said and how people acted, what feeling do you think the winners had about themselves and about the skill or the information on which they were being tested? How do you think the losers felt about both? In the space provided or elsewhere note key words and images from your reflection. _____

_____

_____

_____

_____

....

Many teachers and administrators believe using academic competition in the classroom encourages students to excel. People often argue that our society is based on competition and the only way to learn how to compete—to develop resilience and an open mindset when competing—is to practice competing. For years now, the research in the field has not supported this belief (Bernard, 2004; Henderson, 2013; Johnson & Johnson, 1989; NEA, 2006–2007; Southwick & Charney, 2012; Werner, 2007). Instead, the only time children and young adults feel safe and competent enough to do well in a competition is when they feel good about themselves, when they feel they are capable of winning, and when they know they have at least an *even* chance of doing so. Resilience to competition is not fostered by practicing competing. Therefore, fostering achievement through competition seems most appropriate in situations in which muscle power and physical skill are being tested, when a person is able to pace herself according to the performance of a *comparable* athlete, and when competitors are able to use the adrenaline rush of competition to feed energy to muscles to help push to greater heights. In such classes, when students are fairly evenly matched, being pitted against another may not risk emotional safety in many students.

In contrast to athletic events, competition in classrooms is unhealthy because it often pits one person's cognitive and creative skills against another's. How many can win such a competition? More importantly, how many students would lose? In fact, how many would know they were going to lose even before they began? What does it feel like for a person to experience a frequent reminder that he is not good enough or that she is not as quick or as skilled as her classmates? How would you feel under such circumstances? These are not feelings of safety when learning. In unhealthy competition, there is a shift in focus from the process—from learning—to the outcome: winning. Unhealthy competition dissolves some of the qualities inherent in learning communities: playfulness, wonder, delight, and sensitivity. All these "in-the-moment" experiences are lost when finishing the product (time competition) or the finished product itself (result competition) are what matters. Moreover, competition blocks good creative work because it promotes a defensive posture.

As teachers or students, when we focus on how we are doing *in comparison to someone else*, we lose sight of what is really important—how *we* are doing; we lose sight of what is really important—how we feel about the quality of what are we *doing*. For all but the winners, competition accentuates what we lack, not what we have.

Competition places the judgment and control of quality outside the individual. Yet we have no control over the quality of what others do; we can only contribute to the quality of our own creation. One should not have to lose in order for another to win. Opening our own possibilities so that we can be the best at what *we* do is what learning is all about.

Other serious concerns about unhealthy forms of competition are that they do not enhance connection or they connect students who make up a team but pit them against others. As we know, connection with others in the community—a constructive sense of belonging—is what addresses students' basic needs.

In addition to direct-competition structures, a subtle form of unhealthy competition that is also important to consider getting rid of is students' knowing the evaluative quality of each other's work. To avoid this, we can have students correct their own work. Example: Immediately following an evaluation process that includes multiple choice and short answers, I have students put away their pens or pencils, and I pass out a container of thin colored markers. We go over the answers. They can ask questions to get confusions clarified right away. They put a "C" next to those that are correct and a "?" next to any answer they want me to be sure to double check when I review their work later. This way, they get immediate feedback.

We can also get rid of comparative evaluation in the way we collect and return materials. We can do it upside-down—be sure students write their names on the back as well as the front—or we ask students to put their work in a "Work Done" basket, upside-down. Lastly, we can post only work that is totally free of grades or comments. In learning communities, we want the spirit of learning, the spirit of creation, the spirits of all students to reign.

Shindler (2008) distinguishes unhealthy from healthy competition. In unhealthy competition:

- It feels real. The winners and losers will be affected.
- The competitive goal/reward is valuable/real and is characterized that way.
- The learning task is characterized as a means to an end (winning the competition).
- Winners are able to use their victory as social or educational capital at a later time.
- Competition implicitly or explicitly rewards the advantaged students.
- Over time, students develop an increasingly competitive mindset.

In healthy competition:

- The primary goal is fun.
- The competitive goal is not valuable/real, nor is it characterized that way.
- The learning and/or growth goal is conspicuously characterized as valuable.
- The competition has a short duration and is characterized by high energy.
- There is no long-term effect from the episode.
- All individuals or groups see a reasonable chance of winning.

- The students all firmly understand these points.
- Examples include trivia contests, short-term competitions for a solely symbolic reward, and lighthearted challenges between groups where there is no reward.

Competition Can Have a Possible Benefit Under Healthy Circumstances

Competition can provide a change of pace or an element of fun in learning if it is thoughtfully designed and provided in a manner that relies on a form that Marzano (2007) calls "inconsequential competition." *Each person has an equal chance to win, and the "prize" for winning is having a good time.*

By contrast to unhealthy competitive learning experiences, we know from years of research that, if done well, cooperative learning teams in which students work together to maximize each other's learning can promote the acceptance and the development of positive relationships among community members (Johnson & Johnson, 2009; Johnson, Johnson, & Johnson, 2006; Loguidice, n.d.). As Saphier (2008) reminds us, we want students in our community to build bonds of allegiance and respect for their peers. Students do not build bonds and allegiance with those against whom they compete.

Resources

References for further reading can be found at the chapter's end under "Resources for Cooperative Learning and on Competition."

How Can We Help Community Members Celebrate?

There are other kinds of beginnings we can celebrate. Some beginnings are important every day. Rituals help to open a class. As part of students' integral participation in the learning community, we can create ways for them to be responsible for management procedures. If everyone knows that attendance or lunch count or homework check-in will occur first thing and they have been taught what is expected, then the job is done quickly and efficiently with the coordination of a different student each week. The whole class contributes to the common task. Other routine rituals serve to ease the transition into or out of a particular activity or class. I have used upbeat music to support transitions.

We have already addressed how to begin a new class by setting up a community of learners with a climate of respect and possibility and establishing expectations for the members. Whenever someone new enters, both of these processes need to be revisited—people need to get to know each other, and the new person needs to know what behaviors are expected of him and of others. When this occurs, since most community members have already done this work, the process can be completed at a much quicker pace.

REFLECTION OPPORTUNITY

On a separate piece of paper or in the space provided write your responses.

What might be some ways to support the entrance of a new student into a learning community?

_____

_____

_____

What might be some ways to support the entrance of an adult into the learning community? _____

_____

_____

_____

Think about the implications of what you just have written for preparing the students for a substitute teacher to take over a class. (As we know, this is a time when unconstructive behavior can likely occur.) What might you do with the students in advance of having a substitute come, and what might you have students do for the substitute? _____

_____

_____

_____

The day after the substitute comes, how might you foster the students' reflection about "what went well" and "what could be done the next time to have things go even better"? (Note: We set up our questions so there is no focus on criticism and blaming—we don't want students' brains to be shut down during the refection process—even if something did not work out as hoped. Growth is only possible if we can be open to what we learn from reflecting.) _____

_____

_____

_____

• •

To introduce a new student or a substitute teacher to our class (our grade team, our school), we can use the opportunity to enhance our students' investigative, writing and/or math skills to create a welcoming brochure. We can add their art or photography skills to add to the pamphlet. When students work with us to create a booklet for someone new to the community, they are much more likely to contribute to welcoming and being supportive when someone new enters.

REFLECTION OPPORTUNITY

Think of the groups or teams you have watched. What do many do to energize themselves before they start their work, whether it is heading out onto a playing field, beginning a concert or debate, or opening a store first thing in the morning? In the space provided or on a separate piece of paper write what comes to mind._____

_____

_____

What effect might these activities have on the members' sense of belonging? _____

_____

_____

I have seen teams give a brief greeting or cheer. You can use the same strategy with your class. Rituals pull the group together as a cohesive whole. Share a greeting around to every member, sing a brief song together, or do a rap or chant together. The class can repeat a slogan or have a question–answer ritual, such as calling out, *"Who is awesome?"* to which the group responds in chorus, *"We are!"* These activities help to ask the students to come up with a ritual. The possibilities are endless.

How Can We Help Students Make the Room Their Own?

We Incorporate Student-Created Posters and Exhibits into the Unfolding Curriculum

We design a series of lessons that requires students to "teach" others their portion of the material through the creation of an engaging exhibit, display, or poster that invites community members to interact with the contents. Individual students or teams of students can construct a diagram/poster/display to demonstrate what they have learned. I have seen bulletin board exhibits created by students to communicate expectations established by the class, illustrate issues that were embedded in the Civil War, show "six great ways to make new friends," solve a math problem, and teach how to recycle materials.

We Provide Opportunities for Everyone to "Publish" Work of Which

Each is Proud

Publishing of work done in the room can include models of geometric shapes; books of students' personal narratives, poems, and essays; or a newsletter/newspaper of articles and stories about community members' experiences, perspectives, and insights. There need to be opportunities for *everyone* to publish, although not all may choose to do so. Moreover, there can be no ranking or evaluation of work in public. Equally important, students need to play a role in choosing what piece of their work they wish to have published.

We Infuse the Room with Student Creative Processes and Signatures

In addition to student-created displays relating to curriculum, we can decorate the walls, fill shelves, and provide CD players to share the creative work of the students that may not relate directly to the curriculum content. In any community, there are budding musicians, artists, photographers, computer graphics designers, cartoonists, illustrators, and poets. We can ask them if they would like to share their work with others on the walls, doors, and bulletin boards, not to mention suspended from the ceiling (as long as the items don't distract students from the foci of learning).

We have said learning communities value collaboration, so encouraging joint efforts should be a part of the process. We have also said learning communities value individuals as unique human beings—each has something to offer, so work displayed that would *not* include products that look virtually alike (e.g., 23 penguins made from the same cutout shapes for each part of the body).

> Note: Students need to understand that student and teacher approval is required for any material shared in the room or the hallway outside the room.

In Appendix D at the end of the chapter is a checklist ("Questions to Consider When We Reflect on to What Degree We are Addressing Students' Basic Emotional Needs") to help us remember all the "bricks" we as teachers can use to build a supportive classroom community. I have adapted the format and added to the wording of the original to be sure the list addresses each of the five basic needs.

Application Activity

In Chapters 3 and 5 when we discussed physical environment variables, we said we could look at classroom arrangement and contents to determine whether structure and nurturing that meet basic emotional needs are being provided. With the completion of Chapters 4 and 6, the analysis of evidence can be taken one step further. When we look in a classroom, we can find evidence that structure is being provided, nurturing is occurring, *and they are being done in a way that establishes a community of learners*. What evidence would we see? The chart below provides you an opportunity to answer that question.

On the left side of the chart is a list of strategies that meet basic needs and establish a community that includes some of the strategies we have discussed. For each strategy write the evidence we might find in a classroom. There may be more than one piece of evidence for a strategy. If you need some hints: With which strategies in the chart might you place the following pieces of evidence?

✦ A sign that reminds: "Ask 3 before me." or "Silence is a *must* during fire and lock down drills!"
✦ Student work displayed with no evaluation.
✦ Displays to acquaint community members with each other.

Remember: There may be more than one piece of evidence.

Table 6-7. **Evidence of Strategies that Create a Constructive Learning Community**	
Strategy that Meets Basic Needs & Establishes a Community	**Teaching Evidence One Might See in a Classroom**
Foster connections between the students and you as a person, as well as you as a teacher who facilitates student leaning.	
Foster connections among learning community members.	
Create a warm, supportive class tone that communicates possibility.	
Integrate collaborative structures that provide student-to-student support.	
Integrate collaborative structures into learning experiences and social skills into the curriculum.	
Teach constructive community behavior by example.	
Establish expectations for constructive behavior with community members.	
Find ways to have students infuse their room with their own creative processes and signatures.	

Final Thoughts

When as teachers we are asked what we do, we often say we teach English/language arts, second grade, math, art, or special education. Mathematical problem-solving, participatory citizenship, written and oral communication, and the arts are certainly important—all our curricular content is. But I believe we teach *children*. The content is the medium we use to prepare our students for life. As I reflect on the goal of our work, I often think of what a former student said to my friend after he found her on Facebook and was pleased to connect with her across the country after more than 40 years. As he talked about being in her class, he said, "You caught my heart."[viii] Isn't that what we are all about as we teach—catching the hearts of students? And with their hearts safely in hand, isn't our work about letting them see their possibilities—their undiscovered talents[ix] and skills—and finding strategies to work with them to make those possibilities come to fruition before we send them on their way? This is what these last two chapters have been about for me—how we provide structure and nurturance through our work with students to capture their hearts in our learning community.

Looking Forward

In our efforts to support constructive behavior, establishing a community with students is essential but not sufficient. Therefore, in the next section, we will address how to *maintain* a constructive learning community using variables in both the students' physical and psychosocial environments.

References

Anderson, K. & Forkner, P. (2013). *Resilience and the student experience: Building grit and perseverance in our students.* Handouts from presentation for the New York State College Health Association. Retrieved 2017 from http://www.nyscha.org/files/2015/handouts/WE-2.04%20-%20Resilience%20and%20the %20Student%20Experience.pdf

Armstrong, T. (2002). *You're smarter than you think: A kid's guide to multiple intelligences.* Minneapolis, MN: Free Spirit.

Armstrong, T. (2009). *Multiple intelligences in the classroom* (3rd ed.). Alexandria, VA: Association for Supervision and Curriculum Development.

Armstrong, T. (2016). *The power of the adolescent brain.* Alexandria, VA: Association for Supervision and Curriculum Development.

Aronson, E., & Patnoe, S. (1997). *The jigsaw classroom: Building cooperation in the classroom (2nd ed.).* New York, NY: Addison Wesley Longman.

Bernard, B. (2004). *Resiliency: What we have learned.* San Francisco, CA: WestEd.

Cameron, J. (1992). *The artist's way*. New York, NY: Tarcher.

Carbo, M. (2014, September). Powerful best reading practices for struggling readers, part 7. The reading gamble: Improving the odds for struggling readers. *Instructional Leader* (Texas Elementary Principals and Supervisors Association), *27*(5), pp. 10–12.

Carbo, M. (2017). *Reading styles training manual*. Syosset, NY: National Reading Styles Institute. Retrieved from http://www.nrsi.com/publications.php

Charney, R. (2002). *Teaching children to care* (2nd ed.). Greenfield, MA: Northeast Foundations for Children.

Child Development Project. (1991). *Start the year*. Unpublished manuscript, San Ramon, CA: Developmental Studies Center.

Cole, R., (Ed.). (2008). *Educating everybody's children* (2nd ed.). Alexandria, VA: Association for Supervision and Curriculum Development.

Dean, C., Hubbell, E., Pitler, H., & Stone, Bj. (2012). *Classroom instruction that works: Research-based strategies for increasing student achievement* (2nd ed.). Alexandria, VA: Association for Supervision and Curriculum Development.

Duckworth, A. (2016). *Grit: the power of passion and perseverance*. New York, NY: Scribner.

Dweck, C. (2006). *Mindset: The new psychology of success*. New York, NY: Ballantine Books.

Emmer, E., & Evertson, C. (2017). *Classroom management for middle and high school teachers* [loose-leaf version] (10th ed.). Boston, MA: Pearson.

Emmer, E., & Gerwels, M. (2006) Classroom management in middle and high school classrooms. In C. Evertson & C. Weinstein (Eds.), *Handbook of classroom management* (pp. 407–437). Mahwah, NJ: Lawrence Erlbaum Associates.

Evertson, C., Emmer, W., & Worsham, M. (2017). *Classroom management for elementary teachers* [loose-leaf version] (10th ed.). Boston, MA: Allyn & Bacon.

Gardner, H. (1997). *Extraordinary minds: Portraits of exceptional individuals and an examination of our own extraordinariness*. New York, NY: Basic Books.

Gathercoal, F. (2001). *Judicious discipline* (6th ed.). San Francisco, CA: Caddo Gap Press.

Glasser, W. (1998a). *The quality school: Managing students without coercion* (3rd ed.). New York, NY: Harper Perennial.

Glasser, W. (1998b). *The quality school teacher* (2nd ed.). New York, NY: HarperCollins.

Goleman, D. (2006). *Social intelligence: The new science of human relationships*. New York, NY: Random House.

Good, T., & brophy, J. (2008). *Looking in classrooms* (10th ed.). Boston, MA: Pearson.

Gregory, G., & Kaufeldt, M. (2015). *The motivated brain: Improving student attention, engagement, and perseverance*. Alexandria, VA: Association for Supervision and Curriculum Development.

Henderson, N. (September 2013). Havens of reliance. *Educational Leadership: Resilience and Learning, 71*(1), 23–27.

Herbert, F. (1965). *Dune.* Southborough, MA: Chilton Books.

Hoerr, T. (2017). *The formative five: Fostering grit, empathy and other success skills every student needs.* Alexandria, VA: Association for Supervision and Curriculum Development.

Kohl, H. (2000). *The discipline of hope.* New York, NY: The Free Press.

Jensen, E. (2005). *Teaching with the brain in mind* (2nd ed.). Alexandria, VA: Association for Supervision and Curriculum Development.

Jensen, E. (2013). *Engaging students with poverty in mind.* Alexandria, VA: Association for Supervision and Curriculum Development.

Jensen, E. (2015a). *Guiding principles for brain-based learning.* Retrieved from http://www.brainbasedlearning.net/guiding-principles-for-brain-based-education/

Jensen, E. (2015b) *What is brain-based research?* Retrieved from http://www.jensenlearning.com/what-is-brain-based-research.php

Johnson, D., & Johnson, F. (2016). *Joining together: Group theory and group skills* (12th ed.). Boston: Allyn & Bacon.

Johnson, D., & Johnson, R. (1989). *Cooperation and competition.* Edina, MN: Interaction Book Co.

Johnson, D., & Johnson, R. (1994). *Learning together and alone: Cooperative competitive and individualistic learning* (4th ed.). Boston: Allyn & Bacon.

Johnson, D., & Johnson, R. (1995a). *My mediation notebook* (3rd ed.). Edina, MN: Interaction Book Co.

Johnson, D., & Johnson, R. (1995b). *Reducing school violence through conflict resolution.* Alexandria, VA: Association for Supervision and Curriculum Development.

Johnson, D., & Johnson, R. (1995c). *Teaching students to be peacemakers.* Edina, MN: Interaction Book Co.

Johnson, D., & Johnson, R. (2006). Conflict resolution, peer mediation and peacemaking. In C. Evertson & C. Weinstein (Eds.), *Handbook of classroom management* (pp. 803–832). Mahwah, NJ: Lawrence Erlbaum Associates.

Johnson, D., & Johnson, R. (2009). An educational psychology success story: Social interdependence theory and cooperative learning. *Educational Researcher, 38*(5), 365–379.

Johnson, D., Johnson, R., & Holubec, E. (2008). *Cooperation in the classroom* (8th ed.). Alexandria, VA: Association for Supervision and Curriculum Development.

Jones, V. (2015). *Practical classroom management* [loose-leaf version] (2nd ed.). Boston, MA: Pearson.

Jones, V., & Jones, L. (2016). *Comprehensive classroom management: Creating communities of support and solving problems* [loose-leaf version] (11th ed.). Boston, MA: Pearson.

Kagan, S. (1994). *Cooperative learning* (2nd ed.). San Juan Capistrano, CA: Resources for Teachers.

Kagan, S. (2009). *Kagan cooperative learning*. San Clemente, CA: Kagan Cooperative Learning.

Kagan, L., Kagan, M., & Kagan, S. (1997). *Cooperative structures for teambuilding*. San Clemente, CA: Kagan Publishing.

Kohn, A. (1992). *No contest: The case against competition* (2nd ed.). Boston, MA: Houghton Mifflin.

Kohn, A. (1996). *Beyond discipline: From compliance to community*. Alexandria, VA: Association for Supervision and Curriculum Development.

Lazear, D. (1999). *Eight ways of teaching: The artistry of teaching with multiple intelligences*. Arlington Heights, IL: Skylight.

Loguidice, T. (n.d.). Cooperative and small group learning. *Semantic Scholar*. Retrieved from https://pdfs.semanticscholar.org/f3b6/bc6541b14a8dd0e2c477af635ec7eb2bbcad.pdf

Marzano, R. (2007). *The art and science of teaching: A comprehensive framework for effective instruction*. Alexandria, VA: Association for Supervision and Curriculum Development.

Marzano, R. (2017). *The new art and science of teaching*. Alexandria, VA: Association for Supervision and Curriculum Development.

Marzano, R., Gaddy, B., Foseid, M. C., Foseid, M. P., & Marzano, J. (2005). *A handbook for classroom management that works*. Alexandria, VA: Association for Supervision and Curriculum Development.

Marzano, R., Marzano, J., & Pickering, D. (2003). *Classroom management that works: Research-based strategies for every teacher*. Alexandria, VA: Association for Supervision and Curriculum Development.

McCarthy, B., & McCarthy, D. (2005). *Teaching around the 4MAT® cycle: Designing instruction for diverse learners with diverse learning styles*. Thousand Oaks, CA: Corwin Press.

McGrath, H., & Noble, T. (2013). Building a supportive classroom checklist. In *Different kids, same classroom*. South Melbourne: Addison Wesley Longman Australia Pty Ltd. Retrieved from http://bendigoeducationplan.wikispaces.com/file/view/supportive_classroom_checklist.pdf

Noddings, N. (2003). *Happiness and education*. New York, NY: Cambridge University Press.

Noddings, N. (2005). *The challenge to care in schools* (2nd ed.). New York, NY: Teachers College Press.

Owleus Anti-Bullying Program. Retrieved 2017 from http://www.violencepreventionworks.org/public/index.page

Payne, R. (April 2008). Poverty and learning: Nine powerful practices. *Educational Leadership, 65*(7), 48–52.

Ridnouer, K. (2006). *Managing your classroom with heart*. Alexandria, VA: Association for Supervision and Curriculum Development.

Rimm-Kaufman, S., & Sandilos, L. (2016). *Improving students' relationships with teachers to provide essential supports for learning*. Retrieved from http://www.apa.org?education?k12/relationships.aspz

San Francisco Unified School District. (n.d.). *Restorative practices whole-school implementation guide.* San Francisco, CA: Author.

Saphier, J. (2017). *High expectations teaching: How we persuade students to believe and act on "Smart is something you can get."* Thousand Oaks, CA: Learning Forward, Research for Better Teaching and Phi Delta Kappa.

Saphier, J., Haley-Speca, M., & Gower, R. (2008). *The skillful teacher: Building your teaching skills.* Acton MA: Research for Better Teaching.

Scott, T. (2017). *Teaching behavior: Managing classrooms through effective instruction.* Thousand Oaks, CA: Corwin.

Sharan, Y., & Sharan, S. (1992). *Expanding cooperative learning through group investigation.* New York, NY: Teachers College Press.

Shindler, J. (2009). Examining the use of competition in the classroom. In J. Shindler, *Transformative classroom management: positive strategies to engage all students and promote a psychology of success.* New York, NY: John Wiley & Sons. Retrieved from 'Chapter 18 Competition' at the following address: https://web.calstatela.edu/faculty/jshindl/cm/Chapter18competition-final.htm

Slavin, R.E., Madden, N.A., Chambers, B., & Haxby, B. (2009). *Two million children: Success for All.* Thousand Oaks, CA: Corwin.

Slavin, R.E., & Madden, N.A. (Eds.) (2001). *Success for All: Research and reform in elementary education.* Mahwah, NJ: Erlbaum.

Smith, D., Fisher, D., & Frey., N. (2015). *Better than carrots or sticks.* Alexandria, VA: Association for Supervision and Curriculum Development.

Smith, F. (1998). *The book of learning and forgetting.* New York, NY: Teachers College Press.

Sternberg, R. (1994, November). Allowing for thinking styles. *Educational Leadership, 51,* 36–40.

Sousa, D., & Tomlinson, C. (2011). *Differentiation and the brain.* Bloomington, IN: Solution Tree Press.

Thelan, H. (1981). *The classroom society.* London: Croom Helm.

Thomsen, K. (2002). *Building resilient students: Integrating resiliency into what you already know.* Thousand Oaks, CA: Corwin.

Tucker, C. (2016, September). Don't waste the first week: Establish relationships, not just routines. *Educational Leadership: Relationships First, 74*(1), 87–88.

Wolfgang, C. (2009). *Solving discipline and classroom management problems* (7th ed.). New York, NY: John Wiley & Sons.

Wormeli, R. (September 2016). What to do in week one? How to open the door to a successful teaching–learning dynamic. *Educational Leadership: Relationships First, 74*(1), 10–15.

Resources for Cooperative Learning and on Competition

Aronson, E., & Patnoe, S. (1997). *The jigsaw classroom: Building cooperation in the classroom (2nd ed.).* New York: Addison Wesley Longman.

Cooperative Learning Center at the University of Minnesota. This site offers print and other resources on the Johnson's Learning Together approach to cooperative learning: http://www.co-operation.org.

Good, T., & Brophy, J. (2008). *Looking in classrooms* (10th ed.). Boston: Allyn and Bacon.

Johnson, D., & Johnson, F. (2016). *Joining together: Group theory and group skills* (12th ed.). Boston: Allyn & Bacon.

Johnson, D., & Johnson, R. (1989). *Cooperation and competition.* Edina, MN: Interaction Book Co.

Johnson, D., & Johnson, R. (1998). *Learning together and alone: Cooperative, competitive, and individualistic learning* (5th ed.). Boston, MA: Allyn & Bacon.

Johnson, D., & Johnson, R. (2009). An educational psychology success story: Social interdependence theory and cooperative learning. *Educational Researcher, 38*(5), 365–379.

Johnson, D., Johnson, R. & Holubec, E. (2007). Nuts and bolts of cooperative learning (2nd ed.). Edina, MN: Interaction Book Co.

Johnson, D., Johnson, R., & Holubec, E. (2008). *Cooperation in the classroom* (8th ed.). Edina, MN: Interaction Book Co.

Johnson, D., Johnson, R., & Holubec, E. (2009). *Circles of learning: Cooperation in the classroom* (6th ed.). Edina, MN: Interaction Book Co.

Kagan, Inc. Details regarding the Spencer Kagan's cooperative learning structures are provided at: https://www.kaganonline.com/free_articles/dr_spencer_kagan/

Kagan, S. (2009). Kagan cooperative learning. San Clemente, CA: Kagan Cooperative Learning.

Kohn, A. (1992) *No contest*: *The case against competition* (2nd ed.). Boston, MA: Houghton Mifflin.

Nichols, S., & Sullivan, J. (2009, December 23). *Competition.* Retrieved 2017 from https://www.education.com/reference/article/competition/#A

Sharan, Y., & Sharan, S. (1992*). Expanding cooperative learning through group investigation.* New York, NY: Teachers College Press.

Shindler, J. (2009). Examining the use of competition in the classroom. In J. Shindler, *Transformative classroom management: positive strategies to engage all students and promote a psychology of success.* New York, NY: John Wiley & Sons. Retrieved 2017 from https://web.calstatela.edu/faculty/jshindl/cm/Chapter18competition-final.htm

Slavin, R.E., Madden, N.A., Chambers, B., & Haxby, B. (2009). *Two million children: Success for All.* Thousand Oaks, CA: Corwin.

Slavin, R.E., & Madden, N.A. (Eds.) (2001). *Success for All: Research and reform in elementary education.* Mahwah, NJ: Erlbaum.

Success for All Foundation. This site offers multiple resources regarding the Kagan curriculum-based cooperative learning is http://www.successforall.org.

Weisen, N. (2013). *Creating a culture of inclusiveness in the classroom* [Blog post]. Science of Learning Corporation Cooperative Learning in the Classroom. Retrieved 2017 from http://www.scilearn.com/blog/cooperative-learning-strategies-inclusive-classroom

Resources for Peer Mediation

Asian Pacific American Dispute Resolution Center. (2014). Peer mediators: A complete school curriculum K–8. http://www.peermediators.org/

Block, M., & Blazej, B. (2005). *Resolving conflict with a peer mediation program: A manual for grades 4–8.* Portland ME: University of Southern Maine. Retrieved from http://umaine.edu/peace/files/2011/01/PEER_MEDIATION_FINAL_11.pdf

Johnson, D., & Johnson, R. (1995a). *My mediation notebook* (3rd ed.). Edina, MN: Interaction Book Co.

Johnson, D., & Johnson, R. (1995b). *Reducing school violence through conflict resolution.* Alexandria, VA: Association for Supervision and Curriculum Development.

Johnson, D., & Johnson, R. (1995c). *Teaching students to be peacemakers.* Edina, MN: Interaction Book Co.

Johnson, D., & Johnson, R. (2006). Conflict resolution, peer mediation and peacemaking. In C. Evertson & C. Weinstein (Eds.), *Handbook of classroom management* (pp. 803–832). Mahwah, NJ: Lawrence Erlbaum Associate.

Wolfgang, C. (2009). *Solving discipline and classroom management* problems (7th ed.). New York, NY: John Wiley & Sons.

Resources for Students Supporting Students

Bowman-Perrott, L. (2009). ClassWide peer tutoring: An effective strategy for students with emotional and behavioral disorders. *Intervention in School and* Clinic, *44*, 259–267.

Gartner, A., & Lipsky, D. (1990). Students as instructional agents. In W. Stainback & S. Stainback (Eds.), *Support networks for inclusive schooling.* Baltimore, MD: Brookes.

Harper, G., & Maheady, L. (2007). Peer-mediated teaching and students with learning disabilities. *Intervention in School and Clinic, 43*, 101–107.

Lander, J. (2016, December 20). Students as teachers: Exploring the mutual benefits of peer-to-peer teaching—and strategies to encourage it. *Usable Knowledge.* Retrieved from http://www.gse.harvard.edu/uk/blog/students-teachers

Maheady, L., & Gard, J. (2010). Classwide peer tutoring: Practice, theory, research, and personal narrative. *Intervention in School and Clinic, 46,* 71–78.

McLeskey, J., Rosenberg, M., & Westling, D. (2010). *Inclusion: Effective practices for all students.* Boston, MA: Pearson.

Reading Rockets. (n.d.). Using peer tutoring to facilitate access. Retrieved from http://www.readingrockets.org/article/using-peer-tutoring-facilitate-access

Thousand, J., Villa, R., & Nevin, A. (2002*). Creativity and collaborative learning: A practical guide to empowering students, teachers, and families* (2nd ed.). Baltimore, MD: Brookes.

Veerkamp, M., Kamps, D., & Cooper, L. (2007). The effects of classwide peer tutoring on the reading achievement of urban middle school students. *Education and Treatment of Children, 30,* 21–51.

Website Resources

Antibullying: Owleus Bullying Prevention Program. Retrieved from http://www.violencepreventionworks.org

Learning styles: For more about Bernice **McCarthy's learning styles** questionnaires and/or observation instruments for teachers: http://www.aboutlearning.com.

Mindset: For more information on **Carol Dweck's** Growth and Closed mindsets: https://mindsetonline.com/.

Mindset: For more on Growth Mindset: transformingeducation.org/growth-mindset-toolkit.

Multiple intelligences: Thomas **Armstrong** is the director of the Institute for Learning and Human Development. The Institute's website includes material on **multiple intelligences**: http://institute-4learning.com.

Multiple intelligences: For more on the writings of David **Lazear** and **multiple intelligences** in the classroom: http://www.DavidLazear.com.

Positive discipline: For more information on Jane **Nelson's** and Lynn **Lott's** work with **Positive Discipline:** http://www.positivediscipline.com and/or http://www.empowering people.com.

Reading styles: Marie **Carbo**'s National **Reading Styles Institute** and work: http://www.nrsi.com.

Appendices

. . . .

Appendix A

LEARNING COMMUNITY CONNECTIONS QUILT DIRECTIONS

1. Use the template to make a 6″ or 9″ square of paper. You can use white as your background, another color you particularly like, paper that has a print or design on it, an extra piece of wallpaper, or any other kind of paper you choose.

2. Create a design using your name across the middle or diagonally from corner to corner. You can keep your square as a single frame and add pieces, like a collage, or separate your square into nine equal pieces and then put similar items into each smaller square. The choice is yours. Add pictures, words, stickers, or photos. You can draw, cut out magazine pictures, and download items from software or the Internet—anything that tells about you. (Questions below may help.)

3. Bring your square to class on _____ to help create our class community quilt.

These questions may help you think of what to include, but you are not limited to these ideas.

+ Who are the important people in your life?

+ What is important to you?

+ What do you enjoy doing after and outside of school? Do you have a hobby or something you enjoy doing, such as cooking, baking, painting, drawing, gardening, or fishing? Are you involved in sports, music lessons, or a kind of club?

+ Do you have a special talent?

+ Is there something for which you have won an award?

+ Do you live in an apartment building? A three-family home? On a busy street? In the country?

+ Where is your favorite spot to be?

+ Where is your favorite place to visit?

+ What is your favorite: Subject? Book? Movie? TV show? Play? Musical? Computer game? Instrument to play or hear? Piece of music? Song? Band? Orchestra? Music? Comedian? Sport you play? Sport you watch? Food? Work?

+ What words describe you? Is there anything else you would like us to know about you?

Appendix B

AN INTRODUCTION USING THE EIGHT INTELLIGENCES

Directions: Introduce yourself through *one* of the choices. When it is your turn, tell us what category item you chose. In two or three sentences, tell us what your choice shows us about you.

1. A quotation or an aphorism (a saying, adage, proverb; e.g., a stitch in time saves nine).

    1. The name of (or a quote from) a play, musical, piece of literature, a piece of poetry.

    2. The name of or a line or two from a song.

    3. A gesture or movement.

    4. The name of a sport or the name of a play or position in a sport.

    5. A formula or a mathematical theorem.

    6. A kind of flora (plant) or fauna (animal).

    7. A drawing made by you. Artistic talent is *not* required. Help yourself to our supply of drawing materials.

· ·

Appendix C

COOPERATIVE LEARNING: QUICK STARTERS[i]

1. LEARNING PARTNERS: Ask the students to turn to a neighbor and ask him/her something about the lesson, to explain a concept you've just taught, to explain how to do what you've just taught, to summarize the three most important points of the discussion, to explain the assignment, etc.

2. READING GROUPS: Students read material together and answer the questions. One person is the Reader, another the Recorder, the third the Checker (who checks to make sure that everyone understands, agrees with, and can explain the answers). They must come up with three possible answers to each question and circle their favorite one. When finished, they sign the paper to certify that they all understand, agree on, and can explain the answers.

3. BOOKENDS: Before a video, lecture, or reading, teams of students summarize together what they already know about a subject and come up with questions they have about it. Afterwards, the teams answer the questions, discuss new information, and formulate new questions.

4. JIGSAW: Students form cooperative teams. A team member from each team moves to an Expert Group to study a different part of a topic, lesson, reading, etc. with one student from each of the other teams. This "expert group" practices teaching the material. When ready, each member returns to his home cooperative team to teach teammates what he has learned. Each "expert" then quizzes the cooperative members until everyone on the team is satisfied that everyone knows all parts thoroughly.

5. DRILL PARTNERS: Have students drill each other on the facts they need to know until they are certain that both partners/all team members know and can remember all facts. This works for spelling, vocabulary, math, grammar, test review, etc. Give bonus points on the test if all members score a certain percentage.

6. READING BUDDIES: In lower grades, have students read their stories to each other, getting help with words and discussing content with their partners. In upper grades, have students tell about their books and read their favorite parts to each other.

7. WORKSHEET MATES: Have two students—one whose job is Reader and the other whose job is Writer—do one worksheet. The Reader reads, then suggests an answer; the Writer either agrees or comes up with another answer. When they both understand and agree upon an answer, the Writer writes it. Both get the grade earned for their work.

8. HOMEWORK CHECKERS: Students compare homework answers, discuss any they have not answered similarly, then correct their own papers and add the reason they changed any answer. They make certain everyone's answers agree and staple the papers together. You grade one paper from each group and give each group member that grade.

9. TEST REVIEWERS: Students prepare each other for a test. They get bonus points if everyone scores above a preset level.

10. COMPOSITION PAIRS: Student A explains what s/he plans to write about to student B, while Student B takes notes or makes an outline. Together they plan the opening or the thesis statement. Then Student B explains while Student A writes. They exchange outlines and use them in writing their papers.

11. PROBLEM SOLVERS: Give groups a problem to solve. Each student must contribute part of the solution. Groups can decide who does what, but they must show where all members contributed, or they can decide together, but each must be able to explain how to solve the problem.

12. BOOK REPORT PAIRS: Students interview each other on the books read, then they report on their partner's book.

13. WRITING RESPONSE GROUPS: Students read and respond to each other's papers three times. Teachers can assign questions for students to answer about their group members' papers to help them focus on certain problems and skills:

    a. They mark what they like with a star and put a question mark anywhere there is something they don't understand or think could be stronger.

    b. They mark possible problems with grammar, usage, punctuation, spelling, or format and discuss it with the author.

    c. They proofread the final draft and point out any errors for the author to correct.

14. **REPORT GROUPS:** Students research a topic together. Each one is responsible for checking at least one different source and writing at least three note cards of information. They write the report together, each responsible for seeing that his/her information is included. For oral reports, each must take a part and help others rehearse until all are at ease.

15. **SUMMARY PAIRS:** Students alternate reading and orally summarizing paragraphs. One reads and summarizes while the other checks the paragraph for accuracy and adds anything left out. They alternate roles with each paragraph.

16. **ELABORATING AND RELATING PAIRS:** In pairs, students elaborate on what they are reading and learning by relating it to what they already know about the subject. This can be done before and after reading a selection, listening to a lecture, or seeing a film.

i Source: Johnson, D., Johnson, R., & Holubec, E. (1998a). *Cooperation in the classroom.* Edina, MN: Interaction Book Co.

. . . .

Appendix D

Table 6-8.[i] **Questions to Consider When We Reflect on to What Degree We are Addressing Students' Basic Emotional Needs[1]**	Yes	No	I can do more
Do I meet students' need for safety:			
Do I consistently work to nurture students, to be fair and even-tempered?			
Do I let my students know that I am here to enhance their unique possibilities as a person?			
Do I encourage students to take reasonable risks in their learning, and do I let them know I will support their efforts?			
When I encourage students to try something new, do I let them know that I will support their efforts?			
Do I avoid unfair and/or high stakes competition activities?			
Through my messages and my work with them to establish rules and procedures, have I given my students a clear idea of what is and what is not acceptable in my class?			
Have I established guidelines with the students to provide a learning community atmosphere in which all students feel they can voice their opinions and take risks without fear of ridicule or other disrespectful responses from me other students?			
Do I provide students opportunities to constructively share their feelings and concerns with me and each other, and do I teach them strategies to constructively resolve conflicts?			
When a student does something unconstructive, do I distinguish what the student has done, and who she or he is as a person?			
Are my comments on students' work and my responses to how they work together constructive and specific, so they know what they did right and how to do even better in the future?			
Do I give *all* students—not just those who do best—a variety of opportunities to display their work and to demonstrate their interests and talents? When I do, do I gain permission to do so from each student beforehand?			

i Adapted from Helen McGrath and Toni Noble, Different Kids, Same Classroom. Pearson Australia Group Pty Ltd, 1998.

Do I meet students' need for love/for being cared about:			
Do I let my students know that I care about them as unique individuals?			
Have I supported each student to find ways to uncover or enhance unique qualities or skills?			
Do we take opportunities to celebrate all kinds of happy events in ways the student's religions will permit?			
Do I provide students a model of respect for and valuing of individual differences, Including students' diverse backgrounds?			
Do I make sure I talk individually with each student on a regular basis?			
Do I see a student's disability, talent, interest, quirkiness, as just a *part* of who he is? When a student has difficulty or excels in one area, do I assume she will do the same in all other areas?			
Do I facilitate students' understanding that classmates who happen to have disabilities or particular talents are more similar to others than they are different?			
Do I foster student's use their strengths to address any areas of difficulty?			
Do I meet students' need for belonging:			
Do I quickly learn the name of every student, and do I use their names often in our work together, but not to reprimand in front of others?			
Do I provide opportunities early in the term, class, school year for my students to get to know each other and to get to know me, including my interests and my feelings?			
Do I involve students in making the class rules and in planning class activities and displays?			
Do I work with students to support them in making some decisions about their goals, the nature of their assignments, and how they will be evaluated?			
Do I design opportunities for students to work together and learn from each other, including through cooperative learning experiences?			
Do I work to ensure that every student feels a sense of belonging in the learning community?			
Do I tell students who have been absent that I missed them and I am happy they are back?			
Do I meet students' need for efficacy:			
Do I focus on their strengths and successes, and encourage them to see mistakes as natural in the learning process, rather than as personal flaws or something for which they should be embarrassed?			
Do I design tasks that students feel they are capable of accomplishing?			
Do I consistently foster students' independence?			
Do I take every opportunity to give specific, constructive oral or written feedback to students about their work and how they interact with each other?			
Do I make it clear that mistakes are a useful part of the learning experiences?			
Do I encourage students to challenge my opinions as long as they do it respectfully?			
Do I recognize small steps of progress in my oral and written feedback?			
Do I recognize each student's progress in comparison to what they have previously done, but never in comparison to other students?			
Do I design learning experiences that extend student's thinking?			
Do I offer cooperative learning experiences that foster academic *and* social skill development?			
Do I offer a variety of learning experiences to foster social skill development?			
Do I convey positive expectations and confidence that all students are competent, can learn, can accomplish work, and that I will work with them until they do?			
Do I persevere in my efforts to enhance students' self-esteem, even when I don't seem to be making progress?			
Do I have a system for recording progress that is private and readily available to and frequently shared with each *individual* student?			

Do I give all students an opportunity to develop a variety of talents in a variety of ways?			
Do I work with the students to find ways to share what we are doing though letters home, displays in the school, articles in the school newspaper or on the school website, etc.?			
Do I work constructively with caregivers to support their understanding of their children's abilities and, therefore, what would be reasonable academic expectations?			
Do I meet students' need for joy:			
Do I design learning experiences that are interesting, appropriately challenging and meaningful for students?			
Do we have times when we laugh together (but never at someone)?			
Do we join together to celebrate all kinds of small and large accomplishments, happy occasions, 'good news'?			
Do we take time, even brief moments each day, to have fun?			
Do I include a positive sense of humor in my work with the students, but never sarcasm?			
Are there displays in the room that are esthetically pleasing to the students?			
Do we take even brief time out to give our brains a break and replenish ourselves?			
Do I infuse my teaching with the arts; is there variety in what we do; is there positive energy in our learning community work?			

1   Adapted from McGrath, H. and Noble, T. (1998). Home Group Advisor Handbook found 2016 at: [bendigoeducationplan.wikispaces.com/file/view/supportive_classroom_checklist.pdf]

Endnotes

i   This is the opening line to Frank Herbert's *Dune*.

ii   Thanks to Susan Stokes Ellis (personal communication, February 28, 2016) for this articulated perspective on mistakes.

iii   Owleus's Bullying Prevention Program (2016) can be found at: http://www.violencepreventionworks.org/public/index.page

iv   Charles W. Stokes taught the restorative justice approach to administrators at SUNY New Paltz more than forty years ago (personal correspondence, communication, and unpublished materials [n.d.]).

v   Posted in Fallbrook Elementary School in Pepperell, MA, 2015.

vi   Thank you, Mallory Brideau, for this perspective (personal communication, 2013).

vii   Thank you, Alyssa Serafini, Frances Drake Elementary School, Leominster, MA for these titles.

viii   Thanks to Lynn Sarda (personal communication, 2016).

ix   Thank you, Shelley Stokes Turnbow (personal communication, March 20, 2016), for suggesting "undiscovered talents" be added.

CHAPTER 7

Sustaining Connections and Expectations

I don't teach. I inspire.

—Shari Stokes

What Will This Chapter Discuss?

We have worked hard to establish a community of learners and our expectations for our work with that community. Now our focus is on how we sustain that community and, within it, our ongoing expectations for how students go about learning and how they treat one another as our time together progresses. We have social skills to foster, including the use of problem-solving and conflict resolution strategies. Last but not least, we also want to recognize effort and progress and celebrate together.

Why Is This Important?

Effective instruction includes opportunities to practice, receive constructive feedback, and reflect. The amount of practice depends on the developmental level of the students and the difficulty of the skill or concept. This is true for the teaching of English/language arts, math, and the arts. This is true for the teaching of social skills (Charney, 2002; Evertson, Emmer, & Worsham, 2017; Emmer & Evertson, 2017; Good & Brophy, 2008; Levin & Nolan, 2014). We cannot develop rules with students and expect them to be able to apply them consistently the rest of the time without practice. We cannot teach conflict resolution and assume that each time conflict arises, the students and adults in the classroom will be able to apply the process effectively without practice. Maintenance of community and constructive behavior within it is an important investment. Strategies to support this are essential in any teacher's toolkit.

What Will You Learn?

By the end of the chapter, you will be able to:

- describe each of the strategies to foster constructive behavior and maintain community; and
- identify specific ways you might implement these in your teaching.

What Do You Want To Accomplish?

What goal(s) do you have as you read about sustaining connections and expectations? Write your responses here or on a piece of paper. _____

_____

_____

How Do We Maintain Structure and Nurturance for Students?

We Exude Confidence in Teaching Ability, Classroom Management, and Supporting Constructive Behavior

One way we show this is by using a credible/authoritative (not authoritarian) voice when we are teaching. This is a voice much like those you hear when most news anchor speaks. It is a deep voice, calm in delivery, with no rush of words. The tone stays fairly the same. There are pauses before or after key words. Each sentence ends with the voice dropping down. This is a voice that signals authority. It is not mean, anxious, or worried.

When we are being sociable, on the other hand—before and after class or during quick, appropriate moments in the day—we use an approachable voice. By contrast, this voice has a higher pitch. It "dances" as we speak—the pitch goes up and down and up again. Think of what happens fairly typically when someone speaks to a baby or a puppy. The voice is higher in pitch, the speed is a bit faster, and the voice tends to go up at the end of a statement.

Picture yourself talking to students as they enter class or if you meet them at a game or school concert. What is your voice like? Now imagine you are in front of a class. State a set of directions. Is there a difference?

When it is time to put on our teacher voice, how can we make our voice sound different and give it that authoritative edge? Most men's voices will naturally be lower, but women can make theirs lower by tucking their chin down. That opens the throat and allows the vocal cords to resonate at a deeper level. We *avoid* beginning our sentences with "Well, …". We avoid ending our sentences with "All right?" or "Okay?" in a voice that goes up, as if we are asking for their approval rather than stating something important for them to hear. When we are being authoritative, we pause before or after key words to help the students' brains perk up. We emphasize key temporal words such as "now" and "first," contrast words such as "different," and action words such as "choose". All these elements contribute to a voice that says to students, "Listen. This is important." If you feel you could enhance your authoritative voice, I encourage you to practice it outside the classroom. To do so, I suggest you use a direction you might give to students.

When we use an authoritative voice, we let students know that we mean business, and they can feel safe knowing that we are comfortable setting expectations in our role as their teacher.

Platform: Application Opportunity

On the Active Learning platform under Chapter 7, you have an opportunity to apply what you have learned and in so doing help yourself remember the difference between the two voices.

We Cue Students about Expectations

- ✦ *"For this part of the lesson, please raise your hand."*
- ✦ *"As we do our small-group discussions, keep in mind our rule about listening to others."* [Point to rule on posted rules].
- ✦ *"We are going to talk about _____. One of our rules is that we treat each other with respect. If a visitor walked in as we were talking, what would she see or hear that would show her we respect each other?"*

We Review Expectations Using Teachable Moments

In the midst of a transition, we become concerned that the speed of movement and the noise level are getting out of hand. On the wall is a posted sign that briefly states what is to be done during a transition—what level of noise is appropriate and how the safety of people, materials, and equipment will be maintained. We use a signal that everyone has agreed will mean that talking and walking stop and all eyes turn to the teacher. We ask a student, *"Hernando, can you remind us what we would do during a transition—how loudly we talk and how we move materials and bodies?"* Hernando states two parts of the procedure. We thank him and ask, *"Does anyone have anything to add to help to make the transition safe for all?"*

We Reinforce Expectations

"As you were working in small groups, I wrote some notes about what I saw and heard you doing to listen to each other. Here are some examples."

We Evaluate Expectations with the Students *(Sylwester, 2003)*

Procedures: *"We have a procedure for what to do when you are done with your work and a poster to remind you, if others are still working. Ask yourself: if you were done early today, did you [go down the list]? Is there any other item you think we should add to the list?"*

Class contracts and class rules: A few weeks into our work with students, we look together at the class contract or rules and evaluate the degree to which each feels she is holding up her end of the bargain and the degree to which she feels others are respecting her rights. We ask to have a discussion without the use of names. The focus would be: What are we doing well, and are there any ways we could do even better? With younger children, we can be a model for a response: "I was thinking one way I can help others learn is by writing my directions as well as saying them" or "I am concerned that we are not dealing with our feelings by using words that won't hurt others. How can we do that better?"

For older students, this process can be done anonymously in writing by distributing a copy of a feedback sheet with the opportunity to circle the number (1–5) under each item of the contract to indicate to what degree she feels the community upholds that portion. Note: We need to teach students how to relate their feelings to each item on the 5-point scale (Levin & Nolan, 2014). We ask the students to turn the contract evaluation sheet upside-down, and we shuffle them as we receive them to protect privacy. While the ratings are fresh in students' minds, we discuss which aspects of working together seem to going well, which aspects need more attention, and what might be done. Note the framing of the discussion focus is the same as with younger children. There is no blaming or shaming of anyone, including the teacher. As we facilitate this discussion, we take a very brief moment to eyeball the results so we can provide the class a rough summary of the ratings. We might say, "On _____, most people gave a rating of 3; there were two 4s and one or two 5s. How can we do better in this area—what can you do? What can I do to make this a better learning community?" At the close of the discussion, we can invite anyone who wishes to talk with us privately, if he feels that would be helpful.

We Celebrate When Expectations Have Been Achieved

"At the end of your cooperative team work yesterday, you wrote in your journals at least three ways you were following our rule, 'Help make this a place in which everyone feels safe.' Team speakers, I will give you a moment to review what was written. [Brief pause.] Can someone raise a hand to share one way your team members thought you helped others feel safe as you worked?" As students share, write the items in a way that can be posted as examples. *"We know safety is important. You felt it. I saw each team showing it. Well, done. Give yourselves a silent cheer."*

We Evaluate the Room Arrangement with Students

This can be done with a discussion. We can begin by stating some of the needs we have (in words the students will understand, given their development) such as safety, accessibility, visibility, distractibility, and proximity. Then we ask, *"Is how we have the room arranged working for us? Can we see and hear what we need, get the materials we need quickly and safely, and work without bumping into each other?"* We use a *"Turn and Talk to Your Neighbor"* to involve more in the process. After a couple of minutes, we ask for ideas about how the room arrangement might be even better and evaluate these with the children, using (in our minds) the considerations of safety, accessibility, visibility, distractibility, and proximity.

> Note: We may get a different, useful perception of the quality of the room variables from the students. Given their size and the fact that they may be sitting for much longer periods of time than we are, they have a different view of the room and a different experience of the temperature. (Heat rises).

These opportunities for students to give feedback send a message that we care about them—what they think, how they feel—and that they are an important part of the community. They are given a sense of belonging and value—"My opinion counts here." Their connections to us and to others in the community are strengthened. As a result, they are more likely to follow through on the expectations we have established with them.

ACCESSING PRIOR KNOWLEDGE/EXPERIENCE

Go back in your memories to your experiences in elementary and middle school. In the space below or elsewhere write your answers to these series of questions. What teachers did you (and others) find interesting? Which ones bored you? Remember one you found boring. When he was, what did he do, or what did he not do? _____

_____

_____

Now, remember one you found interesting. When he kept your attention, what did he do? _____

_____

_____

Since we want to avoid being boring whenever possible, instead, how can we hold students' attention during learning experiences?

We Offer Engaging Learning Experiences that Provide Structure and Nurturing for Students

Along with establishing and reviewing expectations through rules and procedures, we know that the most effective way to foster constructive behavior is to provide engaging, meaningful learning experiences. If students are engaged and know how to address their tasks successfully and are given support, encouragement, and useful feedback along the way, it is rare for them to engage in unconstructive behavior.

We Eliminate Threat but Provide Appropriately Challenging Learning Experiences

Learning needs to be something that meets students' basic needs, fosters their intrinsic motivation by challenging them, supports them in becoming better at what they do, and builds their sense of efficacy, their open mindset, and their resilience. We have addressed how we can create such effective learning experiences with key elements in our lesson plans. Now we turn to addressing specific processes that facilitate those lessons.

We Foster Students' Ability to Discuss Ideas Respectfully and Maintain Connections with Each Other

We teach students how to disagree with ideas, not with people. We teach them how to ask for more information if they don't understand. We teach them how to support their ideas with facts and examples, not with put-downs, labeling, or nonverbal communication that suggests the other person is silly, stupid, or ignorant for having certain ideas.

We Ask the Kind of Questions and Respond to Answers in Ways that Minimize Threat and Maintain the Connection Between Us and Students

Our questions can increase students' interest in a topic. The more students know about a topic, the more interest they tend to have (Marzano, 2017). So, we minimize one-right-answer questions. If we do use them, we offer a choice of two or three responses to help provide structure for the students' thinking and maximize success in making a possible answer connect to the question. We give students time to think. If a student's response to our question is correct according to whatever we were expecting, we indicate that. That feedback is useful for all the students. Also, we frequently ask students why they chose that answer.

The correct answer is desirable of course, but only if it is based on appropriate reasoning, because more often than not it is the thinking process that we are trying to help students learn. When a student does not give a correct answer, we work with his answer. As we said before, we use it, in some senses diagnostically, to determine how he is thinking about whatever we are discussing. We can ask how he came to think of that particular answer. If he is confused, we can welcome the opportunity to help refine his thinking (and probably that of other students who have not yet mastered the material). As we do this, we can ask him if *he* would like support from a peer to figure out the answer (because often students who are at the same level of brain development can do a more effective job than we can). If he says yes, we can ask another student to support his thinking. The second student may need some coaching in how to facilitate his thinking rather than giving him the answer.

We give students a question and a moment to think and then ask them to turn to a near neighbor and discuss their responses. Their task is to talk it out until they agree on the answer or have reasons for their disagreement. We let them know ahead of time that we will call randomly on any person in a pair to give the answer for that pair and to give a reason why he feels the answer is appropriate. During the discussion, any partnership having difficulty could ask for help from another pair or from us.

We Offer Learning Experiences that are Brain Compatible and Engaging

We provide a Launch to Prime Students' Brains and Draw Them into the Lesson or into a Particular Learning Experience within the Lesson

Possible strategies to enhance their receptivity include constructive humor, group rituals, verbal or written affirmations, stretching or meditative exercise, and warm-up activities (Dean, Hubbell, Pitler, & Story, 2012; Gregory & Kaufeldt, 2015; R. Hunter, 2014; M. Hunter, 2004; Immordino-Yang, 2015; Jensen, 2005).

We can use a variety of **anticipatory sets** to give the students an enticing preview of what is to come in the lesson (R. Hunter, 2014; M. Hunter, 2004). The minimum would be a review of the lesson agenda. That is helpful, but we can do much more. A narrative—a vignette from a story, a brief essay, or a video— can ready the students. We can use skimming to give students a general impression of material before it is read (Dean, Hubbell, Pitler, & Story, 2012). We can use a graphic organizer (particularly helpful for visual learners). Note: If we use one, we can also fill in additional material with the students as we proceed through the lesson. To engage students' emotions, we can pose a question or present a problem or dilemma that relates to the lesson topic: "Imagine what it would be like if you were never allowed to talk once you left the classroom—not during lunch, or any special, or during recess, or as you were leaving the building at the end of the day. How might that affect you? How might you feel?"

We Offer Opportunities that Engage Students' Thinking and Emotions Throughout the Lesson

We offer learning experiences that provide meaningful content—content that grabs students' attention, curiosity, or emotions and is specific rather than general, novel rather than familiar. Content is remembered to the degree that it is meaningful (Gregory & Kautfeldt, 2015; Heath & Heath, 2007). Meaning is enhanced by connection to familiar information and the nature of the context in which the learning is posed. If we use journals, learning logs, sharing times, and stories, we can enhance personal connections. If we choose content that asks students to address real-life questions to which they can relate, then we enhance meaning in their work (Immordino-Yang, 2015; Jensen, 2005, 2015a).

> *Tell me and I forget. Show me and I remember. Involve me and I understand.*
>
> *—Chinese proverb*

Meaning is enhanced when students can be both active and reflective with the content. At least once, if not more often, in the lesson, students need to actively engage socially, to use movement, and to engage emotionally with the material. They need to process verbally with others or in writing. They need to practice using words and muscles, such as those in their hands, to create a visual illustration of the concept under study. I know a teacher who periodically asked teams of students to create each of the spelling words with their bodies and another teacher who has students act out math problems. After I read a poem by a young person from Thailand who felt like an outsider in her high school, I asked students to give their reaction in a (socially acceptable) physical gesture. One student put her head on the desk. Another created a particularly sad expression on her face and then put her hands over her face. Yet another walked to the door, stepped outside, closed the door, and then looked back in at us sadly through the door's window. A collective gasp could be heard in response.

The more engaged students are, the more likely it is that their behavior will be constructive.

Below is a sample of active engagement activities that are short enough to be used within a lesson. Given the length of a lesson, we could use two or more. Each of these can energize a lesson by providing opportunities for active engagement with the material and a social experience for the students as part of the processing. Saphier and Haley (1993b) provide a number of suggestions with variations.

Pairs Check. [10–20 minutes]. Students work in twos. One person in the pair works on a task while the other serves as coach. They exchange roles for the next task. Then they ask another pair to check their work. If the second pair agrees, the first pair continues. If not, the pairs try to correct the work.

Roundtable. [10–20 minutes]. Ask a question with many possible answers. Using one sheet of paper, students at a table dictate or write a list of answers, beginning with one student and having each person add one answer and then pass it on to the person on the left. No repeats. The product is the result of many minds at work.

We Offer Learning Experiences that Provide Practice and Application with Constructive Feedback that Maintains the Connection between the Students and Us

We Foster Students' Role in Feedback

We teach students how to give constructive feedback to themselves and to others. First, we demonstrate how mistakes are useful feedback that tells them how they are understanding a concept or how they are doing with a particular skill. Then we help students understand the nature of feedback. That way, they are better able to offer it and receive it.

Stone and Heen (2014) distinguish three types of feedback: appreciation (giving thanks, acknowledging positive work or actions), coaching (mentoring with information and communication to support refinement of concepts or skills), and evaluation (to provide a grade or score based on criteria).

Since, more often than not, peer feedback will be in the form of appreciation or coaching, we help students formulate how to be constructive in the words they choose for either purpose. Coaching feedback that answers the questions below helps to build an open mindset that supports the idea that change in competence can occur. Such feedback, thereby, fosters grit and resilience (Dweck, 2006; Duckworth, 2008; Goleman, 1995; Yeager & Dweck, 2012).

- What was done well? What is the basis for that judgment?
- What could be done to provide more or better clarity, quality, etc., and how can I accomplish that?
- What resources—people and material—can help?

Table 7-1 is a sample praise-and-point worksheet designed for a peer to give appreciation and coaching feedback to a writer about a current piece of writing in draft form.

Only telling ourselves or being told what we did wrong is not only discouraging; it is also not instructive. It does not tell us what *to* do. To be able to recognize what we could do better or more of and to be able to grasp how we might make that happen contributes to feeling good about ourselves and our capabilities—it nurtures our feelings of efficaciousness. Useful feedback provides us a means to keep going in a constructive direction—(it structures our efficacious efforts) (Dweck, 2006; Duckworth, 2008; Larrivee, 2009; Levin & Nolan, 2014). If you are concerned that framing evaluation in positive tones will minimize potential for change, look again at the second question: *What could be done to enhance the work?* Asking this question sets up next steps for refinement and improvement and does so with respect—respect for the student as a learner who is always changing, respect for the student as a human being who is of value just because she is who she is.

Table 7-1. **Praising and Pointing Worksheet**

Directions: After you have written your feedback for any of the items below, share your ideas. Then, give the writer this sheet when the two of you are through talking about your feedback.

Writer's Name: _____ Peer's Name: _____ Date: _____

Praising: Choose any that are appropriate.

1. My favorite part of your story was:

2. I enjoyed the character _____because:

3. The best wording was:
I enjoyed that wording because for me as a reader it:

4. I liked the opener or conclusion because:

Pointing: Choose any that are appropriate.

1. I did not understand the part about:

2. Could you tell me more about:

3. I got confused when:

4. This part _____ did not make sense to me because:

5. I would like to hear more about:

. . . .

REFLECTION OPPORTUNITY

How do you feel when you see comments written in red ink on your work? On a separate piece of paper or in the space provided write what comes to mind. _____

_____

_____

. . . .

Color: Does the color of written feedback make a difference?

In our culture, the color red is used to catch people's attention in urgent situations: ambulance or police flashing lights and stop signs are examples. So, many people feel a sense of emergency, anxiety, embarrassment, and shame connected to the color red. Such unpleasant feelings close down the brain. My first suggestion for providing *useful, constructive written* feedback addresses color. We need to use a color other than red to write feedback—a color more typical for written communication. Comments will be just as easy to find if the color contrasts with the student's writing—blue or black (green, purple, brown). The effect of color is a variable to consider. Timing is also important.

Timing: We provide appreciation of hard work and coaching feedback during the *formative* stages on projects that have more than one step. While summative evaluation has its role, fostering constructive student behavior requires providing processes for feedback along the way. We have looked briefly at "praising and pointing" for the writing process, including a feedback sheet in Table 7-1 above. We praise what seems effective, accurate, and on the mark and point to areas that we find confusing, unclear, or inaccurate. Given this coaching feedback, the writer chooses to change whatever he feels would make the final product better. While developed to support writing, I have found that approach constructive for students in any curriculum area.

When providing feedback or fostering peer feedback sessions, we do so after students have had ample opportunity to think through their work. Student work (like the work of an adult) requires continual risk taking. We need to be sure we remember the risk involved. Adult feedback may be destructive, however constructive the wording, if it is offered early in the process, when students' ideas are still in their fledgling form—not yet strong enough to withstand the onslaught. A first draft, a not-yet-formed idea, or a skill that is just beyond acquisition is rarely ready for feedback. Ideas, skills, and creative work all require "safe hatchery," as Cameron (1992) describes it. When student efforts are addressed as ongoing creative work, constructive feedback processes offer the creator the choice to change the product or not as she sees fit.

When judging or evaluating multistep tasks, we wait until the end and *only* when formative feedback has also been offered by us and/or peers.

Language of feedback: We provide coaching feedback that supports and extends the student's thinking rather than providing a "correct version." For example, we ask students to describe how they arrived at a solution. We work with students to garner *joint* feedback. We use respectful language to give feedback when students make mistakes. Again, students need to know (from us) that mistakes are a natural part of learning. We frame mistakes conceptually as data for refining skills, not a part of their personhood. They need to look at their mistakes as information they can assess to determine what needs to be changed. The question is not *wha*t was the so-called mistake but *why did it occur? What* can be done now? Such feedback will reinforce the student's learning, and, after all, learning is what we hope to help promote in each student.

In Table 7-2 is a chart summarizing seminal research by Brophy (1981) illustrating the comparison of *in*effective coaching feedback on the left—what Brophy calls praise—with effective coaching feedback on the right. As you read through the comparisons, consider what makes the difference between each two. For example, the ineffective feedback may have no connection to the student's behavior; specificity or usefulness may be lacking; an inappropriate comparison to another student may be made. In all, the need for safety and a sense of efficacy are compromised.

Table 7-2. A Comparison of Characteristics of Ineffective and Effective Praise[i]	
EFFECTIVE Praise	**INEFFECTIVE Praise**
1. Is delivered contingently	1. Is delivered randomly or unsystematically
3. Shows spontaneity, variety, and other signs of credibility; suggests clear attention to the student's accomplishments	3. Shows a bland uniformity, which suggests a conditioned response made with minimal attention
4. Rewards attainment of specified performance criteria (which can include effort criteria, however)	4. Rewards mere participation, without consideration of performance processes or outcomes
6. Orients students toward better appreciation of their own task-related behavior and thinking about problem solving	6. Orients students toward comparing themselves with others and thinking about competing
8. Is given in recognition of noteworthy effort or success at difficult (for *this* student) tasks	8. Is given without regard to the effort expanded or the meaning of the accomplishment (for *this* student)
9. Attributes success to effort and ability, implying that similar successes can be expected in the future	9. Attributes success to ability alone or to external factors such as luck or easy task
10. Fosters endogenous attributions (students believe that they expend effort on the task because they enjoy the task and/or want to develop task-related skills)	10. Fosters exogenous attributions (students believe they expend effort on the task for external reasons—to please the teacher, win a competition or reward, etc.)

i Jere Brophy, from "Teacher Praise: A Functional Analysis," Review Of Educational Research, Vol. 51, No. 5, p. 26. Copyright © 1981 by SAGE Publications.

Sources of feedback: We design learning experiences so students gain feedback from multiple sources—us, peers, job coaches, the natural consequences of the learning situation itself, and their own self-reflection.

Resources

In addition to the references cited in this section on feedback, a resource that might be of further support in your work is Brookhart's (2017) *How to Give Effective Feedback*. The full reference is at the chapter's end.

We Provide Active Closure to Learning Experiences or to Specific Parts Within Them

With these closure activities, we support students in their construction of personal meaning and schema for the information which allows students to remember the material better and longer. Students also find out what they understand and what they still need to have explained. We surface confusion, misconceptions, or misunderstandings and can adapt future teaching accordingly. Our summarizing at the end does not do the job. Students need to actively engage in the summarizing process or they, and we (in our assessment of their learning), do not gain from it. Below are some ways to engage students in reflecting on and summarizing their learning. Saphier and Haley (1993b) offer many more.

A Note to a Friend. [5–10 minutes]. After an explanation or demonstration, pass out a sheet of paper and ask each student to draw a picture or write a note to a friend showing or explaining the process, rule, or concept they have just learned.

Sort the Items. [5–10 minutes]. Ask the students to place ideas, concepts, pictures, items, or statements into categories you define (e.g., "Which statements are based on fact?", Which animals live in the water and which live on land?).

Draw a Picture or Create a Graphic Organizer. [5–10 minutes]. Direct students to work in pairs to draw a picture or create a graphic summary to organize information on the instruction just provided.

Four Corners. [15–20 minutes]. This is especially useful when students encounter a controversial issue in a story, school life, in their neighborhood, or in the news. State a situation or dilemma, then ask students to go to one of four corners of the room, which are marked "Strongly Agree," "Agree," "Disagree," and "Strongly Disagree." (There can also be a spot in the middle of the room for "Not Sure".) There, the students exchange their opinions or reasoning. Direct one person in each group to share the reasoning to the rest of the class. As students hear others they are allowed to switch their location. Note: For younger students, two spots—"Agree" and "Disagree"—may be enough.

Students who are engaged in brain-compatible, meaningful learning experiences are far more likely to behave constructively. They have few reasons not to.

We Respect the Uniqueness of Each Learner

Differences are normal. We ensure access to learning through a match between lesson design and different students' levels of development, ways of learning, and unique needs.

We Differentiate our Instruction to Match the Needs of All Learners Rather Than Making Students Match a Single Approach

To do so, we ask: How can I provide a variety of learning experiences that, over time, will give students a chance to learn, become competent in key areas, and do so in depth over a breadth of curriculum content? To respond to differences in learning styles, cognitive and emotional intelligences, needs, readiness level, and interests, we plan and carry out lessons that give students multiple options for making sense of new material. We help them tap into their individual learning strengths by offering a variety of learning environments, materials, and ways to access, acquire, and process material and to demonstrate what has been learned (Sousa & Tomlinson, 2011; Tomlinson, 2017.) Tomlinson (2017) suggests that we consider five aspects of the learning experience:

+ Content: What materials will students use, and how do they get them?
+ Process: How will students work with materials to understand and remember skills and concepts?
+ Product: How will students demonstrate what they know or can do?
+ Affect: How will students connect cognition and emotion in the classroom?
+ Learning Environment: How does the classroom function and feel?

We Ask, How Can Technology Support Our Teaching, Including Our Differentiation?

When considering technology, a particularly useful resource is CAST—the Center for Applied Special Technologies, an organization at the forefront of supporting what is known as a Universal Design for Learning. UDL is a set of principles to guide the design of learning experiences (CAST, 2011):

+ teacher adjustments for learner differences should occur for all students, not just those with disabilities;
+ curriculum materials should be varied and diverse, including digital and online resources rather than centering on a single textbook; and
+ instead of remediating students so that they can learn from a set curriculum, curriculum should be made flexible to accommodate learner differences.

Universal Design for Learning's guidelines address the provision of multiple means of:

+ representation;
+ action and expression; and
+ engagement.

Table 7-3 provides an integration of many of the ideas for differentiating instruction I have read about, observed, and utilized, including those of Tomlinson and CAST. As you read the examples in the table, note the use of a variety of technologies to support differentiation. If you would be supported by additional resources, there are many Tomlinson references at the end of the chapter. Hobgood and Ormsby (2011) offer suggestions about technology possibilities to support the learning of students with a variety of needs. For the uses of technology, I also highly recommend a visit to the CAST website [www.cast.org] or [www.udlcenter.org]. Become familiar with the work being done there and what resources are available for you.

Concepts	Examples
Content: Materials used in lessons and how materials are accessed	• Universal Design for Learning[i] principles utilized to make materials accessible; e.g., CAST's UDL[i] Book Builder[ii] (free digital book database and book builder)
	• Recorded tutorials
	• Text with call-out boxes inserted to elaborate on a difficult vocabulary word, idiomatic expression, or complicated idea
	• Materials available at different reading levels, different levels of complexity or abstractness
	• Use of class-based web-site filled with all kinds of materials
	• Materials provided though different mediums: print, video (including closed captions and voice overs), audio sources, including the use of text to voice and voice to text technology
	• Scaffolded materials (including software that allows 'call-out' boxes to provide extra support to guide reading, note-taking, writing)
	• Materials provided in primary languages of students as well as English
	• Materials whose illustrations and text address diversity in all its forms
	• Variety of resources, including photographs, websites, brochures, music/videos, graphic novels
	• Word lists for spelling, virtual and real-life manipulatives, math fact tables, calculators, spell checkers, word translaters, concept maps with or without text, embedded illustrations embedded
	• Pre-teaching of key concepts before students work with materials
	• Demonstration/tutorial (video, audio or teacher) of concept application/skill
	• Digital textbooks with a variety of features—pronunciation guides, text-to-speech, and vocabulary support, features that allow the reader changes in formatting to enhance readability
Process: How students work with materials to understand and remember skills and concept	• Use of individual, paired, small group and whole class learning experiences based on ability/readiness grouping, interest grouping, or grouping by learning profile
	• Procedures taught for working with a variety of materials, at various places in the room, and for various tasks
	• Provision of tiered activities (of varied complexity, sophistication and difficulty) for same content and goals
	• Choices in kinds and complexities of processing, number of variables
	• Students taught process and well as content for producing products
	• Support for product creation; e.g., software that creates graphs and solves formulas from numbers and symbols provided
	• Options for level of difficulty, degrees of scaffolding offered (and chosen)
	• Choices in kind of process required
	• Availability of technology for access channels; e.g., speech recognition or screen reading software; amplification systems; software that highlights words as they are being read, a stylus for tablet use
	• Use of spreadsheets to view and organize data
	• Use of various support systems; e.g., peer or cross-age mentors/tutors, cooperative teams, study buddies, class-based discussion board or chat room
	• Variety in nature and number of practice opportunities based on needs

Table 7-3. **Key Concepts of Differentiated Instruction Based on Students' Learning Profiles**

Table 7-3. **Key Concepts of Differentiated Instruction Based on Students' Learning Profiles** (Continued)	
Product: How students demonstrate what they know or can do	• Models of products at various levels of complexity/sophistication • Rubrics based on both grade-level expectations and individual student learning needs • Students taught how to create a wide range of products • Products in a variety of formats encouraged—audio, video, music, poetry, sketches/plays, software (including PowerPoint presentations) and/or print based, illustrated forms, including graphic novels, graphs, charts, formulas to express mathematical or conceptual ideas • Varied levels of familiarity with context with which application will be required • Choice of product based, in part, on student interests • Choice of creating a solo, paired, small group, cooperative team product
Affect: Students connecting cognition and emotion in the classroom.	• Respectful participation of every student expected and facilitated • Modeling of empathy, respect, constructive conflict resolution by teacher, literary/news/or other individuals • Facilitated discussion of more than one perspective (when students are developmentally able to do so) on an issue or idea • Learning experiences foster the connection between what a student I learning and how a student feels
Learning Environment: Classroom function and feeling	• Students feel ownership of classroom with teacher • Students feel safe, efficacious, that they belong, that people care about their well-being, and there are many moments of satisfaction in learning • A fluid or growth mindset fostered in student and teacher • The learning community focuses on learner-centered, stimulating, engaged learning • Mistakes considered a natural part of learning and seen as an opportunity for feedback for teacher and student • Furniture and equipment arranged to foster a variety of activities in various groupings • Students learn in ability/readiness grouping, interest grouping, or grouping by learning profile • Materials available and arranged for ready use by students

i The Center for Applied Special Technologies (CAST) is the source of Universal Design for Learning (UDL). Additional information can be found at [www.cast.org] or [www.udlcenter.org].

ii CAST can be found at: National Center on Universal Design for Learning, Center for Applied Special Technology, 40 Harvard Mills Square, Suite 3; Wakefield, MA 01880-3233; Tel.: (781) 245-2212, Email: [UDLCENTER@UDLCENTER.ORG; website address is [cast.org].

We Use Multiple Intelligences to Differentiate Learning Experiences

We can offer choices for process, content, and product to students (Armstrong, 2009). To do this, we can consider how we might integrate the following into a lesson:

- ✦ words (linguistic intelligence);
- ✦ numbers or logic (logical–mathematical intelligence);
- ✦ pictures (spatial intelligence);

- music (musical intelligence);

- self-reflection (intrapersonal intelligence);

- a physical experience (bodily–kinesthetic intelligence);

- a social experience (interpersonal intelligence); and/or

- an experience in the natural world (naturalist intelligence).

Armstrong (2009) provides many suggestions for how we can assess the eight intelligences:

- Use anecdotal records or notes. We ask ourselves, "When offered choices in jobs in the room or on a cooperative team, what does the student choose?"

- Talk with former and current teachers may provide information—that a student does better on math and science, for example, than on literature and writing.

- Ask parents/caregivers. They may have valuable information about a student's interests and how time is spent when choices are given.

- Ask students. We can chat with them informally or, having reviewed the intelligences, provide them a list with some relevant information and ask them to circle/check those in which they feel they have strengths.

- Use questionnaires such as Armstrong's (2009) for students to complete or for teachers to use as observation instruments to gather data on students' intelligences.

- Review school records. These might show a pattern of grades that are consistently higher in some content or skill areas.

- Certain tests may provide information about a student's relative strengths in some intelligences (Armstrong, 2009):
    - Linguistic—reading tests, language tests, the verbal sections of intelligence and achievement tests
    - Logical–Mathematical—math achievement tests, the reasoning sections of intelligence tests
    - Spatial—visual memory and visual motor tests, art aptitude tests, some performance items on intelligence tests
    - Bodily–Kinesthetic—sensorimotor tests, some motor subtests in neuropsychological batteries, the Presidential Physical Fitness Test
    - Musical—aptitude tests
    - Interpersonal—social maturity scales, sociograms, interpersonal projective tests
    - Intrapersonal—self-concept assessments, projective tests
    - Naturalist—test items that include pictures of or questions regarding animals, plants, or natural settings

Students who believe we understand who they are and how they learn and work to design learning experiences that address their needs are more likely to behave constructively.

How Do We Maintain the Sense of Community?

We Foster and Maintain Connections Among Community Members

We use learning experiences. One way we can do this is to provide opportunities for students to discuss beliefs (once we have fostered their understanding of how to have such discussions constructively). These activities that connect can be an integral part of our curriculum at any level. For example, the class has just finished a study of animals, biography, chemical properties, or three-dimensional shapes. We can:

+ Give students a list of items (four or five animals, names of people about whom biographies have been written, geometric shapes, chemical properties, etc.).

+ Direct each student to choose one item that she feels she is most like. Older students could write down the reasons for their choices on a sheet like the one below.

+ Direct students to move to a spot in the room designated for that item.

+ Tell students in that spot to share their choice and their reasons with peers.

+ Ask each group to make a list of reasons that eliminates the duplicates.

+ Direct one member to summarize the group's reasons to the whole class.

The sheet below could be given to students.

CORNERS (Think, Write, Move, Share)

As a student/person, I am most like:

+ An oak tree
+ A flowering peach tree
+ An evergreen tree
+ A maple tree

Reasons:

_____

_____

_____

This learning experience gives students a chance to connect with and learn a bit about other community members, an opportunity to discuss beliefs, and an opportunity to summarize what they had learned (which aids retention). We can join in by either choosing the corner that matches us or, when the group is reflecting as a whole, add to the discussion how we are like any of the choices.

We Integrate Collaborative Structures of Cooperative Learning into Our Lessons to Foster Connections, and We Teach Social Skills

There are many collaborative ways that students can support each other and cooperate to get things done. These are informal practices, important in their own right. In the previous chapter, I shared "Cooperative Learning: Quick Starters" with you. We also addressed the cooperative learning process of Learning Together, a formal structure that *requires* students to work effectively together as a *necessary* condition for learning a concept or skill (Johnson & Johnson, 2016; Johnson, Johnson, & Holubec, 2008). The outcome is a result of shared effort. Students sink or (hopefully) swim together (Murray, in Thousand, Villa, & Nevin, 2002).

As we said in Chapter 6, Learning Together is an approach we can use with any curriculum. Moreover, each lesson has social and academic skill objectives specified by the teacher, and there is instruction in *both* academic and social skills. Learning Together has an additional advantage: it fosters group processing of cooperative efforts. Team members need to discuss their progress towards their work goals and their maintenance of their relationships. Additional elements include:

+ Cooperative learning teams should contain students whose abilities are mixed regarding the task on which they will work—ideally, one student with relatively lower ability, two with average ability, and one with high ability. This heterogeneity promotes discussion, including the justification of answers as well as learning from peer teaching—both for those who teach and those who are being taught.

+ We assign roles or we develop an agreed-upon process with the students for the team members to assign roles.

+ Roles are described by us or with the class in discussion: *"If someone were an encourager, what would we see or hear her doing? What would we not see or hear her doing?"* Students' work is supported by written descriptions of their role responsibilities. One way to do this is to give each team a set of 3 x 3 cards with the title of each role typed at the top, the responsibilities listed below, and a "sound bite" example of what that team member would say in the role. For example, the Time Keeper sound bite would be "We only have five minutes left. Let's see if we can wrap up by then."

+ Students are encouraged (after they learn how) to constructively keep each other on task, involve everyone in discussions and other group efforts, support each other to achieve, and provide constructive feedback.

+ A monitoring process that includes individual accountability is designed and taught to students, and an opportunity is provided for members (and us) to evaluate the goals.

Table 7-4 is a template that may support you as you create cooperative learning experiences.

Table 7-4. **Template for Designing a Cooperative Learning Lesson**

1. **Select a lesson focus:** _____

   _____

2. **Determine:**

   - **Goals and criteria for success:**

     Task/Academic: _____

     _____

     _____

     Social/Relationship Maintenance: _____

     _____

     _____

   - **Groups Size:** _____
   - **Member Roles:** _____
   - **Nature of Team Task Steps:** _____

     _____

     _____

     _____

   - **Nature of Positive Interdependence** (e.g., shared materials; consensus required for decision-making; group as well as individual evaluation: _

     _____

     _____

   - **Monitoring Process:**
     - Who: Teacher: _____ Teacher and students: _____
     - What focus: Whole class: _____ Individual teams: _____ Individual students: _____
     - What behaviors: _____
     - How (e.g., team logs, rating or tally sheets): _____
     - Who will provide feedback (without naming names); e.g., teacher to individual team; teacher to class as a whole; team members to team; whole class processing: _____
   - **Materials Needed:** _____
   - **Room Arrangement:** _____

3. **Determine how above decisions will be communicated to class and teams orally and in writing:**

   _____

   _____

   _____

   _____

   _____

   _____

   _____

When We Use Cooperative Learning Experiences, We Differentiate Instruction to Ensure Collaborative Success

Cooperative learning structures are adaptable. To foster students' success in the learning experience and collaborative processes, we can differentiate instruction. Below is a list of some of the ways this might be done. You may have others in mind.

- Lesson Processes
  - differentiated division of labor
  - differentiated time allotment
  - differentiated manner of interaction
  - differentiated structures
  - differentiated role assignment
  - differentiated reward structure
  - differentiate the social skills or the level of social skills required by team members
- Lesson Content
  - choices in level of difficulty of reading materials
  - choices in types of materials to be used. Example: video or audio tapes as well as print materials
- Product
  - particular goals chosen—social or task
  - adaptations within goals—social or task, individual, team or all teams
  - how social or task goal completion may be demonstrated

We Foster Evaluation of Cooperative Learning Experiences with Students to Provide Feedback

The feedback addresses whether the work was done and how well. We give feedback on both, *and* we foster a means for *students* to reflect on and to receive feedback on their development of social skills. When students work collaboratively, they need to have the opportunity to ask questions about the work: "Did we get the job done?" "How did we work together?" "How could our work together improve?" we Can Evaluate Social Skills by Walking Around the Room and providing Oral Feedback

If this seems to disrupt the flow of the work, we can provide written feedback to teams based on our observations. The third means of evaluation can be highly effective—feedback the students provide themselves. Table 7-5 provides an example of a student feedback sheet I developed for a class. You will see that both the task goals and the social goals are included, since they are equally important. You will also see that to save time, the form is designed so that it could be used for a variety of cooperative learning lessons. Because we were carrying out a series of lessons, I filled in the task and social skill goals that were common to all the lessons. I left space to fill in the additional goals of a particular lesson.

Table 7-5. **Cooperative Team Evaluation Form**	Date: _____		
Goals	Ratings		
Task:	Great	OK	Could Have Done Better
1. Made good progress on our work			
2.			
3.			
Social:			
1. Encouraged participation by everyone			
2. Did not evaluate when ideas were being generated			
3.			
One part of our work that we feel good about is:			
One change our team will make so that we work together even better next time is:			
Team Members' Signatures:			

We have already discussed the need for safe, useful feedback. Note the word choice in the form. Students are *not* asked to reflect on what went wrong, but rather what could they do *even better* next time. They need to know *what* to do in order to improve so the feedback will be constructive and useful (Larrivee, 2009; Levin & Nolan, 2014).

Having teams contribute to their own feedback can also give us invaluable diagnostic information. If a team has the same goal for more than a few sessions, we may want to observe the team functioning to see if they need some supportive instruction to help them get over a hump in their work. If several teams have the same goal, a minilesson could be given to those teams or to the entire class, if all would benefit.

There are advantages to the learning process in using and evaluating the work of the same teams over time. Maintaining team membership helps build the sense of belonging. It also helps the students build their skills because they are able to evaluate how well they are working together and *then apply what they have learned* to their work during the next team session. A particularly useful process involves having a team member write the team's ideas in a log or notebook for the evaluation portion of the lesson. The form shown above could be drilled for insertion into a three-ring binder. Then the insights that team members gain from working together one day could be read by the members together just before their work together begins the next time. This enables the team to set a goal for its work based on the evaluation reflection done in the previous lesson. The team-developed goal is added to the evaluation sheet (under the Task or Social Skills portion) at the beginning of the lesson and is one of the foci of the evaluation at the end. Thus, the feedback loop is integrated into the learning experience. Moreover, being conscious of the agreed-upon goal(s) usually enhances the skills of the team members during the lesson.

Good cooperative learning experiences take time to plan. If you are beginning to integrate these into learning experiences, start small. Cheer yourself on. Find a colleague who is also using cooperative structures, and provide support, feedback, and ideas for each other. Ellis and Whalen's *Cooperative Learning: Getting Started* [i] (1990) is particularly helpful when addressing all aspects of cooperative learning experiences. The full reference is at the chapter's end.

We Integrate the Building of Emotional Intelligences Into Lessons

As we said in Chapter 5, five competencies or domains contribute to a student's mindful use of emotions and to maintaining a balance between emotions and reasoning:

+ **Self-awareness:** ability to name feelings and talk about them clearly
+ **Managing emotions:** ability to ease emotions or change moods; ability to resolve a conflict, even if it arouses strong emotions
+ **Self-motivation:** an open mindset of "I can," with a sense of resilience and an ability to maintain inner drive, persistence
+ **Empathy:** ability to grasp what another person is feeling and to "feel" for that person
+ **Social skills:** ability to use emotional intelligence to interact constructively with others of all ages (Goleman, 1995)

We Foster Self-Awareness

With students, we create a safe environment for the sharing of feelings. Then we invite students to share how they feel about an event, a story, or an experience, either in a discussion, journal entry, or learning log. We can discuss how the same event can result in different feelings for different people. Feelings are not right or wrong. People feel what they feel.

We Foster Students' Management of Emotions

We talk with our students about how our brains work and explain that feelings can be managed. We teach them management skills, such as breathing deeply, visualizing a calm place, or counting backwards from 10 until the shift occurs to new brain thinking. Periodically, as we talk about situations filled with feelings— joy, anger, remorse, pride—we include what alternative responses (constructive and unconstructive) they have, how people manage their feelings, and the effect on themselves and others. Students need our help to develop strategies to deal with difficult feelings, such as those that arise during conflicts. As we do this, we use activities and reflections, such as the ones I offer you. We can use literature as sources for our discussion. We can use issues the students are facing, if they are comfortable sharing. We use news events and local events, if age appropriate for the students. We teach students conflict resolution strategies. When they are in the midst of dealing with conflicts, we coach them towards resolution, if our support is needed. When we are in conflicts or in any other difficult situations with students, we provide a model through how we manage our emotions. Equally importantly, we maintain connections with students during difficult times. We show them how people can "hang in" and work through difficulties together.

Because feelings around conflicts are some of the most difficult to manage, let us focus on how we can foster students' addressing these feelings.

REFLECTION OPPORTUNITY

In the space below or on a separate piece of paper, draw what conflict feels like to you.

What kind of feelings does conflict engender in you? Are they relatively easy to experience? If not, you are in the company of a large number of people. Conflict is rarely easy for anyone. Our brains frequently short-circuit our reasoning, and we shift, at least temporarily, into the "fight or flight" response. Even if we can move into our more reasoned brain, resolving conflicts can be trying, even exhausting. Think about how you have felt when a conflict arose. Complete Table 7-6 below. Note: Both the previous reflection and this one could be used in developmentally appropriate ways with students.

	Conditions When Conflict Resolution is Easier for You	Conditions When Conflict Resolution is More Difficult for You
Table 7-6. **Conflict Resolution: Accessing Experiences**		
With Whom		
When		
Where		
Topic		

We Help Students Understand the How People May Respond to Conflicts

Students need to understand that some kinds of conflicts are more difficult for them and others—but the same conflicts are not necessarily difficult for all people. A friend may become really upset about a conflict that another student thinks is "no big deal." Use (in an age appropriate way) of the reflection process above can help students discuss this and understand these differences.

Whatever people feel, taking the time to address the conflict is important.

We Provide Strategies for Resolving Conflicts

The first strategy shown in Table 7-7 could be for younger students or for anyone when the conflict is simple in nature. The second strategy in Table 7-8 is a conflict resolution strategy for conflicts that are more complex.

Table 7-7. **A Strategy for Fairly Straightforward or Simple Conflict**	
The rule: Attack the problem, not the other person	
The goal: Everyone should be a winner; no one should lose!	
Speak in a credible voice and say:	
1. Use the other person's name.	"Evan,
2. Tell how you feel	I feel angry
3. Identify the problem	when you call me stupid.
4. Tell what you want	[please] Stop."

Table 7-8. **A Conflict Resolution Strategy for More Complex Conflicts**

1. **COOL OFF:** When you are angry, you cannot think straight. Count to 10. Take deep breaths.
2. **FIND THE RIGHT TIME AND PLACE TO TALK.** Talk in a quiet place and without others.
3. **TALK:** When you speak, use an authoritative/credible voice as you are describing how you feel and your perception of what happened. Use an approachable voice when you repeat back what you have heard and when you brainstorm and work to reach consensus. Tell the person what you are feeling and why, but do not blame anyone for the problem. Use "I" messages and identify the problem: "When _____, I feel _____." Even though you are upset, if possible, tell the other person you want to work this out with them. Remember you do not have to agree. One at a time tell what happened. Listen to each other's feelings. Ask questions if you need more information. Repeat what the other person has just said to be sure you have that person's perspective and she knows you understand what he was saying.
4. **BRAINSTORM** ways to resolve the conflict. *Without judgment* think of as many ideas as you can.
5. **CHOOSE** a solution that will work for *both* of you. **Reach consensus.** Look for **win/win** solutions.
6. **IMPLEMENT** the solution for a brief while. Take responsibility for carrying out your part.
7. **EVALUATE.** Check back to see if the solution is working the way each of you hoped. Ask: What changes, if any, would make it better.
8. **CONGRATULATE yourselves.** Resolving conflict is not easy.

As we work to enhance conflict resolution skills in ourselves and our students certain reminders (in developmentally appropriate language) can be helpful. See "Reminders About Resolving Conflicts"

Reminders About Resolving Conflicts:

+ Direct your anger towards problems, not people.
+ Frame conflict as a clash of goals, ideas, or beliefs, not people.
+ Address what people say, not the people who say it.
+ Focus your energies on solutions, not blame—on solutions, not excuses. You want a win-win solution for all involved.
+ Always remember that you are looking for solutions, not victories.
+ Resolving conflict is powerful.
+ Resolution creates shared power.

Resources

There are many sources for strategies that can help students learn how to resolve conflicts. Two references I find helpful for teaching conflict resolution and creative controversy are David and Roger Johnson's (1995b) *Reducing School Violence Through Conflict Resolution* and Wheeler's (2004) *Conflict Resolution in Early Childhood*. For teaching alternatives to violence, I have found numerous strategies in Curwin and Mendler's (1997) *As Tough as Necessary: Countering Violence, Aggression and Hostility in our Schools*. Complete references are available at the end of the chapter. Whatever conflict resolution strategies we teach, there are important reminders for students. The box to the left provides essential reminders.

We Foster Empathy

We exemplify someone who empathizes with students and those about whom we are learning. If a student is upset, we listen. We summarize what we believe the student is feeling: "You sound pretty upset about what Shayla just did." We help students understand that people do not have to agree to be able to empathize with one another's perspectives. We offer experiences for the students that build their capacity to be empathic. When we discuss good fiction, biographies, and issues such as war, the environment, slavery, people's rights, diversity, and disabilities, we create learning experiences that foster consideration of the experience for those involved. What does it feel like to be a grizzly bear whose habitat is shrinking drastically, season by season? Ask students to tell the narrative from the bear's perspective as well as from the perspective of someone who does not want the bear to eat the sheep on her/his ranch (Hoerr, 2017).

We Foster Self-Motivation

Students need our support to develop strategies to do for themselves. As we are fostering this, we shift from telling them why they are learning something to having them answer, "Why *are* we learning this?" This supports their taking greater control of their learning. In turn this posters a growth mindset that says, "I can grow; I can change. Who I am today and what I can and cannot do is *not* fixed." We also support students to develop and enhance their strategies to persist—to set reasonable goals (and time frames as they mature and have a reasonable sense of time), to problem solve when difficulties arise, and to cheer themselves on in times of both ease and difficulty (Dweck, 2006; Duckworth, 2008; Goleman, 1995; Yeager & Dweck, 2012).

> Jesse (with great frustration): "It won't work!"
>
> Teacher: *"Would you like some help, or would you like to figure it out?"*
>
> Jesse: "Figure it out."

We Foster Students' Social Skills Beyond Conflict Resolution

As we remind ourselves periodically throughout this book, constructive behavior needs to be taught, just like the skills of mathematics and the language arts. We have said that the inclusion of social skills instruction makes the use of Learning Together so appropriate for our purposes. Examples of social skills that can be taught are numerous. Table 7-9 provides a list of possibilities. Others could certainly be added.

Table 7-9. **Examples of Skills that Can Be Developed through Cooperative Learning**	
Moving desks/chairs into place efficiently	Using members' names
Staying in seat	Using good eye contact
Indicating agreement	Listening to each other
Following directions	Asking team member for help, clarification, explanations
Sitting face-to-face	Dividing up labor equitably
Talking in 24" voices (Speaking in a volume that can be heard by someone 24" away)	Not asking the teacher a question until all agree they do not understand
Encouraging participation	Taking turns
Everyone contributing	Praising others
Distributing materials	Checking for understanding
Sharing materials	Criticizing ideas, not people
Keeping group on task; helping it get back to task	Disagreeing in an agreeable way
Monitoring time	Not 'putting down' other people
Listening	Active listening including paraphrasing
Summarizing	All the skills that go with team member roles, e.g., reader, observer, secretary, summarizer, time keeper, "includer", materials handler, etc.
Reaching consensus	Giving constructive feedback
Describing and owning feelings: "I feel …"	
Taking different perspectives	
Giving help	

Examples in Table 7-10 support our choice of which social and task skills would be appropriate at the level we teach.

Table 7-10. Examples of Task and Relationship Skills by Developmental Level[i]	
Task/Work Skills	
Lower Elementary	Upper Elementary/Middle
• Follow your team's directions • Ask a question, if you don't understand • One person talking at a time • Share both your ideas and feelings • Stay on task • Stay with your team • Be sure everyone has a turn to talk • Share or take turns with materials • Respect materials	• Follow your team's directions and your role directions. • Ask a question, if you don't understand • Be sure everyone understands what s/he needs to do before getting started • Stay focused on your work • Help team members get back on task, if needed • Share your ideas and feelings • Watch the time • Use only 4-feet voices, so you are not heard by groups near you • Treat team members and materials with respect
Relationship/Social/Maintenance Skills	
Lower Elementary	Upper Elementary/Middle
• Use team members' names when speaking to them or about them • Look at your team member when she or he speaks • Listen to other's ideas • Encourage each other to speak • Take turns talking • Disagree respectfully • Respect team members—no 'put downs' • At the end, thank others for the work done	• When you begin, thank everyone for being a part of the teamwork today • Use team members' names when speaking to them or about them • Look at your team member when she or he speaks • Be sure everyone is encouraged to speak • Respond to team member's ideas • Respect team members—no 'put downs' • Disagree respectfully • Resolve conflicts constructively • Work to reach consensus on key decisions • Determine who will take on each team role • Everyone contributes to getting the team work done • At the end, thank team members for the work done

i Adapted from Dee Dishon and Pat Wilson O'Leary, A Guidebook For Cooperative Learning: A Technique for Creating More Effective Schools, p. 57. Learning Publications, Inc., 1984.

We Provide Social Skills Lessons

Because the social skills component is crucial to our focus, let us take a moment to look at how we can develop a lesson to teach the social skills needed for any cooperative learning experience. There are eight specific steps involved in doing this successfully.

Step 1: List the social skills you feel the students need to learn. A question for lesson design purposes would be: What would help them develop constructive collaborative behavior? Choose the skill that would be most helpful to focus on at this point in the students' development.

Step 2: With the whole class, discuss why the skill is necessary in collaborative work.

Step 3: In small groups or as a whole class, brainstorm a list of words that describe the skill. Ask: What does the skill look like? Sound like? If not developed with the whole class, combine lists, eliminating redundancies.

Step 4: With students, turn the list into a T-chart of what is seen/heard if the skill is being used. Post this prominently in the classroom where everyone can refer to the ideas.

Step 5: Select a way for the skill to be demonstrated by the teacher or students. Some possibilities include:

- **role playing** of the social skill by two or more students—a vignette from life, literature, or a movie can be a source for the content;

- a **teacher demonstration** with a script that presents the skill in a serious or lighthearted way; or

- a **skit**—two or more students plan and deliver a short skit that shows how the skill can be used.

Step 6: Create a means for the students to practice the skill, and monitor the results. Choose an activity that is relatively risk free and does not affect their grade.

Step 7: Have student reflect on the success. What went well? What would help them do even better next time?

Step 8: Enjoy! Celebrate adding yet another life skill to one's tool belt.

Students who have the needed social skills, including conflict resolution strategies, are more likely to behave constructively.

We Provide Opportunities for Members to Create a Community Memory

Like individuals who build relationships and a sense of belonging based on the foundation of shared memories, so also, is a learning community fostered by such a process. Photos on display or available in a collection of some kind are examples of how such a memory is created. Stories written about community members or class adventures and then published (by this, I mean bound in a secure form by folks in the school) would be another. After a unit on writing personal narratives, one middle school class I cotaught developed a collection of each member's (including both the

> *Of all the moments we gather in our lives, the ones we cherish most are the moments shared.*
>
> *—Flavia*

teachers') favorite autobiographical vignette. A copy was made for every member in the community. On the cover was a photo of the authors—all the community members. It meant so much to me, I still have it years later.

A primary class wrote a story modeled on the pattern of a book they had read (and reread). Each member contributed a page written in the pattern, illustrated, and signed by the author at the bottom of the page. The pages were bound together, laminated to protect them from wear and tear, and the book was then placed in the reading area for all to enjoy. It was read aloud to the class on more than one occasion—often by popular demand.

We Join Together in Rituals and Celebrations throughout the Life of the Community

There are many benefits of rituals, recognition, ceremonies, and celebrations throughout the life of the community:

- Celebrations nurture:
  - People feel **valued** when they are recognized.
  - Public recognition of tasks accomplished tends to help people feel **competent**.
  - Celebrations are fun and thereby meet the basic need for **joy**.
  - Those who are celebrated feel a **part of the group**.
  - If the celebration is part of closing off the community's work, people feel more **safe** because they are supported through the changes in belonging about to occur; they are eased in feeling sad or cut off from what might have become an important relationship.

- Celebrations provide structure:
  - They **remind everyone of what is valued** by giving the community a chance to review what has been done and to recognize accomplishments.
  - They **remind students what behaviors, skills, and values are important**.
  - They **reinforce appropriate behavior**.

We Help Open Each Class with Rituals

Rituals help to open a class. As part of their integral participation in the learning community, students can be responsible for management procedures. If everyone has been taught the procedures for taking attendance, lunch count, or homework check-in, then the job is done efficiently. The whole class contributes.

Rituals help close a community before the weekend or a vacation. A Quick Whip (a process described on page 137) offers any student who chooses an opportunity to share one good thing that happened during the week or one interesting fact, idea, or process that was learned that week. The list could be posted without names until a new list is created. (We need to be sure to ask permission to post, because this is more public than a verbal sharing in class. It is best to ask before writing the ideas for posting so that after, each student who shares can say whether her idea can be public beyond the Quick Whip.)

We Recognize Changes

A community of learners goes through many changes. One way to foster the sense of community is to recognize these changes. When people enter, we take the time to transition them into the community—to connect them through introductions to others and to go over expectations. This provides an opportunity for a review of the agreed-upon rules and the common procedures. (Since most community members have already done this, the process can be completed at a much faster pace.) When folks leave, we take the time to say good-bye, including a review of the good experiences shared.

We Recognize Happenings Not Connected to Peoples' Comings and Goings

We can have celebrations, ceremonies, and other ways of noting events or happenings:

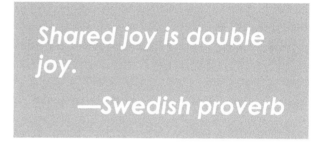

Shared joy is double joy.

—Swedish proverb

+ the coming of winter or spring (with the possibility of a connection to any area of the curriculum);
+ the 100th day of school (with the possibility of connection to all sorts of math activities);
+ changes in development by noting when teeth come out or when people change in height (with the possibility of a connection to science curriculum);
+ changes in families—including changes that inspire mixed feelings, such as older siblings leaving home, births, or the addition of a pet (we can recognize sad changes—perhaps with the support of reading topic-related literature—such as the death of a parent, relative, or pet);
+ a group's or team's success at enhancing the quality of cooperation; or interdependence on a cooperative team—we can have *each* group member receive recognition when the team reaches its goal (e.g., in addition to the score received on individual tests, every member receives five bonus points).

We Foster Recognition in Many Forms

We talk with the students about why ceremonies and celebrations are important. We ask what felt good about the recognition, rituals, and celebrations students have experienced positively. We help them make connections between what they say and the benefits of celebrating. We also discuss why some people are quick to criticize celebrations as being a waste of time or too "touchy-feely." These people may not understand the value, perhaps they do not like the vulnerable feelings that can be experienced at such times, or they may have been told celebrating was prideful. Whether students agree with these perspectives could be the focus of another discussion. Included in the discussion would be the understanding that people feel what they feel. That does not mean that their feelings are "right" and others' are "wrong" or that another's perspective is accurate and ours is not. We state the purpose of the celebration and the connection between what is being recognized and the values we and the students have established that are important to our learning community.

We make celebrations the responsibility of everyone. We consider what to celebrate and how to recognize both large and small contributions and achievements—kindness does not come in only big acts. Incremental growth is worth celebrating. We grab a teachable moment to create a list of adjectives that *describe* or verbs that *show* the action of people upholding the values. Then we take a couple of minutes for students to identify examples they have observed. We can keep a public log posted somewhere in the room to provide further examples. We can remind students that recognition does not need to be a whole class process and brainstorm other-than-whole-class ways of celebrating good work and kind acts; that celebration can be done with large and small ceremonies. Example: Students give a silent cheer for everyone after the class solved that tricky math problem or they do something else that was hard, or they make progress on a complicated task.

Notes: First note–when creating positive rituals and ceremonies, we need to wipe out limits to those being celebrated. There should never be "This is for the best team" or writing down the names of just two people who have been _____ or have done _____ this week. Encouraging everyone to exhibit the values of the learning community works only if everyone feels it is possible and is encouraged for doing so. Second note–celebrations cannot be based on any religious beliefs. On the other hand, we can celebrate people in our communities through other holidays, but with careful considerations. For example, Valentine's Day offers us the possibility of writing about positive qualities in community members, but only if *all* are included.

We Foster the Acknowledgement of Endings

When someone leaves—when a class, team, or learning group that has worked together for a while dissolves—we need to take time to bring closure. Saying good-bye is an important act and how to do it is an important social skill to learn.

We can ask students to think of the good-byes that occur after people have spent time with friends or family. What happens? We hear people talking about what was done: for example, "It was great to have the chance to canoe in that lake this time" or "Baking bread with you was the best, Gram." You also hear people saying things about their relationship: "I'm going to miss you" ("you and our relationship are important to me; distance will not change that"), "Don't forget to write" ("I want us to stay connected, despite the change brought on by distance."). So it is when saying "adios" in a community of learners.

The three important aspects to address are recognition of what was just accomplished or shared, recognition of the relationship between the people, and acknowledgment that both are about to undergo a change.

To support students' development of social skills around closings, we grab this opportunity to teach or review the skills that help people constructively say good-bye. We give students an opportunity to consider the kinds of feelings they might have, including awkwardness and embarrassment, and why those feelings occur. We can also talk about how some people are uncomfortable expressing feelings and may cover them up with joking, teasing, or shutting down and saying nothing. Include how these "cover-ups" can inadvertently hurt other's feelings and why more authentic expressions of the joy and sorrow would be better to employ. We can use the format for teaching social skills we discussed earlier in this chapter. Then we can coach students as needed when "good-byes" are in process.

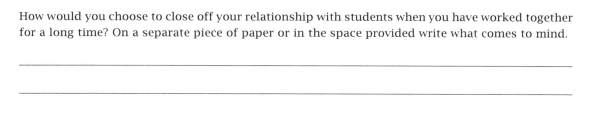

REFLECTION OPPORTUNITY

How would you choose to close off your relationship with students when you have worked together for a long time? On a separate piece of paper or in the space provided write what comes to mind.

_____

_____

Good-byes can be difficult for students and teachers alike. Saying good-bye to one person reminds us of other good-byes in our life, some of which may have been painful. If so, those feelings may never have been resolved. Teaching our students a strategy that supports them in the process of closing off gives them one more social tool for coping effectively in school and in life.

Some Ways Endings Have Been Celebrated

In one school where I supervised a student teacher, the students spent some time talking about what they had learned during the year. Each then put those items that were important on a slip of paper that was carried around the final week of school. Parents, bus drivers, custodians, teachers, administrators, cafeteria personnel, and secretaries were alerted to the activity and encouraged to stop a student and ask: "What is something you remember from this year in school?" Talk about a celebration that connects with others while tying off!

As part of the concepts being studied, one middle school math teacher worked with students to create three-dimensional dodecahedrons—one per student that could be hung from the ceiling. Then the students wrote as many (positive) memories as they wanted—one per face. Some added photos or illustrations they had made or cut from print materials or printed out from the internet.

We can read stories or poems that the students themselves or others have written about looking back or celebrating endings. Students can devise math statements that express how we feel. We and our students can write poetry to describe what we have accomplished and how we feel. To foster poetry writing, we can offer the choice of free verse and one or more structured forms, such as a cinquain. I have included three cinquain patterns below in Table 7-11 to show how the simplicity of the format might lend itself to a celebration of any kind. I have also provided a choice for a pattern that might be appropriate for different student developmental levels.

Table 7-11. **Three Patterns for Cinquain Poems**[i]		
Cinquain Pattern #1*	**Cinquain Pattern #2**	**Cinquain Pattern #3**
Line1: One word	Line1: A noun	Line1: Two syllables
Line2: Two words	Line2: Two adjectives	Line2: Four syllables
Line 3: Three words	Line 3: Three '–ing' words	Line 3: Six syllables
Line 4: Four words	Line 4: A phrase	Line 4: Eight syllables
Line 5: One word	Line 5: Another word for the noun	Line 5: Two syllables

i   Source: Http://Hrsbstaff.Ednet.Ns.Ca/Davidc/6C_Files/Poem%20Pics/Cinquaindescrip.Htm.

We can use any art medium to express how we and the students feel. We can make a collage or create bulletin board displays with the students about what has been learned. We can have the students create bound volumes of work or put finishing touches on portfolios that include narratives about looking back and tying up the work. I have given students a tool bag to support them in the years ahead. I take a lunch-size paper bag and put their names on the front. Inside, I put trinkets that represent some of the important ideas we have addressed in our classes (for example, a tiny owl that represents the wise way to resolve a conflict.) I also put a letter inside that explains the meaning of each of the various objects and how I feel as I look back on our work together as well as my feelings about saying good-bye to them.

• •

Application Activity: Ways to Maintain Connections and Expectations

We have addressed many ways to maintain connections and expectations. These were using collaborative structures, fostering social skill development, solving problems together, celebrating together, reviewing expectations for constructive behavior with learning community members, and offering engaging learning experiences that provide structure and nurturing to learners. Write below or on a separate piece of paper one way you might put each of these ideas into place in your work with students. _____

_____

_____

_____

_____

_____

• •

Final Thoughts

The focus of Chapter 7 has been our work sustaining the learning community through consideration of variables in students' physiological, physical, and psychosocial environment variables. We discussed how to maintain expectations and connections while students do their work, in the midst of conflict, and when their efforts are coming to a close, whether as a team or a class. Last, we talked about the need to celebrate—to celebrate changes, milestones, growth, and accomplishments because, among other reasons, celebrating helps us to recognize and validate important values and important people in our lives. All of these strategies contribute to the establishment and maintenance of constructive behavior in our learning communities.

Looking Forward

In Chapter 8 we will focus on how to foster learning and maintain connections when we encounter some unconstructive student behavior bumps in the road. Our question will be: How can we choose strategies of the caring and empowering kind that will foster constructive behavior in students? We will discuss the kind of reasoning that supports our choices. I will also offer many on-the-spot strategies that can support our choices.

References

Alberto, P., & Troutman, A. (2017). *Applied behavior analysis for teachers* (9th ed.). Boston, MA: Pearson.

Armstrong, T. (1998). *Awakening genius*. Alexandria, VA: Association for Supervision and Curriculum Development.

Armstrong, T. (2009). *Multiple intelligences in the classroom* (3rd ed.). Alexandria, VA: Association for Supervision & Curriculum Development.

Aronson, E., & Patnoe, S. (1997). *The jigsaw classroom: Building cooperation in the classroom* (2nd ed.). New York: Addison Wesley Longman.

Bolman, L., & Deal, T. (1995). *Leading with soul: An uncommon journey of the spirit*. San Francisco: Jossey-Bass.

Brookhart, S. (2017). *How to give effective feedback to your students* (2nd ed.). Alexandria, VA: Association for Supervision and Curriculum Development.

Brophy, J. (1981) Teacher praise: A functional analysis. *Review of Educational Research*, (*51*), 5–32.

Brophy, J. (1998). *Motivating students to learn*. Boston, MA: McGraw Hill.

Caine, R., & Caine, G. (1994). *Making connections: Teaching and the human brain*. Reading, MA: Addison-Wesley.

Caine, R., & Caine, G. (1997). *Education on the edge of possibility*. Alexandria, VA: Association for Supervision and Curriculum Development.

Cameron, J. (1992). *The artist's way*. New York, NY: Tarcher/Putnam.

Center for Applied Special Technologies. (2011). *Universal Design for Learning Guidelines, Version 2.0*. Wakefield. MA: Author.

Charney, R. (2002). *Teaching children to care* (2nd ed.). *Classroom management for ethical and academic growth, K–8*. Greenfield, MA: Northeast Foundation for Children.

Cole, R. (Ed.). (1995). *Educating everybody's children: Diverse teaching strategies for diverse learners*. Alexandria, VA: Association for Supervision and Curriculum Development.

Crum, T. (1987). *The magic of conflict*. New York, NY: Simon and Shuster.

Curwin, R., & Mendler, A. (1997). *As tough as necessary: Countering violence, aggression and hostility in our schools*. Alexandria, VA: Association for Supervision and Curriculum Development.

Dean, C., Hubbell, E., Pitler, H., & Stone, Bj. (2012). *Classroom instruction that works: Research-based strategies for increasing student achievement* (2nd ed.). Alexandria, VA: Association for Supervision and Curriculum Development.

Duckworth, A. (2016). *Grit: The power of passion and perseverance*. New York, NY: Scribner.

DuFour, R. (1998, Fall). Why celebrate? *Journal of Staff Development, 19*(4), 58–59.

Durrand, V. (Ed.). (1990). *Severe behavior problems: A functional communication training approach*. Baltimore, MD: Brookes.

Dweck, C. (2006). *Mindset: The new psychology of success*. New York, NY: Ballantine Books.

Ellis, S., & Whalen, S. (1990). *Cooperative learning: Getting started*. New York, NY: Scholastic.

Emmer, E., & Evertson, C. (2017). *Classroom management for middle and high school teachers* [loose-leaf version] (10th ed.). Boston, MA: Pearson.

Evertson, C. (1991). *Classroom management and organization focusing checklists*. Nashville, TN: Peabody College, Vanderbilt University.

Evertson, C., Emmer, E., & Worsham, M. (2017). *Classroom management for elementary teachers* [loose-leaf version] (10th ed.). Boston, MA: Pearson.

Evertson, C., & Weade, R. (1989). Classroom management and teaching style: Instructional stability in two junior high English classrooms. *The Elementary School Journal, 89* (3), 379–393.

Ferguson, D., & Jeanchild, L. (1992). It's not a matter of method: Thinking about how to implement curricular decisions. In Stainback S., & Stainback W. (Eds.), *Adapting the regular class curriculum: Enhancing student success in inclusive classrooms* (pp. 159–174). Baltimore: Paul H. Brookes.

Gardner, H. (1983). *Frames of mind: The theory of multiple intelligences*. New York, NY: Basic Books.

Gardner, H. (1993). *Multiple intelligences: The theory in practice*. New York, NY: Basic Books.

Gardner, H. (2000). *Intelligence reframed: Multiple intelligences for the 21st century*. New York, NY: Basic Books.

Goldstein, S., & Brooks, R., (Eds.). (2013). *Handbook of resilience in children*. New York, NY: Springer.

Goleman, D. (1995). *Emotional intelligence*. New York, NY: Bantam Books.

Goleman, D. (2006). *Social intelligence: The new science of human relationships*. New York, NY: Random House.

Good, T., & Brophy, T. (2008). *Looking in classrooms* (10th ed.). Boston, MA: Pearson.

Gregory, G., & Kaufelt, M. (2015). *The motivated brain*: *Improving student attention, engagement, and perseverance*. Alexandria, VA: Association for Supervision and Curriculum Development.

Harmin, M. (1994). *Inspiring active learning: A handbook for teachers*. Alexandria, VA: Association for Supervision and Curriculum Development.

Heath C., & Heath, D. (2007). *Teaching that sticks*. New York, NY: Random House.

Hobgood, B., & Ormsby, L. (2011). Inclusion in the 21st-century classroom: Differentiating with technology. In University of North Carolina, Chapel Hill Education Department (Eds.), *Reaching every learner: Differentiating instruction in theory and practice*. Chapel Hill, NC: University of North Carolina, Learn NC. Retrieved from http://www.learnnc.org/lp/editions/every-learner/6776

Hunter, M. (1982). *Mastery teaching: Increasing instructional effectiveness in elementary and secondary schools*. El Segundo, CA: TIP Publications.

Hunter, M. (2004). *Mastery teaching: Increasing instructional effectiveness in elementary and secondary schools* (2nd ed.). Thousand Oaks, CA: Corwin Press.

Hunter, R. (2014). *Madeline Hunter's Mastery Teaching: Increasing instructional effectiveness in elementary and secondary schools*. Thousand Oaks, CA: Corwin Press.

Immordino-Yang, M. (2015). *Emotions, learning and the brain*. New York, NY: W. W. Norton & Co.

Jensen, E. (2005). *Teaching with the brain in mind* (2nd ed.). Alexandria, VA: Association for Supervision and Curriculum Development.

Jensen, E. (2013). *Engaging students with poverty in mind*. Alexandria, VA: Association for Supervision and Curriculum Development.

Jensen, E. (2015a). *Guiding principles for brain-based learning*. Retrieved from http://www.brainbasedlearning.net/guiding-principles-for-brain-based-education/ and http://www.jensenlearning.com/what-is-brain-based-research.php

Jensen, E. (2015b) *What is brain-based research?* Retrieved from http://www.jensenlearning.com/what-is-brain-based-research.php

Johnson, D., & Johnson, F. (2016). *Joining together: Group theory and group skills* (12th ed.). Boston, MA: Allyn & Bacon.

Johnson, D., & Johnson, R. (1979). Conflict in the classroom: Controversy and Learning. *Review of Educational Research, 49*, 51–61.

Johnson, D., & Johnson, R. (1989). *Cooperation and competition: Theory and research*. Edina, MN: Interaction Book Company.

Johnson, D., & Johnson, R. (1994). *Learning together and alone: Cooperative, competitive, and individualistic learning*. Needham Heights, MA: Allyn & Bacon.

Johnson, D., & Johnson, R. (1995a). *My mediation notebook*. Edina, MN: Interaction Book Co.

Johnson, D., & Johnson, R. (1995b). *Reducing school violence through conflict resolution*. Alexandria, VA: Association for Supervision and Curriculum Development.

Johnson, D., & Johnson, R. (1995c). *Teaching students to be peacemakers*. Edina, MN: Interaction Book Co.

Johnson, D., Johnson, R., & Johnson Holubec, E. (1987). *Structuring cooperative learning: Lesson plans for teachers*. Edina, MN: Interaction Book Company.

Johnson, D., Johnson, R., & Johnson Holubec, E. (1994). *The new circles of learning: Cooperation in the classroom and the school*. Edina, MN: Interaction Book Company.

Johnson, D., Johnson, R., & Holubec, E. (1998). *Advanced cooperative learning* (3rd ed.). Edina, MN: Interaction Book Co.

Johnson, D., Johnson, R., & Holubec, E. (2008). *Cooperation in the classroom* (8th ed.). Alexandria, VA: Association for Supervision and Curriculum Development.

Kagan, L., Kagan, M., and Kagan, S. (1995). *Teambuilding: Cooperative learning activities*. San Juan, Capistrano, CA: Kagan Cooperative Learning.

Kagan, M., and Kagan, S. (1992). *Advanced cooperative learning: Playing with elements*. San Juan, Capistrano, CA: Kagan Cooperative Learning.

Kagan, M., and Kagan, S. (1995). *Class building: Cooperative learning activities*. San Juan, Capistrano, CA: Kagan Cooperative Learning.

Kagan, S. (1990). *Cooperative learning resources for teachers*. San Juan Capistrano, CA. Kagan Cooperative Learning.

Kagan, S. (1994). *Cooperative learning* (2nd ed.). San Juan Capistrano, CA: Kagan Cooperative Learning.

Kohl, H. (1998). *The discipline of hope: Learning from a lifetime of teaching*. New York, NY: Simon & Shuster.

Kohn, A. (1992). *No contest: The case against competition* (2nd ed.) Boston. MA: Houghton Mifflin.

Kohn, A. (1996). *Beyond discipline: From compliance to community*. Alexandria, VA: Association for Supervision and Curriculum Development.

Larrivee, B. (2009). *Authentic classroom management: Creating a learning community and building reflective practice* (3rd ed.). Boston, MA: Pearson.

Lazear, D. (1999a). *Eight ways of knowing: Teaching for multiple intelligences.* Arlington Heights, IL: Skylight.

Lazear, D. (1999b). *Eight ways of teaching: The artistry of teaching with multiple intelligences.* Arlington Heights, IL: Skylight.

Lazear, D. (2004). *Higher order thinking the multiple intelligences way.* Chicago, IL: Zephyr Press.

Levin, J., & Nolan, J. (2014). *Principles of classroom management: A hierarchical approach* (7th ed.). Boston, MA: Pearson.

Martin, G., & Pear, J. (2015). *Behavior modification: What it is and how to do it* (10th ed.). New York, NY: Routledge.

Marzano, R. (2007). *The art and science of teaching: A comprehensive framework for effective instruction.* Alexandria, VA: Association for Supervision and Curriculum Development.

Marzano, R., Gaddy, B., Foseid, M. C., Foseid M. P., & Marzano, J. (2005). *A handbook for classroom management that works.* Alexandria, VA: Association for Supervision and Curriculum Development.

Marzano, R., Marzano, J., & Pickering, D. (2003). *Classroom management that works: Research based strategies for every teacher.* Alexandria, VA: Association for Supervision and Curriculum Development.

Murray, F. (2002). Why understanding the theoretical basis of cooperative learning enhances teaching success. In J. Thousand, R. Villa, & A. Nevin (Eds.), *Creativity and collaborative learning: A practical guide to empowering students, teachers, and families* (2nd ed.), 175–180. Baltimore, MD: Brookes.

Ridnouer, K. (2006). *Managing your classroom with heart: A guide for nurturing adolescent learners.* Alexandria, VA: Association for Supervision and Curriculum Development.

Saphier, J., & Hanley, M. (1993a). *Activators.* Carlisle, MA: Research for Better Teaching.

Saphier, J., & Hanley, M. (1993b). *Summarizers.* Carlisle, MA: Research for Better Teaching.

Sharan, S. (1990). *Cooperative learning: Theory and research.* New York, NY: Praeger.

Sharan, S. (1993). *Handbook of cooperative learning methods.* Westport, CT: Greenwood.

Sharan, Y., & Sharan, S. (1992). *Expanding cooperative learning through group investigation.* New York, NY: Teachers College Press.

Slavin, R. (1990). *Cooperative learning: Theory, research and practice.* Englewood Cliffs, NJ: Prentice Hall.

Sousa, D., & Tomlinson, C. (2011). *Differentiation and the brain.* Bloomington, IN: Solution Tree Press.

Stone, D., & Heen, S. (2014). *Thanks for the feedback: The science and art of receiving feedback well.* New York, NY: Penguin.

Sulo, R. (2007). *Activating the desire to learn.* Alexandria, VA: Association for Supervision and Curriculum Development.

Sylwester, R. (1995). *A celebration of neurons: An educator's guide to the human brain.* Alexandria, VA: Association for Supervision and Curriculum Development.

Sylwester, R. (2003). *A biological brain in a cultural classroom: Enhancing cognitive and social development through collaborative classroom management.* New York, NY: Corwin Press.

Thousand, J., Villa, R., & Nevin, A. (2002*). Creativity and collaborative learning: A practical guide to empowering students, teachers and families* (2nd ed.). Baltimore, MD: Brookes.

Tomlinson, C. (2004). *Fulfilling the promise of the differentiated classroom: Tools and strategies for responsive teaching.* Alexandria, VA: Association for Supervision and Curriculum Development.

Tomlinson, C. (2017). *How to differentiate instruction in academically diverse classrooms* (3rd ed.) Alexandria, VA: Association for Supervision and Curriculum Development.

Tomlinson, C. (2014). *The differentiated classroom: How to respond to the needs of all learners* (2nd ed.). Alexandria, VA: Association for Supervision and Curriculum Development.

Tomlinson, C., & Edison, C. (2003a). *Differentiation in practice: A resource guide for differentiating curriculum, Grades K–5.* Alexandria, VA: Association for Supervision and Curriculum Development.

Tomlinson, C., & Edison, C. (2003b). *Differentiation in practice: A resource guide for differentiating curriculum, Grades 5–9.* Alexandria, VA: Association for Supervision and Curriculum Development.

Tomlinson, C., & Imbeau, M. (2013). Differentiated instruction: An integration of theory and practice. In B. Irby, G. Brown, R. Lara-Aiecio, & S. Jackson (Eds.), *Handbook of educational theories* (pp. 1081–1101). Charlotte, NC: Information Age Publishing.

Tomlinson, C., & McTighe, J. (2006). *Integrating differentiated instruction and understanding by design: Connecting content and kids.* Alexandria, VA: Association for Supervision and Curriculum Development.

Tomlinson, C., & Moon, T. (2013). *Assessment and student success in a differentiated classroom.* Alexandria, VA: Association for Supervision and Curriculum Development.

Wheeler, E. (2004). *Conflict resolution in early childhood.* Boston, MA: Pearson.

Wiggins, G., & McTighe, J. (2006). *Understanding by design* (2nd ed.). Alexandria, VA: Association for Supervision and Curriculum Development.

Wolfe, P. (2010). *Brain matters: Translating research into classroom practice* (2nd ed.). Alexandria, VA: Association for Supervision and Curriculum Development.

Yeager, D., & Dweck, C. (2012). Mindsets that promote resilience: When student believe that personal characteristics can be developed. *Educational Psychologist, 47*(4), 302–314.

Zirpoli, T. (2016). *Behavior management: Applications for teachers* (7th ed.). Boston, MA: Pearson.

Website Resources

Cooperative Learning: International Association for the Study of Cooperation in Education. Retrieved from http://www.iasce.net

Cooperative Learning: Johnson, D., Johnson, F., Johnson, R., & Holubec Johnson, E. Co-operative Learning Institute website for the Learning Together structure. Retrieved from http://www.co-operation.org

Cooperative Learning: Spenser Kagan website for a variety of cooperative learning resources. Retrieved from http://www.Kaganonline.com

Cooperative Learning: Richard Slavin website, Success for All Foundation, for resources regarding Success for All cooperative learning structures. Retrieved from http://www.successforall.org

Differentiated Instruction: Carol Tomlinson's website on differentiated instruction. Retrieved from http://www.caroltomlinson.com

Multiple Intelligences: Thomas Armstrong's website for American Institute for Learning and Development for multiple intelligences resources. Retrieved from http://institute4learning.com

Multiple Intelligences: David Lazear's website for multiple intelligences resources. Retrieved from http://www.DavidLazear.com

Research for Better Teaching: website based on the work of Jon Saphier and others. Retrieved from http://www.rbteach.com

Endnotes

i Unfortunately, the Ellis and Whalen book is out of print from Scholastic; however, there are copies in book stores online and from book sellers on line.

CHAPTER 8

Maintaining Constructive Behavior

I've come to a frightening conclusion: I am the decisive element in the classroom. It is my personal approach that creates the climate. It is my daily mood that makes the weather. As a teacher, I possess a tremendous power to make a child's life miserable or joyous. I can be a tool of torture or an instrument of inspiration. I can humiliate or humor, hunt or heal. In all situations, it is my response that decides whether a crisis will be escalated or de-escalated and a child humanized or de-humanized.

—Haim Ginott

What Will This Chapter Discuss?

We have talked about how to get ready for students—how to arrange the room and contents and how to build community. We have also considered how to develop learning experiences that grab students' attention and foster their learning through brain-compatible instruction and differentiation of learning experiences. Now the school year is underway, and school life is in full swing. Suddenly a student does or says something that disrupts our lesson plan. After all our careful planning, why does unconstructive behavior occur? What conditions lead to it? When it occurs, what can we do about it? The answer to these questions will be the focus of this chapter.

Why Is This Important?

Findings from research on teaching are clear: we *can* maximize students' constructive behavior and *prevent* a high percentage of unconstructive behavior. Reduction in disruptions is also correlated with increase in students' learning (Evertson & Emmer, 1982; Evertson & Poole, 2008; Evertson & Weinstein, 2006; Kounin, 1970). If we are aware of potential times when *un*constructive behavior is more likely to occur because of lack of sufficient structure or nurturance—what I refer to as "weak spots"—we can design our instruction to ensure a more successful flow through the day's experiences for everyone. We can also maintain appropriate behavior by being prepared to respond constructively should distractions or disruptions occur.

What Will You Learn?

By the end of the chapter, you will be able to:

+ recognize potential weak spots in advance;
+ design the flow of the lesson and the transitions in and out of learning experiences to proactively prevent weak spots from disrupting learning experiences; and
+ constructively respond on the spot to disruptions.

What Do You Want To Accomplish?

Given these foci, what would you hope to gain from this chapter? Write your responses here or on a piece of paper. _____

_____

_____

When Do Most Unconstructive Behaviors Occur?

There are potential weak spots every day in every classroom and school building when unconstructive behavior is more likely to occur. We have experienced many of them as students, teachers, or both.

. . . .

ACCESSING PRIOR KNOWLEDGE/EXPERIENCE

Take a moment to remember the weak spots you experienced in school when unconstructive behavior was likely to occur. (The behavior might be mildly unconstructive, such as children bounding into a classroom bumping into chairs and, perhaps, each other; dropping items as they hurry to their team's table; or shouting to each other in the hall.) When were the weak spots in a lesson when unconstructive behavior of any kind was likely to occur? When were those weak spots during the school day when unconstructive behavior was likely to occur?

What potential weak spots can occur during a lesson or learning activity? In the space below or elsewhere list those that come to your mind readily:

_____   _____

_____   _____

_____   _____

_____   _____

What potential weak spots can occur during a school day or week? List those in the space below or elsewhere:

_____   _____

_____   _____

_____   _____

_____   _____

Analyze your lists. Do any items seem connected to others, meaning can you group two or more together within or across the two lists? Put a circle around all those that seem to fit into one group, a square around those that fit into another, a triangle around those that fall into a third group, and so on. Some items may fit into more than one group. If this occurs, put more than one appropriate geometric shape around the item.

. . . .

How would you name or categorize your groups? One category that comes to my mind is transitions. Did you have that? Examples of potential weak spots *in a lesson transition* might involve students moving from one learning center to another or from one part of a lesson to the next. Items *during the day or week* might involve students moving from one lesson to the next, moving in and out of the room when going to "specials," to and from lunch or recess, to another room for another subject area, or to special services.

Another category might be interruptions. Examples would be announcements on the loudspeaker, a telephone call, an administrator or teacher entering the room, or student(s) being pulled out for any reason, including services, photographs, health-related needs to be addressed, etc. These can occur any time. If a teacher coming into the room is doing so to gather students to leave the room for some reason, this interruption could also be considered part of a transition—a category we have already discussed. That is why you might have more than one shape around a weak spot item.

Platform: Application Opportunity 8-1

On the Active Learning Platform under Chapter 8, Application Opportunity 8-1 is a list of possible weak spots. You have an opportunity to consider them, see if you would add any from your Reflection list, and then write an example of what you or a student might do under each circumstance.

Why Do Weak Spots Occur?

You have just considered what kinds of unconstructive behavior might occur during weak spots. Now you will have an opportunity to consider what makes the nature of certain times in the school day seem to invite unconstructive behavior.

REFLECTION OPPORTUNITY: WHAT MAKES CERTAIN ASPECTS OF A SCHOOL DAY POTENTIAL WEAK SPOTS?

Table 8-1 gives you an opportunity to consider why weak spots occur. This also gives you an opportunity to review all of the ideas we have shared in previous chapters. In the right column below or on a separate piece of paper write what comes to mind.

Table 8-1. **Reflection: Reasons for Weak Spots**	
Consider what we have said about the need to provide structure and nurturance in our instruction. Below are some categories of weak spots from the list above. Next to each category provide at least one reason why that 'spot' might be weak—what kind of nurturance and/or structure might be absent.	
Potential Weak Spot	**Reason Why that 'Spot' Might Be Weak**
Transitions in a lesson or between lessons	
Unexpected interruptions	
Lack of lesson activity that actively engages student	
Mismatch between instructional strategies and student's physiological variables such as learning style, intelligences	
Compromised physical environment variables such as visibility or accessibility	

Weak spots occur because students' needs aren't being met. More nurturing or more structure is necessary.

How Can We Prevent Weak Spots?

Kounin's (1970) research on management of a whole class to minimize weak spots has provided particularly useful ideas for teachers for many years now. As you read the chart below (Table 8-2), picture yourself in a room of students during a lesson. Imagine what you might do to realize each of the key ideas. What skills do you believe you have in hand already? Which could you improve?

Table 8-2. How Effective Teachers Maintain Constructive Structure: Summary of Kounin Research[i]

Issue	Skills	Definition	Examples	Weak Spot to Avoid
Preventing unconstructive behavior	Withitness	Using behavior that communicates that teacher knows what is going on. Includes prompt, appropriate addressing of unconstructive behavior	• Teacher systematically scans room or changes proximity to students to be aware of potential problems. • Teacher makes eye contact with a student who is about to take out his cell phone to check for messages. The student puts the phone away. A student behind him, who has seen the interaction, decides he's not likely to get away with checking his phone either.	• Allowing an initial distraction (whispering or poking or beginning to take out an inappropriate object to go to the next step, including involving more students in the disruption. • Being unaware that student is on wrong problem, page, computer program or file. • Staying in one spot for extended time so all students are not monitored readily.
	Overlapping	Attending to two or more simultaneous events. Includes responding to needs of other students while fostering a group activity.	• Student approaches teacher while he is listening to another's essay. Teacher places hand on student's arm briefly to both acknowledge her presence, yet her needs to wait until appropriate break in teacher focus. • Teacher distributes materials while explaining the process to be done.	• Without giving students appropriate brief task to complete, stopping whole group lesson to attend to an interruption that cannot be put on hold. • Stopping work with individual student or group to respond to another student who does not have an urgent need.
Managing movement	Momentum	Maintaining activity flow at appropriate pace; ensuring activities are more interesting than competing distractions.	• Teacher gives succinct directions with visuals. • An answer to a student question is taking so much time; others students are losing their focus. Teacher tells the students the question will be addressed later in greater depth and continues with the lesson.	• Over dwelling: Giving more attention than necessary to a set of directions, to a question (either on task or off), or to a student exhibiting a low level unconstructive behavior. • Group fragmentation: Providing directions and addressing questions for individual students rather than doing it at once to whole group.
	Smoothness	Maintaining lesson focus; fostering flow during shifts and transitions; avoiding distractions that lead to confusion.	• Student asks off-topic question. Teacher makes note of question and offers to address it at end of class. • Teacher alerts class of impending transition with '5-minute warning'.	• Over dwelling: Responding beyond what is necessary comment or question. • Flip-Flopping: Starting an activity, then interrupting with distraction from another. • Jerkiness: Teacher suddenly shifts from one topic to another. • Stimulus Boundedness: Distracting students with irrelevant question or comment.

Maintaining group focus	Group alerting	Implementing a lesson in a way that grabs all students' attention and maintains it throughout, even when only some are responding to question or doing a problem	○ Teacher uses 'motivator to grab all students' attention—unusual material or object; provocative question, quick video clip. ○ Teacher uses means of calling on students that has element of surprise; e.g., draws student names from a pencil can; calls on second student to respond to what previous student said. ○ Students not doing problems at the board are asked to turn to near neighbor and share their process and answer to see if there is agreement.	○ Teacher focus is on those responding at board. Students at seats do not have to complete an appropriate task. ○ Some students are called on much more frequently than others. ○ Design of lesson does not engage all students.
	Encouraging accountability	Communicating to students that their participation will be observed and evaluated	○ At the end of discussion and practice of a new skill, teacher directs students to turn to a neighbor and explain the process to him or her. ○ Teacher uses answer boards (dry erase or slate) and has all students write answers to question or solve problem at same time.	○ Students are inactive during lesson. ○ Only a few students are called on to provide answers.
	Higher participation formats	Using activity designs that involve students who are not directly answering a question or giving a presentation	○ While some students work problems at the board, students at their desks are instructed to check the board work to see if they agree by working the problems on paper. ○ Lesson designs include team work to derive an answer and holds each team member accountable for providing rationale behind the answer given.	Students spend an inordinate amount of time listening to answers provided by other students without having to derive the answers themselves or having to provide the reasoning behind their answers.
	Variety and challenge/ Avoiding satiation	Minimizing boring and repetitive tasks so that students do not lose interest in topic or activity.	○ Teacher uses effective and topic meaningful 'motivator to grab students' attention—unusual item, though provoking question, quick clip, etc. ○ Teacher offers variety in types of activities, kinds of materials, student roles, types of presentations, length of activities.	○ Giving lengthy presentation without opportunity for students to apply material. ○ Assigning repetitive drills beyond what is needed for mastery practice. ○ Using same format and materials day after day.

i Based on research reported in Kounin, J. (1970). *Discipline and group management in classrooms*. NY, NY: Holt, Rhinehart, & Winston.

Platform: Application Opportunity 8-2

On the Active Learning Platform under Chapter 8, Application Opportunity 8-2 is a list of weak spots. For each you have the opportunity to consider what need is not being met that may lead to "unconstructive" behavior.

While we can prevent a high percentage of off-task behavior, there will be a few students whose unconstructive behavior will "pop up" every once in a while. What choices do we have then? We have many.

During weak spots, whatever the student is doing is not constructive from the perspective of the teacher but is constructive from the student's viewpoint—it meets one of her basic needs. If, as teachers, we do not find ways for students' needs to be met within a reasonable amount of time, students will find other ways to get those needs met. So would we in similar circumstances. Therefore, I see unconstructive behavior as a warning signal. Something isn't quite right. That means we now have two jobs. The first is to quickly figure out why something isn't right for the student. What triggered the "unconstructive" behavior, and what seems to encourage it to occur? Our second job is to decide how we want to respond, including choosing to ignore what has just happened. Notice I said *respond*, not react. Before we respond, we need enough time to be sure we are in our newer, reasoned portion of our brain when we say or do something as a consequence of the student's behavior.

Job #1 – Ask: "What Triggered the Student's Behavior, and What Does the student Gain by Behaving this Way?"

Another way to phrase this is "What is cueing the behavior, and what is the reinforcement for it?" In Chapter 5, we talked about the fact that behavior doesn't occur unless it is supported by variables internal to the student and external in the setting. We labeled these variables Antecedent (A) and Consequent (C) variables for the behavior (B).

To this A ->B ->C assessment we now add one more important piece of understanding about what supports behavior. We ask "What is this student *communicating* with her behavior?" or "What purpose does this behavior serve? What does it accomplish?" There are four possible answers.

1. **Sensory/stimulation regulation:** behavior that satisfies basic physiological needs; that provides stimulation; that brings feelings of comfort, intrinsic satisfaction, or joy; behavior that increases, decreases, or helps to maintain the current level of whatever stimulation the person is experiencing. This category includes food.

2. **Attention:** behavior that gains someone's attention, help, smiles, or focus.

3. **Tangibles** (things): behavior that provides objects, such as toys, tools, a piece of clothing that "everyone is wearing," a sculpture worked on in art class, a relief map created during geography, or a poem.

4. **Escape:** includes rest, sleep, and avoidance of something unsafe, frightening, or frustrating (Durrand, 1990).

Note: Power comes under attention—"I want your attention when I want it, and I don't when I don't."

To help me remember the categories, I arrange the words so their first letters spell the acronym SATE, which means "satisfied," "to have had enough." Once we have gained what we wanted and thus are sated, we no longer need to behave that way until the need arises again.

What some educators call the "four goals for behavior" fits *my* conceptualization of basic emotional needs. Moreover, I think that each of Durrand's four communicative intents of behavior connects directly to each of the basic emotional needs. That is, a person's behavior is communicating about any of these needs. To help conceptualize this, on the chart below (see Table 8-3) I have summarized possible connections between each of the emotional needs and the intent of any behavior.

Table 8-3. **Connection Between Emotional Need and Function/Communicative Intent of Behavior**	
Need	Function of the Behavior and Related Questions the Behavior Might be Communicating
Safety: Emotional and/ or Physical	*Attention:* Can I get the help I need to feel safe, protected? How can I express what I am feeling (anger, anxiety, fear)? *Escape:* Can I get away from what or who is scaring me/making me anxious, threatening me? How can I get away from the feelings that I don't like? *Sensory Regulation:* What can I do to keep these feelings going? To get these feelings under control? To increase them? To decrease them? *Tangible:* How can I get the things I need in order to feel safe?
Love/Care	*Attention:* Do I matter to my teacher? To my peers? Does my teacher care how I feel? Do my peers? Do the people I want to notice me actually notice me? Will I be treated with respect no matter how well I do this, or no matter how I feel or think about something? *Escape:* How can I get away from my teacher's/peer's criticism, shaming, blaming, disappointment? *Sensory Regulation:* How can I get touched appropriately? How do I get the lighting, heat or kind of seating I need? How can I get away from touch or other sensations (heat, light, hardness or formality of seating) that do not feel good? *Tangible:* How do I get this [item] that will make me feel important/valued? How do I get the materials I need for this assignment?
Belonging	*Attention:* Am I part of this group? *Escape:* How can I get away from this person/these people? *Sensory Regulation:* How can I feel that I am connected to this person/to these people? How can I avoid feeling rejected? *Tangible:* How do I get this [item] that will make me feel part of this team/group? How do I get rid of/hide this item so I can be like everyone else?
Efficacy	*Attention:* How can I get the help I need? *Escape:* How can I get away from these demands because I don't think I can do this or don't know how to do this? How do I avoid looking silly/stupid in front of my friends/classmates/teacher? *Sensory Regulation:* How can I feel confident/competent? *Tangible:* How can I get the tool/materials I need to succeed?
Joy	*Attention:* How can I share these good feelings I have? *Escape:* How can I escape these feelings of boredom, listlessness, discouragement, depression? *Sensory Regulation:* How can I increase or maintain the good sensation/feeling I am experiencing? How can I feel happy/pleased, etc. *Tangible:* How can I obtain that item that will make me happy?

To determine the function/communicative intent of a behavior, I find it helpful to read a student's behaviors backwards:

1. I try to figure out what change occurred by looking at the result of the behavior and then going back and trying to recall what occurred just before the behavior. In other words, I do a quick rewind to see if I can recall what the variables were like for the student just before the behavior occurred (the **A**ntecedent, as we have been calling it).

2. I ask myself "What was the change brought on by the behavior (the **C**onsequent Event or **C**onsequence of the behavior, as we have been calling it)?"

3. I analyze the information.

   a. If the **b**ehavior brought about a "**C**" that reduced the light, noise, etc. around the student, then the function of the behavior was sensory regulation.

   b. If the **b**ehavior gave the student more attention from one or more people, then the function was attention.

   c. If the student obtained an object, the function was a tangible item.

   d. If the behavior enabled the student to get away from the task at hand, the people with whom the student was working, or a place in the room, then the function was escape.

4. I reanalyze the consequences to determine if there was more than one function being served by the behavior.

There are many internal variables we cannot see. Often these have to do with sensory regulation. However, even if we do not know what triggered the behavior and, therefore, why the student wanted or needed that particular result and so acted as he did, we can usually determine the result. However, we need to do our assessment with some caution. Sometimes what we see as a result is not the *intended* result of the student's behavior. Nonetheless, with practice, we can get fairly good at assessing A and C and the function of the behavior by reading backwards.

Note: Nowhere have I suggested that we assign personalized motivation to a student's behavior. Using subjective, evaluative explanations, such as the student is "rude," "thoughtless," or "lazy" does not help anyone, nor does it put us in a position to know what to do next. Again, the occurrence of "unconstructive" behavior is a problem to solve, a student to teach, not a person to blame (Belvel & Jordan, 2003).

As we are doing the on-the-spot ABC and functional analyses, there is a third analysis that is essential: we need to determine to what degree this behavior is a problem for the student, other students, and the task at hand. While the following categorization is highly subjective, I find it helpful to consider whether a student's behavior is distracting, disruptive, or disturbing. Included in my assessment could be questions such as:

+ How long is this behavior likely to occur?
+ How likely is it that the behavior will continue or reoccur?
+ How many people are affected?
+ What kind of effect does the behavior have on the student(s) behaving unconstructively? On others?
+ What is the effect on the learning experience that is unfolding for everyone in the class?

A behavior that is *distracting* is short in duration, a one-time incident, and affects the student and maybe one or two others, but for a brief time only. It is inconsequential. We may not need to respond at all or, if we do, our response will be minimal, and we will be able to carry on fostering the learning experience for everyone. Some call this surface behavior (Larrivee, 2009). Others call it nuisance behavior (Knoster, 2008).

A behavior is *disrupting* if, as the name suggests, the degree of its effect is enough to stop the lesson. One disruptive effect may be on the feelings of others. Another may be the length of time it takes for the behavior incident to stop. As the teacher, we need to be able to restore the well-being of the learning community to what it was before the behavior occurred, so that we and the students can proceed with the lesson.

A *disturbing* behavior is one that is so unusual in its nature, degree, or effect on others that it signals to us that the student needs additional help to support her in functioning successfully in class. Our concern and our response needs to go beyond our on-the-spot response to the student's emotional well-being. This is a situation in which an assessment of the student's needs should occur, and, with that information, there should to be a determination of how to address those needs. Note: If the effect of a "disturbing" behavior may be so unsettling to others, they, too, may need support from us to restore themselves to the way things were before the behavior occurred. *"It can be upsetting to see someone we care about be so upset. I am making sure that people who can help will support Gia in any way possible."*

Whatever our categories, with time and experience we become better at carrying out all four analyses efficiently and effectively. What is most important with these analyses is to be able to quickly determine what, if anything, we need to do to respond constructively and effectively, keeping in mind the goal of ensuring everyone's emotional well-being and fostering constructive learning experiences. When we do need to respond, we also need to determine what level of response would be appropriate. Simultaneously, whenever possible, we need to choose a response that will help students learn how to meet their own needs responsibly.

Job #2 – Ask: How Do I Want to Respond?

When unconstructive behaviors occur, we have many choices for the way we respond on the spot, including the choice to not do anything. Before we discuss our options, I want to review our purposes and goals. These guide the nature of our responses.

Purposes of Any On-the-Spot Response

 + to redirect the unconstructive behavior towards a constructive alternative while simultaneously preserving our right to teach and students' right to learn without unnecessary disruptions;
 + to prevent reoccurrence so that under similar circumstances in the future, the student will choose to engage in purposeful constructive behavior; and
 + to enhance students' repertoire of constructive ways to meet needs, including the development of self-management skills and responsibility.

Guidelines for the Nature of our Response

We need to use these guidelines[i] as we consider our response, whatever its level.

Safety

We must always protect the emotional and physical safety of all learning community members, including those who are being unconstructive. We need to be sure our words and actions are respectful. Whenever possible, we should communicate privately with students about their behavior.

Positive Presumptions and Possibilities

We must always assume that the student is doing the best she can *at the moment*. At the same time, she has within her many *possibilities for growth and change*. Our role is to support her in figuring out how to change, to teach her how to effect change if needed, and to support her progress. Saphier and Gower (1987) encourage us to continually communicate to students in both actions and words: "You can do it. I will stick with you until you do it" (p. 48).

Clarity of Communication

We need to be sure that what we do or say communicates *what needs to be done* rather than what not to do. When we only say what *not* to do, we leave the door open for confusion about what should or could be done.

Least Response Needed

Whatever we choose to do must:

+ be the least intervention necessary to provide the structure and nurturance needed;
+ support the student in addressing the issues;
+ alter whatever physical environment variables need to be adjusted;
+ keep the other students moving along in the learning experience;
+ cause no more, and hopefully less, distraction from the work at hand than what the student was/is doing;
+ let the control be in the hands of the student as much possible (provide the student a sense of efficacy) rather than in our control; and
+ deter a problem from escalating.

Student Efficacy

Our purpose is to teach. What we choose to do should guide the student to examine what is going on and make a more appropriate choice for how to fix it and also how to make amends, if needed. Our focus needs to be on the student's growth—on restoration rather than punishment or retribution for misdeeds. Our focus needs to be on finding solutions, not finding blame.

Teacher Well-Being

We act in a way that will prevent us from harboring negative feelings towards students. We remind ourselves, sometimes frequently, that what the student is doing is not an attack on us any more than a mistake in math or reading is. We cannot take this personally. We need to respond, not react. In the heat of the moment, we need to say to ourselves, "Our 'job' is to teach."

How Can We Respond on the Spot in a Way That Nurtures Students and Provides Structure?

In Some Instances, Student Behavior Requires Our Immediate Attention

Table 8-4 provides a list of such circumstances. While we must respond immediately to the behavior in these situations, we have choices about *how* to respond. Whatever we choose to do should follow our guidelines for treating students with dignity and respect.

Table 8-4. When an Immediate Response is Needed	
Situation	Example
Any learning community member's inner comfort is compromised	An auditory or visual stimulus that exceeds any learning community member's (including a teacher's) tolerance
Student's own physical safety is endangered	Self-injurious behavior
Community members' physical safety is threatened	Any form of fighting
Student's own emotional safety is at risk	Student is about to be or is already flooded with anxiety, anger, overexcitement
Community members' emotional safety is jeopardized	Being called a name that student feels is derogatory; being 'put down' for an idea or opinion, being bullied in any form
Materials or equipment are in imminent risk for damage or are being damaged	One (or more) students are being so rough with manipulatives, art supplies, microscope slide that something is likely to be broken or is already in process of being broken
Maintenance of learning experience flow is thwarted	Any form of distraction (visual, auditory, or olfactory) interruption that is more than momentary or is serious in its effect, including any other item in this list

There Are Times When We Should Delay Responding to the Situation

Grossman[ii] suggests that while it is not ideal to wait, these are the situations when we should consider delaying:

If we have insufficient information

Not only must we be sure we have as much information as is possible to gather before we discuss a situation, whenever possible, in complex or heated situations, we also need to triangulate as much information as possible—that is, try to find more than one source, particularly if it seems to be a "he said, she said" situation.

If there is insufficient time to talk effectively with those involved

We may need to return to teaching all the students or the student(s) may not be able to stop what she/they are doing at the moment to talk. However, if we cannot get together to talk right away, we make specific plans when we will so the student(s) involved know that we care and see the situation as worthy of addressing. We also make sure we get back to the student to address the situation when we said we would.

Disruptive effects of intervening at the moment

One situation when there may not be sufficient time occurs when we need to return to teaching. Pausing at that point would be too disruptive for too many students. We make sure the unconstructive behavior will cease, and we make plans as suggested just above.

Student exposure

If we cannot address the situation privately, we should wait until that is possible.

When students or we are too upset to deal with the situation rationally

We know from our discussion of brain functioning that when people are upset, they cannot use the newer portion of their brain to solve a problem reasonably.

We Have Many Options for Responding to Behavior

The list below is a collection of options I have seen, read about, or used over the years. These strategies begin with low-level responses that are under the control of students and progress to more teacher-directed responses. With any of these responses, I advocate what we described above as "do the least necessary." For example, if there is a distracting behavior, we begin with a nonverbal cue. If that does not suffice, we choose a low-level verbal cue. If the behavior becomes disruptive, we use a directive. If that does not work, we shift to a consequence.

There are many possible responses, not to overwhelm but to provide variety in order to give you options that better match your teaching style. As you read through the list, I suggest you check off those you already have in your tool belt. Then look at those you have checked. Having many options helps. So does variety. If you can add some options, particularly if they expand the variety of your choices, I encourage you to do so. Since there are many possibilities, a tip would be to write down the names of one or two strategies under each category that you want to add to your repertoire when you have the opportunity to apply them. Try these for a week or so. When you are comfortable using them, add a few more, and so on.

Possible Levels of Response

Ignoring a Behavior

If the behavior appears to be short lived and no one is bothered by it to any serious degree.

Low-Level Nonverbal Responses

Since there is no sound involved, these strategies only work if we have eye contact with the student.

Advantages: If they are sufficient to address the situation, nonverbal responses have many advantages (Henley, 2006).

+ Our intervention does not involve others. The learning experience continues, which is one of our goals.
+ Attention is not drawn to the particular student. If attention from others was the motivation, nonverbal intervention foils the plan. The student will not be irritated because our actions go unnoticed by others.
+ The student does not need to be confrontational to save face—to show peers that he has power, not the teacher.

Low-Level Nonverbal Responses-Examples

+ Use the "teacher" look.
+ Change Position(Proximity) in the Room Frequently: Without breaking the momentum of the lesson activity, we move (as naturally as possible) around the room to change the degree to which we are closer to any of the students and to require the students to shift their own positions to stay focused. If the student is talking to another student, we try to position ourselves between them to cut off their ability to see each other.
+ Use Gesture or Nonverbal Cue to Stop or Start a Behavior:
  + Put a finger up to our lips to signal "quiet."

  + Walk to where a student is sitting and point to the spot in the materials where the discussion is focused or where the student can find information to answer a question.

  + Use signals to gain the attention of the whole class, such as a previously learned clapping rhythm or raising a hand high to signal that everyone needs to stop what they are doing and look at the teacher.

Low-Level Verbal Responses-Examples

- ✦ **Change voice volume, speaking emphasis, level of dramatic expression:** Without breaking the momentum of the lesson activity, provide variety in what students hear.

- ✦ **State the relevant rule:** *"When we developed our rules, we agreed that when the bell rang/music stopped, we would be in our seats, not talking, and ready for the first direction."*

- ✦ **Comment (as an observation) on the readiness of some:** *"Folks at four tables are ready, now five, and now everyone is set to go. Great." "Aurora, can you make a choice that will get you ready for the next step?"*

- ✦ **State what we see without judgment or consequence:** *"There are several pieces of paper on the floor and colored pencils out of their boxes."*

- ✦ **Invoke silence:** *"Miki, would you wait for just a moment, please? I am having a hard time hearing what you are saying because there is talking going on."*

- ✦ **Use a private "I" message:** Walk over to students and say in a quiet voice that others are not likely to hear, *"Mike and Bruce, when you talk to each other during a whole class discussion, I can't hear what other students are saying."*

- ✦ **Request a pause:** *"Hang on, BJ. In two minutes, we will take a break, and you will have time to do that then."*

- ✦ **Help with interpreting experiences:** Describe what we believe were the intentions of a student to help the students involved with understanding what happened. Example: As Chad is turning to slide into his seat, his book slips out of his grasp and falls on Nathaniel's foot. As Nathaniel whirls around to say something to Chad, we say, *"Even though that was an accident, I bet that smarts, Nathaniel."* This acknowledges Nathaniel's feelings and, hopefully, gives him enough understanding to stop him from snapping at Chad.

- ✦ **Offer (sincerely) to help:** To two students who are chatting after directions have been given: *"Tanya and Sheryl, is there anything I can help to clarify for either of you?"*

- ✦ **Shift to active student responses:**

  - ◆ **Warn students in advance they will be called on:** *"For the next question, I want Dalia, Sarah, and Colleen to be ready to answer."*

  - ◆ **Call on more than one student for an answer:** After Ronesia gives her answer, say, *"Miranda, tell us if you disagree or agree with what Ronesia has just said and give us a reason."* This is *not* done to catch Miranda off guard but to provide an opportunity for you, too, her to engage in the activity, also.

  - ◆ **Ask all students to weigh in on an answer:** *"If you agree with what Lydia just said, thumbs up; if you disagree, thumbs down. Let me see your thumbs."* We can then ask, *"Jude, your thumb was down. What do you think?"* or *"Kimora, your thumb was up. Why do you agree— what is a reason?"*

  - ◆ **Use response cards, slates, whiteboards** (with no-odor markers, in case of allergies). Each student, pair, or team writes an answer. At the predetermined signal, all slates are shown.

  - ◆ **Provide opportunities for dialogue (e.g., "Turn to Your Neighbor"):** *"Turn to a neighbor or two and create a list of three points you have heard so far"* or *"Come up with four examples of _____."*

- **Provide opportunity for student movement:** To Thomas, who has been getting increasingly restless: *"Thomas, please get the atlases on the bottom shelf and give one to each team."*
- **Provide an opportunity for active processing:**
  - **Use 10-2[iii]:**
    1. After you have presented or demonstrated for 10 minutes, stop for 2. Use this time to let students catch up on their notes and/or clarify what they have learned so far.
    2. Ask them to turn to a neighbor and compare notes to see if they agree, to fill in things they missed, or to discuss things that confused them.
    3. Ask them to create questions that address any issues they uncovered as they were sharing.
    4. With the whole class, go over any issues the pairs found.
  - **Use "Ticket to Leave"[iv]:** A summarizing procedure to use when students are about to leave the room. Pass out a "ticket" the size of a half or quarter sheet of paper. Ask students to jot down one idea or fact they want to remember or a question they have about the topic. They turn in the ticket in order to leave.

Medium-Level Verbal Response with Directives

- **Speak to the entire class:** *"You have 30 seconds to finish whatever you are doing, put materials down, and turn to me for the next direction. Begin!"*
- **Speak to one student:** *"Shannon, we need your ideas. Please put your materials away quickly so you can join us." "Jon, please put all four chair feet on the floor so you don't fall or break the chair." "Brianna, our rule is 'Respect the room and the materials.' Please use the pen tips lightly so they don't break."*
- **Give students choices (privately):** *"Alexia, you seem to be having difficulty sitting next to Germaine. You have a choice. You can either resolve the issues in the next 20 seconds and join our discussion or move your location to a spot that is better for you for the time being."*

Statement of Consequences-Examples

These are communicated privately. *"Jackson, since you have not been using the equipment as directed and with the kind of respect agreed upon in our rules, please work someplace else for a while until you can handle the tools appropriately." "Janelle, you have been reminded twice of the procedure for leaving your team during work time, yet you continue to wander around the room. Please come sit in this seat. In the next five minutes, complete an Individual Problem Solving form, and discuss your solution with me."*

There are three things to remember when communicating a statement of consequences

Step 1: If we do not have a constructive relationship with a student, most of these strategies will not be effective. If students do not feel at least some positive connection to us and the lesson, they may not be willing to engage with us in getting back on track.

Step 2: Few of these strategies will have the desired effect if we don't have a sense of humor—but never one that is directed at the student's expense. A sense of warmth and support is essential. A smile is not required, but it can certainly help if it is authentic and comes from a sense of caring.

Step 3: As we have said, we cannot take "off-task" behavior personally. Student behavior is *not* a personal attack on us. At times, we may be a safe, easy target for unmet needs or frustrations that have nothing to do with us. Unconstructive student behavior is a problem to be solved, not a war that is being waged against us.

Statement of Consequences-Examples

- ✦ **Simple consequence:** *"Diego, can you think of a better way to work with Derek? If you cannot make a better choice, I will make one for you."*
- ✦ **Follow-up consequence:** To Brianna (just above), if she does not stop after the directive: *"Brianna, since you are still using the pen tips roughly, I am going to remove them from your supplies until you let me know you are ready to follow our rule about materials." "Alissa, since you have written a message on the bathroom wall, we will need to get the materials from the janitor so that you can use them to clean up the wall."*
- ✦ **Response with empathy.** Showing our empathy (not necessarily our agreement with the student's feelings) can help to deescalate the situation. Often students just want to be "heard." *"Shayla, I can see you're upset, but you're disrupting our work. If there is something I can do quickly to help or something I can do later, I'd be happy to. In the meantime, take a couple of deep breaths and try to get back on track with our rules. If you can't, then please remember we all agreed the result would be _____."*

> Where did we get the crazy idea that to make people do better, first we have to make them feel worse?
>
> —Jane Nelson

Notice that, whenever possible, we include a reminder of the relevant rule and indicate the consequence our learning community developed. We are *not* including punitive consequences or intimidating measures that have no logical connection to helping students learn alternative behavior.

Earlier in the book, we discussed reasons to avoid punitive measures. They do not teach what we want children and young adults to learn. They hurt rather than help. More often than not, they cause harm to the student and sometimes to other students who observe the punishment. Moreover, these measures are not needed.

People do better when they feel better. Therefore, we use logical consequences, as we discussed previously.

Enhance Consequences by Thinking in Terms of Solutions. Use Problem-Solving Approaches

When we shift our thinking from punishment to consequences, we consider the unconstructive behavior as a sign that something is wrong, a problem to be solved. We then work individually, collaboratively, or with the whole class to find a constructive solution, and we include a means of restitution in our solution.

We can teach our class a procedure to use when a problem arises. Jones and Jones (2016) propose the following steps (however, the number and nature of steps we use will vary greatly, depending on the students' development level):

Step 1: Provide the students with a handout and write the steps on the overhead.

Step 2: Discuss each step and provide a concrete example.

Step 3: Role-play situations in which a student and the teacher use this method for assisting the student in taking responsibility for his or her behavior.

Step 4: Lead a discussion following each role-play.

Step 5: Have the students practice by taking the role of both student and teacher and role-playing several situations.

Step 6: Process these interactions.

Step 7: Provide the class with an example of a violation of a classroom rule, and have each student write a problem-solving plan. (A form that is geared to the developmental level of the students can be used. See Table 8-5 for one example.)

Step 8: Have students share and assist the class in evaluating and, if necessary, modifying several plans.

Step 9: Explain how the problem-solving process relates to the classroom management plan and the difference between verbal and written plans.

Step 10: Quiz students on the steps in the sequence and the classroom management plan (p. 331).

The time invested in teaching this procedure (or a variation for younger students) is well worth it when a problem arises.

Glasser (1965, 1985, 1986, 1990, 1998) suggests a conversational approach between a teacher and student that can support the student in shifting from an unconstructive behavior to a constructive one.

Step 1: Establish a warm, personal relationship with the student.

Step 2: Establish what is being done. Ask: "What are/were you doing?" Focus on the present. Don't spend time trying to determine whose fault it is.

Step 3: Make a value judgment. Ask: "Does this follow our rules? Is it helping you? Others?"

Table 8-5. Individual Student Problem-Solving Form: How I Can Do Better?

Name: _____   Date: _____

Rules we agreed on as a learning community: [To be filled in in advance by the teacher]

1.

2.

3.

4.

5.

As you think about what happened, answer the following questions:

1. Which rule(s) did you not follow? Circle: (1) (2) (3) (4) (5)

2. What did you say or do that did not follow that rule?

3. What was the effect on you, your teacher, or your classmate(s)?

4. Did you try to resolve the conflict in a way that we use in our class? _____ If yes, what occurred (no names)?

5. Is this behavior that breaks one or more rules helping you? If so, in what ways? If not, in what ways?

6. What can you do to help yourself follow the class rules in the future?

7. If anyone was affected by what you did, what can you do to make amends?

8. Who, if anyone, could help you with your plan? How could that person/those people help you?

9. Is there anything else you would like me to know?

Your signature (and the date) show your commitment to making change on your behalf and that of others:

Signed: _____   Date: _____

Step 4: Make a plan to do better. Ask: "How can we work this out? What can be done that would prevent this from happening again?"

Step 5: Get a commitment.

Step 6: Follow up.

Step 7: No put-downs. Don't accept excuses. Don't punish, but don't interfere with natural consequences.

Step 8: Never give up. If the plan doesn't work, revise it until it does.

In addition to all the strategies we have discussed in this chapter and elsewhere, we have a series of strategies that focus on solutions as we support behavior change over a longer period of time. In the next section of the book, we will focus on the ways we can do this.

Reflection: Physical Environment Variables to Prevent Weak Spots

Completing Table 8-6 provides you an opportunity to summarize some of the content we have been addressing in this chapter.

Table 8-6. **Using Physical Environment Variables to Prevent "Weak Spots"**	
What Are Potential "Weak Spots" *During a Lesson* That May Trigger Unconstructive Behavior?	As a Teacher What Can You Do to Prevent These When You Teach?
What Are Potential "Weak Spots" *During a Day* That May Trigger Unconstructive Behavior?	As a Teacher What Can You Do to Prevent These When You Teach?

Application Activity

Picture a situation you have experienced recently in which either you or someone you were observing had to respond quickly to one or more students. Review the on-the-spot strategies provided above. Choose two you have not yet used or observed that would be appropriate to address the student behavior. How could you or the person you were observing have used each of the two strategies (i.e., what could have been said or done that would have been a constructive approach to providing structure for the student[s]?) On a separate piece of paper or in the space provided write your responses to the items below.

Brief description of situation: _____

_____

_____

How one strategy could have been implemented—what would have been said or done: _____

_____

_____

How another strategy could have been implemented—what would have been said or done: _____

_____

_____

Final Thoughts

There Are Certain Negative Strategies That Should Never Be a Part of Our Repertoire

Disparaging Remarks to the Student

An example would be, *"I don't like you when you tease, Uta"*. Personal attacks are not helpful; worse, they are likely to be damaging. Ask anyone about a strong memory she has from school, and you will often find the first memory mentioned is a verbal attack or personal criticism from a teacher. It does not matter how long ago the criticism was leveled; it still smarts. Instead of criticizing the *student,* we need to speak *about the behavior*. We can use an "I" message: *"I feel angry when I hear one student say something that can hurt another's feelings."*

Saying Anything that Would Shame or Embarrass the Student Alone or in Front of Others

An example would be saying any disparaging remark about the student rather than addressing the behavior: *"Zack, you are just like your brother!"* or *"Riley, why are you so mean to other children?"*

Doing More Than Is Needed

An example of this is using a loud voice that gets *everyone's* attention to "call out" a student and tell her to stop chatting with a neighbor during independent work when a *slight* reminder—a teacher "look" or a shift in proximity—would be enough to make the student aware that a change needs to occur. Another example would be "lecturing" the entire class for an extended period of time about a minor refinement in behavior needed to follow a particular class rule.

> *Raise your words, not your voice. It is rain that grows flowers, not thunder.*
>
> *—Rumi*

Responding to the Same Behavior Frequently

If we find we have to speak to one or more students about a behavior frequently, this is a management issue, not a student behavior issue. We need to analyze the contextual variables and figure out how to enhance our management strategies.

Looking Forward

We have focused our discussion on establishing a learning community that meets the basic needs of students so they can learn both academic and social skills. If we have proactively worked to support constructive behavior and responded on the spot constructively, yet the unconstructive behavior persists, what choices do we have? This is the focus of the next chapters: how do we develop a plan to intervene over a more extended period to support behavior change?

References

Belvel, P., & Jordan, M. (2003). *Rethinking classroom management: Strategies for prevention, intervention, and problem solving.* Thousand Oaks, CA: Corwin Press.

Boynton, M., & Boynton, C. (2005). *Preventing and solving discipline problems.* Alexandria, VA: Association for Supervision and Curriculum Development.

Brophy, J. (1982). Classroom management and learning. *American Education, 18,* 20–23.

Brophy, J., & Evertson, C. (1976). *Learning from teaching: A developmental perspective.* Boston, MA: Allyn and Bacon.

Burden, P. (2012). *Classroom management: Creating a successful learning community* (5th ed.). New York, NY: John Wiley.

Cangelosi, J. (1993). *Classroom management strategies.* New York, NY: Longman.

Chandler, L., & Dalquist, C. (2014). *Functional assessment: Strategies to prevent and remediate challenging behaviors in school settings* (4th ed.). Upper Saddle River, NJ: Pearson.

Curwin, R., & Mendler, A. (1997). *As tough as necessary: Countering violence, aggression and hostility in our schools.* Alexandria, VA: Association for Supervision and Curriculum Development.

Dean, C., Hubbell, E., Pitler, H., & Stone, Bj. (2012). *Classroom instruction that works: Research-based strategies for increasing student achievement* (2nd ed.). Alexandria, VA: Association for Supervision and Curriculum Development.

Dreikurs, R. (1957). *Psychology in the classroom.* New York, NY: Harper and Bros.

Dreikurs, R., and Grey, L. (1968). *A new approach to discipline: Logical consequences.* New York, NY: Hawthorn Books.

Durrand, V. (Ed.). (1990). *Severe behavior problems: A functional communication training approach.* Baltimore, MD: Brookes.

Emmer, E., & Evertson, C. (2017). *Classroom management for middle and high school teachers* [loose-leaf version] (10th ed.). Boston, MA: Pearson.

Evertson, C., & Emmer, E. (1982) Effective management at the beginning of the school year in junior high classes. *Journal of Educational Psychology, 74,* 485–498.

Evertson, C., Emmer, E., & Worsham, M. (2017). *Classroom management for elementary teachers* [loose-leaf version] (10th ed.). Boston, MA: Pearson.

Evertson, C., & Poole, I. (2008). Proactive classroom management. In T. Good (Ed.). *21st century education,* 131–140. Thousand Oaks, CA: Sage.

Evertson, C., & Weinstein, C. (Eds.). (2006). *Handbook of classroom management: Research, practice, and contemporary issues.* Mahwah, NJ: Erlbaum.

Fagen, S., & Hill, J. (1977) *Behavior management: A competency-based manual for in-service training.* Burtonville, MD: Psychoeducational.

Glasser, W. (1975). *Reality therapy.* New York, NY: Harper & Row.

Glasser, W. (1985). *School discipline policy.* Materials distributed at an Institute for Reality Therapy workshop, Burlington, MA.

Glasser, W. (1986). *Control theory in the classroom*. New York, NY: Harper & Row.

Glasser, W. (1990). *The quality school: Managing students without coercion*. New York, NY: Harper & Row.

Glasser, M. (1998). *Choice theory: A new psychology of personal freedom*. New York, NY: HarperCollins.

Good, T., & Brophy, J. (2008). *Looking in classrooms* (10th ed.). Columbus, OH: Allyn & Bacon/Merrill Education.

Gordon, T. (1991). *Discipline that works*. New York, NY: Penguin Books.

Grossman, H. (2003). *Trouble-free teaching: Solutions to behavior problems in classrooms*. Mountain View, CA: Mayfield.

Henley, M. (2006). *Classroom management: A proactive approach*. Boston, MA: Pearson.

Hunter, R. (2004). *Mastery teaching as updated by Robin Hunter*. Thousand Oaks, CA: Corwin Press.

Jensen, E. (2005). *Teaching with the brain in mind* (2nd ed.). Alexandria, VA: Association for Supervision and Curriculum Development.

Jensen, E. (2013). *Engaging students with poverty in mind.* Alexandria, VA: Association for Supervision and Curriculum Development.

Jensen, E. (2015a). *Guiding principles for brain-based learning*. Retrieved from http://www.brainbasedlearning.net/guiding-principles-for-brain-based-education/ and http://www.jensenlearning.com/what-is-brain-based-research.php

Jensen, E. (2015b) *What is brain-based research?* Retrieved from http://www.jensenlearning.com/what-is-brain-based-research.php

Jones, V. (2015). *Practical classroom management* [loose-leaf version] (2nd ed.). Boston, MA: Pearson.

Jones, V., & Jones, L. (2016). *Comprehensive classroom management: Creating communities of support and solving problems* [loose-leaf version] (11th ed.). Boston, MA: Pearson.

Knoster, T. (2008). *The teacher's pocket guide for effective classroom management*. Baltimore, MD: Brookes.

Kounin, J. (1970). *Discipline and group management in classrooms*. New York, NY: Holt, Rhinehart, & Winston.

Larrivee, B. (2009). *Authentic classroom management: Creating a learning community and building reflective practice* (3rd ed.). Boston, MA: Pearson.

Levin, J., & & Nolan, J. (2014). *Principles of classroom management: A professional decision-making model.* (7th ed.). Boston, MA: Pearson.

Marzano, R. (2017). *The new art and science of teaching.* Alexandria, VA: Association for Supervision and Curriculum Development.

Marzano, R., Marzano, J., & Pickering, D. (2003). *Classroom instruction that works*. Alexandria, VA: Association for Supervision and Curriculum Development.

Marzano, R., Gaddy, B., Foseid, M. C., Foseid, M. P., & Marzano, J. (2005). *A handbook for classroom management that works*. Alexandria, VA: Association for Supervision and Curriculum Development.

McConnell, M., Cox, C., Thomas, D., & Hilvitz, P. (2001). *Functional behavioral assessment*. Denver, CO: Love.

Nelson, J., Lott, L., & Glenn, S. (2000). *Positive discipline in the classroom* (3rd ed.). Roseville, CA: Prima Publishing.

Redl, F. (1966). *When we deal with children*. New York, NY: Free Press.

Ridnouer, K. (2006). *Managing your classroom with heart: A guide for nurturing adolescent learners*. Alexandria, VA: Association for Supervision and Curriculum Development.

Saphier, J., & Haley, M. (1993a). *Activators*. Carlisle, MA: Research for Better Teaching.

Saphier, J., & Haley, M. (1993b). *Summarizers*. Carlisle, MA: Research for Better Teaching.

Saphier, J., Haley-Spec, M., & Gower, R. (2008). *The skillful teacher: Building your teaching skills* (5th ed.). Acton, MA: Research for Better Teaching.

Scheuermann, B., & Hall, J. (2012). *Positive behavioral supports for the classroom* (3rd ed.). Boston, MA: Pearson.

Shea, T., & Bauer, A. (2011). *Behavior management: A practical approach for educators* (10th ed.). Boston, MA: Pearson.

Sylwester, R. (1995). *A celebration of neurons: An educator's guide to the human brain*. Alexandria, VA: Association for Supervision and Curriculum Development.

Sylwester, R. (2003). *A biological brain in a cultural classroom: Enhancing cognitive and social development through collaborative classroom management*. New York, NY: Corwin Press.

Walker, J., Shea, T., & Bauer, A. (2007). *Behavior management: A practical approach for educators* (9th ed.). Upper Saddle River, NJ: Pearson/Merrill.

Endnotes

i   Some of these are taken from Boynton and Boynton (2005), p. 131.

ii   Grossman (2003) in Larrivee (2009), p. 46.

iii   Saphier & Haley, 1993b, p. 58.

iv   Saphier & Haley, 1993b, p. 61.

NOT LOSING OUR MINDS: POSITIVE BEHAVIOR CHANGE SUPPORT

There are many in the world dying for a piece of bread, but there are many more dying for a little love.

—Mother Teresa

When teachers have put into place the strategies we have discussed that establish and maintain a community of learners, that provide structure and nurture children and young adults, that teach concepts and skills in brain-compatible instruction, and yet these teachers are faced with a student whose behavior they find challenging, what is their response?

- ✦ Do they say, "This is the way this student is; she is never going to change," and they go on teaching?
- ✦ Do they try to increase their power and control over the student or threaten the student to try to force change?
- ✦ Do they punish the student, and when things do not change, do they add on other punishments?
- ✦ Do they isolate the student or try to remove her because "she is a distraction from the real work of the class"?

Have we ever heard a teacher respond in any of these ways? Have we ever responded in any of these ways? I can only speak for myself—I have seen and heard teachers respond this way. I have, too. I do not share that with you easily. Whenever this has happened, I have desperately wished I were able to do otherwise. At this point in my teaching, I have come to understand that the key word for such moments is, in fact, *desperation*. We are caught off guard when our efforts are resisted, when we are challenged. We shut down. As we said in Chapter 3, when we are threatened or afraid, we revert to our old brain. Our attempts at reasoning abort. We want to fight (increase our power) or to flee ("Get this student out of here!"). However, even when we feel most desperate, we do not have to respond by fighting or fleeing. We do have choices, many choices. We can respond with love—with positive regard for the student, even as we support behavior change.

To help us consistently respond constructively, first we need to look at our beliefs. Our beliefs can profoundly affect not only our choices for intervention strategies but also their specific design and the manner in which we implement them. With our beliefs as the foundation, we can build our repertoire of strategies that reflect those beliefs, even in our most desperate moments.

Beliefs About Behavior and Behavior Change Intervention

Do we believe that there are "bad" students whose behavior cannot be changed? Do we believe that an important goal of education is to foster a sense of responsibility for actions? What do we believe? In the Introductions and Reflections Appendices A and B, I provided questions to foster your reflection on what you value and your beliefs. Look at your answers. Are there any you want to revise? Now, in the context of these values and beliefs, consider your beliefs about behavior and support for behavior change. What are they? Below your responses to Beginning Reflection A and Beginning Reflection B or on a separate piece of paper write the title "My Beliefs About Behavior and Long-Term Behavior Change Intervention". Then list your beliefs.

My Beliefs About Behavior and Long-Term Behavior Change Intervention

I share my beliefs because they form the basis of the choices I made in my work and the choices I made in this book, from the detail of word choice to the choice of which strategy to include. As you read my beliefs, see with which you agree and with which you do not.

- I believe human behavior is learned. Because it is, there is no such thing as a good or a bad student—or a defiant one, for that matter; nor is there such a thing as a good teacher or a bad teacher. Inappropriate behavior is almost always not deliberately unconstructive, from the student's perspective. A student has a basic need that is going unmet and is using what we feel is unconstructive behavior to try to meet that need. There may also be a learning problem; the student has learned inappropriate behavior, has never been taught appropriate behavior, or has not sufficiently learned the appropriate behavior.

- Because human behavior is learned, it is possible to change. Human beings can learn alternative behavior. This is true for students. This is true for teachers.

- Because human behavior is learned, a student's culture will affect the behavior and values she learns (e.g., in one culture, she would have learned it is respectful to look at an adult when he is speaking to you; in another culture, she would have learned that looking directly at an adult would be defiant).

- Because what I learned from my culture and experiences will profoundly affect the value I place on any behavior in the classroom, I do not feel that all teachers will agree with my perspective on what constitutes appropriate behavior, nor will all administrators or parents.

- I believe that because my cultural background and experiences affect my response to a student's behavior, I must continually strive to reflect on the degree to which these color the way I perceive students' behavior.

- I believe teachers always have a right and the responsibility to change a student's behavior when that behavior interferes with the student's growth and development, the meeting of basic emotional needs, other students' growth and development and their meeting basic needs, or the teacher's fostering of learning.

- I believe behavior change is not solely the teacher's responsibility; in fact, if the student is involved in designing the intervention, then the change is much more likely to occur. Parents, colleagues, and the staff in the school are all potential support for change and should be included whenever appropriate and possible.

- As a teacher, I believe I *do* need a student's permission/agreement to proceed with a behavior change strategy, *if* the focus is on what I would consider a major change in the student's behavior. This is clearly a judgment call. As a teacher, I do *not* need a student's agreement to proceed *if* the intervention is mine alone; that is, if the focus of change is my instructional strategy or other aspects of the physical environment.

- I believe most forms of punishment are destructive; the exceptions are natural or logical consequences.

- I do *not* believe that the end justifies the means. I hold myself accountable for both the goals and the ways in which I work with students to achieve any goals. I would never choose anything that would hurt a student.

- I believe it takes considerable knowledge and skill to support constructive behavior in students.

- I believe one can be caring *and* support behavior change; I believe caring for students is essential.

- I believe that one must be ethical when addressing student behavior and when supporting behavior change.

Goals For Any Long-Term Behavior Intervention

Given your beliefs, what are your goals for any behavior change support plan? On a separate piece of paper or in the space below or write your goals.

_____

_____

_____

_____

_____

_____

_____

_____

_____

_____

My Goals Are that Any Intervention I Implement Should

+ enhance the student's autonomy, empowerment and self-concept, including a sense that the locus of control for her behavior is within her;
+ build the student's understanding of essential concepts and social skills, including self-control;
+ enhance the student's ability to cope independently when problems arise, to work to resolve them, and restore the situation whenever needed and possible, and to carry on constructively when the resolution is not ideal;
+ enhance the student's disposition and ability to work respectfully and collaboratively, to weigh choices effectively, to take responsibility for addressing his needs and being responsive to addressing other's needs;
+ enhance the student's ability to lead a life that is physically and emotionally safe and healthy, self-affirming, productive, and fulfilling;
+ enhance the student's desire for ongoing, life-long learning;
+ be under the control of the student to the maximum extent possible, rather than the control of others; and
+ employ the most natural and least intrusive effective means of supporting change.

In the next four chapters, we will go through each of the steps we as teachers need to take to develop systematic and effective long-term behavior change support plans. We will address how we gather useful information; how we assess that information to support our reasoning; and how we use all that we know to develop constructive plans that will support behavior change.

CHAPTER 9

Gathering Information To Support Behavior Change

We don't see things the way they are. We see them the way we are.

—The Talmud

What Will This Chapter Discuss?

To effectively support change, we need to mitigate against our natural biases ("the way we are") by gathering *objective* information on the nature of the behavior. Also, because we are ecological in our approach, we need to gather objective information about the context within which the behavior occurs to determine which variables might be contributing to the appearance of that behavior. This chapter will address a number of strategies we can use to gather both kinds of information. To be able to gather objective information, we will consider the following:

  + How can we determine the **nature of the behavior**?
  + How can we determine the variables in the context(s) in which the behavior **appears** that may contribute to its occurrence?
  + How do we determine the variables in the context(s) in which the behavior *does not appear* that may contribute to the *lack* of its occurrence?

Why Is This Important?

Why devote a chapter to gathering information? You may know the adage that begins, "An ounce of prevention … ." In this case, the warning is not to help us prevent inappropriate behavior in students but rather to prevent us from behaving unconstructively as we succumb to our own haste to fix things. Before we can begin to support change in the behavior of children and young adults (and ourselves as their teachers), we need to take time to gather information. **If we do not have sufficient information, we may not be able to make an accurate assessment of the situation.** As a result, we are likely to choose an intervention that does not appropriately support the behavior change. Moreover, without initial information, our ability to monitor and refine the change process is limited. To finish the adage above, we would say, "An ounce (a few moments) of data gathering is worth a pound of intervention." The "pound" refers to the many unnecessarily costly hours we spend on ineffective strategies because the intervention was not based on an accurate and thorough picture of the behavior and monitoring of the change process.

Certainly, there are occasions when there is no time to collect information, such as when a student's behavior puts the student or others in danger. In such serious situations, obviously, we must act quickly to ensure safety. However, with the exceptions of emergencies, collecting prior information is essential to effective intervention.

A second important point about gathering data has to do with the nature of the data. Information needs to be gathered about the behavior itself, but information also needs to be collected on variables in *all three of the student's environments*: the physiological, the physical, and the psychosocial environments. These data give us the much-needed ecological perspective that provides a thorough assessment of the variables that may be contributing to the occurrence or the lack of occurrence of a behavior. We need a variety of techniques in our toolbelt to be able to choose the one that best matches our needs for information.

A third essential aspect of our data gathering is that we try to be as objective as possible. As the opening quote suggests, our view of what is occurring is profoundly affected by our own values, beliefs, and resulting perceptions of the people and the situational variables. As we know from our discussion of brain functioning, our thinking (perceiving) is also influenced by the emotions we are feeling at the time. Objective data help to mitigate against the natural subjective filters that affect our ability to see or hear the behavior as it is actually occurring.

Lastly, if we are precise and objective in our choice of words, we can better elicit students' participation in the process because they will clearly understand what we are describing and be less likely to feel defensive, which can come as a result of subjective descriptions of their behavior.

What Will You Learn?

By the end of the chapter, you will be able to:

+ describe ways to collect objective quantitative and descriptive data on the occurrence of a behavior; and
+ describe ways to gather many kinds of information on variables in the student's three environments (internal, external, and interpersonal) that may contribute to the occurrence of that behavior.

What Do You Want To Accomplish?

What goal(s) do you have as you read about gathering information to support behavior change? Write your responses here or on a piece of paper. _____

_____

_____

_____

ACCESSING PRIOR KNOWLEDGE/EXPERIENCE

In the space provided or elsewhere describe the kind of information, if any, have you gathered on a student? _____

_____

What were the sources? _____

_____

As we address ways to gather information, consider which of your strategies you feel are "keepers" and which you want to revise or substitute.

What Steps Do We Take to Collect Information?

Step 1: We objectively describe a TARGET BEHAVIOR that would be an appropriate focus for supporting positive change. We objectively describe a GOAL BEHAVIOR towards which we hope to support change.

Step 2: We determine what kind of data to collect about the target and goal behaviors.

Step 3: We determine the appropriate methods to gather many kinds of information about those variables in the student's three environments that might affect the occurrence or lack of occurrence of the target and goal behaviors.

Step 4: We collect quantitative and descriptive information about the target and goal behaviors.

Step 5: We gather together information from many sources about the variables in the three environments that might affect the occurrence/lack of occurrence of the target and goal behaviors. If needed, we make adjustments in our methods and return to an earlier step to continue with the process.

Step 1: Objectively Describe the Target and Goal Behaviors

A problem well defined is half solved.

—John Dewey

The target and goal behavior definitions must have specific beginnings and ends. Neither can be a broad series of behaviors. Each needs to be described in terms of what can be seen or heard. Table 9-1 lists verbs we frequently use to describe behavior. On the left side are those that are not observable, internal events—we cannot come to a reasonable agreement on what constitutes evidence that any of these particular behaviors occurred. By contrast, the verbs on the right are objective.

Table 9-1. **Verbs Used Frequently**		
Verbs that are <u>NOT</u> Observable or CAN<u>NOT</u> be Heard		**Verbs that <u>ARE</u> Observable or <u>CAN</u> Be Heard**
appreciate	hear	speak
assume	imagine	alphabetize
be sensitive	know	arrange
become aware	learn	ask
believe	like	chop, mix, stir, etc.
comprehend	realize	answer a question

Platform: Application Opportunity 9-1

On the active learning platform under Chapter 9 is an Application Opportunity (9-1) that provides practice distinguishing between objective words that describe behavior and those that do not.

Determining whether or not verbs can be seen or heard is fairly clear. Listening and thinking are internal states and are, therefore, not observable. For other verbs, the issue is not whether the action could be observed; rather, does the verb *alone* delineate what could be seen? An example is the verb *apply*. More specificity is needed. How do we know what the application would entail? What constitutes "application"? "Apply paint to a surface" would provide details that are observable. "Apply a concept" needs more detail. "Use" is another verb that lacks specificity. We can certainly see someone use a tool, but *how* the person uses that tool is really what needs to be observed.

If the verb alone does not describe an action that can be seen or heard, adding a definition for an "unseen" or "unheard" verb can make the description objective. Platform Application 9-2 provides an opportunity to apply "Can you see or hear it?" to evaluate actions and their definitions.

Platform: Application Opportunity 9-2

On the active learning platform under Chapter 9 is an Application Opportunity (9-2) that provides practice distinguishing whether definitions of behavior are objective or not. In each sentence, you will circle the underlined words you can see/hear.

To enhance objectivity, we can *start* with more general terms and then add specifics. Example: We are concerned because a student seems to lack focus on the activity at hand. To begin, we could write the Target Behavior in general terms, such as: "Luca focuses on materials other than those of the lesson." The Goal Behavior would be: "Luca will actively engage in the learning experience." Then we need to clarify each more specifically by asking: *What would I see and/or what would I hear?* Below are my definitions of Luca's target and goal behavior and the specifics I am looking for to determine if the observed behavior meets either more general descriptor. Do you think the specifics for each definition are objective enough?

Definition of the target behavior: Luca focuses on materials other than those of the lesson. By that I mean:

- ✦ Luca looks at materials other than those in the lesson;
- ✦ Luca shares ideas that are on topics other than the lesson focus;
- ✦ Luca writes ideas that relate to concepts other than the lesson focus;
- ✦ Luca writes ideas in a form other than that directed in the lesson.

Definition of the goal behavior: Luca actively engages in the learning experience. By that I mean:

- ✦ Luca looks at the materials in the lesson;
- ✦ Luca offers at least one idea to the discussion that relates to the topic at hand;
- ✦ Luca looks at another student's face when that student is speaking;
- ✦ Luca completes all written assignments, following the directions and criteria in the learning contract.

If we have subcategories, these need to be what will be seen or heard, and these need to be mutually exclusive; in other words, there is no overlap between them. This means that if other people are watching a student, most (if not all) could agree that a behavior fits into a particular subcategory.

A third essential element is the use of positive words. This means the definition states *what happens* rather than what does not. Example: Instead of "Macy does not raise her hand and wait for the teacher to address her," we need to describe what we see or hear: "When asked a question, Macy keeps her hands in her lap and shouts out the answer before she is called on by her teacher."

A fourth characteristic of objective definitions is that they exclude adverbs or adjectives because both parts of speech are subjective.

- ✦ Example: "Logan walks so slowly over to the carpet, he is frequently late for Morning Meeting" includes the words "so," "slowly," and "frequently"—all highly subjective terms. Instead we write what we *see*. "When the teacher announces Morning Meeting, Logan takes about two minutes to walk to the carpet and arrives after greeting has begun."

Not everyone will agree with what we choose to include in our definition of a behavior. This is not required. What *is* required, however, is that we are clear about what we mean, so that when others look at our data they know what *we* determined constituted the particular behavior and its dimension would be frequency.

Step 2: Determine the Kind of Information Needed

Determine Which Dimension(s) of the Behavior Will Be the Focus of the Change

There are five dimensions of behavior: duration, frequency, latency, magnitude, and topography. Three dimensions have to do with time. How often the behavior occurs is called its frequency. The length of time a behavior occurs is called its duration. The length of time it takes for a behavior to occur once it has been cued or requested is called latency. The other two dimensions, magnitude and topography, focus on the nature of the behavior—its force/intensity and the form it takes. If you are helped by viewing comparisons, Table 9-2 provides distinctions among dimensions.

Table 9-2. Dimension Distinctions	
Dimension	**Definition**
Frequency—may be stated as Rate	**Frequency:** Number of times of the behavior occurs
	Rate: Number of times the behavior occurs during a specific time frame or number of opportunities
Duration	Amount of time between when the behavior begins and ends
Latency	Length of time that passes between a request, signal, or cue for a behavior and when the behavior begins or occurs
Magnitude	Force or intensity with which a behavior is demonstrated
Topography	The physical form of the behavior, what the behavior looks like, sounds like

In terms of timing, we can divide behavior into two groups. There are those behaviors that occur in a moment (countable) and those that take a longer time (continuous stream). I distinguish the two by snapping my finger. If I am able to do so by the time the behavior is finished, then it is a countable behavior and its dimension would be frequency.

✦ **Examples for frequency:** A blink; saying "Yes" or "No."

For behavior that goes on for a while, the dimensions of interest are duration (how long the behavior occurs) or latency (how long it takes before the behavior occurs, once it is cued).

✦ **Examples for duration:** Studying for a test; washing hands.
✦ **Example for latency:** How long after the teacher directs the class to begin their independent projects does Elissa walk around the room before she sits in her chair and begins to work?

This distinction between countable and continuous-stream behavior can get murky if we add other quantitative variables to our behavior focus. For example, if we are collecting information about how long Mark works on math problems, then we are considering continuous-stream behavior—the length of time he worked. If we are focused on his completion of math problems, we have shifted our attention to the result and turned the focus into a count of problems completed. Therefore, we have to ask ourselves repeatedly, *What is the focus?* If we are looking at how long it takes him to begin to write the answer once he has read the problem, then our focus is latency. Only clear target and goal behavior definitions enable us to determine the nature of the dimension or dimensions on which we choose to focus.

Important Details about Collecting Information on the Five Dimensions

Dimension Focus

We may be interested in more than one dimension for the target and the goal behaviors.

Collecting Data on Frequency

If the length of the observations *is the same*, then noting the **number of times** a behavior occurs each session is appropriate. However, when the data collection sessions *are not the same length* or the *opportunity to exhibit the behavior is not consistent across sessions*, the frequency of a behavior needs to be expressed in **rate**—the number of times the behavior occurred per a unit of time or opportunity.

- ✦ **Example of rate per time:** Cleo poked Judy four times per minute in the 10-minute lesson and six times per minute in the 12-minute lesson.
- ✦ **Example of rate per opportunity:** One day the teacher asks 16 questions. The next day, she asks 22. On Day 1, Thad shouts out 10 out of 16 times—a rate of approximately 62%. On Day 2, he also shouts out 10 answers. He has the same frequency for both days; however, there is a different *rate*. What is that rate? (Divide the number of times he did it by by the number of opportunities.)

Collecting Data on Duration

For continuous-stream behavior, we usually want to know not only how *long* the behavior occurs but also its frequency during a particular length of time.

Collecting Data on Latency

With the dimension of **latency**, we are interested in **duration,** but the focus is the duration of time that passes between when the behavior was cued—"supposed to" occur—and when it did occur, not the length of time the behavior itself occurred.

Collecting Data on Magnitude

The way to distinguish magnitude from other dimensions is to see if it can be inserted into the following sentence:

Elena _____ so _____ that _____.

         (behavior)   (adverb)   (what happens)

- ✦ **Examples:** "Elena shouted so loudly that she could be heard in the next two rooms", and "Elena bit herself with such force that she broke the skin on her arm."

Collecting Data on Topography

With topography, our focus is the nature and the form of the behavior rather than how often it occurs, how long its duration, how long it takes for it to occur once cued, or the effect/strength of the behavior. For example, each student's handwriting has its own form. We might wish to support change so the form is more legible. Each person's response, when the person is frustrated, has its own form. We might want to foster change in the form of a student's behavior—moving from pounding a fist on a table or desk (target behavior) to expressing feelings verbally in a socially acceptable way (goal behavior).

Now that we have chosen which dimension is the focus of the desired behavior change, we are ready to choose the kind of data we need.

Determine Whether Quantitative or Descriptive Information Is Needed to Assess the Nature of the Behavior Dimension on Which You Are Focusing

It is important to remember that information is not equivalent to measurement. We have to be careful not to use these two words interchangeably.

If we want to **measure** a behavior dimension, we need to collect **quantitative** information/data that uses numbers to indicate what is occurring. For the dimensions of frequency, duration, and latency, quantitative information is most useful:

- **Example of duration:** It took him 45 minutes to complete the problems.
- **Example of frequency:** Ezekiel completed six sentences.
- **Example of latency:** Three minutes after the teacher asked the students to return to their tables, JoAnne returned to hers.

If we want to **"tell a story"** about the dimension of a behavior or the effect of a behavior, we need to collect **descriptive** information/data that uses words (a narrative form), not numbers, to talk about the nature of what is occurring. For the dimensions of topography and magnitude, descriptive information is more useful.

- **Examples of topography:** "These are the choices Tom made for his lunch each day: he ate vegetable soup for lunch on Monday; a hotdog and a hamburger—both on buns with a side of chips—on Tuesday; and a submarine sandwich with meat, tomato, and lettuce on Wednesday."
- **Example of magnitude:** "Sue erased the sentence on her paper so hard, the paper tore in half."

While there is no quantitative data in these last two descriptions, the information provided would nonetheless be helpful. We do not call descriptive data a **measure** of a dimension because the data are not based in our number system. However, the nature of the change in a behavior (or lack of it) can be determined by analyzing the degree of change over time in the descriptions of the behavior.

There are times when both kinds of information—measurement and description—help us support behavior change. The choice is ours, based on the nature of the behavior focus.

Step 3: Consider the Choices of Data Collection Methods. Choose One that Gathers the Kind of Information is Needed About the Target Behavior

Methods of Collecting Quantitative Data

Frequency Count

We can count how frequently a behavior occurs within a particular time period.

Steps to Record a Frequency Count

Step 1: **Record the time when the data collection begins.**

Step 2: **Each time the behavior occurs, make a tally of some kind.**

Step 3: **Record the time the data collection ends.**

Step 4: **Subtract the beginning time from the end time to determine the total time, observed in minutes.**

An example of a counting sheet to help us record frequency appears in Table 9-3.

Table 9-3. Example of a Counting Sheet[i]

Student _____   Date_____

Setting & Context _____

Behavior _____

Time the count began _____; Ended _____. Total time _____ (minutes)

1 2 3 4 5 6 7 8 9 10 11 12 13 14 15 16 17 18 1 20 21 22 23 24 25 26 27 28 29 30

Total number of behaviors _____   Total time in minutes: _____

Rate per minute _____   (The formula for rate is number of occurrences divided by number of time units.)

---

i Based on research in J. Kounin, Discipline and Group Management in Classrooms. Holt, Rinehart and Winston, 1970.

A frequency count can also be used to determine the number of opportunities/practice sessions required for success. The is often referred to as **Trials to Criterion.**

✦ **Example:** "Sally needed five chances (trials to practice swinging the bat) before she hit the ball."

As with percent of opportunities (see below), the data gathered for trials to success requires also counting the number of times Sally *tried* to do the behavior before she was able to succeed.

Another useful measure of frequency is **rate**, or *how frequently* the behavior occurred *in a particular time frame*. We compute this by finding the *number of occurrences divided by the total number of time units*. A time unit could be 30 seconds, a minute, etc. As we have said, rate as a measure helps us if we cannot observe *for the same amount of time each time we do the recording*. Rate allows us to have the data collected be comparable.

If we are observing a behavior whose occurrence *is dependent on specific opportunities*, such as raising a hand *to answer a teacher's question in a lesson,* we need to express the frequency of the behavior in terms of **percent of opportunities**. *Given 10 times to turn his work in when directed to do so, Toby did so five times (frequency) or 50% of opportunities.* To convert the count to percent of opportunities, we take the number of occurrences of a particular behavior, divide it by the number of opportunities. Regardless of the length of the observation, if a student was given a chance to respond to questions 13 times in one lesson and five times in another, and in *each* lesson, she just responded five times, then converting the frequency of her responses to the percentage of responses she made gives us comparable data.

Below, in Table 9-4, I have provided a series of tips to support your collecting countable behavior.

Table 9-4. **Tips to Record Countable Behavior**
• We can use a **wrist counter, hand-held calculator, iPhone software applications** available to record the frequency of a particular behavior—even for each student in a class.
• We can **make slashes** on a small 'sticky' note inside our hand, on a piece of paper on a clipboard, in the corner of a board.
• We can put pieces of masking tape on our arm, the side of our desk, a clipboard, etc.
• If we have a pocket, we can **shift a small paper clip** from the supply to the 'tally' pocket.
• **A colleague** can come into our class and be a counter; at another time we can reciprocate.
• We can use a **counting sheet**. Table 9-3 above provides an example. We can also have the student use a counting sheet. The advantage of having the student do it is that we are free to concentrate on teaching. An advantage for the student is that she gains immediate feedback on her behavior. The possible disadvantage is that the student may lose track of the count while focusing on the lesson. (Of course, teachers can lose count, too.) If a student counts, the act of counting may have an effect on the behavior. (Hopefully, a positive one.) Therefore, *if we need a count that is baseline*—the frequency with which the behavior occurs prior to our intervention, then having the student count (with its possible effect on the target behavior) would not be ideal. On the other hand, having the student count may be a useful strategy during the intervention phase of the behavior support plan.

Sometimes students can be the ones to count behavior. They can use the counting sheet. They can also use a countoon—a combination of a recording sheet and behavior change strategy illustrated by a cartoon. Figure 9-1 provides an example of a hand drawn countoon. As you can see, the countoon consists of: (1) the "What I Do" picture sequence (i.e., the goal behavior); (e.g., in the example below, "I wait to be called on before speaking"); (2) the "My Count" column, where the data is collected; and (3) the "What Happens" column (e.g., "If I do this 10 times, I can pass out paper") (Kunzelmann, 1970). The student draws a circle around the succeeding number each time the goal behavior occurs. Because the countoon include both a count and a consequence, it is best used for what seem like straightforward behavior support plans for which we believe having the student count her behavior would alone be enough to encourage change, knowing that a positive result would occur. However, since a countoon does provide a count of behavior, I included it here.

Figure 9.1: Example of a "Countoon"

Recommendation: Whether you are measuring frequency, rate based on time, rate based on number of occurrences, percent of opportunities, or number of times required to reach a criterion for success, instead of making a slash, write the *actual time* the behavior occurs. That will provide frequency and the timing of the behavior—two bits of data for later analysis.

Time Duration

Some behavior takes longer than a moment to run through a complete cycle. Staying on task is one example. Singing a song would be another. To collect data on the timing of these, we use the technique of Time Duration. We note each time the behavior begins and then when it ends.

Steps to Record Time Duration

Step 1: **Record the time data collection begins.**

Step 2: **Note the specific clock time when the behavior occurs in minutes and seconds and ends in minutes and seconds.**

Step 3: **Note the specific time when data collection ends** for that session.

Important point about recording the duration of a behavior: The ability to note seconds is essential. This will allow greater clarity in the data, since the duration of a behavior can be less than a minute.

Time Duration To Measure Latency

To measure latency, we note the seconds (and minutes) that pass between the cue/prompt or request for particular behavior and when that behavior actually occurs.

Steps to Record Time Duration of Latency

Step 1: **Note the time (in minutes and seconds; e.g., 10:22.25) the request, cue, prompt, or signal is given.**

Step 2: **Note the time (in minutes and seconds; e.g., 10:27.20) the corresponding behavior occurs**, if at all.

Step 3: **Subtract the time of #1 from time of #2** to determine the latency.

Instruments That Measure Response Strength

As teachers, we rarely have the need to quantify the effect of a behavior on the environment, except, perhaps, in certain sports.

Work Sample (or Portfolio)

Samples of student work can provide quantitative information, such as how many problems the student finished in a particular time length or how many correct versions of the letter "a" the student could write.

Methods of Collecting Descriptive Data

Running Narrative

A running narrative provides a continuous written record of all we observed—what we saw and heard in a given time period. Because our memory provides an imperfect record of events, a running narrative completed in a particular time and context is a much more accurate source of information (Carroll, 1978, 1977a). Table 9-5 provides an example portion of a Running Narrative Record.

<table>
<tr><td colspan="3" align="center">Table 9-5. Example of a Portion of a Running Narrative Record[i]</td></tr>
<tr><td colspan="3">Observer: Alison Corner Time: 10:35–10:55. Date: _____ Setting: Classroom: Grade 4; number of children: 24 sitting in four rows of 6 each. Agenda/Context: Math Actors: P = Peter; T = Teacher; AC = Another Child Target Behavior: Off Task behavior including, calling out answers without waiting to be called on; out of seat; closing book; putting book in desk; putting pencil anywhere but on paper and writing as directed; looking out window. Goal Behavior: Doing whatever directed by teacher, including waiting to be called on before speaking; going to the board when ask to by the teacher. Layout is 4 rows of 6 desks facing the board. Peter's position: Last in row by window. [Map has been omitted from this copy of the record.]</td></tr>
<tr><th>Time</th><th>Narrative</th><th>Notes</th></tr>
<tr><td>10:35</td><td>T erasing blackboard.

Children clearing desks.

P sliding math book under desk between feet.</td><td></td></tr>
<tr><td>10:36</td><td>T begins math lesson using blackboard to illustrate points.

P's book now closed on desk—he watches T. P paying attention

T asks for volunteer to do problem on board.

P calls out the answer (correct). Hand stays on desk.</td><td>P paying attention

Correct, but no hand raised</td></tr>
<tr><td>10:37</td><td>T asks P to raise hand and wait to be called on.

P smiles.

AC does problem on the blackboard.</td><td>T response</td></tr>
<tr><td>10:38</td><td>P looks out the window as teacher continues the lesson.

P raises hand and calls out, "Can I go to the Boys' Room?"

T knits eyebrows and turns mouth down. "Alright, quickly!"

P smiles as he leaves room.</td><td>P paying attention?

Needs movement or escape?

T response to off task</td></tr>
<tr><td>10:42</td><td>P returns. Slides hands across desks of last row as returns to seat.

T "Peter, please sit down quickly."</td><td>For stimulation or attention?

T response</td></tr>
</table>

	Table 9-5. **Example of a Portion of a Running Narrative Record**[i] (*continued*)	
10:43	T asks for volunteer to come to blackboard to do problem. P calls out answer (incorrect). T asks P to come to blackboard. P claps his hands once as he gets out of his seat.	T cue, but for action, not answer Calls out whether correct or not T response
10:44	P goes to blackboard, does problem correctly, returns to seat.	*Called* out wrong, but *did* it correctly

i Used with permission from Alison Corner, personal communication, 2015.

Recording a running narrative is *not* something we can do while teaching. We must arrange for someone else to do the teaching and free us to do the observation or record for us while we teach. Often, 15 to 20 minutes is enough. Thirty minutes is probably too long because the process takes dedicate focus, and the human brain tires after 20 or so minutes and cannot continue with the degree of accuracy needed.

Steps to Record a Running Narrative

Step 1: On a sheet of paper, create a table with one row at the top and three columns below on which to write the record of what is happening. An example appears in Table 9-6 below. Divide the table vertically so the left column is quite narrow; the second should be about one-half or more the width of the page; the right should be about one-quarter of the page. Label the left column "Time"; the second column "Narrative"; and the right column "Notes."

	Table 9-6. **Sample Form for a Running Narrative Record**	
Observer: _____ **Date:** _____ **Time-Begin:** _____ **End:** _____		
Setting: _____ **Agenda/Context:** _____		
Behavior Foci (target and goal): _____		
Actors: _____ **Map** can be found on page: _____		
Time	Narrative	Notes

Step 2: Provide essential information. Complete the top of the form.

Step 3: Sketch a ground plan or map of the physical setting. This drawing serves to orient the scene to the observer's location and helps develop ways to identify the actors in the narrative. It is also useful during the recording state as notes are taken about the actors while events unfold. In the final report, include a note indicating where the map can be found. The map should always include the following information:

- The location of key physical features, including fixed and moveable furniture and equipment.

- Activity zones, if they are apparent.

- The location of the actors in the narrative. If possible, use initials. If not known, use descriptive devices (yellow hair, red plaid shirt, etc.). When actors, objects, or zones are identified by numbers, initials, etc., include a list of these devices and their meanings in a legend next to the map.

- The location of the observer.

If at any time an identified actor or the observer moves, an arrow from the original location to the new one will indicate the change.

Step 4: Record "Time." Periodically (and whenever a new interaction or a key behavior occurs), write the clock time in the left column. If there is a change in setting or actors, indicate this in the narrative and note the time it occurs.

Step 5: Write a skeletal account or record of what is happening in the "Narrative" column. Over time, you will probably come up with your own system of notation that will jog your memory and keep the events in the correct sequence. The ultimate goal is to develop notation devices and skills that permit us to make notes *without* looking at the paper at all. Write whatever is observed and heard as completely as possible; otherwise, the memory may be quite faulty. We may be able to listen while writing, but no one can observe a class while looking down and writing. This is why using a "shorthand" version of words is essential. Remember, if a change in setting or actors occurs, indicate this in the narrative.

Step 6: Add notes. Write any thoughts, questions, comments, or hypotheses about the patterns observed in the "Notes" column. Placing these subjective ideas in a separate column keeps the narrative more objective and minimizes bias that can occur when subjective information is included in the narrative.

Step 7: Write out the full narrative account as soon as possible, certainly *before* sleeping. Sleep fogs our memory. The "Narrative" column should be a record—as detailed as possible—of the actions directly seen and heard.

Remember, this is a *technical account*[i] of an observation. Think of the narrative as a script for a play. It includes only the verbal statements and actions of the actors/people. Nothing subjective should appear in the narrative. In other words, anything not directly seen or heard by the observer goes in the "Notes" column. Notes include motives we ascribe to the actors, judgments about the appropriateness or inappropriateness of actions, questions we might have, and other kinds of comments named below. Consider this record the first *draft* of the running narrative account. More editing will be needed.

Step 8: Editorially sort the account as soon as possible, and certainly before sleeping. Carefully read the entries in the "Narrative" column. If there are statements of what the student or teacher did *not* do, change them to what those people *did* do. **Example:** Rather than writing "The student did not speak," write "The student was silent." **Lift out words that do anything other than state the actions seen and heard. Enter these in the "Notes" column. Read the Notes to spot any actions that are embedded but not recorded in the "Narrative" column. Enter those actions at the appropriate point in the running narrative.**

Four kinds of items should be removed from the "Narrative" and written in the "Notes":

- ♦ Statements that attribute motives or psychological states to actors. **Example:** "Maria raised her hand to win approval."

"Maria raised her hand" is observable and therefore belongs in the "Narrative" column. The wording "to win approval" is an inference and, therefore, belongs in the "Notes" column, perhaps rephrased as a question: "Did she do this to win approval?" because we do not know her internal motive.

- ♦ Statements that link an action to a cause. **Example:** "The teacher's silence made the children nervous."

Instead of directly linking these things, we should first write "The teacher was silent." The next sentence would be "The students squirmed." That the silence *seemed to* cause something is an inference and belongs in the "Notes" column. In our "Notes" column, across from this portion of the narrative, we might record "The children seemed nervous when the teacher was quiet", or better still, "I wonder why the children squirmed. Were they nervous?"

- ♦ Statements that ascribe value (worth or appropriateness) or lack of value to actors or their behaviors. **Example:** "The troublemaker fouled it up again."

"Troublemaker" and "fouled it up again" are judgments and, therefore, do not belong in the "Narrative" column. Instead, we would use the "Narrative" column to report what the student specifically *did.* In the "Notes" column, we would write "This is the second time he has done this during science class."

- ♦ Statements that indicate a count or sense of time. **Example:** "For the third time, the teacher …" or "Finally, she turned around."

The reader can count the number of times something occurred without any underlying subjective judgment that a statement like either of those above may contain.

Step 9: Editorially clarify the account. Read the two columns again and make whatever changes are necessary for **each entry to be as clear as possible.**

- ♦ Locate and modify two kinds of unclear language in the "Narrative" column. The first is the use of pronouns or phrases where the noun referent (e.g., "the student") is unclear. You must specify which student is being referred to or whether you are referring to the teacher or the student. The second source of unclear language is the use of the passive voice (e.g., "The question was answered"). This also leaves the actor unspecified. **Instead, specify who acted:** "Orlando answered the question."

♦ Be sure that **entries in the "Notes" column have corresponding actions entered in the "Narrative" column.** **Example:** In the "Notes" column, we might have written "Why did Keelan make a face when she answered his question?" but there was no corresponding behavior written in the "Narrative" column. Keelan's mouth turned down and his eyebrows knit together should be then added to where it belonged in the sequence of events in the "Narrative" column.

♦ **Phrase entries in the "Notes" column so that they pose hypotheses, ask questions, or denote patterns observed** as specifically as possible. This increases their future usefulness. Questions in the form of "What happens when ...?" are useful because they point out possible patterns in the A->B->C sequence. Their answers provide with descriptions in the form of "This ... happens when ... happens."

♦ **Remove adjectives and adverbs in the narrative and the notes.** Each time I find these, I ask myself, ***What can I write that I saw or heard?*** **Example:** I need to state how long something went on, rather than using *quickly* or *slowly*. *Quickly* can mean different things to different people. It's too subjective.

Step 10: Polish the narrative as much as possible ***before sleeping.*** Often moving items from one column to another requires rephrasing entries so they will be readable to someone else weeks later. When the editing is complete, the narrative should be a record of one or more specific actors doing some specific behavior. Given what we know about the distortions of memory, there is one extremely important rule for polishing our records: *if something is not in the written record, most likely it did not happen.*

Step 11: Polish entries in the "Notes" column. These notes represent our best effort to understand the events we observed. They provide information to consider regarding our hypotheses, statements of patterns observed, and questions about subjective aspects of the observation. They also provide a yardstick that permits us to compare our understanding of this event with the realities of our next observation (if we choose to do another) as well as clues about what to look for the next time.

The narrative must be closed after 24 hours! We *cannot go back and add more information*. However, the "Notes" column is always open. Frequently, a review of the "Narrative" column gives rise to new questions and descriptions of patterns in the "Notes" column.

Tips for creating a clear, useful record, including the map:

♦ When typing the report, create a table with three columns. Each time a new episode of a behavior or an interaction occurs, create a new row to type that information. Any related subjective information or questions would be typed directly across in the same row in the "Notes" column. This allows the narrative and related notes to be aligned in the report. Also, indicate the clock time in the extreme left column. This gives the reader a sense of how much time has passed during various segments of the observation.

- If a change in setting or actors occurs, indicate this in the narrative and annotate the time it happened. Use a *different* colored pencil/pen/font to add the location of the new actors in the map.

- If a change in location of an already-identified actor occurs, draw an arrow on the map from the original location to the new one.

- If a change in setting occurs, sketch a second map to provide the information and the location of the actors.

If you want to use the Running Narrative Record to collect descriptive data *and* to collect quantitative information on the count or duration of the behavior, there is an efficient way to do so. In a fourth column on the far left, simply add "Behavior Count" and provide space to indicate a tally mark whenever the behavior occurs *in the timing of narrative*. An example is provided in Table 9-7 below. That same column could be labeled "Duration" to provide space to indicate how long each episode of the behavior lasted. If we want both count and duration, then adding two columns enables us to record these, as is shown in Table 9-7. Any of these additions to the original Running Narrative Record allows us to collect rich information about the target and goal behaviors to support change.

			Table 9-7. **Narrative Form with Space for Quantitative Data**		

Observer: _____ Date: _____ Time-Begin: _____ End: _____

Setting: _____ Agenda/Context: _____

Behavior Foci (target and goal): _____

_____

Actors: _____ **Map** can be found on page: _____

Behavior Count	Behavior Duration	Time	Narrative	Notes

Expanded Anecdotal Record

I designed this method of collecting information based on the Anecdotal Record form, in which a person writes an account of a particular *incident* of a behavior. The Expanded Anecdotal Record enables the collection of additional information that fosters an ecological perspective and also helps the recorder and reader determine patterns. This, in turn, enables us to intervene more effectively. The inclusion of "Narrative" and "Notes" columns reduces both observer and reader bias. The Expanded Anecdotal Record form appears in Table 9–8 below.

Table 9-8. **Sample Expanded Anecdotal Record Form**							

Observer: _____ **Date:** _____ **Time-Begin:** _____ **End:** _____

Setting: _____ **Agenda/Context:** _____

Behavior Foci (target and goal): _____

_____

Actors: _____ _____ **Map** can be found on page: _____

Additional Information			Narrative			Notes
Count/Length	Actors	Time	Before	Behavior	After	

Steps to Create an Expanded Anecdotal Record

Step 1: Turn the paper into horizontal "landscape" mode.

Step 2: Fill in the top of the Expanded Anecdotal Record.

Step 3: Create three major columns. The middle and rightmost columns are where we write "Narrative" and "Notes," just as we did for the Running Narrative record.

Step 4: Subdivide the "Narrative" column into three sections labeled "Before," "Behavior," and "After."

Step 5: Rather than recording everything observable, when the target behavior occurs, record the nature of the behavior in objective terms in the "Narrative" column.

Step 6: Fill in all the columns as soon as possible:

- In the appropriate columns, objectively record anything that happened just prior to the behavior and just after the behavior.

- Fill in the columns under "Additional Information."

- Write any subjective information under "Notes."

Step 7: Attach a map to indicate the location of the observer and to visually represent key information in the physical and psychosocial environments.

Work Sample

Another method of obtaining useful information about behavior is to look at the product it produces. For example, some students write with such crowded letters that we cannot read what they have written. In a fine arts class, a student may not work the air bubbles out of their clay pieces sufficiently; as a result, their pieces explode in the kiln. Other students sort silverware or machine bits into containers so quickly that many pieces do not make it into the correct bin. In each instance, looking at the product, the Work Sample, provides useful information about the *result* of a behavior.

All of the Methods Designed for Collecting Descriptive Information Also Have the Potential for Gathering Quantitative Information

The two kinds of data collection methods are compared in Table 9-9. Do you see any pattern?

Table 9-9. **Methods of Data Collection**	
Methods that Provide Descriptive Data	Methods that Provide Quantitative Data
	Frequency Count
	Time Duration
Running Narrative	Running Narrative
Running Narrative with space for a behavior count added to the form	Running Narrative with space for a behavior count added to the form
Running Narrative with space for a record of the behavior's duration added to the form	Running Narrative with space for a record of the behavior's duration added to the form
Running Narrative with space for a behavior count and a record of the behavior's duration added to the form	Running Narrative with space for a behavior count and a record of the behavior's duration added to the form
Expanded Anecdotal Record	Expanded Anecdotal Record
Work Sample/Portfolio	Work Sample/Portfolio

While we addressed six methods in the left column under the category of those that provide descriptive data (and principally, they are designed to do that), these methods can offer us both kinds of data. Therefore, if we are looking for *quantitative measures* of behavior, we can choose from a descriptive data collection method that can also provide the measurement needed *and gather much richer information*.

We can choose from eight data collection techniques. All can potentially provide quantitative measures about a behavior. Six can also offer descriptive information about a behavior.

Step 4: Part A—Collect the Quantitative and/or Descriptive Data About the Behavior

Collect Data More Than Once

The usual rule of thumb is to obtain three data points. The rationale for sampling at least three times is that few, if any, of us are consistent in our behavior. People's interactions with all their environments change from day to day, if not moment to moment. If we have only one source of data—quantitative or descriptive—on a student, we will not have a complete picture of the person. Even worse, we will likely have an inaccurate one. Being ethical in our work with students includes ensuring that our data is a reasonable sample of their behavior. At least three observations using the same method for gathering data enables us to determine if what we saw on Day 1 is sufficiently similar to Days 2 and 3 to warrant our assumption that the data is a valid sample of the student's typical behavior.

Collect Data in More Than One Agenda and/or Setting

When we collect data at least three times, we collect data twice with the physical environment variables staying as consistent as possible. On the third opportunity, we collect the same kind of data (frequency, duration, etc.) but in a situation in which one of those variables is changed. This enables us to compare results and find possible patterns.

Minimize Bias

To be ethical in our data collection, we minimize bias as much as possible. We want to be sure we see things as *they* are, not as *we* are. We must guard against two kinds of bias. The first kind is that which exists as we *observe*. The second is that which occurs as we *record* data.

Observation bias: When we observe in any situation, our brain cannot possibly take in everything. As a result, we naturally begin to tune out certain aspects. We gravitate towards observing what we consider to be interesting aspects of any situation. We may tend to watch girls more than boys, teacher-to-student interaction more than student-to-student interaction, or verbal behavior more than nonverbal behavior. This bias is naturally built into our inability to completely observe everything that is going on in a situation.

Observer bias: Everything we know and have seen in the past colors what we perceive in any given moment. We filter the information we take in through our personal lens of life. (Remember our quote at the beginning of the chapter: "We don't see things the way they are. We see them the way we are.") This means we not only screen *out* data; we also quickly interpret what we see. Example: We had a difficult experience with a large 13-year-old in the past and, therefore, now feel threatened by the size and demeanor of some middle school boys. We may therefore, see an eighth-grade male suddenly standing up as an instance of aggressive posturing; whereas someone else might see it as a boy standing up and shaking both legs as if to relieve muscle cramps or release pant legs caught in an uncomfortable position.

IN SUMMARY: When we record, we cannot possibly write everything we see and hear. What gets written is only a portion of what was occurring. In addition, as the opening quote of the chapter reminds us, whatever gets written is filtered through who *we* are.

To minimize the effects of both sources of bias, we state the focus and we separate objective data from subjective judgments. In a focused observation, we define what we are observing to tell others what we *choose to have in our lens. We cannot say whether or not other behavior is going on, although it may be.* Moreover, whichever method of data collection we use, we always *separate the objective description of what we see and hear from our subjective comments, notes, questions, judgment, interpretations, etc.* The forms for writing down data that are presented in this chapter are intended to help. If we let the behavior *tell the story, then presumably anyone observing that student at that time on that day* would have collected a similar set of data.

There is a third way to minimize bias. We only give others the objective data that has been recorded. Phrased another way, when first sharing a written report, we do not give them subjective data. We let the person reading the data analyze the information for patterns before being presented with our analysis. Someone reading a narrative may not see the patterns we do, or they may see patterns we do not. That person may have different concerns and may ask different questions. We should not bias his view of the behavior with ours. Moreover, allowing him to analyze the data *before* we share our perspective means we may gain a different analysis from a fresh pair of eyes, or we may have the opportunity to hear that someone else shares our view. Either way, richer analysis or shared analysis, the student wins. We want the most considered examination of the data possible in the time available, and we want that analysis to be as reliable as possible. Then we can proceed to the next step with reasonable confidence in our work. Once the other person has analyzed the objective data, we can share our subjective interpretation, *if it seems helpful.*

Always Include Essential Information in Any Data Collection Records

Any observation record needs to include the date, the beginning and ending time of the observation, the name of the observer, the actors, setting, context/agenda, and one or more maps. Why is all this information essential? Let us consider each piece of information.

Observer's Name

This provides the source of the data. Should there be any questions or need for further clarification or information, the observer can (hopefully) be located.

Date

An observation is a sample of behavior at a moment in time. Whenever we look at data, we need to know when in time this sample was taken. Was the data obtained a while back? Circumstances may change, and these in turn can contribute to behavior change or differences in the nature of someone's behavior. Anchoring the data in time may also help us to determine patterns if we have other data from that same time period or other information about what was occurring in the student's life at that point. The date could tell us that this data was gathered the day before the Junior Prom when all the student stayed up late to finish the decorations, or the date could indicate that the observation was don the day everyone was waiting for the announcement of when school would close because of terrible weather. If we looked at the hall pass log for the morning of the observation, we could see that Travis had a bad headache that day and had taken acetaminophen.

Actors

We know that informal interactions with others, both verbal and nonverbal, and even people's proximity can affect a person's behavior. When we analyze patterns of behavior in order to design an intervention, the richer the data about the actors involved, the more accurate our assessment will be. As a result, the more likely it is that we will design an appropriate intervention.

Setting and Context/Agenda

What occurs in a band rehearsal (context) does not necessarily occur in a science lab. The playground (setting) can be a place where all sorts of behaviors occur that we do not see in a classroom. Stating the setting and agenda provides information that illuminates possible variables in the physical environment that can affect behavior.

Time

Length of observation: Providing the times the observation began and ended sets the boundaries for the information therein. While the behavior may also have occurred before or after the observation, we do not know the details because the observer was not keeping a record then.

Time of day: With a single observation, we might *hypothesize a correlation* between the time of day and the behavior observed. With *repeated observations* at different times of day, we might *see a pattern* of behavior that relates to time of day. Time of day may also provide us additional information about setting and context as we said when (above) we considered the importance of knowing the date.

Timing of behavior in minutes and seconds: This tells us the frequency and, if appropriate, the length of a behavior as well as when in the sequence of events the specific behavior occurred. This might show us a pattern in terms of what triggers the behavior.

Map

A map of the observation area provides a visual representation of the setting and the location of key persons identified to the greatest extent possible. This information helps us to identify possible variables in the physical and psychosocial environments that may have an impact on the focus behavior. The location of the observer helps determine what she could/could not see.

Step 4: Part B—Collect Information about Variables Surrounding the Behavior that May Contribute to its Occurrence

Note: If the answers to questionnaires are not private or confidential and students are not able to read the questions or cannot write, we or an appropriately trained person can become the scribe for the student.

We can gather information informally about students as we get to know them. We can also gather information from students, either orally or in writing, through questionnaires and inventories. We can create our own questionnaires and inventories to use with our particular group(s) of students. If we choose to write questions, we can do so by considering appropriate variables from the research addressed in Chapter 3.

Example: A special education teacher[ii] designed a questionnaire with fewer than 10 statements, such as:

"This is how I feel when I work by myself."

"This is how I feel when the teacher works with me alone."

"When I need to read something, this is how I feel."

Under each statement were five faces with expressions ranging from frowning to smiling to indicate a scale of *least like me* to *most like me*.

We can also use questionnaires available in the field. One whose content addresses concepts from this text was written by Jones and Jones (2001). The full reference can be found at the end of the chapter.

Student records can be helpful. Most schools have a form, completed by a guardian, that includes any number of important pieces of information, such as the medications the child is currently taking, including those for allergies, depression, seizure disorders, etc. Students' records may contain useful information about physical disabilities and medical conditions, any one of which might contribute to a student's behavior or lack thereof. The student's file might also contain recommendations from professionals who have carried out formal testing or from professionals in the field of counseling services.

If your school system does not have such a form, I encourage you to work with your building administrator to form a team with other staff, including the school nurse and guidance counselor or individuals in equivalent roles, to create one.

If the student is taking a medication, you can ask the school nurse or school doctor about the potential side effects. Your local druggist, libraries, and reliable Internet sites can be sources of useful information regarding the effects of a particular medicine on a child or young adult.

Note: For those fairly new at this sleuthing work, remember this information is confidential. Information we gather is not to be a part of a conversation in the Teacher's Room.

Illnesses and absences are also important to consider. Has the student been absent frequently? Is there a pattern to the absences? For example, do more occur on Mondays or after holidays?

What about the student's academic history? In what curriculum areas, if any, does this student seem to excel?

What, if any, are the areas of relative difficulty? With what teaching styles does the students seem to have the most success? With which does he have the least success?

Checklists can be helpful. As we teach, we watch students all the time. To help us organize the information we gather from these observations, we can use a checklist, either one that we develop based on any of the concepts addressed in Chapter 3 or one designed by a professional.

Make Needed Adjustments and Return to an Appropriate Earlier Step to Continue with the Process

Often when we begin to analyze the data about a student's behavior, we find that our focus was not as targeted as we thought or the description of the behavior is incomplete. We realize there are additional observable aspects to the student's behavior that we did not include in our definition. At other times, we have lots of useful data, but analyzing it leads to additional questions that need to be addressed. In either case, before proceeding, we go back to the appropriate step and refine our data gathering process to match the needs of the situation. This may seem obvious. However, we must remember that intervening to support behavior change is an *ongoing* process that often requires refinements along the way. When things do not go smoothly, some teachers tell me they feel as though they are not doing it correctly or that they have somehow failed. I reassure them that this need to shift and adjust is almost inherent in the process. When it happens in your work, as it inevitably will, consider yourself getting closer and closer to determining what the student needs and therefore to being that much more likely to succeed in supporting behavior change.

Recommendations for Choosing Among Data Collection Methods

Choose a Method that Allows You To Gather More, Rather Than Less, Information

Once we have in mind all the choices that are appropriate matches for the behavior focus, we need to decide how much information we want. The methods we have just discussed vary widely in the amount of information they enable us to gather.

The use of some form of focused *running narrative* account *as at least one source* of information provides us with more, rather than less, information. With a narrative in hand, we can look for patterns of behavior in and around the student(s) whose behavior, or lack thereof, is the concern. We might see that the behavior occurs/does not occur with certain people or at a certain time in the learning experience. We might notice this behavior was a pattern of response if, for example, it frequently occurred when the teacher asked a question or gave directions.

While using an expanded anecdotal record does provide more information than just a frequency count or a time-du-ration technique, it also creates a narrative that is interrupted. The danger with starting and stopping a narrative is that when it is stopped, a lot can happen that was not considered significant at the time. The significance was only noted when it was seen to be a pattern in the narrative.

There is another drawback of/to the expanded anecdotal record. Because we begin recording based on what we believe to be the behavior "event," we may not begin early enough in the sequence of events to obtain the full picture. Therefore, any technique that includes a *running* narrative would be preferable because a running narrative collects a more complete story of the variables surrounding the behavior as well as the behavior.

Choose Methods that Gather Quantitative and Descriptive Data

The more *descriptive* information we have about a behavior, the more effectively we can be ecological (and thorough) in diagnosing the variables that appear to be contributing to it. This makes it possible to design a change strategy that will truly foster change. The *quantitative* information reveals how much behavior is actually being exhibited and when. This also supports objectivity about the behavior. (I have occasionally learned from data that the unconstructive behavior was *not* incessant, even though I felt as though it was!) Also, it may be happening more frequently at particular times. These patterns help with assessment, and when I implement the support plan while still collecting additional data, I can clearly see if my intervention is having the effect I hoped.

If Possible, Collect Data about Both the Unconstructive Target and the Constructive Goal Behaviors at the Same Time to Enhance Efficiency

Often, we can set up our collection systems to do so. On the other hand, if we are collecting data on a constructive behavior that may or *may not* be exhibited in the same setting or context as the unconstructive behavior, we *will* need to collect information about the goal behavior (using the steps in Table 9-10 on the left side) and on the target behavior in a different setting (according to the steps on the right).

Example: Whenever Jayden finishes his independent work in math, he talks to his neighbors, even if they are still working. We are aware that in social studies, he does not do this. Rather, he pulls out a book and reads. We would want to obtain some descriptive information in the subject areas where his chatting occurs to analyze variables that might contribute to the unconstructive behavior being exhibited. We would also want to collect descriptive information in history about variables that may contribute to the constructive behavior. Then we can compare these variables.

Another circumstance that requires additional data occurs when we are not sure what behaviors might be natural alternatives for the unconstructive behavior. In this situation, we would gather data in different settings to look for clues about possible cues and reinforcers and about the constructive behaviors that already exist in the student's repertoire. These could perhaps be used as substitutes for the unconstructive behavior.

If Necessary, Get Help Collecting Data

Some methods of obtaining information can be difficult to carry out while teaching. Others, such as any form of a running narrative, are impossible to do while teaching. If we create a form for data collection and explain the essentials about the method, colleagues, a paraprofessional, or an aide may be able to help. We can create a reciprocal relationship with another teacher; if that person collects information for us, we do the same for them. We also know that in some instances, students can collect data on their own behavior. Some teachers videotape classes and take notes later.

The Big Picture: Steps 1–4

While the steps we take to collect information prior to designing a behavior change support plan are similar whether we hope to increase or a decrease a behavior, there are some distinctions in the steps and the thinking processes that underlie each. I have included both sets of steps in Table 9-10. Since the methods we utilize when our focus is on increasing a behavior should also be employed when we decrease behavior, those are provided on the left. Note: When we discuss how to support behavior change in the next chapters, you will more fully understand why I encourage this two-pronged approach of increasing constructive behavior to decrease unconstructive behavior.

Table 9-10. Steps to Take When Collecting Information Prior to Intervention	
When Increasing a Goal Behavior	**When Decreasing a Target Behavior**
Step 1: Begin with the end in mind: Choose a specific behavior as the goal. Define the goal behavior clearly and objectively. Include relevant dimensions.	Step 1: Begin with the end in mind: a) Target the specific behavior to decrease. Define it clearly and objectively. Include relevant dimensions. b) Determine a constructive alternative—incompatible or a substitute—to the unconstructive behavior. c) Define the behavior to increase clearly and objectively. Include relevant dimensions. **Note**: This last step may not occur until after we determine what alternative behaviors the student already has in his repertoire.
Step 2: Determine the kind of quantitative and descriptive information needed about the behavior and the variables around the behavior in the 3 environments.	Step 2: Determine the kind of quantitative and descriptive information needed about behaviors (to decrease and to increase) and the variables around both in the three environments and to determine alternative behaviors in student's repertoire, if a substitute behavior is to be increased.
Step 3: Consider the choices of data collection methods. Choose one(s) that will gather the kind of data needed about the target and goal behavior.	Step 3: Consider the choices of data collection methods. Choose one or more that will gather the kind of information needed about the target behavior to decrease *and* about the alternative goal behavior to increase:
Step 4: **Part A** Collect the data—descriptive and/or quantitative—about the goal behavior to increase.	Step 4: **Part A** Collect the quantitative and descriptive data about the behavior to decrease and about the goal behavior to increase. **Note**: If we are collecting data on a substitute or alternative (rather than an incompatible) behavior, there may be circumstances—other than when the unconstructive behavior occurs—when the constructive behavior is likely to occur. If so, include data collection on the goal behavior during such contexts and agendas.
Step 4: **Part B** Collect descriptive information about variables surrounding the behavior that may contribute to its occurrence. If the behavior does not yet occur, collect information about the variables that exist and do not exist in the student's environments that would contribute to the behavior's constructive occurrence.	Step 4: **Part B** Collect descriptive information about variables surrounding the unconstructive behavior that may contribute to the occurrence of that behavior. If there are agenda in which the alternative behavior does occur or the unconstructive one does not occur, collect information about variables that may contribute to the occurrence of the substitute or alternative behavior, or to the lack of the unconstructive behavior.
(Make adjustments as needed and return to the appropriate step to continue on with the process, if needed.)	

Application Activity: Choices When Collecting Data

Think of a behavior you have seen recently that you believe is not constructive. Imagine that you are in a position to help support behavior change with that person. Write your definition of the target (unconstructive) behavior as objectively as possible. Then write your definition of the goal (alternative) behavior. For each describe what you would see and hear. Remember to eliminate all the adverbs and adjectives in your definitions.

Target Behavior Definition: _____

_____

Goal Behavior Definition: _____

_____

Review your data collection choices. Choose the quantitative data collection method you believe would be most helpful.

_____

_____

Which means of collecting descriptive data do you believe would be most helpful?

_____

_____

I encourage you to discuss your answers and reasoning with someone who is knowledgeable enough in this area to respond supportively to your application of data collection concepts.

Final Thoughts

We collect information for two purposes. The first is to learn about the occurrence of target and goal behaviors. The second is to learn about the variables in the person's ecosystem that may contribute to the occurrence of the behaviors or the lack thereof. Our choice of data collection methods will depend on: a) the nature of our target and goal behaviors; b) whether we want to collect descriptive data, quantitative data, or both (I strongly recommend both); and c) the richness of the data we need/want about the target behavior. Numerical data helps us to be objective. Descriptive data provides richer information that helps identify the variables that seem to contribute to the occurrence of the target and goal behaviors. Any form of a running narrative account provides richer information than numerical data alone.

Looking Forward

Now that we have addressed how to collect quantitative and descriptive data, we are ready to shift to the assessment stage of supporting behavior change. We will look at several means of analyzing patterns among variables. This will help us design a behavior support plan that is more likely to be successful.

References

Alberto, P., & Troutman, A. (2017). *Applied behavior analysis for teachers* (9th ed.). Boston, MA: Pearson.

Armstrong, T. (2009). *Multiple intelligences in the classroom* (3rd ed.). Alexandria, VA: Association for Supervision and Curriculum Development.

Buber, M. (1971). The education of character. In J. Strain (Ed.), *Modern philosophies of education* (pp. 486–497). New York, NY: Random House.

Carroll, T. (1975). *Systematic observation for competency-based teacher education* [mimeograph]. Buffalo, NY: Center for Studies of Cultural Transmission.

Carroll, T. (1977a). *Producing a running narrative account of an observation* [mimeograph]. Worcester, MA: Clark University.

Carroll, T. (1977b). *Making an observation schedule* [mimeograph]. Worcester, MA: Clark University.

Covey, S. (1989). *The seven habits of highly effective people*. New York, NY: Simon & Shuster.

Emmer, E., & Evertson, C. (2017). *Classroom management for middle and high school teachers* [loose-leaf version] (10th ed.). Boston, MA: Pearson

Evertson, C., Emmer, W., & Worsham, M. (2017). *Classroom management for elementary teachers* [loose-leaf version] (10th ed.). Boston, MA: Allyn & Bacon.

Jones, V., & Jones, L. (2001). *Comprehensive classroom management: Creating communities of support and solving problems* (6th ed.). Boston, MA: Allyn and Bacon.

Jones, V., & Jones, L. (2016). *Comprehensive classroom management: Creating communities of support and solving problems* [loose-leaf version] (11th ed.). Boston, MA: Pearson.

Kunzelmann, H. (Ed.) (1970). *Precision teaching: An initial training sequence*. Seattle, WA: Special Child Publications.

Lane, K., & Beebe-Frankerberger, M. (2004). *School-based interventions: The tools you need to succeed*. Columbus, OH: Merrill.

Littky, D. (2004). *The big picture: Education is everyone's busin*ess. Alexandria, VA: Association for Supervision and Curriculum Development.

Martin, G., & Pear, J. (2015). *Behavior modification: What it is and how to do it* (10th ed.). New York, NY: Routledge.

Szymanski, E. (1994). Transition: Life-span and life-space considerations for empowerment. *Exceptional Children, 60*(5), 402–410.

Touchette, P., MacDonald, R., & Langer, S. (1985). A scatter plot for identifying stimulus control of problem behavior. *Applied Behavior Analysis, 18*, 343–351.

Zirpoli, T. (2016). *Behavior management: Applications for teachers* (7th ed.). Boston, MA: Pearson.

Endnotes

i   Amber Dutton, thanks for pointing out the technical nature of the Running Narrative Record report (personal communication, 2015).

ii   Veronica Kenney (personal communication, n.d.).

Figure Credits

CHAPTER 10

Assessing Data

*If I had an hour to solve a **problem**, I'd spend 55 minutes thinking about the **problem** and 5 minutes thinking about solutions.*

—Albert Einstein

What Will This Chapter Discuss?

Now that we have collected both quantitative and descriptive data about a student's behavior and the variables that may contribute to it, we are ready to shift to the data assessment stage, where we, in Einstein's words, "think about the problem." In this stage, we analyze our information to: 1) determine the nature of behavior, and 2) discover patterns among variables in the student's three environments that may contribute to the occurrence of the unconstructive behavior and to the occurrence of an alternative or opposite constructive behavior.

Why Is This Important?

Our role of teacher gives us the opportunity to hold up a mirror of possibility for students to help them see what they can become. Nowhere is this role more important than in our efforts to support behavior change. Analyzing the data helps to gain perspective on when the behavior focus occurs. Our assessment also supports our three analyses—A->B->C, ecological, and functional—of the patterns that contribute to the occurrence of the unconstructive behavior. We can also learn what variables contribute to the occurrence of the alternative constructive behavior. Knowing how often and/or how long a behavior occurs and under what conditions it seems to occur enables us to design a behavior change support plan that is effective. Our success is enhanced because our data allows us to design an intervention that *encourages* or *enhances* variables in *any* of the student's three environments and *diminishes* or *removes* variables that do not enhance constructive behavior or that seem to foster unconstructive behavior. We do all this work so we have a full toolbelt to help the student realize her potential.

What Will You Learn?

By the end of the chapter, you will be able to describe:

- ✦ how to objectively determine under what conditions the unconstructive behavior occurs and what conditions, if any, the alternative constructive behavior occurs; and
- ✦ the steps to complete the three data analyses—A->B->C, ecological, and functional—that enable us to hypothesize:
  - ◆ which particular antecedent variables in the student's three environments trigger (cue) the unconstructive and constructive behavior (if the latter, in fact, occurs) and which do not;
  - ◆ which consequent variables in the student's three environments encourage (reinforce) the constructive and unconstructive behaviors and which do not;
  - ◆ which variables in the student's three environments do not encourage the constructive and unconstructive behavior to occur again (extinguish) and which variables discourage the behaviors from occurring again (punish), given the same circumstances.

What Do You Want To Accomplish?

What are your goals regarding assessing data and developing hypotheses about variables that impact student behavior? Write your responses here or on a piece of paper. _____

_____

_____

What Steps Will Help Us Reach Our Two Assessment Goals?

Step 1: We Look for Patterns Within the Quantitative and the Descriptive Data

- During what time of day or on what days in the week do the target and the goal behavior occur most/least frequently?
- Within what settings do the target and goal behaviors occur most/least frequently?
- During what agendas do the target and goal behavior occur most/least frequently?
- Within what learning environments, during what sequence of events, and in response to which instructional strategies does the behavior occur most/least frequently?
- With which actors—adults and peers—do the target and goal behavior occur most/least frequently?
- Do any changes in occurrence seem to happen when the student is in school for consecutive days or when the student is not in school for consecutive days?

While the baseline data in Table 10-1 only provide quantitative information, see if you find any patterns that address these questions.

	Table 10-1. Quantitative Baseline Data on Giving Answer Before Being Recognized by Teacher									
11										
10										
9										
8										
7	M				M					
6							M			M
5		M						M		
4		E	M	M	E		M		M	
3	E		E	E		E	E			E
2								E	E	
1										
	2/1	2/2	2/3	2/4	2/5	2/8	2/9	2/10	2/11	2/12

Number of times in 20 minutes. S gave answer before being called on by teacher (left axis label)

Dates data were collected during Math (M) at 8:00 AM and English Language Arts (E) at 10:AM—both whole class discussions

What patterns, if any, did you notice?

I noticed a higher number of callouts in one subject, and those callouts were higher in number at the beginning and end of the school week.

The answers to the Step 1 set of questions help us determine the *general* patterns in the data. These patterns show us in which contexts the target and goal behaviors are most/least likely to occur. Then we can do more in-depth analyses on certain contexts to look for the variables in the student's three environments that may contribute to the behavior's occurrence or lack of it. We can also collect more data on the behavior during those contexts to help us with our analyses.

Step 2: We Carry Out an Ecological Assessment

We look at our descriptive data from anecdotal notes, questionnaire responses, checklists, student records, and information gleaned from colleagues, parents, and the student herself to consider all that we know about the variables in the student's physiological environment. We develop as clear and thorough a picture of this student as possible.

We Ask Physiological Environment Variables Assessment Questions

✦ What are the aspects of her temperament, interests, learning needs, and strengths? What is the state of her health? What substances, pharmaceutical or otherwise, are in her system? What skills and concepts already exist in her memory upon which her learning can be built?

✦ Given the characteristics of this learner, what does she require in order to have her basic emotional needs met and to be successful in any learning situation?

✦ What variables might exist that would interfere with her emotional needs being met and would prevent her from learning successfully? As a result of the presence and interaction of all these variables, what might contribute to the occurrence/lack of occurrence of that behavior?

Answers to these questions help us figure out *which variables within the individual might have existed just as the behavior was about to be exhibited* and would, therefore, potentially have interacted with variables in the student's physical and psychosocial environments to trigger the behavior. We also want to look at how the student's physiological environment variables would be affected as a result of the behavior being exhibited, so we integrate our descriptive data with the quantitative data.

✦ What changes occurred in her physiological environment, from the cue to the consequence, as a result of the behavior?

✦ Would these changes encourage her to exhibit/not exhibit this behavior in particular contexts?

With this information in mind, we look at the variables in the student's physical environment and psychosocial environment. First, we look for patterns among the variables within each of these environments. Then we look at the interaction of variables in two and all three environments.

We Ask Physical and Psychosocial Environment Variables Assessment Questions

In Table 10-2, I have provided a list of questions we need to consider as we do an ecological analysis. There are many questions. Many. The intent is to be thorough, not to overwhelm those doing the assessment process. As we analyze our quantitative and descriptive data, we can move through the questions readily until we find those that seem to best relate to the nature of the data before us. I do encourage us to consider *all* the questions, however briefly. If we do not, we may miss a key insight about behavior patterns that would support behavior change. People are complex. Their behavior is complex. If we are going to hold up the mirror of possibility for students, we need to be thorough in our enhancement of their efforts to change.

Table 10-2. Questions to Ask When Assessing the Relationship Between the Behavior and Variables in the Student's Physical and Psychosocial Environments

Physical Environment Instructional Variables:

- Does the behavior appear to occur more often during transitions between activities or classes?
- What kind of activity appears to immediately precede the behavior? What kind of activity exists when the behavior occurs? What activity immediately follows the activity where the behavior occurs; e.g., is it teacher-directed or student-directed? Whole group discussion? Small group, individual, or 1:1 work with an adult? Is the focus a particular subject or concept or skill set?
- When the behavior occurs:
  - Are materials/activities perceived by student as being inappropriate; e.g., "This is baby stuff" or "This is kindergarten work" or "This is for girls!"?
  - Do the materials/activities seem too easy/too difficult for the student, or is the student asked to perform a task that she has previously failed or feels is in a subject he can't do ("I'm not smart in math")?
  - Are directions for the activity clearly understood by student? Do these include a cue (that is clear to the student) for the appropriate behavior?
  - Does the student receive reinforcement (from the student's perspective) or other positive feedback for appropriate constructive responses to the directions or the instructional activities?
  - Is the pace of instruction too rapid or too slow for the student?
  - Have the same materials/activities been used for a long stretch of time or for several days in a row?
  - Is the activity lacking in student engagement?
  - Does the student have some meaningful activity (from the perspective of the student) to do?
- Does the behavior appear to increase or decrease after the teacher exhibits a specific instructional behavior towards the student or after the teacher/other adults respond in a specific manner?

Physical Environment Non-Instructional Variables:

- Does the behavior occur at a specific time of day (just before lunch, just after gym)?
- Does the behavior occur in a particular part of the room or school?
- Does the behavior occur when the student is sitting in a particular seating arrangement or in a particular kind of chair?
- Is the area appropriately lit for this student's needs? Is there any glare that appears to bother this student?
- Is student able to see instructional materials and the other foci of instruction (board, other students' faces, teacher's face)?
- Does student appear to be bothered by:
  - The lighting in the room, or a particular kind such as fluorescent lights?
  - The temperature of the room?
  - The noise in room or a particular kind of stimulation such as music?
  - Total quiet?
  - Facing stimuli that may be distracting (hall, window, computer screen, or other students)?
  - An odor appears to affect the student's behavior?
- Do changes in or disruptions to the schedule appear to increase/decrease the behavior?
- Do changes in the physical arrangement of the class appear to increase/decrease the behavior?

Psychosocial Environment Variables: Number and proximity of students/adults, behavior of others towards student:

- Do changes in the number of students or adults in the room/area affect the student's behavior?
- Does student behave more appropriately when specific people are present or absent?
- Does the behavior occur only in the presence of specific adults? Specific students?
- Does the behavior occur only when student is close to or away from specific students?
- Does the behavior occur only when others have exhibited a specific behavior towards the student?
- Does the behavior appear to increase/decrease when other students or adults respond to the student in a specific manner?

We Assess the Interaction Among Variables in All Three Environments

After we have a sense of the physical and psychosocial environment variables that exist, we examine them along with the information we have on variables in the student's physiological environment and consider the degree to which is there a match between the needs of the student (her physiological environment) and the nature of the other two environments. What might be contributing to the occurrence of the "unconstructive" behavior?

- Is there a physiological need that is not being addressed?
- Is there a demand in the physical or psychosocial environment that cannot be met by the variables in the student's physiological environment and is, therefore, contributing to the student's feelings of frustration, embarrassment, or anxiety, which, in turn, might be cueing the behavior?
- Is the student's response to this mismatch between internal need and external demand what prompts the "unconstructive" behavior?

As We Assess We Remind Ourselves that the Behavior May Not Be "Unconstructive" to the Student

It may be the only way the student knows how to get a need met. To help the student develop more "constructive" behavior, we must understand the interactions among variables in order to:

- determine where the interactions create positive energy in the student's ecosystem, because we want to design an interaction that capitalizes on that dynamic; and
- determine where the interactions create tension or negative energy in the student's ecosystem, because we want to design an intervention that alters that dynamic.

We Look at the Ecological Variables that Exist, Both When the Target and the Goal Behavior Are Exhibited and When They Are Not

Determining the variables around each behavior provides us an important piece of the puzzle. If we know what contributes to the occurrence of the target unconstructive behavior, we can work to diminish that. In addition—and this is a powerful piece of supporting change—if we know what contributes to the occurrence of the alternative goal (constructive) behavior, we can enhance that.

Step 3: We Carry Out an ABC Assessment

In Step 3, our purpose is to develop an even more specific hypothesis about the interactions of variables in all three environments. We do this by trying to determine the specific *antecedent* and *consequent* events (or conditions) and their effect on the student's behavior.

In Chapter 5, we discussed the principles of behavior. We talked about the role of conditions that come before (i.e., that are antecedent to) a behavior and that trigger the occurrence of a behavior, whether or not that behavior is constructive. We also talked about consequent conditions, those that occur *soon after* a behavior and offer something pleasant or get rid of something unpleasant. These are likely to encourage behavior to occur again when circumstances are similar. In contrast, unpleasant consequent conditions following soon after a behavior are likely to decrease its occurrence. These events can be unpleasant in and of themselves, or they can remove something pleasant. If we keep these basic principles in mind as we analyze the sequence of events surrounding a target behavior, we can often determine the nature of the antecedent (A) and consequent (C) events in relation to the behavior (B) as well as their effect on the person who exhibited the behavior.

When we look at all our data to do an ABC assessment, the first step is to look for patterns between the quantitative and descriptive data. To do so, we ask four questions. Each question has two parts.

Step 1: When the target behavior occurs most frequently:

♦ What antecedent variables are present in the physical and psychosocial environments that seem to set the behavior in motion?

♦ What consequent variables are present immediately afterwards that encourage it to occur again under similar circumstances, consequent conditions, or events?

Step 2: When the target behavior occurs least frequently or not at all:

♦ What variables are present or absent in the physical and psychosocial environments so that the behavior is not triggered (antecedent conditions or events)?

♦ What variables are present or absent in the physical and psychosocial environments after the behavior occurs so that the student is not encouraged to exhibit it again (consequent conditions or events)?

Step 3: When the goal behavior occurs:

♦ What antecedent variables are present in the physical and psychosocial environments that seem to set the behavior in motion?

♦ What consequent variables are present immediately afterwards that encourage it to occur again under similar circumstances, consequent conditions, or events?

Step 4: When the goal behavior occurs least frequently or not at all:

♦ What variables are present or absent in the physical and psychosocial environments so that the behavior is not triggered (antecedent conditions or events)?

♦ What variables are present or absent in the physical and psychosocial environments after the behavior occurs so that the student is not encouraged to exhibit it again (consequent conditions or events)?

Case Study: We feel that Crispin's chatting with other students when independent work is to be done should be decreased. He is not finishing what he needs to do during that time period. If we look at the variables that exist in his three environments, we can hypothesize about what triggers (cues) the chatting and, once it has occurred, what encourages (reinforces) it. This would tell us how the physiological variables and needs are addressed by the variables in his physical and/or psychosocial environments and, therefore, what variables we need to decrease so that the chatting occurs less frequently or not at all.

Crispin sits at the same table each afternoon for independent work time. For three days, we collect data on his chatting. We make a note that he is at the same table (physical environment variable), and there are always three other students there (general psychosocial environment variables). On two of the days, he is with Ross, Joelee, and Karen (more specific psychosocial variables). On Day 3, he works next to Bodie, Brian, and Cathy. On Days 1 and 2, there is chatting among all for 14 of the 21 minutes. What might we hypothesize is cueing and reinforcing his chatting?

On Day 3, he chats (target behavior) during independent work time for less than three minutes. During independent work time, Crispin remains silent (goal behavior) and completes each of the assigned tasks. This occurs for a little more than 18 minutes. On Day 3, we note that after everyone chatted briefly (one minute) as he or she sat down, Bodie, Brian, and Cathy all kept their heads down for the rest of the 21 minute time period and seemed pleased (based on what they said at the end) with what they accomplished when it was time to return to their desks to share with the rest of the class. We also note that once, when Crispin began to talk, Brian put his hand up as if to say "no" while he kept reading his book. Now that we have looked at the variables around both the target and the goal behavior, what might we hypothesize?

In this case, as we look at the ecological assessment variables in the context and setting (when chatting does and does not occur), we see the same table. Same activity. Same length of work time. Same number of children with Crispin. What was different on Day 3, when the chatting occurred less frequently? In a collapsed version of our four questions from just above:

+ Was there an absence of any cue for the target behavior, such as other children willing to chat?
+ When the target behavior of chatting occurs, is there any reinforcement for it?
+ When the target behavior occurred, was it ignored (extinguished) or punished?
+ What variables encouraged the goal behavior to occur—either by triggering it or reinforcing it?

There were different children on Day 3. How did that change the variables for Crispin? What might you hypothesize?

It is possible that Crispin's need to connect with other children Day 3 is at such a low level that a couple of minutes at the beginning of the work time was sufficient, when he was not encouraged to talk for a longer period of time. Perhaps his need to connect with the three children with whom he worked on the third day was not as great as when he worked with Ross, Joelee, and Karen. Perhaps the cue of Bodie's, Brian's, and Cathy's working helped to trigger Crispin's focus on task. More data about these patterns could enhance our hypotheses, but we have questions we can pursue by collecting more data.

Knowing what is going on around the individual, both when the target and goal behaviors occur and when they occur infrequently or not at all, is essential.

We have looked at the variables that exist in the three environments, both before the behavior is exhibited and immediately afterwards. Having laid that groundwork, we are now ready to take the next step that will lead us to greater detail, to a higher level of specificity in our assessment.

I find it helpful to do the assessment in chart form. Below is the A->B->C Assessment Form.

Table 10-3. A-B-C Assessment Form					
Observer: _____ Date of Assessment: _____					
Setting: _____ Agenda: _____					
Actors: _____					
Target Behavior Focus: _____					
Goal Behavior Focus: _____					
Map can be found on page: _____					
Date & Time	Antecedent 'A'	Behavior 'B'	Consequence 'C'	Student's Reaction/ Response	Hypothesis: Given the student's reaction, the consequence seems reinforcing or punishing *for the student*

At the top of the form, I have provided room for the information we identified as essential for recording any observation, including a column on the left for the date and time of the incident. At a minimum, the time the behavior occurred would be recorded here. If the behavior is a *continuous* one, the time the behavior ended would also be written. We take the information we have from a running narrative record or an expanded anecdotal record and fill in the "Antecedent," the "Behavior," and the "Consequence" columns of the A-B-C Assessment Form. On the right of the form, I have added two more columns that I believe are essential to our ABC assessment. The first is the student's reaction to the consequence, because we can only hypothesize about the nature of the consequence (pleasant or unpleasant) by observing the student's response. Remember: A person's response, whether a smile, frown, laughter, etc., may not give us a completely accurate picture. The only way we *really* know if a consequent condition is pleasant (reinforcing) or unpleasant (punishing) is to see whether the behavior occurs again or less and less frequently. Measuring the change in frequency or duration of a behavior over a series of data collections can help us determine, given these antecedents and consequences, if the frequency of the behavior stays the same, increases due to reinforcement, or decreases due to a sense of punishment.

Platform: Application Opportunity

On the Active Learning Platform under Chapter 10 is an example of an ABC Assessment Form for you to complete, given the information already supplied on the form.

Step 4: We Carry Out a Functional Behavior Assessment

While the information about antecedent and consequent events is helpful, an additional assessment will support us even further in designing an effective behavior change support plan. The ABC assessment helps get us ready for this third and final assessment. In the Functional Behavior Assessment (FBA), we look at what seems to be the purpose of the behavior. Sometimes people refer to the purpose as "the communicative intent of the behavior," meaning what the behavior is *saying without words*. (This Functional Behavior Assessment process is *required* in the Individuals with Disabilities Act [IDEA] of 2004 Public Law 108–446.)

When we look for the function of a behavior, we are still looking for A->B-> C patterns, but we are focusing in particular on the consequences. We ask: What did the behavior provide the student? That is, is the student trying to obtain something or get away from something?

ACCESSING PRIOR KNOWLEDGE/EXPERIENCE

Do you remember the four functions of behavior? On a separate piece of paper or in the space below write as many as you remember. We used the acronym SATE to help us remember.

S _____

A _____

T _____

E _____

The four functions or communicative intents are stimulation/sensory regulation, attention, tangibles, and escape. As we said above, the student might be trying to obtain something, such as attention, stimulation, or a tangible item. He may be trying to get away from or lessen something (such as a sensation), avoid unwanted attention, remove himself from a tangible item, or escape from a difficult situation or person.

Step 5: We Determine if Data Is Sufficient and Designing a Behavior Support Plan Is Appropriate. We Make Needed Adjustments

Often, when we begin to analyze the data about a student's target and goal behaviors, we find that our focus was not as appropriate as we originally thought or the description of the behavior is incomplete. There are additional observable aspects to the student's behavior that we need. When this occurs, we change definition and then collect data that has the revised definition as the focus. Another adjustment may be needed if we notice gaps in the information. Then we collect the missing data. At other times, we may have a lot of useful data, but assessing it leads to questions. If so, we need to ask those questions and then determine if we need additional or different data to answer them.

When we have the information we need and we are ready to analyze the data, we have two foci. The first is to determine what, if any, patterns we can find. We have already discussed how to analyze the data for patterns. The second focus is to determine if the patterns require intervention. To determine if designing a behavior support plan is appropriate, we look at the effect of the behavior on the student as well as the effect of the behavior on others in the learning community. Questions that can guide our analysis include:

- Does the behavior appear to keep the student from meeting her basic needs?
- Does the behavior appear to be emotionally or physically harmful to the student?
- Is the behavior age appropriate? (This question is a tricky one because while some behavior, such as teasing, may be typical of students at a certain age, it may *not* be constructive.)
- Does the behavior appear to keep the student from developing reciprocal social relationships with other students?
- Does the behavior appear to keep the student from developing an effective working relationship with the teacher and any other adults working in the room?
- Does the behavior keep the student from asking for help?
- Does the behavior keep the student from seeking feedback when needed?
- Does the behavior appear to keep the student from making reasonable progress in learning concepts and skills?

Application Activity: Ecological, A-B-C, and Functional Analysis of Patterns

In Table 10-4 below is the complete version of the Running Narrative Record from the previous chapter for you to apply what you have just learned. First, analyze the narrative for patterns in the antecedent conditions and consequences of Peter's target behavior. Then analyze the narrative for patterns in the antecedent conditions and consequences of Peter's goal behavior. Complete both parts of the ABC Assessment Form (Table 10-5) below the running narrative to support your assessment process. I have provided a couple of examples for the target behavior portion.

<table>
<tr><td colspan="3" align="center">Table 10-4. Example of a Running Narrative Record[1]
as it appeared in brief in Chapter 9 Table 9–5</td></tr>
<tr><td colspan="3">Observer: Alison Corner Time: 10:35–10:55. Date: _____ Setting: Classroom: Grade 4; number of children: 24 sitting in four rows of 6 each. Agenda/Context: Math Actors: P = Peter; T = Teacher; AC = Another Child Target Behavior: Off Task behavior including, calling out answers without waiting to be called on; out of seat; closing book; putting book in desk; putting pencil anywhere but on paper and writing as directed; looking out window. Goal Behavior: Doing whatever directed by teacher, including waiting to be called on before speaking; going to the board when ask to by the teacher. Layout is 4 rows of 6 desks each facing the board. Peter's position: Last in row by window. [Map has been omitted from this copy of record.]</td></tr>
<tr><th>Time</th><th>Narrative</th><th>Notes</th></tr>
<tr><td>10:35</td><td>T erasing blackboard.

Children clearing desks.

P sliding math book under desk between feet.</td><td></td></tr>
<tr><td>10:36</td><td>T begins math lesson using blackboard to illustrate points.

P's book now closed on desk—he watches T. P paying attention

T asks for volunteer to do problem on board.

P calls out the answer (correct). Hand stays on desk.</td><td>P paying attention

Correct, but no hand raised</td></tr>
<tr><td>10:37</td><td>T asks P to raise hand and wait to be called on.

P smiles.

AC does problem on the blackboard.</td><td>T response</td></tr>
<tr><td>10:38</td><td>P looks out the window as teacher continues the lesson.

P raises hand and calls out, "Can I go to the Boys' Room?"

T knits eyebrows and turns mouth down. "Alright, quickly!"

P smiles as he leaves room.</td><td>P paying attention?

Needs movement or escape?

T response to off task</td></tr>
</table>

	Table 10-4. Example of a Running Narrative Record[i] **as it appeared in brief in Chapter 9 Table 9–5 (Continued)**	
10:42	P returns. Slides hands across desks of last row as returns to seat.	For stimulation or attention?
	T "Peter, please sit down quickly."	T response
10:43	T asks for volunteer to come to blackboard to do problem.	T cue, but for action, not answer
	P calls out answer (incorrect).	Calls out whether correct or not
	T asks P to come to blackboard.	T response
	P claps his hands once as he gets out of his seat.	
10:44	P goes to blackboard, does problem correctly, returns to seat.	*Called* out wrong, but *did* it correctly
10:45	P looking out window.	
	T finishes lesson and explains assignment.	
	T passes out paper.	
	P asks if he can sharpen his pencil.	Needs movement or escape?
	T tells P he can sharpen it, if he will then sit in his seat and do the math problem.	T response
10:46	P sharpens pencil.	
	P returns to desk, holds foot out in aisle as child walks by.	To trip child? Attention or escape?
	AC2 walks around P's foot to own desk. AC2 eyes ahead.	AC2 response is to ignore
10:47	T "Peter, have you started your math?"	T cue or response?
	P "Yes." Sitting down.	
	P looks at page in book.	
	P "These are hard."	
10:48	T "Maybe if you had been listening, you'd understand."	T response
	P looking at problems. "These are dumb."	Had two correct before. *Are* these too hard?
10:50	P looks at book. Begins to write first problem.	
	Closes book. Puts in desk.	
	T "Peter, take out that math book."	T response

i   Used with permission from Alison Corner, personal communication, 2015.

Table 10-5. A-B-C Assessment Form Completed for Peter's Target and Goal Behavior

Target Behavior: Off Task behavior: including, calling out answers without waiting to be called on; out of seat; closing book; putting book in desk; putting pencil anywhere but on paper and writing as directed; looking out window.

Date & Time	Antecedent 'A'	Behavior 'B'	Consequence 'C'	Student's Reaction	Hypothesis: Given student's reaction, consequence seems reinforcing or punishing *for student*
Date unknown; time is 10:36.	T asks for volunteer to do problem on board.	P calls out the answer (correct). Hand stays on desk.	T asks P to raise hand and wait to be called on.	P smiles	P seems happy, so T response is probably reinforcing.
Date unknown; time is 10:37	Teacher continues the lesson	P raises hand and calls out, "Can I go to the Boys' Room?"	T knits eyebrows and turns mouth down. "Alright, quickly!"	P smiles	P smiles, so being able to leave the room is likely to be reinforcing.

Goal Behavior: Doing whatever is directed by teacher e.g., waiting to be called on before speaking.

Date & Time	Antecedent 'A'	Behavior 'B'	Consequence 'C'	Student's Reaction	Hypothesis: Given the student's reaction, the consequence seems reinforcing or punishing *for student*

Ecological/ABC Assessment Questions for the Analysis of Patterns

Now, consider your answers to these four questions as part of your analysis. (You can write your answers, or not as would be of benefit to you.) Then, as a synthesis of all your analyses, in the space provided or on a separate piece of paper write your responses to the questions that appear under Results of Your Ecological/ABC Assessment below.

Step 1: When the target behavior occurs most frequently:

♦ What antecedent variables are present in the physical and psychosocial environments that seem to set the behavior in motion?

♦ What consequent variables are present immediately afterwards that encourage it to occur again under similar circumstances, consequent conditions, or events?

Step 2: When the target behavior occurs least frequently or not at all:

♦ What variables are present or absent in the physical and psychosocial environments so that the behavior is not triggered (antecedent conditions or events)?

♦ What variables are present or absent in the physical and psychosocial environments after the behavior occurs so that the student is not encouraged to exhibit it again (consequent conditions or events)?

Step 3: When the goal behavior occurs:

♦ What antecedent variables are present in the physical and psychosocial environments that seem to set the behavior in motion?

♦ What consequent variables are present immediately afterwards that encourage it to occur again under similar circumstances, consequent conditions, or events?

Step 4: When the goal behavior occurs least frequently or not at all:

♦ What variables are present or absent in the physical and psychosocial environments so that the behavior is not triggered (antecedent conditions or events)?

♦ What variables are present or absent in the physical and psychosocial environments after the behavior occurs so that the student is not encouraged to exhibit it again (consequent conditions or events)?

Results of Your Ecological/ABC Assessment

1: Do you see any patterns in either the antecedents to or the consequences of Peter's target behavior?

Antecedent event patterns that may set the target behavior in motion: _____

_____

Consequent event patterns for the target behavior that may or may not encourage it to occur again: _____

_____

2: Of those antecedents, is there anything that seems to encourage Peter's target behavior to occur and, once it occurs, is there anything to encourage it to occur again? _____

_____

3: Do you see any patterns in either the antecedents to or the consequences of Peter's goal behavior?

Antecedent events that may set the goal behavior in motion: _____

_____

Consequent event patterns for the goal behavior that may or may not encourage it to occur again: _____

_____

4: Of those antecedents is there anything that seems to encourage Peter's goal behavior to occur and, once it occurs, is there anything to encourage it to occur again? _____

_____

· ·

Below is a brief version of my ABC assessment:

1: Target behavior—patterns of antecedent conditions:

It is possible that the context of math class and the way it is taught may contribute to the behavior, but without comparable data being collected in another subject area, I cannot say more.

One antecedent is the teacher asking for a volunteer (10:36 and 10:43).

Another antecedent may be internal. Peter seems to need to move around or perhaps take a break. (I gather that from looking at what he does when he is off task.)

2: Target behavior—patterns of consequent conditions:

When Peter calls out, the teacher responds, or he is able to do what he has asked to do, including move around.

3: Goal behavior—patterns of antecedent conditions:

There is an absence of antecedent events to trigger the goal behavior. The teacher *does not cue* the key aspect of the goal behavior, which is hand-raising. Sometimes she reminds Peter to raise his hand, but that is not a cue because it occurs *after* the moment when the constructive behavior should ideally have happened. (I am *not* suggesting we ignore a student's request to use the bathroom. An alternative would be to talk with Peter in advance and set up an agreed-upon system that includes clear cueing and reinforcement. This could be verbal, if Peter waited to be called on, and ignoring him if he didn't. In addition, designating a good time for bathroom use would be a part of the agreement.)

4: Goal behavior—patterns of consequent conditions:

There is no evidence of positive consequences for Peter's goal behavior.

Functional Assessment of Patterns

Below in Table 10-6 is a Functional Assessment Form I designed to help me with my work. Using your answers to item 2 on the Results of Your Ecological/ABC Assessment fill in as many of the fours rows you can under Target Behavior; that is, fill in the Behavior column for any behavior that seemed to be reinforced for Peter, and fill in the Consequence column for what teacher or student behavior you hypothesize seemed to be reinforcing for Peter and/or what change in Peter's Physiological Environment might have occurred as a result of his behavior. Then, complete the last column in the assessment form to hypothesize the Possible Function of each of Peter's behaviors you included under Behavior.

Given your analysis of the consequences of his actions, below or on a separate piece of paper write what you hypothesize is the function/are function(s) of Peter's behavior.

1: _____

2: _____

One function, I would hypothesize, is stimulation/sensory regulation. A second one would be escape. I would also hypothesize a third one: attention from the teacher.

We have now completed all three analyses on our quantitative and descriptive data: ecological, ABC, and functional. Table 10-7 and Table 10-8 provide summaries of the questions we ask about variables in all three of the student's environments as we carry out these important assessment processes. Table 10-7 looks at the questions from the perspective of the kinds of data collected; whereas, Table 10-8 provides the analysis from the perspective of the antecedent and consequent events and variables that may contribute to the occurrence of the behavior.

Table 10-6. Functional Assessment Form For Behaviors that Were Reinforced
(for completion on Peter's behavior)

Observer: _____ Date of Assessment: _____

Setting: _____ Agenda: _____

Actors: _____

Target Behavior _____

Time	Antecedent Setting Event 'A'	Behavior 'B'	Consequence or Consequent Condition 'C'	Student's Reaction/ Response	Hypothesis: Given student's reaction, consequence seems reinforcing for student	Possible Function(s) of Reinforced Behavior: Sensory Regulation; Attention; Tangibles; Escape

Goal Behavior _____

Time	Antecedent Setting Event 'A'	Behavior 'B'	Consequence or Consequent Condition 'C'	Student's Reaction/ Response	Hypothesis: Given student's reaction, consequence seems reinforcing for student	Possible Function(s): of Reinforced Behavior: Sensory Regulation; Attention; Tangibles; Escape

Table 10-7. **Nature of Data and Related Assessment Questions**

	DATA ON BEHAVIOR			DATA ON VARIABLES SURROUNDING BEHAVIOR		
	When Behavior Occurs	How Behavior Occurs			Ecological Assessment	
	Frequency/Duration/Latency	Magnitude	Topography	Physiological Variables	Physical Variables	Psychosocial Variables
ASSESSMENT QUESTIONS (DATA)	◦ When in the day does the behavior occur most frequently or for longer time periods? When does it occur least frequently, or for shorter time periods? ◦ In what setting(s) does it occur most frequently or for the longest time period? In what setting does it occur least frequently or for shorter time periods? ◦ Under what agenda(s) does it occur most frequently or for the longest time period? Under what agenda does it occur least frequently/or for the shortest time periods? ◦ With what actor(s) does it occur most frequently or for the longest time period? With what actors does it occur least frequently, or for the shortest time periods?	◦ When in the day is the behavior stronger? Weaker? ◦ In what setting is it stronger? Weaker? ◦ Under what agendas it is it stronger? Weaker? ◦ With what actors is it stronger? Weaker?	◦ Are there any conditions under which the 'look' of the behavior changes; e.g., time of day, setting, agenda, with particular actors?	◦ What student's physiological environment variables might have an effect on the student behavior, e.g., health, learning style &/or needs, disabilities, talents, intelligences, previous learning or lack of learning, emotions?	◦ What variables in the setting e.g., furniture, equipment (or lack of it), heating, light, seating arrangement, location in room, might affect student's behavior; i.e. to what degree does the make-up of the setting match student's physiological needs? ◦ To what degree does the agenda match student needs, interests, strengths? ◦ What aspects of the teacher's instructional strategies might have an effect on student's behavior; to what degree do instructional strategies match student's physiological needs?	◦ What variables in the student's social interactions with other students or teacher might have an effect on the behavior?

ABC Assessment: What appears to be the **antecedent condition** for the behavior, if it is occurring–what specifically cues the behavior? If the behavior is not occurring, what cues are missing? Have any been utilized? Which, if any, have been successful? What appears to be the **consequent** condition for the behavior? What effect does is seem to have on the student, i.e., does the student perceive it as reinforcing or punishing?

Functional Assessment: Given the change from the variables just prior to the behavior and those existing after the behavior occurred, and given the effect of the behavior for the student, what function(s) does the behavior appear to serve? **S**ensory regulation, **A**ttention, **T**angibles, **E**scape?

	Table 10-8. **Integrating Ecological, ABC, and Functional Assessment Questions**	
ANTECEDENT VARIABLES	BEHAVIOR	CONSEQUENT VARIABLES
Physiological Environment Variables: Just prior to the behavior what variables exist in the student's physiological environment that might relate to variables in either of the other two environments and to this behavior; e.g., emotions, temperament elements, learning style, disabilities, talents, health, medicines, toxic substances, mood disorders, neurological conditions, what student has/has not learned, physiological and emotional needs?		**Physiological:** What, if any, variables in the student's physiological environment change as a result of the behavior or as the result of what occurs immediately after the behavior? Variables might include: physiological or emotional needs that seem to be met by the behavior; needs for sensory regulation, attention or escape that seem to be met by the behavior? What function, if any, does the behavior seem to serve?
Physical Environment Variables: Just prior to the behavior what variables exist in the student's physical environment that might relate to the other two environments and affect this behavior; e.g., student location in setting or proximity to other student(s) or teacher, agenda, arrangement of objects, furniture, teacher instructional strategies, curriculum content and materials? [These may be referred to as 'setting events'.]		**Physical:** What, if any, variables in the student's physical environment change as a result of the behavior or as the result of what occurs immediately after the behavior, e.g., student location in setting or proximity to other student(s) or teacher, agenda, arrangement of objects, furniture, teacher instructional strategies, curriculum and materials? What function, if any, does the behavior seem to serve?
Psychosocial Environment Variables: Just prior to the behavior what variables exist in the student's psychosocial environment that might relate to the other two environments and to this particular behavior; e.g., other student behavior, teacher social behavior. [These may be referred to as 'setting events'.]		**Psychosocial:** What, if any, variables in the student's psychosocial environment change as a result of the behavior or as the result of what occurs immediately after the behavior; e.g., other student's behavior, and teacher social behavior. What function(s) do these variables serve?
Interrelationship Between Variables in the Physiological and Other Environments: When variables in any environments interact, is there a need/tension to be resolved; e.g., is there a mismatch between variables in the physiological environment and learning task requirements, or are there variables in the physical or psychosocial environment that might interfere with the student's accomplishing the task?		**Interrelationship Between Variables in Physiological and Other Environments:** As a result of the behavior, does a change occur in any of the student's three environments that affects the student's physiological environment?
In Summary: What variables or interaction(s) among variables in any of the three environments seem to cue, prompt, trigger the behavior to occur, or what variables are absent so there does not appear to be a cue?		**In Summary:** What consequence (change in variables) seems to encourage the behavior to continue or to increase, or what consequence seems to decrease the occurrence of the behavior? What function is served by the behavior?

Integrative Summary: How do variables interact to create conditions that encourage the behavior to occur by addressing a need or serving a function? If the behavior does not occur, what could cue the behavior and what could occur as a result of the behavior that would create a positive effect by addressing a need or serving a function?

Final Thoughts

Using both quantitative and descriptive data gives us a more complete sense of the patterns of interactions of variables in all three of a student's environments. We need numerical information. We also need information about the nature of the behavior and the variables surrounding it.

There are advantages of using an ecological perspective during the assessment phase of supporting behavior change. Now that we have had an opportunity to analyze data using an ecological perspective, I hope the appropriateness of this approach will be apparent. If we had not looked at all three environments, we would have missed valuable information. Our assessment can only be as thorough as our data enables it to be.

The more complete the assessment, the more likely the intervention design will be appropriate. The more appropriate the design, the more likely it will be a match for the student. The more the intervention is a match for the student, the more likely it will be successful. I began the chapter with Einstein's quote because I agree; spending dedicated time to think about the problem by assessing the data is essential.

Looking Forward

We have collected and assessed our data, and we have considered whether what we have learned warrants intervention. If we believe behavior change would be constructive for the student, we are ready to design our behavior change support plan. Chapters 11 and 12 will take us through the steps of developing effective plans.

References

Alberto, P., & Troutman, A. (2017). *Applied behavior analysis for teachers* (9th ed.). Upper Saddle River, NJ: Pearson.

Chandler, L., & Dahlquist, C. (2014). *Functional assessment* (4th ed.). Columbus, OH: Merrill.

Maag, J. (2018). *Behavior management: From theoretical implications to practical applications* (3rd ed.). Boston, MA: Cengage Learning.

Miltenberger, R. (2016). *Behavior modification: Principles and procedures, international edition* (6th ed.). Pacific Grove, CA: Brooks/Cole.

Scheuermann, B., & Hall, J. (2012). *Positive behavioral supports for the classroom* (3rd ed.). Boston, MA: Pearson.

Shea, T., & Bauer, A. (2012). *Behavior management: A practical approach for educators* (10th ed.). Boston, MA: Pearson.

Umbreit, J., Ferro, J., Liaupsin, C., & Lane, K. (2006). *Functional behavioral assessment and function-based intervention: An effective, practical approach*. Columbus, OH: Merrill.

CHAPTER 11

Fostering Constructive Behavior

*Our students give us the opportunity to
be the teachers we wished we had.*

—Shari Stokes

What Will This Chapter Discuss?

Once we have identified an unconstructive behavior that we believe should be changed, what can we do? The most effective strategy involves a two-pronged approach. We must increase or establish an appropriate behavior that is an alternative to the unconstructive one while simultaneously using the appropriate methods to decrease the unconstructive behavior. This chapter addresses how to increase or establish an appropriate behavior, which helps us to affect change in the right direction and takes us halfway towards our goal.

Why Is This Important?

So often when we want to stop an unconstructive behavior, we want an approach that is quick. We think in terms of how to get rid of it, period. If, however, we try only to stop the unconstructive behavior, we will rarely succeed in the long run. It is also possible that we may succeed in stopping the unconstructive behavior but our strategy will inadvertently have a ripple effect. We rarely succeed because we haven't addressed what encouraged the student to behave in a certain way in the first place.

Example: Serita wants attention, so she turns to her neighbor to chat about what is going on during independent work time. If we are successful in getting her to stop chatting, we have not addressed her need—only *how* she was addressing it. She is likely to try to meet her need another way, perhaps by chatting with peers at another time during the lesson.

The second problem with *just* stopping an unconstructive behavior is that we may succeed but at the same time create other problems.

Example: When we tell a student to stop asking questions that do not relate to the discussion, the student may stop asking what *seem* like off-track questions, but she may stop asking any other questions, too.

To counteract our strong tendency to address unconstructive behavior by trying to make it cease immediately, we need a more successful way to think about supporting behavior change and the strategies that will enable us to respond more constructively.

What Will You Learn?

We have choices when we use positive strategies to support behavior change. By the end of the chapter, you will be able to:

+ describe how to foster the establishment of a behavior;
+ describe how to increase the frequency or duration of a student's constructive behavior;
+ describe how to lessen the time between cueing a desired behavior and having a student manifest it;

- describe how to support change in the nature of a behavior; and
- describe ways to decrease or eliminate an unconstructive behavior by increasing a constructive behavior.

What Do You Want To Accomplish?

What do you want to learn about how to increase a behavior to support positive change? Write your responses here or on a piece of paper. _____

_____

_____

_____

We cannot control a student. What we *can* control to a considerable extent are those variables surrounding the student (the cues and reinforcers for what we feel is unconstructive behavior as well as possible cues and reinforcers for encouraging constructive behavior), and we can profoundly affect a student's behavior by doing so. The strategies we will consider are supported by research, best practices, and my years of experience teaching, supervising, and working with teachers in the field (Alberto & Troutman, 2017; Belvel & Jordan, 2003; Henley, 2009; Maag, 2018; Martin & Pear, 2015; Marzano, Gaddy, Foseid, Foseid, & Marzano, 2005; Knoster, 2014; Knoster & Drogan, 2016; Scheuermann & Hall, 2016; Shea & Bauer 2011; Wheeler & Richey, 2013; Zirpoli, 2016).

How Can We Arrange Antecedent Conditions to Foster Constructive Behavior?

How Can We Address Antecedent Conditions in the Student's Physiological Environment?

We Address Variables that May Interfere with the Student's Receptivity to Change

One purpose for addressing variables in this environment is to ensure that the student can be open to the behavior change intervention, not to mention the learning experiences beyond. First, we look at the student's emotional needs. Does he feel safe and cared about? Does he experience a sense of well-being and have a sense of belonging in the context within which we are supporting behavior change?

Note: In the data collection phase of the intervention (Chapter 10), we discussed giving the student a questionnaire or interviewing him to determine to what degree he felt his needs were being met. This data could help.

Is the goal of the intervention a behavior he feels competent to perform? We must address any unmet need, or most cues will likely not be effective.

Is there a chemical imbalance (such as bipolar or attention deficit disorder) interfering with the student's learning or with forming constructive friendships? Has medication been considered to address these imbalances[i]? Is a medication making the student drowsy or agitated? How might this be addressed? If we do not address any of these kinds of issues in the student's physiological environment, it will be difficult to support behavior change.

We Capitalize on the Student's Capacities

As we think about setting the stage for supporting behavior change, we have student variables that are our allies. These are what the student brings to the intervention in terms of interests, learning strengths, and intelligences. We can use what we know to help us choose a trigger for the behavior. Example: If the student is a visual learner, having a poster that indicates appropriate voice level for the current activity or a set of written steps with a place for the student to check off each completed step would be more effective than an auditory cue.

How Can We Arrange Antecedent Conditions in the Student's Physical Environment?

We Create a Physical Environment in Which the Student's Basic Needs Are Met

We have the most control over variables in the student's physical environment. We need to ask ourselves if there are ways to foster a context of safety, belonging, being valued, feeling efficacious, and feeling good about learning that we have not yet implemented. A review of the strategies discussed in Chapters 5, 6, and 7 may help us to address any as yet unmet needs.

We Arrange Furniture and/or Equipment, Lighting, and Temperature to Match the Student's Learning Needs

As we noted earlier in the text, some students prefer hard seats. Others do better sitting in less formal furniture. Some need natural lighting, while others are fine with florescent lights. Some need bright lights, yet others prosper under less intense lighting. Some like it warm and some do not. Some students are helped by having a moderate amount of noise around them, and others need quiet to concentrate. We need to ask ourselves if this a student for whom a change in any of these physical environment variables would foster the learning and development of constructive behavior.

We Teach Prerequisite Concepts and Skills

Determining a likely antecedent and an effective reinforcement for appropriate behavior may not be enough to ensure success. Sometimes a behavior change support plan is not successful because the student does not have the prerequisite concepts or skills. To teach specific prerequisite skills, we design a "preintervention" to help him learn these. Example: Before we teach students how to resolve conflicts, they need to learn how to identify and name the feelings they have.

> Note: To teach the prerequisite concepts, skills, or the behavior itself, we can follow the instructional sequence of any effective lesson we addressed in Chapter 6.

We Arrange Variables to Cue the Appropriate Behavior

Are there clear clues in the physical environment, such as seating arrangements and signs, that constructively "call out" to the student, "Do this here!" Examples: If we want to increase independent work while minimizing the students' opportunities to talk to others, we must consider whether or not there is enough space between seats (if this is physically possible) to cue that this is a time to do solo work. If we want to increase constructive use of time once assigned work is completed, we must provide a clearly visible list of possibilities and a variety of activities to suggest what could be done during "choice" time that we review periodically with students. If we want the student to contribute to team discussions, we must help students position themselves so that they are knee to knee and eye to eye to foster such collaboration.

How Can We Create a Match Between Variables in the Student's Physiological and Physical Environment Variables?

We Consider Whether We Have a Match Between Our Instructional Strategies and the Student's Learning Style and Needs

Does this student prefer variety in learning experiences or a patterned set of routine learning experiences? Is this student more successful at a task if there is a high degree of structure or a low degree?

We can infuse lessons with opportunities to learn through the intelligences in which this student shows strength. We can learn about current strategies to address the specific needs of an individual with a disability. We can use Universal Design for Learning principles to make a learning experience available to this particular student while at the same time making the experience available to all.

How Can We Arrange *Antecedent Conditions* in the Student's Psychosocial Environment?

We Think About the Social Variables We Hope will Cue and Encourage the Constructive Behavior

We consider which student(s) would provide a good example of a desired constructive behavior and arrange to have them sit near a student who needs to learn this behavior. We consider the level of collaboration that would be best for this student. Some students do better working on a task independently, while others prefer to work with a partner or in a team. Another important consideration is with whom the student prefers/prefers not to work. We may not always be able to choose pairs and team members that are wholly suited, but when trying to change behavior in a student, we must consider the best collaborators for supporting that change.

How Can We Most Effectively Use *Cues* in Any Environment?

Given all the variables we have considered, the cue must be appropriate for the student and the behavior desired. The cue must be clear to the student. The cue must occur close in time to when the desired behavior is to be exhibited—preferably *just* before it. When we are first fostering a constructive behavior, the cue must occur each time the behavior is to occur.

We must plan a safety net of prompts in case the cue does not work—see Chapter 11's Appendix A for additional options and support in considering how to use them.

How Do We Choose the Nature of a Cue or Prompt?

We Consider the Student's Learning Style and Needs

Examples: Some students benefit from having cues they can hear, such as the human voice saying specific words, a chime, or a piece of music to indicate that an activity requiring particular behavior is about to take place. Cleanup and silent reading time are times these students benefit from auditory cues. Other students benefit from visual cues, such as the gesture of pointing a finger to a watch or the clock, a colored card in a slot that indicates the appropriate voice level for an activity,- or specific objects arranged in a specific way. Still other students need to feel a gentle touch on the shoulder to help them shift gears and exhibit the needed behavior.

We Ask the Student What Would be Helpful

Examples: A colleague (with whom I cotaught in a middle school class) and I were designing a plan to support the increase of a student's attention to verbal direction. Because this student looked around a lot, we asked him if he thought he would easily see either of us rub our fingers down the side of our noses to remind him to focus on what was about to be said. He thought he would. When it came time to give directions, one of us would move into his line of sight and rub the side of our nose. The resulting change in his attention made a big difference in his ability to follow through on directions. Another student wanted us to *say* something to focus her attention. We all agreed that just before giving directions, a teacher would say, "This is important."

We Try Out Cues While Observing the Effect and Refine Our Choice Accordingly

I suggest having a couple of backup cues in mind so that it's easy to move to plan B (or C), if needed. On the other hand, if we find we have to repeatedly use lots of prompts to enhance the cue despite feeling that the student should have reached the learning goal, this is probably a clue that the student has not yet really learned the concept or process/skill. In this case, we need to help her build the skill or develop the concept more completely.

How Do We Fade Cues?

To enhance students' locus of control and support them in becoming constructive, autonomous human beings, we need to fade the cue as soon as the student is able to proceed successfully without it. If we wait too long to fade the cue, the student may become dependent on it. On the other hand, if we move too quickly, the student may not exhibit the behavior consistently enough to create a habit, or may make mistakes in the way he exhibits the behavior so that reinforcement does not occur.

To successfully ease back on the cue, we must consider both which aspects we will fade and the progression of steps we will take to foster success. Like so many of our instructional strategies, fading is like a dance between teacher and student. The choreography is data from our ongoing observations. We take a step to reduce the cue, and we observe how a student responds. We reflect and proceed or revise our step. If more in-depth information on how to fade cues and prompts would be helpful, see Chapter 11's Appendix A.

How Can We Arrange Consequent Conditions to Support Constructive Behavior?

When we support the development of new behavior, having antecedent events in place that trigger the constructive behavior and removing those that cue unconstructive behavior is essential but not sufficient. We must also consider a *consequent* condition to ensure that the desired student behavior leads to a change that is pleasurable to the student. This creates motivation for the change. The positive experience also reinforces the process of change over time. With any learning, any change, people progress and then regress. Such "fits and starts" are natural. However, if we want to avoid discouraging the student through this process, the new behavior *must* lead to a positive outcome. Ultimately, *the student* needs to want to change; the success of the change must be in *her* eyes, or the support plan will not be effective.

ACCESSING PRIOR KNOWLEDGE/EXPERIENCE

In the space provided or elsewhere write what you recall about how we reinforce effectively: What kinds of reinforcement are there? What are the principles behind successful reinforcement? _____

_____

_____

What Kinds of Reinforcement Do We Have Available?

Did you remember there are two? Positive reinforcement presents something that is pleasurable to the student. Negative reinforcement removes something unpleasant and, therefore, the student also experiences pleasure. Because the result is pleasant *in either case*, reinforcement encourages the behavior to be exhibited again under similar circumstances.

	What is done to create the consequent condition	
Table 11-1. **Comparison of Positive and Negative Reinforcement**		
The Effect of the Consequent Condition from the Perspective of the Student*	Positive: Add something	Negative: Take something away
Reinforcement	*Positive* Reinforcement: Something pleasurable is added right after behavior.	*Negative* Reinforcement: Something unpleasant is taken away right after behavior.

*Note: What is pleasurable for one student may not be for another, so we must always say a consequent condition is reinforcing *for this particular individual*.

Reinforcement is a powerful tool because it gives the person exhibiting the behavior *immediate feedback on what behavior is successful*. Reinforcement can help establish a behavior that has not occurred before. Reinforcement can increase the occurrence of a behavior. Reinforcement can maintain a well-established behavior. Moreover, because the result is pleasant and, therefore, meets basic emotional needs, the student is open to the learning experience and the change it produces.

How Can We Most Effectively Use *Reinforcement* in Any Environment?

Reinforcement Works Only If It Follows the Behavior We Are Trying to Establish or Increase

We must ensure that students experience reinforcement immediately and consistently when a skill is first becoming part of their repertoire. Also, just like the choice of cue, the reinforcement chosen must be individualized. When we choose a reinforcer, we cannot assume that what we like or most students like will necessarily be reinforcing for a particular student. We can help ourselves determine what is reinforcing by observing to see what the student seems to respond to favorably: Is peer approval or adult approval likely to bring a smile? Is a choice of an activity a source of student pleasure? (Later, we will talk about using information from our functional assessment to add to the possible choices for a reinforcement.)

Extrinsic Reinforcement Needs to Be Paired with Natural Reinforcement

If we want students to be increasingly independent, constructive members of society, we cannot keep them dependent on contrived/unnatural reinforcement. Therefore, we always need to pair the unnatural reinforcer with a more natural one. Reinforcers are natural if they are readily available as an organic part of the particular class environment because they occur within the class schedule, and they are not overly intrusive. Examples of natural reinforcers include privileges, activities, and social reinforcers, such as a smile, a "That's kind of you," or "You stuck to it and are making progress." The pairing of the two kinds of reinforcers gives credence to the natural reinforcement, and, ultimately, the unnatural one can slowly but surely be removed while the natural one remains in place.

Natural reinforcers offer many advantages. We want students to be successful in the world without the need for contrived reinforcers. In addition, when students learn to anticipate a natural reinforcer, they learn natural reinforcement schedules that are available in their organic timing. In this way, natural reinforcers prepare students for what occurs in the real world, both in the nature of the reinforcement itself and in the timing of when it occurs in relationship to the behavior exhibited.

- -

REFLECTION OPPORTUNITY

What kinds of natural reinforcers were available for students with whom you have worked? Did you use these? If so, how effective were they? Given the principles we addressed, why do you think this might be the case? In the space provided or elsewhere write your answers.

_____

_____

_____

- -

We Need to Ensure that Students Experience Reinforcement for Successive Approximations of a skill When It Is First Being Learned

We reinforce behavior that is closer and closer to the goal of the behavior change. Even if the student's attempt to demonstrate the goal behavior has not yet reached the criteria for success, providing positive reinforcement for the attempt motivates the student to keep trying.

Example: Jeremy can stay focused on his project work for about a minute. Ultimately, we feel it would be of benefit to him to be able to work on it for 15 minutes. The leap from 1 to 15 minutes is too great to support successful behavior change, so at first, we reinforce his being on task for 2 minutes; then, after a series of successful work periods of 2 minutes, we shift to 4 minutes. After that length of on-task behavior becomes possible for him, we shift to 7, and so on.

Example: Leeza can complete seven math equations. After that, she begins to look around the room, chat with near neighbors, wander to the pencil sharpener, etc. Given her skills in math and other variables, we feel she is ready to extend the number completed. In addition to other aspects of the behavior support plan, we reinforce eight for a few days and then increase the number every few days until she reaches the criterion of 15.

How Can We Shape Behavior Change?

We Choose Reinforcers Based on Essential Information

We Use Functional Assessment Results to Choose Reinforcement

We can observe the function of the behavior and use that information to set up the reinforcement of the constructive behavior. We will address this process later in the chapter. If the constructive behavior exists, but at a low level, then we can take the information from our analysis about which function(s) the constructive behavior serves and try to enhance this/these.

We Gather Ideas from Other Useful Sources

We set up a menu of possible reinforcers and invite the student to choose. We can ask the student to suggest what would be reinforcing. We can ask the student's parent or guardian or a colleague what they see as reinforcing for the student.

We use social reinforcement to support the student's refinement of skills and concepts. When using social reinforcement, we are conscious of the *purpose*. We distinguish support from feedback. Therefore, we choose the *words* with thought and the tone of voice with careful consideration. The purpose of support is to encourage and cheer the student on. As we have said, the purpose of feedback is to give the student useful information that fosters continued progress. While good feedback is supportive, short, one-word or brief statements of support do *not* give useful feedback, except to say, "Whatever you are doing is on the mark—keep on going." Students need both encouragement to keep up their ongoing learning and useful information to refine their work.

We Use Social Reinforcement Constructively

As we said in Chapter 5 when discussing effective reinforcement, we need to:

- distinguish the student from the behavior and reinforce the behavior;
- focus on the student's success, not on our needs as a teacher;
- communicate privately;
- be specific;
- communicate naturally;
- communicate with appropriate words; and
- vary the nature of the social reinforcement.

We Use Contrived "Unnatural" Reinforcement Only as Long as is Necessary to Teach the Constructive Behavior. We Shift to Natural Reinforcement as Soon as the Student is Ready

We use contrived reinforcement at first, if needed, to provide additional motivation to get change started. We do not want students to be "stuck" with needing contrived reinforcement in order to learn and progress. The change will not ultimately be successful if the student is not able to become pleased internally with what has occurred.

We choose the nature of reinforcement we use dependent upon the following:

- The reinforcement is something that the student will find reinforcing: To borrow (and put a twist on) an old aphorism, what is good for the goose is not necessarily good for the gander, and may not even be good for another goose.
- The student wants/needs the reinforcer when we are about to offer it. The student must be sufficiently "deprived" of the reinforcer for it to work.
- The reinforcement is being offered at a level appropriate to the student's needs at this time. This refers to the degree to which the reinforcer responds to a lower-level primary need (food, water, rest) versus a secondary need (praise, privilege, credits) or the degree to which the reinforcer is extrinsic (lower level) versus intrinsic. (If you want more information on levels of reinforcement, see Appendix B of this chapter.)
- The timing of the reinforcement ensures that the student grasps the relationship between the behavior and the consequence. The student needs to understand that being reinforced is dependent on her exhibiting the constructive behavior. If the behavior is one for which frequency is the goal when we first intervene, we need to establish a one-to-one relationship between constructive behavior and reinforcement. On the other hand, if the behavior goal is an increase in duration, there needs to be reinforcement within a fairly short duration of the constructive behavior.
- The reinforcer corresponds in value to the effort required by the student. If the student hasn't really tried to demonstrate the constructive behavior, but we have offered something relatively minimal in value to the student, our reinforcer does not support the behavior change.

✦ **The reinforcer addresses the function of the unconstructive behavior.** In Chapter 10, we used a functional assessment to determine the motivation for unconstructive behavior. If we use what the student was hoping to get from her unconstructive behavior as the reinforcement for the constructive behavior, we will have a powerful reinforcement indeed. Example: During small-group work, students do a lot of chatting about things other than the topic at hand. Our assessment indicates that the function of their behavior is attention. We work out an informal contract with them: if they are able to stop talking (off-task) and are able to get their project work finished according to the directions and the criteria of the particular steps on which they are working, with the extra time available from their efficient work, when the work is done, we can take a three-minute break for people to chat.

✦ **The reinforcer does not undermine other areas of the student's life in class or the life of the learning community.** Giving a student a "no homework" pass as a reinforcer is usually inappropriate. It suggests that having no homework is a positive condition while simultaneously suggesting that homework is a form of punishment. This is not a message we want to give to students.

We Have Two Overarching Ideas We Must Keep in Mind if We Want to Be Successful in Supporting Behavior Change

Success Teaches

I cannot emphasize this point enough. We need to be sure a student experiences recognizable cues and reinforcement to achieve progress towards the ultimate goal, *particularly* if the behavior being learned is a complex or multistep skill.

Fluency in a Skill Must Be Reinforced in Successive Approximations before Accuracy Is Reinforced

For successful learning, students need to become fluent in a skill before we address accuracy. If we jump in too quickly to evaluate for accuracy, students shut down, and learning (as well as self-esteem, in many cases) is threatened.

Example: Have you ever watched a toddler learning how to walk? What do those around her do as she makes her first attempts to get up onto her feet? They certainly do *not* become critical when she falls down. They encourage any attempt she makes. They also do not wait until she can walk around the room without falling before they clap or coo at her hard work. We need to provide this kind of reinforcement with students. Social skills, like any other skills, take time and refinement to become an integral part of a person's behavior schema. Students need challenges, but they need to experience reasonable amounts of success to keep them striving to meet those challenges.

As someone is learning a new skill or learning how to apply a new concept, two important questions come into play: *How am I doing?* and *How can I do this even better than I am now?* Therefore, for us as teachers, the two corresponding questions become these: *How can we give students useful information about their work?* and *How can we support their movement to that next level?* Providing useful, constructive feedback, as discussed in Chapter 7, should help with this process.

What Constructive Strategies Support an Increase in Behavior?

Guided Practice

This strategy gives students an opportunity to practice a new skill with the guidance that ensures success. Guided practice takes many forms, including teacher-led learning experiences, cooperative learning experiences, and peer tutoring sessions. The basic steps of this strategy are (Maag, 2018):

Step 1: Model: Present the task and ask for a response.

> Example: *"Nev, you are upset with Andy. We have talked about how important it is to be able to deal with our feelings and let people know (respectfully) how we feel about what they did. Let's practice." "Remember, the pattern is, 'When you _____, I feel _____.' What can you say to Andy?"*

Step 2: Lead: Immediately respond with a prompt of the correct answer.

> Example: *"Andy, when you …"*

Step 3: Test: Have the student respond, and give him feedback immediately on his response.

> Example: *"Yes, you remembered to say what the person did and how you felt. You also used the word 'when' instead of saying he made you felt a certain way. Well done, Nev."*

Repeat these steps until the student has the skill somewhat in hand. As soon as the student is ready, repeat the steps, but increase the amount of time before offering the correct response prompt. Continue to increase the time delay of the correct response prompt. As soon as possible, fade out the prompt so the student is responding correctly quickly and independently with natural reinforcement.

> Example continued: *"Try it one more time. This time, let's see if you have all the parts on your own."*

> [Student speaks.]

> *"Yes! You remembered on your own all the parts of what to say. It is not easy to tell people how we feel. I hope you feel good about what you have just done. Now you are ready to tell Andy."*

Contracts

Contracts not only support positive behavior change; they build students' skills at managing their own behavior by giving them the power to work collaboratively with the teacher to support the development of a constructive behavior. Contingency contracts describe the relationship between the student's behavior and what will happen if the student reaches a predetermined criterion of success. Any form of constructive reinforcement can be integrated, including activities, privileges, and natural reinforcers. A contract is most effective when it is *negotiated between* teacher and student. As with rules, if the student is involved in creating the contract, she understands what she has to do to live up to her side of the agreement. Therefore, she feels more committed to its success. Homme (1970) developed the idea of contingency contracting using basic tenets that are still appropriate today. The contract is positive, clear, fair, rewards accomplishment rather than obedience, and is used systematically. As with all successful reinforcement, An initial contract requires and rewards small approximations. The reinforcement occurs as soon as possible after the goal behavior occurs—initially on a one-to-one basis until the behavior change is firmly established.

There Are Seven Steps to Develop a Written Contract

Step 1: Explore the rationale for the contract with the student. Identify the behavior that should be changed. Explain why. *I've noticed that you can do your math well, but you seem to be having difficulty getting your work done on time because you are chatting with your neighbors about anything other than math. This also seems to distract them from doing their work. I'd like to help you find a way to stay on track.*

Step 2: Work with the student to carefully define the behavior. Be sure everyone agrees on precisely what we would see and/or hear. Discuss the criterion by which that behavior would be considered successful *at this point in time.* (Once progress has been made and seems to be well established, you and the student can decide how the criterion might be revised.)

Step 3: Agree on the initial rate and level of reinforcement for the change.

Step 4: Agree on the time/date when the behavior will be evaluated and the reinforcement (hopefully) earned.

Step 5: Prepare the contract.

Step 6: Have both parties sign the contract, and choose a specific date when the contract will be revisited to consider any needed adjustments.

Step 7: If either party does not live up to her end of the contract, we recognize this as an indication that the contract is not working and needs to be revised.

There are levels of contracts. In the first level, we determine the behavior required and the reward to be given. We know from our previous discussion that having the control in the teacher's hands is not the most productive form of intervention, so while this is a possibility, I would not recommend it for most situations with individual students. Instead, I would advocate for a discussion of the behavior change goal, the rationale, and an exploration of possible consequences that the student would find sufficiently reinforcing to support the change.

The last level of contract has the roles in reverse. This level puts the behavior, the evaluation, and the reinforcement in the hands of the student. The student is able to use the process as a means of (systematic) self-management. As we have said, this self-management is the ultimate goal of any behavior change support plan.

The levels in between the first and last shift the responsibility from teacher to student. How we move through those levels depends on the developmental level of the student and her needs. While we begin at the level that would be most appropriate to ensure success for the student, over time, we want to achieve the gradual fading of teacher control and the simultaneous strengthening of student control until the student is managing herself and the reinforcer is a natural one.

Contracts can be used alone or in conjunction with other intervention strategies. They can also be used with an individual or with more than one student at a time. Below is an example of a contract written by an elementary teacher for her class. As you read it, consider which level of control the teacher chose. What is the nature of the reinforcement?

Table 11-2. **Example of a Class Contract**[i]

Thursday, September 28

Dear Children,

After school today as I was thinking about you, I smiled when I remembered the interesting ideas you had as we discussed "A Wrinkle in Time". I wondered how I could help you become better listeners when we talk as a while class. I came up with these ideas that I think will help during whole class discussions:

> *Hands and bodies still*
>
> *Eyes on the speaker*
>
> *Raise a hand to get a turn and wait to be called on before speaking*
>
> *Talk only to the whole group*

I will remind you about the rules for the next few days each time we have a discussion about our book. We will also ideas about to help you remember, and I will post your ideas. Soon you will be able to remember them on your own.

Tape this chart to your desk. Mark yourself each day after we finish talking about "A Wrinkle in Time. Mark X if you remembered. Mark O if you forgot. By the end of next week, if you can fill in at least three boxes with an X, we will have a mini celebration.

I am cheering you on,

Ms. X

When we talked about "A Wrinkle in Time":	F	M	Tu	W	Th	F
I kept my hands and body still.						
I kept my eyes on the person speaking.						
I raised my hand when I wanted a turn to speak (and I waited quietly to be called on before speaking).						
I spoke only to the whole group.						

Table 11-2: Adapted from Margaret Bruell.

In Chapter 12, you will find an example of an entire grade-level contract written for middle school students. This contract included both reinforcement and punishment.

What Ethical Considerations Shape Our Choices?

Our first ethical responsibility is to consider the *nature of the goal*. For whose sake are we seeking this change in behavior? While it can be tempting to support a change that will benefit a teacher or other students in the class, these benefits alone are not enough for any behavior support plan goal. The key issue is how this change will contribute to the child's education, to the development of his character, "the person as a whole both … now and … what he might become" (Buber, 1971, p. 486).

Our second ethical responsibility is to consider the *nature of the strategies* chosen. Are our means ethical?

Our third ethical responsibility is to consider how we behave as we implement the strategies we have chosen.

Take a moment now to reread your philosophy statement from Beginning Reflection B. Complete the reflection below.

REFLECTION OPPORTUNITY

What beliefs do you want to consider as you design an intervention? Make a list below or on a separate piece of paper.

_____

_____

_____

_____

_____

Reread your philosophy statement once again. On a separate piece of paper or in the space provided list those aspects of your beliefs you want to have in mind as you implement an intervention.

_____

_____

_____

_____

_____

How Can We Design an Intervention to Support an Increase in a Behavior?

Below is a series of steps for an intervention that is designed to establish or increase a constructive behavior. Note that while some of the steps may be written as though this process is to be done alone, I do not believe that you need to do it alone or that this would be in the student's best interests. At any point, you might naturally and productively include not only the student but also the student's parent/guardian and your colleagues.

Step 1: Determine the desired constructive behavior that is the end goal of the intervention. Be specific. Determine what the prerequisite skills are for the goal behavior. Determine if these skills are in the student's repertoire. If not, make a plan for teaching them.

Step 2: Determine what variables exist in the physiological environment to support the change and how you can constructively use the student's strengths, intelligences, learning styles, etc. to help ensure success in the design. Determine what variables in the student's physiological environment might interfere with the success of the intervention. Consider how these should be addressed to support the change process.

Step 3: Using any available data, determine what antecedent condition/cue would likely trigger the constructive behavior for this student. If there is no useful data, consider how you will gather that data and involve others, including the student, to determine the antecedent cue. If you use a contrived cue, determine the natural cue you will pair with this contrived one. In case the cue is not effective, determine what alternative cues and prompts would be helpful to have at the ready. Determine the steps you will take to fade the prompts as the student makes progress during the intervention.

Step 4: Determine what consequent condition would reinforce the constructive behavior. If you feel the power of a primary reinforcer is needed to ensure the initial change, pair it with a natural one, including a social reinforcer. Determine what consequent conditions in the physical and psychosocial environments need to be addressed to support an increase in the constructive behavior once it has been exhibited. Decide how you and others will address these variables.

Step 5: Before you begin, take time to reflect. Consider if the design of the intervention is such that the student will learn from it and be empowered by what is learned. If this intervention is successful, will it build the student's character? Will it increase her independence? Will it empower her to work constructively with others? Will it enhance her life? Last but not least, ask yourself if the intervention is a realization of your philosophy. When you implement it, will your actions be—to quote Ralph Waldo Emerson—"a picture book of your creeds"?

How Can We Introduce an Intervention to Increase or Decrease a Behavior?

Successfully setting up a behavior change intervention takes time. Not only do we need to analyze our data and think about possibilities before we talk with the student, we also need time to meet with the student privately. As rushed as we are as teachers, spending this time is well worth the investment. Here are steps to follow in your discussion with the student.

Step 1: Explain the need for a behavior change. In Chapter 9, we discussed the possibility of having the student collect data. Whether he has or has not, we can involve him constructively in the diagnostic process. One way is to share the data with him (without our notes or any other means of interpretation) and invite his analysis. If he is not able to analyze the data, then we can share our perception of the data.

- Talk with the student about why you think a behavior change is needed. (We briefly considered one example above when we addressed establishing a contract with a student.)

  Example: *"Kip, here are some patterns I have observed: _____"* or *"Cameron, this is what I often see when you are working with others on your project: _____."*

- If the student can understand the data, share the *baseline* data in an objective, descriptive manner or invite the student to describe what he sees in the data.

  Example: *"Kip, when _____ happens, I have seen you _____* (unconstructive behavior). *"In fact, in the last week I have counted ___ times that this happened."*

- Foster the student's grasp of the effect of the behavior.

  Example: *"What happens, Kip, when you chat while your group is supposed to be doing an experiment?"* or *"Cameron, when you do this, what happens?"*

  If the student has difficulty responding, you might foster his reflection by gently asking such questions as *"How do others respond?"* or *"What happens to the teamwork/class/your work when you do this?"*

- Share your perception of the effects of the unconstructive behavior. This step is optional. If the student has already indicated an understanding that his behavior is not constructive, then you may choose not to add your perspective, you may add any other consequences you have observed, or you may simply agree.

It is essential that this conversation takes place without shaming or blaming. You want to maintain or enhance self-esteem. The focus is on sharing information as the basis for defining a problem that will be solved by working together to support and celebrate change.

Step 2: Gain student's agreement to work with you to support change.

Example: "Skylynne, I would like to help you change this behavior so that _____" or "You are often kind, Davida. I have seen you help other people. Let's find a way to bring out your kindness even more."

Step 3: Target the behavior change focus: With the student, target one specific behavior for the focus of change. Together, create a description that is clear to both of you and any other adults who will be supporting the change. Use the *"Can you see it, or hear it, or feel it?"* test to be sure the behavior is defined in objective terms. You can add smell, if the behavior has to do with cooking, or the use of chemicals or other materials in which odor plays a role.

Example: "Tina Marie, you have decided you want to be able to work longer at a time. Let's imagine I was looking at you through a camera while you were working. What would I see you do? If my camera could record, what would I hear you say? Let's make a list so that both you and I know what we mean when we say 'work longer.'"

Step 4: Determine the function of the behavior: Talk about the purpose of the unconstructive behavior. Use a motivation scale, if that would be illuminating. If you are not sure of the function, ask with a slight pause after each question. (In the example below each question addresses one of the functions of behavior. Can you determine which?).

Example: "Chelsie, do you think you are doing _____ because you want to feel, calm things down, or add a little excitement to what is going on?" [Pause.] "Because you want someone in the class or me to pay attention to you?" [Pause.] "Because you are trying to get something you want or feel you need to have?" [Pause.] "Because you don't like to write stories or because you don't want to sit where you do when you write?" If the student has difficulty answering, you could say, "Since right after you do it, this happens_____, I think you want to_____. Does that make sense to you?"

Step 5: Determine the constructive behavior focus: Given the function(s) of the behavior as a basis, brainstorm possible alternative constructive behaviors. Weigh the merit of each until you both agree on one that seems promising. Remember, doing the constructive alternative must be reinforcing for the student—must address the function of the unconstructive behavior, or eliminate its need, or the change won't occur.

Step 6: With the student, determine if the constructive behavior is one he can exhibit already. If not, choose a way to teach the behavior and any prerequisite skills that might also be needed.

Step 7: Change the environmental variables/the setting events. Talk about changes in the environment that would support the change to the alternative behavior changes in the physical environment and changes in the psychosocial environment. To the degree that the student is cognitively able to reason with you, empower the student as you do this.

Example: "Do you think it would be easier for you to _____ if we _____?" or "Would _____ help you remember to do this?"

Step 8: Determine the antecedent conditions. Talk about the specific cue(s) that will be used to elicit the constructive alternative.

Example: "I have noticed, Ashlee, that in other situations it seems most helpful to you when you are told something directly. Would you like me to specifically tell you when the time comes? Is there another kind of signal that would be more helpful to you?"

Step 9: Determine the consequent conditions. Choose the reinforcement *with* the student. You can chat or use a questionnaire or prepared interview form. Do this in the context of supporting the student's efforts to change. Remember, you are modeling a process that you hope the student will learn to use whenever she senses that change is needed. In your discussion, include considerations of whether the reinforcer is in balance with the effort required to make the change. Will it be enough? Is it too much? Will it meet the need that triggered the unconstructive behavior in the first place?

Step 10: If you are going to use a contract, follow the steps outlined to design one jointly.

Step 11: Talk about who else might support the change: Are there other people whose participation in the intervention would feel helpful to the student?

> **Example:** *"Roberto, I've noticed that you enjoy talking with Mr. _____. Would you like to share your progress with him?"*

> **Example:** *"Trish, you seem to work well with Ms. ____. Is she someone with whom you'd like to share your successes?" or "Is she someone you'd like to have a few moments of time with, if you can get your work done on time?"*

Often, even a few minutes of time with key people can be a powerful reinforcer. The key person may be a nurse, bus driver, administrator, previous or current teacher, aide, coach, lunchroom staff member, or teacher in one of the specialty areas—any adult who works in the school. I had a middle school student who worked well with a particular teacher and felt more successful in her class than during any other time of the day. When I asked him if he would like to have anyone else involved, he wanted to use her as the reinforcement—but he didn't say it that way. What he *did* say was that he wanted her to know when things got better. At first, he was uncomfortable talking with her about it, so he asked if I could write a note that he could give it to her as he entered class. Then, as he made progress, he was able to shift to my writing less often, then from a written note to his telling her. In the end, he would just occasionally tell her how well things were going. Another student (in an elementary class) wanted the opportunity to walk down to the office with a note he could give to the office secretary. For yet another student, it was a couple of minutes chatting with the custodian that became the means of celebrating the progress.

A middle school guidance counselor with whom I worked had pizza lunches every other week to celebrate all sorts of good news with students. The group did not talk about why they were there in order to preserve confidentiality about their changing behavior. Instead, they talked about sports, the latest music, or whatever was important to them. The guidance counselor was effective in using these informal moments to help the students get to know each other. Not only was he reinforcing them for their constructive behaviors, he was also building community and fostering the students' self-esteem.

Step 12: If needed, work with the student to foster the development of the prerequisite skills and the skills of the new behavior.

Step 13: With the student, determine the time you will meet again to talk about the progress of the intervention and to determine what changes, if any, are needed.

Example: *"George, I want us to talk again so that we can look at how things are going and figure out if there is anything that you or I need to do to make this change even more successful. Do you think meeting at the end of the week would be soon enough?"*

Step 14: Begin! Don't forget to pair any contrived reinforcer with a natural one when you implement the support plan, and continue to collect data, or have the student collect it, throughout.

Step 15: With the student, analyze the data to determine if the change is moving in the desired direction. Remember that if you are using extinction as part of the intervention, there may be an increase in the unconstructive behavior until the student realizes that the old reinforcer does not exist.

When analyzing behavior with students, we may learn that the student behavior is prompted by hurtful behavior from someone else. At those moments, I believe we need to say something. We need to let children and young adults know that their safety is of utmost importance to us. In essence, we need to say, "I do not know why people do that, but I believe that it is wrong. Children and young adults should never be treated that way."

Then we need to do whatever is appropriate to protect the student from the behavior, prevent it from ever happening again, and support change in the person who exhibits/exhibited this behavior. Some people make excuses for inappropriate behavior. I have heard statements such as "She has it coming to her after all the times she has done that" or "Oh, children this age do this kind of thing"—referring to teasing or excluding another student. People may do all sorts of things, but that doesn't make their actions right. We know how to intervene in ways that enable *both* the bully and the victim to be safe.

If we ever have any reason to believe that a student is being emotionally or physically abused at home or in school, we are required by law to report our suspicions to protect the child from such heinous behavior to the person designated in each school for reporting such concerns.

How Can We Help the Student Move Towards Generalization?

Usually, the student needs to exhibit the goal behavior in more than one setting and context. However, *generalization rarely occurs automatically*. More often than not, it needs to be supported as part of the behavior change support plan. How might we do this? When the student's constructive behavior seems to become a part of her repertoire in one setting, we help her recognize the need to use the behavior elsewhere. We also ensure that the cues and the reinforcement for the constructive behavior will exist in the other setting(s) and that she is alert to the nature of those cues.

Examples: *"Erin, you have been doing such a good job of asking for help when you need it. Look at the difference it has made in this class. Do you remember what it was like before? What changes do you see? I think you are ready to try this strategy in math class. What will Ms. Gonzales say that will tell you to listen carefully because she is about to give the assignment directions?"*

As we talk about strategies for generalization, our choice of words can be based on what motivates the student.

Examples: If this student likes challenges, we could smile and say, *"Are you up for the challenge of now doing this when we are reading, Elyse?"*

Example: If the student likes attention, we could say, *"Johan, this will give you a chance to ask Ms. Longusa any questions you have."*

How Do We Reflect on the Degree of Success of an Intervention?

Success is never final. Failure is never fatal. It is courage that counts.[ii]

Before we discuss reflecting on success, I think we need to put our work into context. If we have tried a way of supporting change and discovered that the intervention is not working as we hoped, have we failed? Not at all. I think of Edison, who was asked if he was discouraged that he had tried over 200 ways to create the filament of a light bulb and none had worked. He responded that he wasn't—now he knew over 200 materials that *didn't* work. So it is with supporting change. There is no one right answer. Humans are incredibly complex beings. So are the contexts in which we teach and learn. Sometimes we are not successful with our first design, so we go back to the drawing board and refine the pieces.

Behavior evolves. Supporting its change is a work in progress. I think the most useful perspective is to consider *where we are* and *where we want to go and then find a constructive way to get there.*

We Use Data Analysis

To consider the effects of the intervention thus far and design next steps, we look at quantitative data. We analyze what the data tells us regarding the direction the change seems to be taking and what correlates with that change. Earlier in the book, when we addressed collecting data to support our work, I stated how essential it was to continue to collect the same kind of data during the implementation phase of the behavior change support plan. We do this to get feedback—quantitative evidence of the degree to which the intervention is succeeding, that change is occurring in the direction we hoped. As we have said, visual illustrations of data are particularly useful. Below, in Table 11-3 (*Comparison of 20-Minute Baseline and Intervention Data for Target Behavior*) is a sample of data collected prior to intervention (baseline data that we looked at in Chapter 10) and then the same kind of data collected once the intervention had begun.

Table 11-3. Comparison of 20 Minute Baseline and Intervention Data for Target Behavior

Number of times in 20 mins. S gave answer before being called on by teacher

Baseline

	7/2	7/3	7/4	7/5	7/8	7/9	7/10	7/11	7/12
11									
10									
9									
8									
7							M		
6	M		M			M			
5		M		M	M			E	E
4	E		ME	E		M			M
3		E			E	E	E		
2									
1									

Dates data were collected during Math (M) at 8:00 AM and English Language Arts (E) at 10:00 AM—both whole class discussions

Intervention

	7/15	7/16	7/17	7/22	7/23	7/24
11						
10						
9						
8						
7						
6						
5						
4	M		ME	E	E	
3	E	ME		M		E
2						M
1						

Dates data were collected during Math (M) at 8:00 AM and English Language Arts (E) at 10:00 AM—both whole class discussions

Comparing the intervention data (on the right) collected on the *target* behavior in math and in English/language arts with that gathered during baseline (on the left), what patterns in the two data do you see, if any? Do you see an increase, a decrease, or approximately the same amount of target behavior recorded? If there are any changes, are there any variables that seem to correlate with those changes: Is the change subject specific? Does the time of day make a difference? Does attendance or lack of it seem to affect the behavior? Does the passing of time in general seem to correlate with some change? (Note the dates highlighted in gray that indicate the second week of intervention.)

While it may be tempting to look only at the target behavior data to see if there is concrete evidence that it is decreasing, we are using an ecological model. This means we need to analyze one more set of data to thoroughly determine what patterns are occurring with the goal behavior—the constructive alternative. That data is shown below in Table 11-4.

Table 11-4. Comparison of 20 Minute Baseline and Intervention Data for Goal Behavior

Number of times in 20 mins. S raised hand and waited to be called on before giving an answer

Baseline Data

#	3/2	3/3	3/4	3/5	3/8	3/9	3/10	3/11	3/12
11									
10									
9									
8									
7									
6									
5									
4									
3									
2									
1	E	ME	E	E	ME	ME			
0	M		M	M			ME	ME	ME

Dates data were collected during Math (M) at 8:00 AM and English Language Arts (E) at 10:00 AM—all were whole class discussions

Intervention Data

#	3/15	3/16	3/17	3/22	3/23	3/24
11						
10						
9						
8						
7						
6						
5					M	
4	M		M	M	M	
3		M	M			
2						
1			E			
0	E	E		E	E	

Dates data were collected during Math (M) 8:00 AM and English Language Arts (E) 10:00 AM—all were whole class discussions

Once again, as we reflect on the data, we can ask questions. Comparing the intervention data collected in math and in English/language arts with that gathered during baseline, what patterns in the two data of the goal behavior do you see, if any? If there are any changes, are there any variables that seem to correlate with those changes: Is the change subject specific? Does the time of day make a difference? Does attendance or lack of it seem to affect the behavior? Does the passing of time in general seem to correlate with some change? (Note the dates highlighted in gray that indicate the second week of intervention.)

As we analyze both sets of data, we see that the target behavior has decreased in math and the goal behavior has increased in math, whereas the target behavior has stayed approximately the same in English and the occurrence of the goal behavior has also stayed the same in English. Another pattern is that after the weekend, the target behavior increased in English, both during the baseline and the intervention phase.

We have seen variance between the target behavior in math and English. We also see variance in the goal behavior in math and English. These exist during both the time of baseline data collection and during intervention. Does this mean we should then consider what is *wrong* in English? No. Behavior occurs because it is supported. There is at least one cue (and perhaps more) for the behavior, and one or more consequent conditions are encouraging the behavior—constructive or not—to occur again. Therefore, the important questions are:

    ✦   What is happening in math that supports the goal behavior?

    ✦   How can we take those positive variables in any of the student's three environments in math and help them to occur in English?

As we consider these questions, it is important to talk with the student.

    Example: *"We need to improve how we are supporting you in remembering to raise your hand and wait to be called on before answering. This is some data I have collected. What do you see when you look at the number of times you raised your hand in math? What about English? How can we make this better for you?"* A follow-up question might be: *"What happens in math that helps you remember to not call out?"*

If time of day makes a difference, changing the student's schedule might make a difference, but that may also be difficult to implement. Other changes, however, might be positively powerful enough that the time of day would no longer be a variable that affects behavior. For example, are there characteristics of the kinds of activities in math that support the change that can be used in English? So goes the process of analysis and modification.

To repeat: behavior does not occur if it is not supported. We need to look at the variables in the student's three environments to determine how the target behavior is being cued and reinforced and diminish the power of both. At the same time, we need to look at what cues and reinforcers are happening for the *goal* behavior that encourage it to increase. If there are no clear patterns to help affect change, then perhaps we need to go back and collect more data or a different kind of data.

It helps to keep in mind that we are teaching an alternative behavior. In some cases, this may be a totally *new* behavior. If the target behavior isn't decreasing—which is what is happening for this student in English—we have some questions to ask: What function is the behavior serving? What need is being met when the behavior occurs? Concurrently, we need to ask how the target behavior is *not* being reinforced in math. How is the function of the goal behavior being addressed so that the unconstructive behavior *is* decreasing and the constructive behavior *is* on the rise? We can have an intervention that decreases the target behavior (calling out) but does *not* increase the goal behavior (waiting to be called on before talking). Instead, the student just stops contributing. We often think that a decrease in an unconstructive behavior automatically means an increase in a goal behavior. If the goal behavior is not the opposite of the target behavior and the goal behavior is not triggered and reinforced, then this may not happen.

What Questions Can We Ask to Support the Ongoing Design of an Intervention?

Below is a list of questions that are more conceptual in nature. They help us reflect on the nature of the intervention as a whole and then on each of the A, B, and C parts of the intervention as students move through the various stages of learning. Many of these questions are helpful to use (in a developmentally appropriate form) with the student when we have a conversation to monitor and evaluate progress. We can also use them to problem solve as we refine the intervention.

When we consider the nature of the intervention as a whole, we can ask:

- Is the student actively involved in the *ongoing* design and implementation of the intervention?
- Are the student's basic emotional needs being met?
- Is the intervention having a positive effect? Is it enhancing the student's ability to learn and adding to the learning environment for those in the class? Is it enhancing the student's social relationships? Is it offering a change that the student values?
- When the change in behavior does not seem to be occurring or is not evolving at an expected rate, we can look at the antecedent conditions, the nature of the goal for the behavior itself, and the consequent conditions and ask ourselves, is each appropriate?

If antecedent conditions do not seem to be effective eliciting the constructive behavior, we can ask:

- Are there still triggers for the unconstructive behavior that need to be addressed? If so, what can be done to weaken these triggers?
- Is the cue of an appropriate type and at an appropriate level, not more contrived or less contrived than needed to trigger the constructive behavior?
- If the cue alone is not effective in eliciting the constructive behavior, what additional prompts are needed to support this particular student's success in exhibiting the constructive behavior?
- Are the conditions (variables) in the physical and psychosocial environments sufficiently powerful to trigger the constructive behavior? Are these variables more compelling than those that trigger the unconstructive behavior? If not, what can be done to strengthen these variables?

If the student is having difficulty performing the constructive behavior, we can ask:

- Are the student's basic emotional needs being met so that he has not shut down to the learning process?
- Does the goal behavior need refinement because it is not realistic?
- Do prerequisite skills need to be taught?
- Do aspects of the constructive behavior need to be taught?
- Do we need to reteach or review the problem-solving, reflective-thinking steps that foster the occurrence of the behavior?

If the consequent conditions do not seem to be effective reinforcing the constructive behavior, we can ask:

- Does the student actually find this consequent event for the constructive behavior reinforcing?
- Is the reinforcement sufficiently powerful? If not, what can be done to strengthen it?
- Is the reinforcement being given *as soon as possible after* the constructive behavior (contingent upon its occurrence) so that the student connects it to the constructive behavior?

- Does the student connect the reinforcement to the appropriate behavior?
- Is the reinforcement at an appropriate level (not more or less contrived than needed)? If not, how can it be modified?
- Are there still reinforcers present for the unconstructive behavior that are competing with those for the constructive behavior? If so, how can we address this? How can those reinforcers be weakened or removed?

When the student is acquiring the new skill:

- Is there a shift towards more natural cues that elicit the constructive behaviors? If not, how can we foster this?
- Are the variables in the student's physical and psychosocial environments being addressed so that the variables that trigger the constructive behavior are consistently more powerful than those that trigger the unconstructive behavior? If not, how can we foster this?
- Is there a shift towards more natural reinforcers that can foster the constructive behavior? If not, how can we foster this?

When the student is transitioning to proficiency:

- As soon as the student no longer needs them, how do we plan to fade the cues over time?
- Have we been pairing the contrived cue with a natural one in anticipation of shifting to a more natural one? If not, how will we pair the reinforcers now?
- How do we plan to shift implementation of the reinforcement? How will we increase the time length of behavior required (for continuous stream behavior) or the ratio of number of behaviors to reinforcer (for countable behaviors)?

When the student is transitioning to maintenance:

- How will we shift to natural cues and reinforcers?
- How will we support memory of the skill, if needed?

When the student is transitioning to the generalization stage:

- How will we give the student more opportunities to exhibit the skill at different times, with different people, in different contexts and settings?
- How will we help the student prepare to apply the skill in a new arena?
- Are we ensuring that there are clear cues for the constructive behavior in the new contexts and settings?
- Are we ensuring that there are clear reinforcers for the constructive behavior in the new contexts and settings?
- Are we ensuring that there are reinforcers for any appropriate adaptations that the student makes in the behavior?
- Are we shifting towards natural reinforcers as soon as the student is ready to have that happen?

As a student progresses through the stages of learning a new skill, we need to continue using the original contrived reinforcer—but only intermittently—to support the persistence of the new behavior. To do this, we simply increase one of these three things: the ratio of the number of behaviors required before the reinforcement is earned; the length of behavior required before the reinforcement is earned; or the length of time required before the reinforcement is earned.

Once again, it is important to remember that there is no failure as we support change. There may be frustration, disappointment, and/or perhaps a bit of internal impatience. Change, however, is an ongoing process—not only the student's change but also our change as we use different strategies to support the student's learning and growth. This is not always an easy process for any of us. Two ideas may help foster how we think about the process of change as we help students and ourselves design (and redesign) behavior support plans. The first is, for change to occur the courage to change or persist at changing needs to be stronger than the fear of the change or the fear that the change will not be successful. Whether or not fear and courage are a factor, the second idea is that the reinforcement to change has to be stronger than the reinforcement for continuing things as they are.

. . . .

Application Activity: How Can We Shape Behavior Change?

Below are some examples of student behaviors that could be shaped. Write how you might reinforce successive approximations to the end goal.

Table 11-5. Examples of Student Behavior that Could be Shaped			
Current Student Behavior	The goal you believe would be constructive	The behavior you begin reinforcing to support change towards the final goal	The behavior you reinforce *next* to support change towards the end goal
1. Completes 2 out of 10 math problems			
2. Can participate in a team activity for 1–2 minutes before arguing about rules			
3. Takes 40 minutes to complete task she could reasonably complete in 20 minutes			
4. During clean-up picks up one item [out of many possible] and puts it away			
5. Writes essays that are 1/2 page long when assigned [and capable of writing] at least 3 pages			
6. Walks to sink, runs water over hands, dries hands, throws towel in trash.			

. . . .

We can shape the number of responses required (Items 1 and 4). We can shape the time required—we can require more or less time to complete a task (Item 3). We can shape the topography of a behavior (Items 2 and 6). We can shape how much of a behavior is required before we reinforce it (Item 5). (If you are interested in what ways I might shape each item, see the text's Appendix A Answer Key—AKTable 11-5, *Chapter 11: Examples of Student Behavior that Could be Shaped—Answers.*

Final Thoughts

We have considered ways to increase constructive behavior and how to do so constructively. We have looked at the nature of the cues in all three environments that trigger both constructive and unconstructive behavior and how we might adjust them to support positive change. We also looked at the nature of a behavior's consequent conditions and how we can alter them to support constructive change.

Looking Forward

Next, we will consider how to decrease unconstructive behavior. Once again, we will be analyzing what comes before and after the behavior in order to see what can be changed. We will analyze the role of punishment and its effects, but we will avoid all forms of punishment unless it has natural or logical consequences.

References and Resources

References and resources for Chapter 11 have been combined with those for Chapter 12 and can be found at the end of the Chapter 12 narrative.

. . . .

Appendix A

USING PROMPTS TO TRIGGER CONSTRUCTIVE BEHAVIOR AND HOW TO SHIFT FROM A MORE INTRUSIVE TO A LESSER ONE

Prompts are a second round of antecedents. They can also help a student do the behavior in a particular way. While we have many choices, because one of our goals is to enhance the student's sense of positive control, we want to use the least intrusive prompt. Therefore, I have arranged the list of choices from least intrusive to most (although 1, 2, and 3 are at the same level). We use the least intrusive prompt possible. Then, as the student's behavior suggests *that* level of support is no longer needed, we shift to a prompt that is even less intrusive.

1. **Gestural:**

    ♦ We point to a place in the chapter where the student needs to focus.

    ♦ We crook our finger and point it towards us to signal a student to come to us.

2. **Visual:**

    ♦ We provide additional written directions.

    ♦ We offer a picture illustration of the steps to be taken.

3. **Environmental:** We make specific arrangements in the physical or psychosocial environment variables and use those arrangements to indicate where (and perhaps when) the behavior is to be performed.

    ♦ On a 3 x 5 card, we make a list of steps to be taken and post it on the student's desk or table.

    ♦ We place a carrel on the top of a table or desk and tell the student that the exam needs to be taken there, where there will be less distractions.

4. **Indirect verbal prompt:** We speak in a way that implies a behavior should occur.

    ♦ *"Are you making a choice that is constructive right now?"*

    ♦ *"It would be terrific if all the students on team B could find a place to sit down quickly and quietly."*

    ♦ *"I have said that it is time for us to begin to read. So everyone should have a book in hand ready to do so."*

5. **Direct verbal prompt:** We speak directly to the student.

    ♦ *"As you leave, don't forget to hand me your 'Ticket to Leave' with one idea or fact you learned in class today."*

    ♦ *"For this next activity, take out your science lab book and a pencil."*

6. **Direct nonverbal, auditory, or tactile prompt:**

    ♦ We put a pager on vibrate for the student to keep in his pocket or on his desk so the sound or sensation prompts the student to elicit the behavior. This might be used to encourage the student to participate in 15-minute discussion more than once.

    ♦ We use a timer that goes off to indicate when the transition to the next activity will begin.

7. **Model:** Right after or during our directions, we demonstrate the desired behavior that students already know and encourage their imitation.

   ♦ We tiptoe in an exaggerated fashion to get the materials needed for the cooperative learning activity and encourage the "materials handlers" on each team to do likewise (but perhaps not in such an exaggerated fashion!).

   ♦ We come in the door with a coat on as if we were a student entering the room at the beginning of the day, hang the coat up on a hook in the cubby (in the room), place our permission paper in the right box, and sit down at our desk.

8. **Minimal physical prompt:** We provide a slight physical contact just to get the student going or to guide the student.

   ♦ We gently rest our hands on the student's shoulders while simultaneously pointing to the spot on the page where the math problem we are addressing exists. **Note:** This should only be done when we know in advance that the touch would not be perceived as unsafe.

   ♦ We gently tap under the student's upper arm to encourage her to raise her hand to have her idea recognized.

9. **Partial physical prompt:** We physically start the student on whatever needs to be done, *then release the touch so that the student completes the task independently.* **Note:** We should always let the student know before we touch her.

   ♦ *"Nancy, I am going to get you started by grasping the bat with you. Then I will release it as soon as you begin your swing."*

   ♦ *"Marcel, I am going to put my hand over yours to show you how to move your hand to start writing the cursive 'Z,' and then I will let go."*

10. **Full physical prompt:** We physically move the student through the entire task (e.g., using hand over hand). **Note:** We should always let the student know before we initiate this prompt.

    ♦ *"Dalia, I'm going to put my hand over yours to show how someone can hold this mouse to make the cursor move to the right place on the screen."*

    ♦ *"Chip, I'm going to put my hand over yours to show you how to write the letter 'q' in the sand tray."*

Appendix B

ADDITIONAL INFORMATION ON LEVELS AND TYPES OF REINFORCEMENT

		Table 11-6. **Additional Information on Levels and Types of Reinforcement**		
Level	Type of Reinforcement	Description	Category of Reinforcer	Examples
Lower (more basic)	Primary Reinforcers	Reinforcers that meet a biological need. They are not learned; they are an integral part of the person's neurological make-up.	1. Edible 2. Sensory	1. Food; liquids 2. Sleep (including rest or escape from stimulation); attention*; protection from elements that would be uncomfortable to the senses; sensory stimulation: proprioceptive experiences, e.g., bouncing, rocking. spinning; visual experiences, e.g., movement of toys, blinking colored lights, words, photos; auditory experiences, e.g., listening to music or a voice; tactile experiences, e.g., feeling a vibration, touching soft, rough or smooth materials, rubbing fingers together; taste experiences enjoying liquid or solid food; olfactory experiences, e.g., enjoying different kinds of smells or smells associated with positive experiences.
Higher (learned)	Secondary Reinforcers These are *learned* reinforcers.	Reinforcers that are learned (and, therefore, are also called conditioned reinforcers). What is reinforcing for one student may not be for another	3. Tangible (material) 4. a) Privilege b) Activity 5. Generalized 6. Social	3. Stickers, small prizes; e.g., pencils, easers, metal 'buttons' with pictures or sayings, sport team names or logos on them to wear or put on a book bag. 4. a) Being line leader; being the person who runs a piece of equipment, use of special equipment or supplies; b) Being able to take out extra books, CD's, DVD's. 5. Tokens, points, credits. 6. Anything that provides evidence of personal value or approval such as written or verbal praise, smile or gesture ('thumb up'), physical contact, proximity, e.g., letting a student sit next to the teacher or other important person in a group.

***Note:** Some theorists would question my placing attention in the primary reinforcer category. I believe that attention is a basic need. Most of us have heard of the failure to thrive of babies because they were left in their cribs, were not held, and were not talked to–in other words, they did not receive attention beyond the 'basic' needs of being fed and having their diapers changed. Knowledge of the importance of attention has led neonatal units in hospitals to include attention as part of the 'prescription' for health for the babies in their care. The babies are held and talked to. In my opinion, that is enough evidence to support the inclusion of attention as a basic need.

Endnotes

i   Note: I am not suggesting teachers should <u>recommend</u> medicating a student. In particular, medication for ADHD should not be seen as a quick fix. It should only be *considered* (not recommended) after other forms of intervention have been implemented and not deemed successful enough. Then we need to have a thoughtful discussion with the student's caregiver and other appropriate people about the possibilities and difficulties of medication.

ii This quote has been said to come from the words of Winston Churchill, Sam Rayburn (Speaker of the House for 17 years), and several coaches. My research has not enabled me to attribute it to any one person.

CHAPTER 12

Decreasing Unconstructive Behavior

[All children deserve] a champion—an adult who will never give up on them, who understands the power of connection, and insists that they become the best that they can possibly be.

—Rita Pierson

What Will This Chapter Discuss?

In Chapter 11, we learned that the *most* effective method for decreasing behavior involves a two-pronged approach—increasing a substitute, alternative, or opposite constructive behavior while simultaneously decreasing the unconstructive behavior. Now that we have talked extensively about strategies to establish or increase a constructive behavior, we will focus on the second prong of our approach: strategies to decrease an unconstructive behavior. We do not need to be punitive to support a decrease in a behavior. If we want an unconstructive behavior to occur less often, we must eliminate conditions that encourage its occurrence.

Why Is This Important?

As we have said, we need a consistently constructive way to support behavior change that enables us to decrease unconstructive behavior or eliminate it altogether.

What Will You Learn?

By the end of the chapter, you will be able to:

+ describe at least two strategies that address antecedent conditions to decrease constructive behavior;
+ describe at least two strategies that address consequent conditions to decrease constructive behavior;
+ describe at least two strategies that address the behavior itself to decrease constructive behavior;
+ explain why the use of punishment, other than logical or natural consequences, is not constructive; and
+ explain why the use of most punishment strategies is counter to our goals for our work with students.

What Do You Want To Accomplish?

What goal(s) do you have as you read about strategies for decreasing unconstructive behavior? Write your responses here or on a piece of paper.

_____

_____

_____

How Can We Use Our Assessments to Support Behavior Change?

Since we know behavior is affected by variables in all three student environments, we use our assessments—ecological, ABC, and functional—to determine which variables appear to have an impact on the unconstructive behavior. First, we integrate the ABC and ecological assessment information. We look at the Antecedents to the unconstructive behavior in each of the student's three environments. What physiological, physical, and psychosocial variables might have a *fueling effect* and trigger the unconstructive Behavior? Next, we analyze what effect the behavior had. What Consequences did the student experience in each of her environments as a result of the unconstructive behavior? Another way to phrase this is: What did the student gain by exhibiting this behavior? Having determined the variables that are the As and the Cs, we can then do a functional assessment. Whatever change occurred in any of the student's environments between the Antecedent and the Consequence tells us the function(s) of the unconstructive behavior. We notice the effect of the unconstructive behavior first and then go back and try to figure out what Antecedents would bother the student enough for her to take action to effect the change that occurred. If we know what variables fueled the unconstructive behavior and what change the student was trying to effect, then we can work with the student (and others) to reduce or eliminate the triggering effect of those variables or help the student find a constructive way to address that effect the in the future.

How Can We Address Antecedent Variables to Support Change?

We Address the Specific Antecedent Cue for the Unconstructive Behavior

We can remove the cue altogether or change it sufficiently so it no longer triggers as it once did. However, simply decreasing an unconstructive behavior by removing the cues for it is not the most efficient, effective strategy. That alone is frequently not enough to effect lasting change.

We Strengthen a Specific Cue for an Alternative Constructive Behavior

In addition to diminishing or removing the cue for the unconstructive behavior, we need to provide a strong cue for an alternative *constructive* behavior. If we are not able to remove the cue for the unconstructive behavior, the strength of the cue for the constructive behavior has to be much more powerful than the cue for the unconstructive one.

We Cue the Student to Exhibit the Constructive Behavior by Reinforcing Peers Who Already Exhibit it

This strategy is a variation of the "strengthen a cue" strategy. The intent is to have our reinforcement of peers function as a reminder of what behavior is appropriate. If the student wants teacher attention, the teacher reinforcement of peers serves as an enticement for him to do the same in the hopes of obtaining that same attention. When he does exhibit the behavior, we need to reinforce it immediately. However, reinforcing peers should be pursued with caution: we do not want to repeatedly compare a student with others. This can cause embarrassment to those being recognized, particularly within certain cultures and at certain ages. If we keep our recognition more general, we avoid this issue.

Example: When the student has a job such as Materials Manager on a cooperative team, we can say: *"The material managers of two teams are ready. A point each to those teams. Ah, now three are."* If an additional positive "punch" is needed, we could add, *"Three teams have now earned a point for being ready. A point will be given to any other team that is ready in the next 30 seconds."* (This cue-and-reinforcement strategy assumes that the points will lead to some future recognition the students know and feel will be fun.)

How Can We Address Consequent Variables to Support Change?

We Remove the Reinforcer for Unconstructive Behavior

Once we determine the function of the behavior we can eliminate the reinforcer. If our attention or a peer's is the reinforcer for the unconstructive behavior, we can eliminate the attention. If access to materials is the reinforcer, we can remove them. If escape from some aspect of a learning experience is the reinforcer, we can change the nature of the lesson content, materials, student grouping, timing, or instruction so escape is no longer reinforcing.

We Reinforce a Progressive Decrease in Unconstructive Behavior

We can reinforce a decrease in the frequency of an unconstructive behavior, its duration, or both. You may wonder if reinforcing a decrease in behavior runs the risk of *appearing* to sanction a certain amount of that behavior when, in reality, the goal is to eliminate it. One way to address this while also reinforcing successive approximations is to increase the incentive for moving closer and closer to the end goal.

We Reinforce Other Constructive Behavior When the Unconstructive Behavior is Not Occurring

In a situation in which a student is likely to exhibit the unconstructive behavior, *but he does not*, we reinforce him for what he is doing that is constructive. While in other intervention strategies we focus on a specific behavior to reinforce, in this case we reinforce any constructive behavior that occurs in place of an unconstructive one. Example: We are supporting Declan's decrease in interrupting *other students*. In small-group work with us, he reads a passage when requested, he writes notes on paper, he listens to our comments, and he writes answers to questions posted on a whiteboard. We reinforce these behaviors. Since other students did not speak, there was no opportunity to reinforce the goal behavior of "wait until others finish speaking before sharing your idea."

The advantage to this strategy is that it includes the reinforcement of appropriate behavior. However, while the larger category of appropriate behavior includes any alternatives to unconstructive target behavior, the connection between the reinforcer and a *specific* constructive *alternative* to the unconstructive behavior may be weak. The term "other behavior" does not provide the specificity that supports lasting behavior change. What behavior can the student exhibit *instead of* the unconstructive behavior? What specifically *is* a constructive alternative? We need to make this clear with the student and reinforce it, too.

We Reinforce an Incompatible Alternative to the Unconstructive Behavior

When we reinforce an incompatible alternative to an unconstructive behavior, the trick is to find a behavior that will effectively compete. Earlier in the book, you tried selecting a behavior that would successfully compete with each of the unconstructive behaviors in the chart below. Think of additional competing behaviors and add them to Table 12-1 below. The first has been filled in for you.

Table 12-1. Possible Constructive Behavior That is Incompatible with an Unconstructive Behavior	
Unconstructive Behavior	Constructive Behavior that is Incompatible
Hitting someone	While hands down at his sides, telling someone he is angry about what she is doing or asking someone to stop what she is are doing that is upsetting him.
Calling out answers	
Screaming	
Running in the hall	
Clowning around during a discussion	
Nose picking* in public	

*Note: Yes, nose picking is a 'gross' example, but I cannot count the number of times teachers have used that as a focus for a behavior change support plan. I certainly understand why.

We Enhance the Effectiveness of the Reinforcement for the Competing Constructive Behavior

Several previous strategies have included reinforcement of the alternative, substitute, or opposite to the unconstructive behavior. In order for any of these options to be successful, we must be sure that what we choose to reinforce the constructive behavior is more powerful than whatever is reinforcing the unconstructive behavior. We examined several ways to do this in Chapter 11.

We Create a Contract with the Student

We can design a contract with the student to reinforce the less frequent occurrence of the unconstructive behavior. Under "Create a Contract" in Chapter 11, we discussed the process we can use and the elements of an effective contract.

How Can We Address the Nature or Timing of the Behavior When What the Student Wants is Constructive?

We can teach the student how to constructively obtain what is wanted. Example: Ana waves her hand with great enthusiasm and frequently says, "Oh, oh, oh!" when she has an idea to share in group discussion. We work with her to silently raise her hand and maintain it in a motionless fashion until she is addressed.

We work with the student to find a way to support (and reinforce) his being patient and postponing getting what he wants until an appropriate time. Example: Hamad wants to briefly walk around to dissipate his increasing tension and anxiety. He needs to wait until the whole class is given a "brain break" or other opportunity to move out of their seats. We teach him how to breathe slowly and deeply and to clench and release muscles to foster his patience while he waits for an appropriate time to walk about.

How Can We Address the Function of Attention and Obtaining Tangibles?

The strategies we have already addressed support us in addressing an "unconstructive" behavior when its function is attention or tangibles.

How Can We Address the Function of Sensory Regulation?

We Provide Variety in Learning Settings, Materials, Teaching Strategies Within a Lesson, and Kinds of Responses Required

We orchestrate variety or offer students choices to meet their needs. Planning for variety and offering of choices are also opportunities for us to consider both how students learn through their multiple intelligences and the importance of differentiating instruction.

We Address the Stimulation Level of the Shift Required by Two Contiguous Parts of a Lesson, Two Lessons, or Two Contexts

When students are moving from a high stimulation activity, such coming in to a class from lunch, recess, physical education, an assembly program, or a bus ride, often many cope more successfully if the first activity we facilitate is moderate in stimulation level rather than low. The first task does not have to be very long. In fact, it can be a transition process that leads into the quieter lesson.

We Consider the Length of Time a Student Spends at a Particular Level of Stimulation

If the required stimulation level is difficult for the student—whether it is working at a specific task or during the "wait time" needed at some point in the learning process—, we shorten that portion of the learning experience for her, if not for all students. If the stimulation level is just what the student needs to work well on a task, whenever possible we lengthen that portion of the learning process.

We Provide Structure that Supports Students in Addressing the Variety of Stimulation Levels that Occur Every Day in a Class

We provide predictable routines, directions, activities, room arrangements, materials, and equipment. We control the environment to prevent extreme and/or sudden variations in stimulation among learning experiences and during transitions. We let students know ahead of time when changes are going to occur so they are not caught off guard and can, thereby, cope more effectively with a new teacher, new learning experience, or a change in the schedule.

We Respond to Different Stimulation Level Needs Simultaneously

One strategy we use is alternating high-stimulating tasks with moderate and low ones so that students have a chance to experience the level of stimulation that best suits their needs. To help those who need support during the transition between activities with these different stimulation levels, we can use presignals to warn students that change is about to occur and thus to ease them through transitions. Between a high a low stimulation level activity, we can include a brief, moderately stimulating activity, such as a couple of rounds of "Simon Says" or a few stretching exercises. Providing a calming process at the end of a high-stimulation learning experience can also help (e.g., we can ask students to close their eyes, take a deep breath, and recall one idea they want to remember; picture themselves doing the process they just learned; draw a picture in their mind's eye of _____. If they need more help with what they just learned, they could picture who could provide it, when, and how they could ask that person for that help).

Another essential strategy is to teach students coping mechanisms to ease themselves through transitions to different stimulation levels, such as deep breathing or self-piloting, that are constructive in the school setting, that they can employ independently, and are useful throughout life.

How Can We Address the Function of Escape?

The function of escape is particularly powerful. Any behavior that allows a student to remove himself or be removed from a situation is being fostered by negative reinforcement—the desire to escape an unpleasant feeling associated with a setting, a task, an individual, or a group of people. More often than not, a student tries to escape when, from his perspective, his basic need for safety or efficacy is at risk and he cannot figure out a way to address that. Escape behavior is a hard-wired response of protection. We need to determine why the student feels the need to escape and how to address the variables to help the student to act constructively.

The desire to escape is often paired with the function of sensory regulation because the student is trying to cope with intense internal feelings of anxiety, frustration, depression, or shame—to name just a few examples. Once we know from what the student is escaping, we have many options.

We Help the Student Determine Which Kinds of Learning Experiences Seem Best Suited to that Individual's Learning and Stimulation Needs

We support students' discovery of needs, interests, and strengths. We helps students begin to build the kind of information that is essential to the development of constructive self-advocacy, coping mechanisms, and, therefore, resilience.

We Reduce the Negative Impact of Variables in the Student's Physiological Environment *or* of a Mismatch Between Variables in the Student's Physiological and Physical Environments

We support the student in addressing the particular variable or coping with a given condition that has the negative impact. We can work alone with the student and we can work with other professionals and the student's parent/caregiver to effect change. We need to ask (and we can ask the student directly): What is it about this setting/context/student arrangement/task, etc., that makes her want to escape? Then, to the degree possible, we can address any mismatch and help the student develop coping mechanisms.

We Build Constructive Behavior Momentum

We have the student do two or three tasks at which she feels competent—the types of tasks we already know that she typically completes readily—before we ask her to do the lesson that seems to precipitate escape behavior.

We Build Success

We arrange the learning sequence of the whole class lesson so that the student experiences incremental and ongoing success.

We Reinforce Partial Task Completion so that Encouragement Comes Frequently

To build the student's feelings of competence we support the strategies the student is using to cope with completing the task.

We Give Frequent Constructive Feedback that Supports the Student's Successful Completion of the Task at Hand

We foster the student's thinking and problem solving by offering useful information to help shape the student's efforts towards success.

We Change the Nature or Sequence of the Instruction or the Activity

We manage the level of stimulation in the task. We give directions in smaller chunks, tasks in *shorter* spurts, or smaller instructional pieces to ensure the student's success. We intersperse activities, materials, groupings, and curricular foci that the student prefers into those he does not. We offer choices.

We Let the Student Know Ahead of Time that if He has Worked Appropriately, He Can Have Brief Breaks in the Middle of the Whole-Class Activity When We Give the Signal

These breaks can help dissipate the tension students experience as they work on tasks. A break could be an action that the student chooses from a list developed with us. Note: Brief "brain breaks" for the entire class can also help any student's brain process what has just been learned (Immordino-Yang, 2015).

We Provide Presignals and Safety Signals

We provide the student with cues before the activity and prompts during the activity that give her information about what she can expect in a way that promotes her self-control and tolerance of the activity or facilitates her asking for help with the task.

We Use the Design of the Physical Environment to Support a Constructive Means of Coping

We use the location of equipment and materials to provide a space that helps the student cope with whatever uncomfortable sensation she is experiencing as she faces the task she would like to escape.

We Address Variables in the Student's Psychosocial Environment

We enhance the positive impact or we reduce the negative impact of these variables. We provide variety in group work: we change the students with whom the student is working, or the number of students involved, or which particular students are in a given group, or the closeness of one or more students.

How Can We Use Extinction as a Strategy?

· ·

ACCESSING PRIOR KNOWLEDGE/EXPERIENCE

In the space provided or elsewhere write what you recall about extinction and its effect as a consequent condition: _____

_____

_____

· ·

To review: when extinction occurs, all variables that may be reinforcing a behavior are removed prior to the occurrence of the behavior, not as a result of it. Since the behavior no longer causes something pleasurable, it is less likely to occur over time because it loses its purpose. How long it takes until the behavior disappears completely varies greatly from situation to situation.

Extinction is not punishment. Extinction does not *result* in something unpleasant occurring after the student behaves in a particular way, as occurs with punishment. Extinction *is* like punishment in that both lessen the likelihood that a particular behavior will occur. However, with extinction, no pleasurable consequence occurs, whereas with punishment, an unpleasant experience occurs.

We Keep the Function of the Behavior in Mind as We Consider Using Extinction

Extinction works best in response to an unconstructive behavior whose purpose seems to be to gain attention or use attention to escape doing a task. If a student is sighing heavily or complaining in response to a reasonable request or tattling (not asking us to help solve a problem) to get our attention, or if a student is clowning around instead of doing the task at hand, or engaging us in an argument about the details of an assignment rather than getting to work, then walking away without providing the attention while simultaneously paying attention to something or someone else is one way to decrease the behavior. On the other hand, if the function of an unconstructive behavior is to escape by leaving the room, obtain something tangible within reach, or regulate stimulation, then extinction would not be the intervention of choice.

Student's Usual Responses to Extinction Occur in Two Phases

During the **first phase** of a student's response, which occurs immediately after the reinforcer no longer exists, the unconstructive behavior almost always increases in rate or intensity (Alberto & Troutman, 2017). This makes sense. The student is wondering if he should engage in the behavior for a longer period of time or do it more intensely to get the desired response. A period of experimentation occurs. How long the student goes through this first phase depends in large measure on how consistently the behavior was being reinforced before extinction occurred. When one-to-one reinforcement stops, the brain is able to figure out the change quite quickly. However, if the student was reinforced for the unconstructive behavior only every so often, without any particular pattern, it may take longer to extinguish the behavior. It is important for us to not give up extinguishing the unconstructive behavior during this first phase. If we hang on and if the other students hang on so there is no positive consequence for the unconstructive behavior—then the second phase is likely to occur. During the **second phase**, the unconstructive student behavior begins to decrease if the reinforcer has consistently been absent. Important Note: *If we cue the alternative constructive behavior ahead of time and then reinforce it when the student exhibits it, this experimentation may take far less time or not occur at all (Shea & Bauer, 2012).* See below for further details.

Before We Use Extinction, We Need to Setup an Intervention to Cue and Reinforce an Alternative Behavior

There are two reasons why this setup is particularly important. The first is that, as we have said, just showing students what NOT to do doesn't teach them what to do constructively instead. The second equally important reason is that if we use the two-pronged approach by both extinguishing the unconstructive behavior *and,* in advance *of putting the intervention in place, we set up a surefire way to elicit and reinforce an alternative constructive behavior* using the attention that the student desires, extinction-induced aggression rarely occurs.

We Can Use Time-Out Procedures Based on Extinction

Time-out, *if done constructively*, can be part of a positive behavior change support plan that contributes to decreasing behavior designed to gain attention or tangible items. Time-out decreases a behavior by denying a student positive reinforcers for a particular period of time. The reinforcers are removed from the student's physical and psychosocial environments as a result of the unconstructive behavior, or the student is removed and thus does not have access to the reinforcers.

There are Levels of Time-Out

While professionals in the field agree that there are three levels of time-out, they describe many different category systems for these levels. Also, what is included at each level varies from professional to professional. I am combining all that I have learned to describe what we can do with the time-out strategy.

Level One Time-Out

This is the least intrusive time-out, which I call *observational time-out*. This occurs when the situation itself is altered or the student is removed *slightly* so that what was reinforcing her is no longer available *but she remains able to see and hear* what is occurring in the class. The distinguishing characteristics of Level-one are:

+ the student is *not* removed from the view of the learning activity and may not even be moved from the spot where the unconstructive behavior occurred; and
+ a change in variables is made in the student's physical or psychosocial environment so there is no reinforcer for the unconstructive behavior.

Example for a student: Maeve might have all materials in front of her removed but she would stay in place, or she might be asked to sit on the perimeter of the activity, out of the line of sight of the other students, so that she would not receive attention from her peers during the time-out.

Baroque music, particularly Mozart, has 60 beats per minute. Therefore, hearing it tends to help people return their heart rates to normal and, thereby, contributes to a sense of calm.

Example for an entire class: If the sensory stimulation level was exciting (reinforcing) for the students but it had become so high that a shift was necessary to help them maintain control of their behavior, we might ask them to return to their desks temporarily, remove all materials on top, and sit quietly for a few moments. We might encourage them to close their eyes or take some deep, slow breaths. We might turn the lights off to reduce stimulation. We turn on some soothing music.

Level Two Time-Out

I call this level exclusionary in-class time-out. The distinguishing characteristics of Level-two are:

+ the student is moved to another part of the room so that she is no longer a part of the activity and cannot see what is going on; and
+ the student can hear what is going on.

Hopefully, what the student hears will be enticing enough that she will want to rejoin the group as soon as she is able to make a positive change.

Example: Maeve shouts at her classmate in a manner that is neither constructive nor appropriate. When this happens, she is directed to go to a spot in the room (where she cannot see what is going on) selected with her ahead of time. She will stay there until she is sure that her behavior will be appropriate.

Level Three Time-Out

I call this level *out-of-class time-out.* The distinguishing characteristics of Level-three are:

   + the time-out spot is a quiet place in another room nearby in when there is adult supervision; and
   + the site is selected in advance so the transition to an out-of-class time-out is as seamless as possible.

We can usually prevent this level of agitation in a student by maintaining awareness of each student's needs as we are building our learning community. However, should a moment of great agitation occur, having a spot where the student can be safe but not reinforced with attention or tangible items is important. However, sometimes a student is so agitated that remaining in the classroom is not productive. Moving her to a new setting is constructive because it gives her time to regain control.

For some professionals, there is a fourth level of time-out—seclusionary time-out—in which the student is separated from everyone else and nearly all stimulation. I do *not* recommend this. Separating the student from the community can threaten her basic need for belonging. I believe this extreme strategy does not impose a logical consequence for unconstructive behavior. Instead, seclusion leads to such negative feelings that the student may believe adults are not available to support, teach, nurture, or provide the necessary structure. The student may even feel a need to engage in further unconstructive behavior in an effort to seek revenge. I mention seclusionary time-out only so that you will be aware of it. If you would like further discussion of this form of time-out, resources would include Alberto and Troutman (2017) or Maag (2018). References can be found at the chapter's end.

The First Three Levels of Time-Out Can be Constructive Under Certain Circumstances

These three levels are appropriate when they are used as a logical consequence to a behavior and when the time away from the learning experience is minimal. Consider this scenario: Maeve grabs something from a classmate (the function of her behavior is a tangible item). We direct her to return the item and sit a bit away from the group until she can follow the agreed-upon class rule to communicate respectfully. This intervention is logical. If she temporarily cannot act in a constructive manner within the group, she needs to remove herself from the activity until she can. This process becomes constructive if we also tell her to come back and join the group as soon as she feels she is ready. Hopefully, what she is able to do when she returns will reinforce her being a part of the group. Our goal is to teach. In this case, we are helping her learn the following:

   + There are boundaries for our behavior and there are consequences for what we do.
   + When you need to regroup, take time to do so.
   + Listen to yourself to determine when you are ready to rejoin whatever is going on.

These learnings are important ones for all of us to have as we proceed through life.

You might ask, "What do we do if Maeve comes back too soon (meaning before she has returned to her thinking brain and can be constructive in her actions)?" We tell her that her behavior is telling us that apparently, she needs more time to gather herself. She needs to return to the time-out space. We add a minute or two on to the previous time Maeve was in time-out and tell her that after _____ minutes, if she feels ready, she is welcome to return. *If,* however, *attention* was the function of the unconstructive behavior, we keep our conversation with Maeve very brief so that little attention is gained and the behavior is not reinforced. We try not to look at her as we state what we observed and the consequence; thereby giving her as little direct attention as possible.

We Keep in Mind These Essential Elements to Ensure That Time-Out is Constructive

Our Words and Tone of Voice Must Convey Our Constructive Perspective

As is true with all procedures, how we behave with the student makes all the difference. We need to be calm and explain that this intervention is providing a useful alternative. We are not angry, nor are we banishing the student. We are not breaking our connection with her.

What is Going On in the Class Must Be Something to which the Student Will Want to Return

If the lesson is not enticing, then time-out can become an escape—a place the student will *want* to be—so the student will act up to be able to leave.

The Place Where the Student Goes for Time-Out Must Not Be Reinforcing in Any Sense

Where the student sits and what the student is doing there must be less interesting than what is going on in the classroom. This ensures that the student will not want to *stay* in time-out. The student will want to leave the "dull" time-out to rejoin the group, so the student will be reinforced *negatively* (by the removal of something unpleasant) for returning.

Upon Returning, the Student Must Be Integrated Naturally and Readily

There can be no shaming, blaming, or embarrassment in front of peers. What's done is done. A matter-of-fact, quietly spoken "It's good to have you back" from us makes reentry a constructive step.

The Level of Time-Out Depends on the Function of the Behavior

Directing a student to take time-out (Level-one) in a spot where she can hear and see all the interesting things going on in the class is effective *if* the function of the unconstructive behavior is to obtain tangible items or sensory regulation. However, *if* the function is attention, then directing the student to a place where she can hear but *not be seen* (Level-two) and, therefore, cannot receive any attention from others in the classroom is appropriate.

The Length of Time a Student Spends in the Time-Out Spot Should Be Determined by the Student or by the Student and the Teacher

The criteria for the student's return is the student's apparent readiness to be a constructive member of the community. The younger the child, the shorter the time span should be. When we determine the timing, we also need to be sure that the student is not spending so much time away from the activity that he cannot successfully reenter and succeed in whatever the class is doing. In addition, we do not want the time-out to be so harsh that the student becomes disheartened or angry. The intention of any strategy is to teach a different behavior. Feeling disheartened or angry will not contribute to learning constructive behavior. When we involve the students in the decision-making, we empower the student to work towards better and better self-monitoring and behavior enhancement.

A Reminder of What to Do During Time-Out Needs to Be Available to the Student

A small poster or booklet of steps to calm oneself or a problem-solving form available in the time-out space can provide the student with structure for what to do while there.

We Need to Remember Certain Cautions about Using Time-Out

If the Function of the Behavior is Escape, Time-Out is Not the Strategy of Choice

Sometimes we forget, particularly if we or other students would like a time-out to momentarily shield us from the unconstructive behavior.

*The Use of Time-Out **Alone** is Not Effective*

Time-out does *not* teach the appropriative behavior. Whenever we use time-out, we need to debrief the student as soon as possible and ensure that the student understands why the time-out was necessary. We encourage her to describe, or if needed, we describe the behavior that *would have been* appropriate at that moment, as opposed to whatever she did. We also need the other prong of our two-pronged approach, which is a cue and reinforcement of an alternative constructive behavior.

How We Address Transitioning the Student to Time-Out Matters

If the student's unconstructive behavior is motivated by attention, she could receive lots of reinforcement while being removed, unless we direct her in an efficient manner while giving her as little direct attention as possible. We must minimize eye contact and speak only briefly and clearly. One way to avoid giving the student a lot of attention is to establish the time-out process in advance, either individually with a student or with the entire class. This includes explaining in simple terms that if anyone feels like acting unconstructively, that is a cue to step away and take some time to regroup before saying or doing something regrettable. If this cue is missed by a student, we will quietly say that student's name and nod or point in the direction of the time-out spot, where self-control can be regained. If the student is going to stay where he is, simply removing materials and sharing our observation in a quiet tone of voice can be sufficient.

Example: *"Harry, we agreed that we would respect the materials we use. What you just did was not respectful handling of _____. I will return these in a couple of minutes, if you feel then that you can follow our class rules."* We then return a few moments later to ask if everything is all set and the student is ready to work with the materials constructively.

Time-Out Loses its Effectiveness if the Time Away is Too Long

One rule of thumb for a reasonable time period is no more than half of the student's age, up to 5 minutes. If any student remains in time-out for a longer period of time, the usefulness gets lost. Our goal is to have the student contribute constructively to the learning experience *going on in the class*.

If the student has chosen to remain in the time-out location because she feels she needs a lot of time to regroup, then this should be a signal to us that a brief time to cool down away from the action is *not* what this student needs. Instead, this student needs additional support to develop the skills needed to collect herself and return to a lesson.

Time-Out is a Strategy We All Need in Our Repertoire

As we have said, the purpose of time-out is to help students learn that anyone can feel overwhelmed by feelings, unsure of what to do, or feel like reacting rather than responding to a situation. When these things happen, anyone might act unconstructively. Instead, we need to recognize it is a cue to take some time and temporarily remove ourselves from the situation to regroup, so that we do not use words or actions that hurt ourselves or others.

Teachers need to recognize the cue, too. I learned this from the students in my self-contained elementary school special education class when I first began teaching. I had just returned to the room after being asked if I would witness a student being paddled. In Ohio at that time, paddling was legal, but it had to be witnessed. I calmly and professionally refused, but I was clearly shaken. As I write about it all these years later, I am still upset. I told my students why I was upset—that while I knew paddling was legal in schools, I did not think it was right. In fact, I did not think anyone should treat anyone else that way. My eight boys, aged seven through 12, sat there listening intently. Then one quietly said, "I think you need a time-out." I thought to myself, *Now, there's a good idea.* I agreed. I asked my students to read books for a few minutes while I sat at a desk we had designed as a place people could go to work quietly or to regroup. After I had this opportunity to decide how I would follow up on the paddling, I stood up, thanked them for helping me, and told them I had figured out a way I could respond respectfully to the situation. Then I told them it was time to finish the sentences they were reading and put their books back in their desks. We went on our way.

Note: The use of time-out for us, as teachers, must be used but rarely and only if we have a procedure in place so that our students can continue on while we briefly put some of our attention elsewhere.

When Might We Use Punishment?

ACCESSING PRIOR KNOWLEDGE/EXPERIENCE

Think back to a time when you felt punished for something. What had you done? How did you feel about the punishment? How did you respond? What do you remember that you learned from the experience? In the space provided or elsewhere write what your recall.

_____

_____

As we address the many forms of punishment, keep this experience and other experiences with punishment in mind.

A Quick Review: Kinds of Punishment

As we had said in Chapter 5, there are two kinds of punishment. Positive punishment means something unpleasant is presented to the student following a particular behavior. Negative punishment removes something pleasant. With both kinds, the student is displeased, experiences the punishment as unpleasant, and will decrease the unconstructive behavior under similar circumstances.

Within positive punishment and negative punishment, there are two other categories of punishment we have mentioned before: natural consequences and contrived consequences. See Table 12-2 below.

Table 12-2. **Comparison of Positive and Negative Punishment**					
Nature of the Consequent Condition from Student Perspective	What Is Done to Create the Consequent Condition				
	Positive: Something is added		Negative: Something is taken away		
Punishment	_Positive_ **Punishment:** Something _unpleasant_ is added right after behavior.		_Negative_ **Punishment:** Something _pleasant_ is taken away right after the behavior.		
	Natural Punishment	**Contrived Punishment**		**Natural Punishment**	**Contrived Punishment**	
		Logical	**Not Logical**		**Logical**	**Not Logical**

To review, natural punishing conditions occur organically. For example, if we eat too much food, we feel uncomfortable afterwards, which is a positive natural punishment. If we move too fast, we may drop and break something we value, which is a negative natural punishment because something important to us was removed by our actions. Unlike natural punishment, Contrived punishing conditions are created by others. Of these, the constructive ones are logical consequences because these show the cause–effect connection rather than the power of a person of authority. You may remember that logical consequences have other constructive characteristics. They do not involve a judgment about the student's character, nor do they shame and blame the student. They *do* ask the student to take responsibility for her behavior. They *do* communicate that the student is in control of her behavior and the consequences of her actions. As a result of their characteristics, logical consequences teach (Dreikurs & Grey, 1968; Levin & Nolan, 2014).

. . . .

REFLECTION OPPORTUNITY

Can you think of an example of a logical positive punishment and an example of a logical negative punishment that would occur in school? Write your two examples in the space provided or on a separate piece of paper. _____

_____

_____

For me, a logical positive punishment would be earning a lower grade because I turned in a paper late. I have to say "for me" because for someone else, a low grade might be a status symbol. A logical negative punishment would occur if I were so busy talking to a friend that I missed the audition for a play in which I hoped to act.

. . . .

Why Should We Avoid Using Most Forms of Punishment?

Punishments that are not logical include those that occur without clear and appropriate reasoning that *connect* the punishment to the consequence and those whose severity does not match the degree of the unconstructive behavior. Examples of unconstructive punishment include requiring a student to write "I will not toss my paper across the room into the basket" 50 times, or keeping a student after school because she spoke without raising her hand.

Illogical Kinds of Punishments are More Difficult for the Brain to Figure Out Because of the Negative Feelings Attached to Them

I encourage you to look back at the beginning of Chapter 2 about brain functioning to refresh your understanding. Sometimes students are not sure whether they *did not do* something they should have or if they actually *did* something wrong. As a result, students are not likely to come up with an appropriate alternative behavior themselves. Their reasoning may also be situation specific; that is, they may learn not to exhibit this behavior in *this* situation or *this* setting or only with *this* person rather than not to exhibit the behavior at all. In other words, students may try to determine how not to get caught rather than learning how to behave in a constructive manner to obtain what they want or need.

Because of the Negative Feelings Attached to Punishment, Students May Avoid the Person Who Administered It

How can we facilitate learning if students are trying to avoid working with us?

Because of the Negative Feelings Attached to Punishment, Students May Avoid the Context in which the Other Person Administered It

If a student is punished without logical consequences in a science class, then he may not want to go back to that class again. How can students learn under such circumstances?

When Punished, Students Have Not Learned Appropriate Behavior, Only What Behavior to Avoid or What Person or Context to Avoid

They do not know what *to do* to behave constructively.

Punishment Rarely, if Ever, Eliminates Behavior; at Best, It Suppresses It

What triggered the behavior in the first place will trigger a replacement behavior to address the same function until the student learns a substitute behavior that connects that trigger/cue with a consequent condition that is pleasurable for her. We want that connection to be to a *constructive* behavior.

Often, After Students are Punished, the Emotions They Experience Linger

Students are frequently more tense, fearful, or withdrawn and, therefore, more stressed. They may be angry and resentful over being treated in such a manner. They may even feel vengeful; as a consequence, the punishment results in aggression against the person who punished them or displaced aggression (such as bullying) against others who appear to be weaker. Moreover, after punishment, the student's brain stays alert in case additional unsafe experiences lurk around the corner. Clearly, if we are interested in students' learning, the post-punishment emotional state is particularly counterproductive.

The Student Who is Punished and Others Who Observe the Punishment May Use the Punishing Tactics on Others

Do we want to be this kind of model for others? Is this the way we want people to treat each other? Is this what we want students to learn?

What We Consider Punishment May Be Reinforcing for a Student

If a student desperately wants attention, she may learn that the fastest way to grab our attention is by acting unconstructively. While it may not be what we would consider a pleasant form, punishment does provide attention to the student. Under such circumstances we can be trapped into continuing our punishment when, in fact, it is not effective at changing the unconstructive behavior. Quite the opposite.

Why is Punitive Punishment Tempting to Use?

We Punish Because We are Hurt or Upset

The student has done something that creates unpleasant feelings. Perhaps we feel as though we are not appreciated, or our efforts are in vain, or this student is picking on a weak spot, and we are convinced the student's behavior is deliberately calculated to "bug" us. Whatever the cause, we feel vulnerable and want to lash out, so we hurt back to relieve our feelings, tension, or agitation. We punish to regain power, to feel strong, once again.

Punishing when and because we feel vulnerable actually turns even more power over to the student. He sees that we have lost our objectivity. We also run the serious risk of losing that student's respect and the respect of any students who are aware of what is happening. We also run the serious risk of losing our relationship with the student or creating an unproductive one.

We Punish Because We were Punished Punitively

If we feel threatened, punishment is a model in our memory traces. Lacking an alternative when our quick-reaction response is triggered by threat, we, too, punish.

We are Reinforced for Punishing

We might get frustrated if student behavior has interrupted the lesson flow. We may become anxious when students do something wrong. We worry that they will not turn out all right. We worry that their behavior is a reflection of our teaching. We may become frightened if we feel their behavior threatens our competence or power. For any of these reasons, we want to do something quickly to stop what is going on. Swiftly punishing in a punitive manner is a fight response that relieves our unpleasant physiological tension. Because we have removed an unpleasant sensation in our bodies, our punishing action is reinforced.

We Incorrectly Believe the Punitive Punishment was Successful

If we punish, the unconstructive behavior usually stops, at least for a while. This is another example of negative reinforcement because the unpleasant event (the unconstructive student behavior) is removed, and this results in a more pleasant situation for us. Never mind that the behavior may happen a little later in a slight variation or crop up somewhere else. We punish, and the behavior stops (for the moment).

Below in Table 12-3 is a visual illustration of this series of events. Both rows need to be read together—what is the B (behavior) for the student is simultaneously the A (antecedent) for the teacher's behavior.

Table 12-3. Interrelated Events that Reinforce Teacher Use of Punitive Punishment

	Antecedent	Behavior	Consequence	Short-Term Result	Long-Term Result
Student	Whatever cues the behavior	Student unconstructive behavior	Student spoken to sharply by teacher (punitive punishment)	Student's unconstructive behavior stops briefly. Note: BUT if the behavior function was attention, S was reinforced. If there were other functions, they were not addressed, and S was not taught alternative behavior to address function(s)	Student unconstructive behavior will occur again.

	Antecedent	Behavior	Consequence	Result
Teacher	Student unconstructive behavior	Teacher speaks sharply to S (punitive punishment)	Student's unconstructive behavior stops—at least for a while, so Teacher is reinforced.	Teacher likely to use punitive punishment again

Essential Points We Need to Remember About Punishment:

Unless Natural or Logical Consequences are Used, Punishment Does Not Teach

When punitive punishment is used, the unconstructive behavior is likely to occur again, and so the cycle repeats—and repeats. Therefore, reinforced though we may be, the usefulness of punishment is an illusion. Both we and our students lose far more than we gain when it is used.

We Do Not Have to Use Contrived Aversive Punishment to Support Behavior Change

We have evolved from our early primate days. We are using our cerebral cortex more and more, so the quick fight response of our lower brain does not have to be activated. We do have alternatives, ones we know are far superior. We can trust our reasoning. If we wait long enough for the reasoning of the higher-level cerebral cortex to take over, if we recall the relative ineffectiveness of punitive punishment, we give ourselves enough time to depersonalize the threat aspect and construct a more reasoned, effective response that teaches.

What Unconstructive Strategies are Used by Some to Decrease Behavior?

While I believe we should *not* use these strategies, I do think we need to be familiar with them. Then, if one is suggested, we understand what is being discussed, why it is not constructive, and why the other strategies we previously addressed would be the choice to make. The strategies are summarized in Table12-4 below, along with the reasons why I believe they should not be used to provide us all a rationale for their abandonment.

Table 12-4. *Un*constructive Uses of Punishment		
Type	Description	Drawbacks to Use
Positive-Practice Overcorrection	Immediately after exhibiting an unconstructive behavior, the student is required to practice an alternative constructive behavior in an *exaggerated manner* or *for an extended period of time.* Examples: a) Iris runs down a hall, so the teacher has Iris walk particularly slowly (exaggerated fashion) down that same hall 8 more times. b) Guadalupe does not "regroup" when she completes a subtraction problem, so her teacher has Guadalupe solve fifteen additional problems (extended period of time) to "get it right" while the teacher states the steps each time.	Because of the exaggerated quality to the practice or the extended time period of the practice, the constructive behavior becomes associated with unpleasant feelings. "I hate doing this!" Also the person in power who requires this overcorrection procedure may become associated with these feelings. "I hate her because she made me … ."
Restitutional Overcorrection	Immediately after exhibiting an unconstructive behavior, the student is required to **correct the situation or restore the environment not only to its original condition,** *but also beyond.* Example: Nick was not only to wash the table where he spilled some paint, but all the other tables in the room.	Restitution or restoration is an important principle to help instill in any student; however, the punishing quality of the OVERcorrection risks all sorts of unconstructive associated feelings such as shame and embarrassment.
Response Cost	Immediately after exhibiting an unconstructive behavior, **a specific number of reinforcers that have already been earned by the student are taken away.** Example: Solita has earned ten tokens for raising her hand and waiting to be addressed before answering 10 times. The next minute she forgets and blurts out a comment. One token is taken from her.	• When hard work has been invested in behavior change, losing a reinforcer that was earned by the constructive behavior is not only disheartening. It is also, illogical and unfair. • If constructive behavior has earned a reinforcer such as points and those points are later removed for a different behavior, we are connecting the punishment—the removal of points—to the originally constructive behavior. One could say, that behavior no longer counts.

Many of these strategies were designed more than 40 years ago to support change with individuals who have severe disabilities. Although I continue to see them included in textbooks today (Alberto & Troutman, 2017), we have come a long way in our understanding of instructional strategies. We understand the brain's neurological processes far better and the probable reasons for such behavior. We do not need to use these punishing techniques to decrease behavior in instances when these are neither logical nor natural. We have many constructive alternatives that are educational in nature and respect human beings in their design.

"Gray" Area: When an Intervention Combines Reinforcement with Punishment

When I worked in a middle school, the assistant principal developed a contract with all the eighth-grade students. The contract involves both positive reinforcement and punishment—response cost. A copy appears in Table 12-5 below.

Table 12-5. **Example of Intervention that Combines Reinforcement and Punishment**[i]
NAME:
Grade 8 Cooperative Privileges MARCH 17 – APRIL 11
Okay grade eight, YOU ASKED FOR IT!!!!!! For this session, you have the chance to earn … A PIZZA PARTY!!!! The pizza party will be scheduled DURING CLASS TIME!!! It won't be easy. You must read all the "fine print" and be extremely familiar with the rules, because they are very different from before. Make your teams and get ready. In order to earn a pizza party for your team, you need to have 40 POINTS. All teams already have 50 POINTS, so if you don't blow it, you can get the pizza!!
YOUR TEAM CAN'T EARN MORE POINTS, BUT IT CAN LOSE POINTS. Here's how:
Speaking or acting in a non-friendly way
Tardy
Rudeness to an adult
Late for class
Not following lunch rules
Running in halls
Failure to offer proof of weekly team meeting
Failure to answer oral quiz questions about these rules
Failure to have these rules in your possession
Fine Print: Any adult in the school can report any team member to Mr. XXXX (the Assistant Principal) regarding the above rules. His decision (as always) is final. Above rules are in effect from 7:55 a.m. until 3:00 p.m. Team members must contribute some money to pizza, exact amount to be negotiated. Teams must find a parent in each homeroom willing to deliver pizza to school on specified date.

i   Thank you, David Nihill, personal communication and copy of contract (1991).

Rather than having the students earn points for appropriate behavior (positive reinforcement), the system is based on the threatened loss of points (negative punishment; more specifically, threatened response cost) for inappropriate behavior. The assistant principal said that the system was created this way for practical purposes. Previously, when the contract was just reinforcing (points were awarded), the faculty and the assistant principal could not guarantee the reliability of so many adults awarding points to such a large number of students for so many different behaviors. Moreover, it was difficult to tally points for so many students to determine who had reached the goal. Having only to subtract points made the system less complicated. Since more students complied than did not, far fewer students required faculty input and signatures on points lost. Also, a comparatively small number of students had points lost to be tallied.

I do believe that if it such a contract is presented to the students in an encouraging way, the culture of positive possibilities can be maintained, and the threatened punishment can be reframed in a constructive light. One could say, "You are students who act constructively. Here is our way of celebrating that. We expect that you will be able to keep your points without any problem. That is why the system is set up the way it is. Now, show us your constructive way of getting through the day."

As the contract is constructed now, it falls under the category of punishment, but I placed it in this gray area because the contract does simultaneously include a reinforcement for appropriate behavior. Also, because I was familiar with the student population, I knew the contract was likely to be successful. Therefore, the students had a much higher probability of being reinforced than of experiencing response cost.

- -

FOOD FOR THOUGHT: "NONCOMPLIANT"? "DIFFICULT"?

A while ago, I was at a wedding. The bride and groom were important to me, as were all the events unfolding during the reception. I was enjoying the music and the rare opportunity to dance with my husband. In between the dance numbers, I was having good conversations with people with whom I rarely have a chance to talk, and I was enjoying the delicious food. I had every motivation to stay in the room. However, the volume of the band was too high for comfort. As I became more and more overwhelmed by my efforts to screen out the music, conversations became increasingly difficult for me to hear. After a while, I felt as though my head was going to explode. Despite the fact that every other aspect was drawing me into the activities in the reception, I got up and left for a brief while.

If someone had directed me to stay in the room and I had followed the direction, I would have become increasingly uncomfortable and eventually agitated. I would have stopped talking because I could no longer screen out the irrelevant noise. I would have covered my ears and likely begun to close my eyes and lower my head to screen out some of the stimulation, which, as time went on, would become more and more difficult for me to process. Soon, I would have found a powerful reason to leave, probably saying I needed to go to the bathroom right away.

Was I being rude as I increasingly closed myself off from the experience as time went on? Was my shutting-down behavior "unconstructive"?

Change the surroundings and the specifics of this scenario, add a few more peers who are engaged in the process, and you have a scene that can occur in any classroom. Clearly, the term unconstructive is subjective. When we judge a behavior unconstructive, we believe that behavior is not conducive to the student's well-being or learning (or that of others) or to achieving our teaching goal at the moment. However, from the student's perspective, the behavior may be a constructive attempt to address his needs. As I work with students to support behavior change, I remind myself of this experience, particularly when I am facing what is, for me, a difficult behavior to address.

We Need to Remember that Student's Behavior is Constructive from Their Perspective

Students are meeting a need the best way they know how at the moment. We can support them in finding an alternative choice that meets their needs but does so in a way that is also constructive for their whole community.

How Do We Address Bullying, a Complex Unconstructive Behavior?

Bullying is one of the most serious unconstructive behaviors. Bullying in schools is defined as "unwanted, aggressive behavior among school aged children that involves a real or perceived power imbalance. The behavior is repeated, or has the potential to be repeated, over time. Bullying includes actions such as making threats, spreading rumors, attacking someone physically or verbally, and excluding someone from a group on purpose" (U.S. Department of Health and Human Services, n.d.)

We know that bullying has an impact on the victims, but it also effects those who bully (Mishna, 2009; Shea & Bauer, 2017). In addition, bullying has an effect on those who witness it, particularly if they do not respond. The effects can be on social interaction or physical, psychological, and emotional health as well as a student's ability to progress academically (Teaching Tolerance, 2017; Jones & Jones, 2016).

REFLECTION OPPORTUNITY

Think for a moment about bullying. How would you describe the kinds of people who bully? What is their gender? Have they been bullied? Do they have difficulty academically, socially, or emotionally? Do they tend to bully just during their school years, or does their bullying carry on after they graduate from high school? Write your description in the space provided or on a separate piece of paper.

_____

_____

_____

There are some misconceptions about bullies. We often think that bullies have been bullied and so they are doing what was done to them. We think of bullies as people who have difficulty in school and seem to have poor relationships with adults, and, perhaps, with most other students. These perceptions are an accurate understanding of the dynamics behind *some* bullying, but only some (Teaching Tolerance, 2017; National Youth Violence Prevention Resource Center; Jones & Jones, 2016).

Research suggests that there appear to be two different bully types. One type is proactive, while the other reactive (Wood & Gross, 2003, as cited in Jones & Jones, 2016). Proactive bullies are often competent students. They may be leaders in school sports. Being more powerful than others is a part of their sense of self. They believe they are bigger, tougher, or stronger. Their actions that push others around reinforce their self-concept. They may not even be aware that they are bullying. What they lack is empathy. They do not understand the degree to which they affect others when they bully, so they have no remorse about what they have done. In many instances, these are children and young adults who do not have warm relationships with adults at home. There were no caring models, so these students have not learned empathy.

Reactive bullies, on the other hand, act abusively towards others in what appears to be a reaction to perceived threatening situations. They are likely to want positive relationships with adults, but they lack them. They seem to have quick tempers and yet are likely to express remorse after they bully. Acting abusively isn't something they consider to be a part of their day-to-day actions, an act that lets others know they are powerful. In fact, while they do not feel particularly powerful, a perceived threat will bring out their power. Sadly, it will not be in a constructive way.

Another misconception is that *only* the victim suffers. It is true that there can be terrible consequences for those who are bullied. What is sometimes unknown or forgotten is that there are also negative effects for the bystander. Also, for the bully. Regardless of the style, those who become habituated to behaving in a bullying way will often go on to bully as adults. As a result, they often run into difficulty in the workplace and in relationships. Moreover, they may violate laws. According to Utterly Global Youth Empowerment (n.d.), students in grades six to nine who were bullies are 60 percent more likely to have a criminal conviction by the age of 24.

We Need to Address Bullying for Everyone's Sake, Including that of the Bully

If we look at bullying from the perspective of our A->B->C sequence, we see a student who either perceives a threat (reactive bully-internal cue/trigger) or is someone who wants to feel powerful (proactive bully-internal cue/trigger). The bully looks around and finds a student who *looks* less powerful (external cue/trigger). This could be someone shy or anxious in demeanor, more socially isolated, who has a visible disability, or has a slighter or shorter body size (Graham & Hendricks, 2015). The bully seizes the opportunity to feel more powerful and acts (behavior). If he perceives he has overpowered the other person, either because the other student backs away or someone cheers him on for what he did, he is reinforced and will try it again. Moreover, if no one responds negatively to what he has done or works to prevent it from happening again, he is encouraged–reinforced–to try it again.

Bullies are also reinforced for physically overpowering others in some sports. Consider ice hockey, football, and some of the pushing that goes on during a basketball game, even though it is not supposed to be a contact sport. Many in our culture cheer on those who hit hard. In our larger culture, we reinforce power, particularly in boys and men. To the contrary, we do not reinforce it in girls and women. Those of the female gender who are strong and athletic are often called tomboys. So many young girls feel they cannot show strength or they will be teased. On the other hand, when those of the male gender don't appear to be powerful in a physical sense, people may make fun of them, call them wimps or female names (as if being female is weak or undesirable), or shame them some other way in front of others.

What Can We Do to Stop the Cues and Reinforcement for Bullying?

Because the proactive bully does not feel remorse, supporting him to change his behavior is more difficult than changing the behavior of the reactive bully. Helping both kinds of bullies develop empathy and connect with others diminishes the chances of bullying. Simultaneously, the strategies for changing behavior in bullies are the same strategies that we use to change other behavior. We must diminish the strength of the cue/trigger for the bullying behavior and weaken the reinforcement for the bully's actions.

How We Can We Weaken the Cues for Bullying

+ *Everyone* in the school needs to know about the dynamics of bullying, as well as its effects, in order to diminish the attraction of trying to overpower others for the bully and, perhaps, one or more bystanders. Some schools have used playback theatre, in which adults act out student's bullying experiences to help everyone understand these in a new way (Salas, 2005). Other possibilities include using characters from literature, movies, or videos and facilitating role plays as a source for discussions to help students grasp how the victim, the bystander, and the bully feel before, during, and after an incident. Fostering empathy for the victim and the bystander and facilitating understanding that the habit of bullying tends to be carried over into adulthood with higher rates of criminal behavior (Cole, Cornell, & Sheras, 2006, as cited in Jones & Jones, 2016) are all important foci of such dialogues.

+ We need to counter the difficulty bullies have connecting, which makes it easier for them to think of others as faceless targets for whom they have no concern. Therefore, we must build their capacity to connect to help mitigate against the bullying behavior. Cooperative group work that includes the teaching of social skills, peer coaching, and tutoring can make connections between students who might otherwise remain faceless. Cross-age activities can help. Multiage advisories can help. Cross-age academic work can help, too. In a school where I worked, eighth graders who had just finished studying biography as a form of writing interviewed and wrote biographies for first graders. Bus drivers and teachers noticed there was less of what I call "cock of the walk" behavior on the part of the eighth-grade boys. There was also more connecting and even protecting of the younger children by all the eighth graders. This stands to reason. If you know someone, you are more likely to care about how they feel.

+ Students need to be taught strategies to help them present themselves more assertively so they are less likely to be seen as potential targets. Also, teaching how to connect with peers in ways that encourage students to walk together will help add strength to those who do not appear to be strong.

+ Halls, busses, bathrooms, and sports activities need to be supervised in ways that are respectful to students but do not allow opportunities for bullying to occur (Kemp-Graham & Hendricks, 2015).

How We Can Diminish the Reinforcement for Bullying?

✦ No one in the school can encourage bullying behavior. Recent research (Sparks, 2016) on peer-led anti-bullying shows encouraging results. Having key students in the school publicly speak out against bullying, but not against the people who did it, helped reduce the incidents. What was interesting was that it was not the most popular students or those identified by teachers as leaders who made the difference; rather, it was those who other students named as being people they *respected*.

✦ Students need to be taught how to react to bullies in a way that communicates strength without threat rather than acceptance so bullies do not have the feeling of power over others.

✦ Knowing that bystanders and the school community won't tolerate bullying also lessens the likelihood that it will occur.

✦ Peer victimization rarely involves just an aggressor and a victim. Usually there are bystanders. How these people respond contributes to either the solution or the problem. We have to teach bystanders to react in a way that communicates strength without threat to the bully. Otherwise, bystanders become unwitting accomplices.

✦ A system that makes it possible for victims and bystanders to safely report bullying incidents to adults must be available.

✦ All students need to know what they can do and to whom they can turn for support at school and elsewhere to address the issue, should it arise. We also need to ensure that adults always follow through constructively *not punitively* to address the situation.

✦ There needs to be an ongoing school-wide effort to develop a culture that accepts all people but does not accept all behavior—one that does not expect and does not tolerate bullying or other aggressive behavior (Jones & Jones, 2016; Manning & Bucher, 2013; Shafer, 2017). That is the warm and caring community we have been discussing all along.

✦ The larger the school, the more essential it is for faculty and administration to talk about how to structure the physical and the social environment to help students connect with each other and with teachers. In many schools, the youngest students, who are often smaller and more timid, are placed in their own hall or wing for their first year in that school: kindergarten children in an elementary school, fifth or sixth graders in a middle school, or freshman in a high school. Part of the school-wide effort should be a process for teaching emotional social skills from grades kindergarten up through high school, starting with the recognition and naming of feelings, speaking assertively, and interacting constructively with others (Brackett & Rivers, 2014).

✦ When adults respond to an act of bullying, they need to use restorative-justice practices rather than punitive responses, or they will not teach the bully how to become a contributing rather than a detracting member of the community (Smith, Fisher, & Frey, 2015*)*.

A principal part of the solution is being proactive. It is much more effective to prevent bullying than it is to address it once it happens (Shafer, 2017).

How We Address the Bully's Needs so that Bullying Is Not Necessary

First and foremost, we establish a climate in each of our classes in which warm and caring relationships with adults are natural for all students. We know how important these are for the many reasons we have discussed in earlier chapters. Moreover, a sense of warmth and community can break down the alone-ness—the sense of isolation that students feel in the bigger school building—which can feed the bully's feeling that his behavior will go unnoticed and the victim's feeling that she is all alone, vulnerable, and without recourse. In addition, such relationships provide much-needed models of empathy and help fill the void of caring some students feel with the other adults in their lives that can trigger bullying behavior.

In addition to helping possible bullies feel that someone cares about them, we must help them find other ways to feel competent and powerful. We have discussed the strategies we can employ to meet the students' needs for efficacy and how to avoid those that do not. Bullies need to be taught how to resolve issues in other ways when they feel threatened. Teaching conflict resolution strategies is a must. Peer mediation programs also support constructive ways to address conflicts.

Part of the solution has to be a school community-wide effort. We need to build a school culture (including parents/caregivers) in which bullying is not tolerated, there is vigilance by all to prevent it, *and* none sees it as an acceptable behavior—even those who might be tempted to try it. There are many programs that help schools address the complexities of bullying. Addressing all the possible strategies is beyond the scope of this text. On the other hand, there are many resources available to support antibullying efforts. Please see a sample of those under "Resources for Addressing Bullying" at the chapter's end.

IMPORTANT POINTS FOR CONSTRUCTIVELY DECREASING BEHAVIOR

✦ The strongest intervention is one that combines cue and reinforcement for increasing a constructive behavior while at the same time decreasing the cue and reinforcement for an unconstructive behavior. Therefore, we should always reinforce an alternative for the behavior being decreased.

✦ As part of a behavior change support plan, we should only take actions that address *all* the student's basic needs.

✦ After the constructive behavior has been established and appears to be part of the repertoire, we should continue to cue the appropriate behavior. The student may be ready to move to a less intrusive cue, but we need to be sure there is a clear cue. In particular, we always cue the behavior if there is a shift in expectation within an activity or between activities.

✦ After the constructive behavior has been established and appears to be part of the repertoire, we should continue to reinforce the constructive behavior. The student may be ready to move to a less intrusive or more natural reinforcer, but we need to be sure there is a clear reinforcer for the behavior—including an intrinsic one. In particular, we should always be sure to reinforce the behavior if there is a shift in expectation within an activity or between activities.

Application Activity: Analysis of Teacher–Student Interaction

Consider the following scenario and write your answers to the questions in the spaces provided, or on a separate piece of paper, if needed:

Shushila blurts out questions without raising her hand and waiting to be called on. When she does, Mr. Petri always reminds Shushila to raise her hand. After this, Mr. Petri scolds Shushila for not raising her hand. Then Mr. Petri answers Shushila's question. For a while after Mr. Petri responds to Shushila, she doesn't blurt out, but then the blurting occurs again. This has gone on now for several weeks. Analyze this use of what Mr. Petri calls "punishment" to correct Shushila's behavior.

1. Of the four possibilities, what is the function of Shushila's behavior? _____

2. Is the teacher's intervention effective? _____

3. How can you tell? _____

4. When asked, Mr. Petri says that his strategy is a combination of first cueing as an antecedent to the desired behavior and then afterwards punishing the inappropriate behavior by presenting a noxious consequence (the scolding). Is he cueing? Does his so-called cue come before the constructive behavior is desired? _____

5. Is his response to Shushila's behavior punishing *for her*? _____

6. Mr. Petri feels that, in a while, the blurting-out behavior will completely stop. He just needs more time to make the strategy work. Do you agree? _____

7. What are your reasons? _____

8. Do you think the consequence is reinforcing or punishing **for Shushila**? _____

9. How do you know? _____

10. What **teacher** behavior is being reinforced? _____

11. What is the reinforcer **for the teacher behavior**? _____

12. How do you know the teacher is being reinforced? _____

The answers to the activity can be found in the text's Appendix A Answer Key under Chapter 12 C12AK: Analysis of Teacher – Student Interaction – Answers.

What Mr. Petri does not realize is that the nature of the consequences for Shushila is not what he thinks it is: punishment. Rather, he is reinforcing her behavior by giving her attention. By stopping her shouting out, at least briefly, she is reinforcing his behavior. 'Round and round' they go. This cycle of unending back-and-forth behavior between teacher and student is often called the "Criticism Trap."

· ·

Application Activity: How Can You Support Yourself as You Support Change in Others?

If you get frustrated or discouraged, what can you do to continue being constructive in your efforts?

_____

_____

_____

With any learning, growth, or change, people tend to go two steps forward and one step back. While mistakes and back steps are natural, if we as teachers are going to keep from getting discouraged through the times of regression, then the behavior change process needs to be experienced positively by us. We, too, need the energy provided by reinforcement. Sometimes the change we see in the student is sufficient to keep us going. Sometimes it is not. When it is not, we need to build in ways to cheer ourselves on. Talking with a colleague about the fits and spurts may help. Sometimes positive statements to ourselves help: "Remember: last week, this constructive behavior only happened three times; this week she did it eight. That's progress," or "Three days ago he shouted out 4 times during our discussion; today it was two. Reminding all to raise their hands at the beginning is working."

· ·

Final Thoughts

Each of our students brings different strengths and needs to the learning experience and to classroom life. One-size teaching does not fit all. There is so much that we know from the field about effective teaching strategies that there is no longer a need to teach everyone the same way. *Is it not possible to use teaching strategies that not only fit the student but bring delight?* When I say delight, I mean delight for students *and* for us as teachers. The more we are able to offer choices in the learning and assessment process—the more we are able to adapt and adjust for students to meet their needs—the less likely we are to have students who need to exhibit unconstructive behavior and the more likely they (and we) will enjoy and benefit from the teaching–learning process.

The non-punitive strategies we have been discussing in this chapter can be used with students behaving constructively. Many of the strategies we have just discussed including those to address stimulation needs and to prevent the need for escape are effective practices for any part of school life. Were these strategies an integral part of the learning experience, they would prevent many unconstructive behaviors from occurring because they would make learning experiences meet students' basic needs.

Success teaches. The best way to support behavior change is to ensure, insofar as it is possible, that our teaching elicits the constructive behavior and, once it has occurred, that a positive result from the student's perspective is produced. If we have many instances of trigger → behavior occurrence → positive result, then we foster the emergence of constructive behavior patterns and habits. If we want a behavior to decrease, the best way to support behavior change is to ensure, insofar as it is possible, that our design does not elicit the unconstructive behavior and, once it has occurred, that no positive result from the student's perspective is produced. The most powerful way to decrease a behavior is to *also* cue and reinforce a constructive alternative.

The purpose of fostering behavior change is to support students in becoming caring, responsible people in a democratic society who act constructively wherever they go. As Goodlad, Souder, and Sirotnik (1990) remind us, education serves to enculturate students with society's values and prepare them for community life and citizenship. Of the many strategies we have available, how do we encourage ourselves to choose the ones that address students' basic emotional needs and lead them in positive ways to become more mature individuals, to develop interdependent relationships with others, and to lead a life that is physically and emotionally safe and healthy, self-affirming, productive, and happy? If, by chance, we start going down the unconstructive path, how do we have the strength to stop and remember what we believe are our values regarding how one person treats another, our beliefs about the potential for growth and change in any student, and our goals for our teaching so we can take a deep breath, shift gears, and change what we are doing? Perhaps one way we can maintain constructive strategies is to keep in mind John Ruskin's words: *"When love and skill join together, expect a masterpiece."*

Within our love is our empathy for the student. Within that skill is our patience. The student is behaving on purpose—*her* purpose. She has learned to act that way because her behavior functions to fulfill a need, so she is reinforced to continue using that behavior. Our role—indeed, our responsibility—is to teach her a new way to meet the need or a new way to help dissipate that need. Then she can behave constructively. On purpose.

With each lesson we design, each conversation we have with a student, and each behavior change support plan we develop, we hold up a mirror of possibility. While we cannot control a student's perception of self, we can certainly offer a positive perception through what we say and do. The choice is ours. Will they see possibility?

Looking Forward

Teachers need celebrating, too. This brings us to the last section of the book, "Illuminating Our Souls," an opportunity to reflect on what we have accomplished in our work together and what we hope to accomplish in the days ahead. As we said in Section II, an effective learning experience provides people with an introduction to what they will be learning and, in the last step, an opportunity to summarize and reflect on what they have just learned. We opened this book by launching ourselves into the topic in the Introduction and laying the conceptual background for our work together in the first section of the book. We will now draw our work to a close.

References

Alberto, P., & Troutman, A. (2017). *Applied behavior analysis for teachers*. (9th ed.). Upper Saddle River, NJ: Pearson.

Belvel, P., & Jordan, M. (2003). *Rethinking classroom management: Strategies for prevention, intervention and problem solving*. Thousand Oaks, CA: Corwin Press.

Berliner, D., & Rosenshine, B. (1987). *Talks to teachers*. New York, NY: Random House.

Brackett, M., & Rivers, S. (2014). Transforming students' lives with social emotional learning. In R. Pekrum & L. Linnebrink-Garcia (Eds.), *International Handbook of Emotions in Education* (pp. 368–388). New York, NY: Routledge.

Buber, M. (1971). *I and thou*. New York, NY: Free Press.

Chandler, L., & Dalquist, C. (2015). *Functional assessment: Strategies to prevent and remediate challenging behaviors in school settings* (4th ed.). Boston, MA: Pearson.

Charles, C. (2014). *Building classroom discipline* (11th ed.). Boston, MA: Pearson.

Charney, R. (2002). *Teaching children to care*. Turners Falls, MA: Northeast Foundation for Children.

Curwin, R., Mendler, A., & Mendler, B. (2008). *Discipline with dignity* (3rd ed.). Alexandria, VA: Association for Supervision and Curriculum Development.

Dreikurs, R., & Grey, L. (1968). *Logical consequences*. New York, NY: Hawthorne Books.

Evertson, C., Emmer, W., & Worsham, M. (2017). *Classroom management for elementary teachers* [loose-leaf version] (10th ed.). Boston, MA: Allyn & Bacon.

Glasser, W. (1992). *The quality school: Managing students without coercion* (2nd ed.). New York, NY: HarperCollins.

Goodlad, J., Soder, R., & Sirotnik, K. (Eds.). (1990). *The moral dimension of teaching*. San Francisco, CA: Jossey-Bass.

Henley, M. (2009). *Classroom management: A proactive approach* (2nd ed.). Boston, MA: Pearson/Merrill.

Homme, L. (1970). *Contingency contracting*. Champaign, IL: Research Press.

Hopkins Medicine. (2017). *Attention-Deficit/Hyperactivity Disorder (ADHD) in children*. Retrieved from http://www.hopkinsmedicine.org/healthlibrary/conditions/mental_health_disorders/attention-deficit_hyperactivity_disorder_adhd_in_children

Hunter, M. (1982). *Mastery teaching*. El Segundo, CA: TIP Publications.

Hunter, M. (2004). *Mastery teaching* (2nd ed.). Thousand Oaks, CA: Corwin Press.

Hunter, R. (2014). *Madeline Hunter's Mastery Teaching: Increasing instructional effectiveness in elementary and secondary schools*. Thousand Oaks, CA: Corwin Press.

Jensen, E. (2013). *Engaging students with poverty in mind.* Alexandria, VA: Association for Supervision and Curriculum Development.

Jones, V. (2015). *Practical classroom management* [loose-leaf version] (2nd ed.). Boston, MA: Pearson.

Jones, V., & Jones, L. (2016). *Comprehensive classroom management: Creating communities of support and solving problems* [loose-leaf version] (11th ed.). Boston, MA: Pearson.

Kauffman, J., Mostert, M., Trent, S., & Pullen, P. (2011). *Managing classroom behavior: A reflective case-based approach* (5th ed.). Boston, MA: Pearson/Allyn and Bacon.

Kemp-Graham, K., & Hendricks, L. (2015). The socio-emotional and financial costs of bullying in the United States. *Journal of Bullying and Social Aggression, 1*(1). Retrieved from http://sites.tamuc.edu/bullyingjournal/article/the-socio-emotional-and-financial-costs-of-bullying/

Knoster, T. (2014). *The teacher's pocket guide for effective classroom management* (2nd ed.). Baltimore, MD: Paul H. Brookes.

Knoster, B., & Drogan, R. (2016). *The teacher's pocket guide for positive behavior support.* Baltimore, MD: Paul H. Brookes.

Levin, J., & Nolan, J. (2014). *Principles of Classroom management: A hierarchical approach* (7th ed.). Boston, MA: Pearson.

Littky, D. (2004). *The big picture: Education is everyone's business.* Alexandria, VA: Association for Supervision and Curriculum Development.

Maag, J. (2018). *Behavior management: From theoretical implications to practical applications* (3rd ed.). Belmont, CA: Wadsworth.

Manning, M., & Bucher, K. (2013). *Classroom management: Models, applications and cases* (3rd ed.). Boston, MA: Pearson.

Martin, G., & Pear, J. (2015). *Behavior modification: What it is and how to do it* (10th ed.). New York, NY: Routledge.

Marzano, R., Gaddy, B., Foseid, M. C., Foseid, M. P., & Marzano, J. (2005). *A handbook for classroom management that works.* Alexandria, VA: Association for Supervision and Curriculum Development.

Marzano, R., Marzano, J., & Pickering, D. (2003). *Classroom management that works: Research-based strategies for every teacher.* Alexandria, VA: Association for Supervision and Curriculum Development.

Maslow, A. (1972). *The farther reaches of human nature.* New York, NY: Viking Press.

Menzies, H., Lane, K., & Lee, J. (Winter, 2009). Self-monitoring strategies for use in the classroom: A promising practice to support productive behavior for students with emotional or behavioral disorders. *Beyond Behavior,* 27–35.

Michenbaum, D. (1977). *Cognitive behavior modification: An integrative approach.* New York, NY: Plenium Press.

Michenbaum, D., & Goodman, J. (1971). Training impulsive children to talk to themselves: A means of developing self-control. *Journal of Abnormal Psychology, 77*, 115–126.

Miltenberger, R. (2015). *Behavior modification: Principles and procedures* (6th ed.). Pacific Grove, CA: Brooks/Cole.

Mishna, F. (2003). Learning disabilities and bullying: Double jeopardy. *Journal of Learning Disabilities, 36*(4), 336–347.

National Youth Violence Prevention Resource Center. *Bullying facts and statistics.* Retrieved 2017 from http://www.yellodyno.com/pdf/safeyouth.org_bullying_facts_statistics_2001.pdf

Noddings, N. (2005). *The challenge to care in school: An alternative approach to education* (2nd ed.). New York, NY: Teacher College Press.

Premack, D. (1959). Toward empirical behavior laws: Positive reinforcement. *Psychological Review, 66*, 219–233.

Rosenshine, B., & Stevens, R. (1986). Teaching functions. In M. L. Wittrock (Ed.), *Handbook of research on teaching* (3rd ed.). New York, NY: MacMillan.

Savage, T., & Savage, M. (2010). *Successful classroom management and discipline: Teaching self-control and responsibility.* (3rd ed.). Thousand Oaks, CA: Sage.

Scheuermann, B., & Hall, J. (2016). *Positive behavioral supports for the classroom* (3rd ed.). Boston, MA: Pearson.

Schlozman, S. (2002, February). Quit obsessing. *Educational Leadership, 59*(5), 95–97.

Shafer, L. (2017, March 21). Developing a school culture that prioritizes the social-emotional wellbeing of every student (and adult). *Useable Knowledge.* Retrieved from http://www.gse.harvard.edu/news/uk/17/03/schoolwide-sel-prevent-bullying

Shea, T., & Bauer, A. (2012). *Behavior management: A practical approach for educators* (10th ed.). Boston, MA: Pearson.

Smith, D., Fisher, D., & Frey, N. (2015*). Better than carrots or sticks: Restorative practices for positive classroom management.* Alexandria, VA: Association for Supervision and Curriculum Development.

Sullo, B. (2007). *Activating the desire to learn.* Alexandria, VA: Association for Supervision and Curriculum Development.

Szymanski, E. (1994). Transition: Life-span and life-space considerations for empowerment. *Exceptional Children, 60*(5), 402–410.

Teaching Tolerance (n.d.). *Basics on bullying.* Retrieved from http://www.tolerance.org/bullying-basics

Topper, K., Williams, W., Leo, K., & Fox, T. (2017). A positive approach to understanding and addressing challenging behaviors. In V. Jones & L. Jones (Eds.), *Comprehensive classroom management* (10th ed.). Boston, MA: Pearson.

Turnbull, A., Turnbull, R., Wehmeyer, M., & Shogen, K. (2016). *Exceptional lives: Special education in today's schools* (8th ed.). Columbus, OH: Merrill.

Umbreit, J., Ferro, J., Liaupsin, C., & Lane, K. (2006). *Functional behavioral assessment and function-based intervention: An effective, practical approach.* Columbus, OH: Merrill.

U.S. Department of Health and Human Services (n.d.). What is Bullying? *StopBullying.gov.* Retrieved from www.stopbullyingnow.hrsa.gov/kids/effects-of-bullying.aspx

Utterly Global Youth Empowerment. Statistics: Research, facts and statistics on bullying. Retrieved from http://antibullyingprograms.org/Statistics.html

Wheeler, J., & Richey, D. (2013). *Behavior management: Principles and practices of positive behavior supports* (3rd ed.). Boston, MA: Pearson.

Wood, C. (2007). *Yardsticks* (3rd ed.). Turners Falls, MA: Northeast Foundation for Children.

Zirpoli, T. (2016). *Behavior management: Applications for teachers* (7th ed.). Boston, MA: Pearson.

Resources for Addressing Bullying

Adler, M., Katz, A., Minotti, J., Slaby, R., & Storey, K., (2008). Bystander quiz from *Eyes on Bullying, What Can You Do?* Retrieved from www.eyesonbullying.org/pdfs/toolkit.pdf

Center for the Study and Prevention of Violence: http://www.colorado.edu/cspv/index.html

Colorosa, B. (2008). *The bully, the bullied, and the bystander.* New York, NY: Harper Collins.

Crowe, A. (2012). *How to bullyproof your room.* Turners Falls, MA; Northeast Foundation for Children.

Cyberbullying Research Center website: http://www.cyberbullying.us

Moss, P. (2013) *Say something.* Thomaston, ME: Tilbury House. This book and related materials can also be retrieved from http://www.witsprogram.ca/schools/books/say-something.php

Safe Youth. Retrieved 2017 from http://www.Safeyouth.org

Salas, J. (*1995*, September). Using theatre to address bullying. *Educational Leadership, 63*(1), 78–82.

Shafer, L. (2017, March 21). Developing a school culture that prioritizes the social-emotional wellbeing of every student (and adult). *Useable Knowledge.* Retrieved from http://www.gse.harvard.edu/news/uk/17/03/schoolwide-sel-prevent-bullying

Smith, D., Fisher, D. & Frey, N. (2015). *Better than carrots or sticks: Restorative practices for positive classroom management.* Alexandria, VA: Association for Supervision and Curriculum Development.

Sorrel, D. (2015). Adult and childhood bullying in schools. *Journal of Social Aggression and Bullying.* Retrieved from http://www.sites.tamuc.edu/bullyingjournal/article/adult-childhood-bullying-schools/

Sparks, S. (2016, September 16) Peer-led anti-bullying efforts yield payoffs. *Education Week 64*(4), 8. Retrieved from http://www.edweek.org/ew//articles/2016/09/14/peer-led-anti-bullying-efforts-yield-payoffs.html

Teaching Tolerance. (n.d.). *Basics on Bullying.* Retrieved from http://www.tolerance.org/bullying-basics

Teaching Tolerance. (n.d.). *Bullying Tips.* Retrieved from http://www.tolerance.org/activity/bullying-tips-students

Teaching Tolerance. (n.d.). *Anti-bullying Resources.* Retrieved from http://www.tolerance.org/toolkit/anti-bullying-resources

U.S. Department of Health and Human Services (n.d.). What is Bullying? *StopBullying.gov.* Retrieved from www.stopbullyingnow.hrsa.gov/kids/effects-of-bullying.aspx

Website Resources for Supporting Constructive Behavior

Association for Positive Behavior Support: http://www.apbsinternational.org

Beach Center on Disability: http://www.beachcenter.org

Behavior Doctor Seminars: http://www.behaviordoctor.org/index.html

California Department of Education Positive Environments, Network of Trainers (PENT): http://www.pent.ca.gov/index.htm

Center for Effective Collaboration and Practice: http://cecp.air.org

Center for Evidence-Based Practice: http://www.challengingbehavior.org

Center for the Study and Prevention of Violence: http://www.colorado.edu/cspv/index.html

Center on the Social and Emotional Foundations for Early Learning: http://www.vanderbilt.edu/csefel/

Cyberbullying Research Center website: http://www.cyberbullying.us

National Center on Education, Disability, and Juvenile Justice: http://www.edjj.org

National Center on Mental Health Promotion and Youth Violence Prevention: http://www.promoteprevent.org/about-national-center

New Hampshire Center for Effective Behavioral Interventions and Supports: http://nhcebis.seresc.net

New Jersey Positive Behavior Support in Schools: http://www.njpbs.org/index.htm

Online Academy, University of Kansas: http://uappbs.apbs.org

Schoolwide Information System (SWIS), Educational and Community Supports of the University of Oregon: http://www.pbisapps.org

The Technical Assistance Center on Positive Behavioral Intervention and Supports: http://www.pbis.org

University of Missouri: http://kidtools.org/index.ph

CLOSING

Great is the art of beginning, but greater the art of ending.

—Longfellow

When we talked about building a community, we said that supporting students through beginnings and endings was an important aspect of constructive teaching. We started our work with the narrative and activities in the Introduction designed to ready us for our journey. How shall we finish off all that we have done? We have discussed two important parts to fostering endings: looking back to review what was accomplished and celebrating the work that has been done. We will do both.

Summarization Review

First, let us look back to review what we have accomplished in our thinking together about supporting constructive behavior in students. What have been some important ideas? One for me is: all people have basic needs that must be met if those people are to learn and grow constructively. What might be yours? To foster your thinking, I encourage you to go back and do a quick walk through the text by looking at all the "What Will This Chapter Discuss?" sections.

Which ideas do you want to be sure to remember? I encourage you to write them either book or on a separate piece of paper _____

_____

_____

_____

_____

_____

Here are some of the lessons I have learned from the students with whom I have worked all these years. I think the following ideas are essential if we are to be successful in our efforts to support constructive behavior. As you read them, write (either here in the book or on a separate piece of paper) one or more strategies you want to remember next to any topic.

Hold up a mirror of possibility: _____

_____

Think ecologically: _____

_____

Meet basic needs: _____

_____

Nurture and provide structure: _____

_____

Plan and act proactively: _____

_____

Connect: _____

_____

Teach social skills, including those that foster collaboration: _____

_____

Support change constructively: _____

_____

Reflect: _____

_____

If I were to summarize all that I have learned over the years, I would borrow these words from Goethe: "Treat people as if they were what they [could] be, and you help them to become what they are capable of being."

Next Steps

You Teach Who You Are. Who Do You Want to Be in the Days Ahead?[i]

As you consider each question, I encourage you to write your ideas either here in the book or on a separate piece of paper.

What ideas and strategies of your own did you find reinforced what you want to be sure to maintain? ___

_____

_____

What new strategies do you want to implement? _____

_____

_____

> ## "You are what you take the time to become."
>
> ### —Joseph Sheen

How might you design a brief plan for implementing your strategies? How might you do this? Who might support your efforts? What resources would be helpful to have in place? _____

_____

_____

Where will you keep your plan so it will be easy to find when you are ready to check in and reflect on your progress? _____

_____

Teaching and, with it, supporting constructive behavior, is *not* an easy process. In fact, the more I share what I know is needed, the longer this guidebook becomes. As teachers, we find ourselves in all sorts of challenging situations. Is teaching exciting? Yes. Does it ask us to be all that we can be? All the time. Do we get incredibly frustrated? Yes, you bet. Is it awe inspiring? Yes! Teaching is all this and more.

I have yet to meet a student who came to school saying, "Today I am going to have a bad day." Even in their most anxious or frustrated moments, students want to learn, want to learn how to learn, and want to learn how to learn more. It is up to us to work with them to find a way to teach them how. So, if we are support constructive behavior in others, whose behavior actually needs to change?

Our behavior as the teacher needs to change. When we change the relevant variables in students' three environments, including our behavior, then we support more constructive behavior. The strategies are ours to implement. How we manage the variables affects the degree to which students will be fostered to meet their fullest potential. One of my favorite poets, Rumi (a 13th-century mystic from what is now Afghanistan), suggests: *"Yesterday I was clever, so I wanted to change the world. Today I am wise, so I am changing myself."*

We are the mirror of possibility. What we do helps shape the degree to which any student reaches his or her potential.

Celebration

We have been on quite a journey. You have considered many ideas and, depending on your learning style, you have participated in activities, analyses, and reflections. Congratulations for all your efforts.

I, too, celebrate my work during my part of this journey of thinking, learning, reflecting, writing, and editing. For someone who nearly dances when she is teaching, taking sabbaticals to just write was difficult, indeed.

So here's to both of us for our parts in this process of looking at how we can provide structure and nurturance for others. We have worked hard on behalf of the students with whom we work.

A Farewell

I hope that in some way this book has helped you to feel supported as a teacher. You have my best wishes for your efforts in the future. I cheer you on. Take care of yourself and the students with whom you share your life.

I leave you with a gift. My father gave this to me years ago when he and I were both teaching.

Thus a Child Learns[ii]

Thus a child learns:

>by wiggling skills through his fingers and toes into himself,
>by soaking up attitudes of those around him,
>by pushing and pulling his own world.

Thus a child learns:

>more through trial and error,
>more through pleasure than pain,
>more through experience than suggestion,
>more through suggestion than direction.

Thus a child learns:

>through affection
>through love
>through patience
>through understanding
>through belonging
>through doing
>through being.

Day by day the child comes

>to know a little bit of what you know,
>to think a little bit of what you think,
>to understand your understanding.

That which you dream and believe … becomes the child.

As you teach, may you dream and believe and work with great caring, always using your head and heart.

And may you walk in peace and beauty,

—Shari Stokes

December 21, 2017

Endnotes

i   Adapted from Palmer, P. & the Center for Courage and Renewal. (2007). *We teach who we are—The courage to teach guide for reflection and renewal.* San Francisco, CA: Jossey-Bass.

ii   Written by Fred Moffitt, EdD, New York State Department of Education (n.d.). Thanks for this one, Dad.

ANSWER KEY

Chapter 3

. . . .

C3AK Four Considerations for Room Design—Answers

The four considerations you want to keep in mind when arranging the furniture, equipment, and objects in a room to address students' physiological variables and basic needs, provide structure, and nurture students are:

1. *Accessibility*

2. *Visibility*

3. *Proximity*

4. *Distractibility*

In Chapter 5 we will add a fifth.

. . . .

Need	Instruction that *would* meet the need	Instruction that would NOT
Emotional & Physical Safety	• Create an organized, physically safe learning climate; • Use strategies that match learning styles, address needs; • Use brain compatible teaching approaches; • Use activities that are engaging for all students; • Provide variety in activities, e.g., use music, movement; • Use curriculum that respects students' cultures, celebrates diversity; • Address individual issues privately instead of in group; • Get permission before displaying work; • Keep evaluation private, including that which ranks students; • Use kind, positive humor; • Use reinforcement, constructive feedback, not criticism.	• Have a disorganized or unsafe room arrangement; • Use "one size fits all" instruction; • Use the same processes most of the time; • Use competitive structures; • Use ranking for evaluation; • Speak critically about student publicly; e.g., to another teacher or student. • Make evaluation of student work public; • Display student work without permission. • Use sarcasm or ridicule; • Use materials that omit the contributions of cultural groups or represent them disrespectfully.
Belonging	• Use "ice breakers" to help students learn about/get to know others; • Use cooperative learning structures; • Use flexible social configurations/settings; • Use learning buddy to dialogue during lesson; • Assign responsibilities that contribute to the group/class; • Use peer activities, e.g., constructive peer editing.	• Pit students against others; • Single out student(s) publicly for judgment. • Speak negatively about one student to others • Minimize opportunities for students to learn about each other; • Use only individualistic structures for learning.
Personal value	• Develop rules as a class; • Use student input to make content or activity choices; • Use activities that engage students in areas of interest; • Use strategies that address individual needs; • Use tasks that allow personal perspective, opinion; • Validate effort as well as progress; • Do not reject inaccurate idea; help shape to 'right' answer; • Value student's ideas; • Foster sharing of beliefs, customs.	• Tell the students the class rules; • Make all the decisions and do all the management tasks yourself; • Boss rather than lead or foster; • Use large group instruction most of the time; • Discount or ridicule student's ideas; • Single out a student who needs help; • Make one student's success be dependent on another's failure, e.g., "Well, Leah doesn't know the answer; do you, Amy?"

C3AK Table **3-7. The Role Instruction Can Play[i] in Addressing Basic Emotional Needs—Possible Answers**

Need	Instruction that *would* meet the need	Instruction that would NOT
Efficacy	• Share responsibilities, e.g., attendance, lunch count; • Teach the procedures before they are required; • Keep needed materials where readily available to students; • Design experiences that address 'real world' problems, examples; • Design activities that enable students to be in charge; • Design experiences that facilitate success; • Ready students for lesson, e.g. access prior knowledge; • Instruct just a stretch above student level of functioning; • Ask students to review directions in own words; • Model, provide examples to foster learning; • Offer choices, opportunities for decision-making; • Provide opportunities for practice before assessment; • Make evaluative criteria clear in advance of assessment; • Use criterion-based evaluation; provide rubrics; • Provide opportunities to share, publish, display work; • Prepare student for how to share before they share.	• Instruct beyond students' stretch; • Lecture at students; • Address private issues publicly; • Criticize publicly; • Criticize instead of providing constructive feedback; • Expect perfection; • Expect accuracy before fluency is achieved; • Use comparative evaluation; • Use evaluation criteria or processes that are not known to students in advance.
Fun, joy, recreation sense of well-being	• Create experiences that excite curiosity; • Provide choices that captivate interests; • Model excitement about discovery, learning; • Encourage positive humor; • Integrate hands-on activities, movement, creativity in lessons; • Design experiences that nourish the learner; • Have students create bulletin board and other displays; • Celebrate student's strengths.	• Provide no variety in nature, pacing, social configuration, setting, timing, momentum, materials; • Use rigid, authoritarian strategies; • For in-school and homework assignments rely on text and paper and pencil learning; • Control everything.

C3AK Table **3-7. The Role Instruction Can Play[i] in Addressing Basic Emotional Needs—Possible Answers (Continued)**

i   For their many ideas, my thanks to the undergraduate and graduate students at Fitchburg State and to the teachers in the field with whom I have worked.

Chapter 6

<table>
<tr><td colspan="2"> 6-7. Evidence of Strategies that Create a Constructive Learning Community—Summary Chart of Possible Answers</td></tr>
<tr><td>Strategy that Meets Basic Needs & Establishes a Community</td><td>Teaching Evidence One Might See in a Classroom</td></tr>
<tr><td>Foster connections between the students and you as a person, as well as you as a teacher who facilitates student leaning.</td><td>Greet Students at the door; have welcoming display; use questionnaires to learn about students' learning needs, strengths and interests.</td></tr>
<tr><td>Foster connections among learning community members.</td><td>Have students create name cards so everyone learns each other's names; chat with students about activities and interests outside school.</td></tr>
<tr><td>Create a warm, supportive class tone that communicates possibility.</td><td>Welcome mistakes as a natural part of learning; cultivate a discipline of hope with the words you use.</td></tr>
<tr><td>Integrate collaborative structures that provide student-to-student support.</td><td>Create a homework buddy system to provide support; offer 'Help Wanted'/I Can Help process; train and foster peer coaches; train and foster peer mediators</td></tr>
<tr><td>Integrate collaborative structures into learning experiences and social skills into the curriculum.</td><td>Use Cooperative Learning Quick Starters; teach conflict resolution strategies; coach/mentor students in using the constructive conflict resolution strategies they have been taught.</td></tr>
<tr><td>Teach constructive community behavior by example.</td><td>Eliminate shaming and blaming; work with students to solve the problem.</td></tr>
<tr><td>Establish expectations for constructive behavior with community members.</td><td>Have anti-bullying discussions/activities along with a contract that everyone signs.</td></tr>
<tr><td>Find ways to have students infuse their room with their own creative processes and signatures.</td><td>Facilitate student designed display of curriculum content; Have display areas for work of which students are proud.</td></tr>
</table>

Chapter 11

C11AK Table 11-5. Examples of Student Behavior that Could be Shaped

Reminder: We can shape the number of responses required (items 1 and 4). We can shape the time required—we can require more or less time to complete a task (item 3). We can shape the topography of a behavior (items 2 and 6). We can shape how much of a behavior is required before we reinforce it (item 5)

Current Student Behavior	The goal you believe would be constructive	Step 1: The behavior you begin reinforcing to support change towards the final goal	Step 2: The behavior you reinforce once the student is successful with Step 1	Step 3: Reinforcement of goal Behavior
1. Completes 2 out of 10 math problems	*Completes 10 out of 10 math problems*	*Completes 4 out of 10 math problems*	*Completes 7 out of 10 math problems*	*Completes 10 out of 10 math problems*
2. Can participate in a team activity for 1–2 minutes before arguing about rules	*Participates in a team activity for 2–4 minutes complying with rules*	*Participates in a team activity for 4–6 minutes complying with rules*	*Participates in a team activity for 6–8 minutes complying with rules*	*Participates in a team activity for 10 minutes complying with rules*
3. Takes 40 minutes to complete task she could reasonably complete in 20 minutes	*Completes task in 20 minutes*	*Completes task in 33 minutes*	*Completes task in 28 minutes*	*Completes task in 20 minutes*
4. During clean-up picks up one item [out of many possible] and puts it away	*During clean-up picks up seven items and puts them away*	*During clean-up picks up three items and puts them away*	*During clean-up picks up five items and puts them away*	*During clean-up picks up seven items and puts them away*
5. Writes essays that are 1/2 page long when assigned [and capable of writing] at least 3 pages	*Writes essays that are 3 page long when assigned at least 3 pages*	*Writes essays that are 1 page long when assigned at least 3 pages*	*Writes essays that are 2 page long when assigned at least 3 pages*	*Writes essays that are 3 pages long when assigned at least 3 pages*
6. Walks to sink (does not use soap), rinses, dries hands, throws towel in trash.	*Walks to sink, uses soap on all parts of hands and fingers (tops and inside), rinses, dries hands, throws towel in trash.*	*Walks to sink uses soap on palms of hand only, rinses, dries hands, throws towel in trash.*	*Walks to sink uses soap on palms and insides of fingers only, rinses, dries hands, throws towel in trash.*	*Walks to sink, uses soap on all parts of hands and fingers (tops and inside), rinses, dries hands, throws towel in trash.*

Chapter 12

. . . .

Application Activity: Analysis of Teacher–Student Interaction—Answers

Shushila blurts out questions without raising her hand and waiting to be called on. When she does, Mr. Petri always reminds Shushila to raise her hand. After this, Mr. Petri scolds Shushila for not raising her hand. Then Mr. Petri answers Shushila's question. For a while after Mr. Petri responds to Shushila, she doesn't blurt out, but then the blurting occurs again. This has gone on now for several weeks. Analyze this use of what Mr. Petri calls "punishment" to correct Shushila's behavior.

1. Of the four possibilities, what is the function of Shushila's behavior? Attention (and perhaps escape).

2. Is the teacher's intervention effective? No.

3. How can you tell? The student's behavior doesn't stop. After a short while, Shushila calls out again.

4. When asked, Mr. Petri says that his strategy is a combination of first cueing as an antecedent to the desired behavior and then afterwards punishing the inappropriate behavior by presenting a noxious consequence (the scolding). Is he cueing? Does his so-called cue come before the constructive behavior is desired? No.

5. Is his response to Shushila's behavior punishing *for her*? A cue occurs *before* the desired goal behavior, not afterwards. Teacher talk after a behavior becomes a source of attention, reinforcement. Also, if the teacher response were a punishment from Shushila's perspective, she would either not exhibit the behavior any more or, minimally, exhibit it less and less to avoid the punishment.

6. Mr. Petri feels that, in a while, the blurting-out behavior will completely stop. He just needs more time to make the strategy work. Do you agree? No.

7. What are your reasons? His intervention isn't effective for the reasons given in #5 above. Also, he is not providing antecedent events that cue the behavior and then reinforcing it when Shushila does it.

8. From the entire summary, do you think the consequence is reinforcing or punishing for Shushila? Reinforcing.

9. How do you know? She keeps calling out.

10. What teacher behavior is being reinforced? All of it.

11. What is the reinforcer for the teacher behavior? Shushila stops for a little while immediately after the teacher response.

12. How do you know the teacher is being reinforced? The teacher keeps scolding, reminding, and answering.

Mr. Petri and Shushila are caught in a cycle of behavior and response on the part of both that many in the field have come to call the "criticism trap." The behavior of each reinforces the behavior of the other—thus, each is caught in but also creates a trap for the other. What Mr. Petri is doing in response to Shushila is not punishment; it is reinforcement because it provides the attention Shushila wants. Therefore, the "punishment" actually encourages her unconstructive behavior! Because Shushila stops for a while, Mr. Petri is reinforced to continue to scold Shushila.

INDEX

caring and love, 18. *See also* Care/caring

characteristics, 19

feel competent, 18

joy, play, recreation, merriment, 18. *See also* Joy, play, recreation, merriment

role of instruction and, 77, 78

safety, 18–19. *See also* Emotional safety; Safety

ways to meet, 19–20. *See also* Nurturing

Emotional safety. *See also* Safety

need for, 63–64

role of instruction and, 77, 78

Emotions, 34–36, 92

examples, 34–35

management of, 201–202

overview, 34–35

role in thinking, memory, and learning, 35–36

safety, research on brain functioning and, 36

self-management of, 36

Empathy, 36, 92

fostering of, 249

response with, 238. *See also* Responding to behavior

Empowerment, 100

Environmental prompts, 332

Environments, 24. *See also* Physical environment; Physiological environment; Psychosocial environment

in community of learners, 132

interconnectedness of, 26

variables, 25–26

questions related to, 25

Equipments, arrangement, 108–109, 306

Escape, 229, 292

function of, 344–346

Ethical considerations, 318

Expanded anecdotal record, 268

Expectations

establishing, 143

by contract, 144–145

by creating procedures, 151–153

by rules, 145–146

evaluation of, 182

reviewing of, 184

Experiences, 20. *See also* Learning experiences

in physiological environment, 114

Explanation, teaching strategies, 76

External conditions, 114

External cue/trigger, 362

Extinction, 117

as strategy, 346–352

intervention setup before, 347

phases of usual responses to, 347

time-out. *See also* Time-out

cautions about using, 351–352

elements, 350–351

levels of, 348–350

procedures, 348

Extrinsic reinforcement, 311

F

Familiarity, 87

Farewell, 379–380

FAS (Fetal Alcohol Syndrome), 52

Feedback, 199–201

coaching, 187, 189

color of, 189

language of, 190

peer, 187

praise-and-point worksheet, 187

praising and pointing, 189

sources of, 190

students' role in, 187

Fetal Alcohol Syndrome (FAS), 52

Fight or flight response, 202

Fixed mindset, 37

Flexible seating arrangements, 106–107

Focus, setting, 110

Follow-up consequence, 238

Ford, Henry, 37

fostering constructive behavior and reinforcement, 313–314

Four goals for behavior, 229

Frequency, 256

Frequency count, 259–261

Fueling effect, 339

Full physical prompt, 333

Functional behavior assessment (FBA), 291

Furniture, 306

G

Gardner, Howard, 42

Generalization, 323

Gestural prompts, 332

Ginott, Haim, 221

Goal behavior, 254, 255, 293

patterns of antecedent conditions, 298

kinds of, 353–354
logical negative, 354
logical positive, 354
misconception about success of, 357
natural, 353–354, 357
negative, 116, 353–354
positive, 116, 353–354
punitive, 356–357
reinforcement for, 356
unconstructive uses of, 358–359
Punitive punishment, 356–357

Q

Quality of mood, 39
Quantitative information/data, 259, 270
Questions
  classroom designing and, 101
  intervention design, fostering constructive behavior and, 328–330
    antecedent conditions, 328
    consequent conditions, 328
Quick Whip
  how to use the process, 137
  uses, 137, 208
Quilt square activity, 135

R

Rate, 258, 260
Rate per opportunity, 258
Rate per time, 258
Reactive bullies, 362
Receptivity, enhancing of, 185
Recognition, 209–210
Recreational drugs and related substances, 52
Reducing School Violence Through Conflict
    Resolution, 204
Reflection, 375
Reinforcement, 310–311, 313
  effectiveness of, 342
  effective use of, 311
  extrinsic, 311
  for bullying, 363–365
  for punishment, 356
  for successive approximations of skill, 312
  function of escape, 344–346
  intervention that combines punishment and, 359–360

natural, 311
negative, 115, 310
of incompatible alternative to unconstructive behavior, 341
peers, 340
positive, 115, 310
social, 312
types of, 334
unnatural, 313
Reinforcers, 115
  for unconstructive behavior, removal of, 340
  selection of, 312–313
Research
  on brain functioning, emotional safety and, 36
  on temperament, 39
Resources, compiling of, 155
Responding to behavior
  clarity, 232
  delay, 234
  guidelines, 232
  least response, 232
  levels, 235–241
  low-level nonverbal responses, 235–237
  medium-level verbal response, 237
  negative strategies, 242–243
  on-the-spot response, 231–234
  options, 234
  problem-solving approaches, 239–241
  safety, 232
  statement of consequences, 237–238
  student efficacy, 232
  teacher well-being, 233
Rest, 49
Restorative approach, 149–151
Rhythmicity, 39
Rhythmic/musical intelligence, 43
Rituals, of community, 208
Room arrangement variables, 72–74
  accessibility of high-traffic areas, 73–74
  elimination of distractibility, 73
  proximity of students and teacher, 73
  visibility of teacher(s), students, and lesson foci, 73
Room content variables
  classroom contract/rules/pledge/charter/
      constitution, 68–69
  curriculum standards/learning targets, 70
  posted procedures, 69
  posted signs cue, 69–70

rules posting, 107
  use of signage, 107
  through instruction, 75–78, 112–114
    assessment information gathering, 113
    curriculum content, 75
    lesson topics integration, 112–114
    teaching strategies, 75–76
Student responsibilities in classroom, 152–153
Student(s)
  and teacher, proximity of, 73, 104
  retention and transfer facilitation, 111
  values, 38
  visibility in classroom, 73, 103
Student-student social interactions, 86–87. *See also* Group(s)/group members
Student-teacher social interactions, 88–90, 366–367
  effects, 89–90
Summarization (closing), 76, 111, 375
  review, 376–378
Support, 20
Synchrony, 36, 84

T

Tangibles, 228, 292, 342, 350
Target behavior, 254, 255, 293
  patterns of antecedent conditions, 297
  patterns of consequent conditions, 297
Teacher(s)
  and students, proximity of, 73, 104
  desk location, 66
  student-teacher social interactions, 88–90, 366–367
  values, 38
  visibility in classroom, 73, 103
Teacher well-being, responses and, 233
Teaching
  effective, 23–24. *See also* Nurturing
  instructional strategies, 75–77
Team Accelerated Instruction for Math, 157
Technical account, 265
Technology, use of, for teaching, 192–194
  differentiated instruction based on students' learning profiles, 193–194, 194–195
"Tell a story", 259
Temperament, 39–42
  research on, 39
  role of, 39
  styles, 39
  vs. behavior styles, 39

Temporary illness, 49
Thinking, emotions role in, 35–36
Threshold responsiveness, 39
Time duration, 262–263
Time, observation, 273
Time-out, extinction and
  alone use of, effectiveness, 351
  cautions about using, 351–352
  elements, 350–351
  levels of, 348–350
  observational, 348
  procedures, 348
  time, importance of, 352
  transitioning, 351
  words and tone of voice, 350
Timing in day, 65
Tolerance, 20
Topography, 256, 258
Toxic substances
  ingested, 51
Transitions/transitioning, 224
  time-out and, 351
Trials to Criterion, 260
Triune Brain Theory, 34

U

Unconditional positive feelings, 19–20
Unconstructive behaviors, 223. *See also* Constructive behaviors; Weak spots
  decreasing, 337–368
    antecedent variables, addressing, 339–340
    application activity, 366–367
    attention or tangibles, function of, 342
    bullying, 361
    consequent variables, addressing, 340–342
    extinction, using, as Strategy, 346–352
    function of escape, 344–346
    importance, 338
    intervention with reinforcement and punishment, 359–361
    nature or timing of behavior, addressing, 342
    objectives, 338
    overview, 338
    punishment, 353–358
    sensory regulation, function of, 343
    strategies, 358–359
    use of assessments to support, 339
  elimination of, 116–117

Understanding, checking for, 76
Universal Design for Learning (UDL), 192
Unnatural reinforcement, 313

V

Value(s), 38–39
  personal, role of instruction and, 77, 78
  student, 38
    as individual, 65
  teacher, 38
Variables
  ecological, 287
  interaction among, 287
  physical environment, 25
    assessment questions, 285–286
    categories, 62
    effects on behavior, 61–79
    importance, 62
    instruction, 62, 75–78
    learning styles, 47
    objectives, 62
    overview, 62
    room arrangement, 62, 72–74
    room contents, 62, 67–73
    room variables, 63–67
  physiological environment, 24–25
    application activity, 54
    assessment questions, 285
    brain functioning, 33–34
    disabilities, 47–48
    effects on behavior, 31–55
    emotions, 34–36
    health factors, 49–53
    importance, 32
    intelligences, 42–44
    learning styles, 44–47
    mindset, 37–38
    objectives, 32
    overview, 32–33
    social intelligence, 36–37
    temperament, 39–42
    values, 38–39
  psychosocial environment, 25
    assessment questions, 285–286
    effects on behavior, 83–93
    importance, 84
    learning styles, 47
    negative impact, 344
    objectives, 85
    overview, 84
    physiological and physical environments and, 91–93
    social skills learned outside school, effects of, 90–91
    student-student social interactions and, 86–87
    student-teacher social interactions and, 88–89
  questions related to, 25
Ventilation, classroom, 104–106
Verbal cues, 114
Verbal/linguistic intelligence, 42
Visual cues, 114
Visual prompts, 332
Visual signal, 151
Visual/spatial intelligence, 42
Voice of teacher, 181

W

Weak spots
  occurance, 224
  physical environment variables, 241
  prevent, 225
  reasons for, 225
  triggers, 228–231
Well-being
  balance between nurturing and structure and, 22
  role of instruction and, 77, 78
  room variables in physical environment and, 67
Work sample (or portfolio), 262, 270